KT-463-505

A2
Economics

Ray Powell

Philip Allan Updates, an imprint of Hodder Education, an Hachette UK company, Market Place, Deddington, Oxfordshire OX15 0SE

Orders
Bookpoint Ltd, 130 Milton Park, Abingdon, Oxfordshire OX14 4SB
tel: 01235 827720
fax: 01235 400454
e-mail: uk.orders@bookpoint.co.uk

Lines are open 9.00 a.m.–5.00 p.m., Monday to Saturday, with a 24-hour message answering service. You can also order through the Philip Allan Updates website: www.philipallan.co.uk

© Philip Allan Updates 2009

ISBN 978-0-340-94751-7
Impression number   5 4 3 2 1
Year   2013 2012 2011 2010 2009

This textbook has been written to support students studying AQA A2 economics. The content has been neither approved nor endorsed by AQA and remains the sole responsibility of the author.

The front cover is reproduced by permission of Comstock Images/Alamy.

All Office for National Statistics material is Crown copyright, produced under the terms of PSI Licence Number C200700185.

Printed in Italy.

Hachette UK's policy is to use papers that are natural, renewable and recyclable products and made from wood grown in sustainable forests. The logging and manufacturing processes are expected to conform to the environmental regulations of the country of origin.

Contents

Foreword

Welcome back to economics and your second year of A-level study. At the start of my *AQA AS Economics* textbook I stated that my most important objective is to help you achieve the highest possible examination grades.

However, I have a second objective, namely to turn you into a good economist. In an important sense, my two objectives come together at A2. To achieve the highest A* grade for the overall A-level (AS + A2), you have to be a good economist. The A* grade requires a mark of 90% at A2, together with a mark of 80% for the whole AS and A2 course. In future years, top-rated universities such as Cambridge, Oxford, the London School of Economics, Bristol and Warwick are likely to require A* grades rather than the basic A grade that was the highest on offer before 2010.

Of course, most students end up earning grades that fall some way short of A*. My books are meant for all AQA economics students, and aim to help you to gain high rather than low grades in all your economics exams. To help you to get the most out of your studies, I have included extension material in most of the chapters of the book. This goes beyond the immediate demands of the A-level specification, introducing you to new theories and to developments of existing theories. There are also many case studies in the book. These enable you to link theory to up-to-date events taking place in the UK and the international economy.

Synopticity

I have tried to present A2 economics as a coherent whole, building on what you learnt at AS. Wherever possible, I have avoided unnecessary repetition of material you learnt a year ago at AS. However, do remember that the A2 exam papers are synoptic. To prepare for the synoptic nature of the questions, make sure you note the 'What you should already know' section at the beginning of each chapter (apart from Chapter 1).

Synopticity means that questions in an A2 examination paper require reference to knowledge and economic theory from one or more of the other AS or A2 units. Synopticity may be vertical, horizontal or diagonal. A Unit 3 examination question is vertically synoptic when it tests knowledge learnt in Unit 1. Two examples of such subjects are supply and demand and elasticity. Likewise, a Unit 4 examination question testing knowledge learnt in Unit 2 is vertically synoptic. Examples include national income, the multiplier and *AD/AS* analysis.

Horizontal synopticity requires the application of a macroeconomic concept or theory from Unit 4 to a microeconomics question in the Unit 3 examination (or vice versa). For example, a question on poverty (in Unit 3) could test knowledge of how fiscal policy (a Unit 4 topic) may reduce poverty. Diagonal synopticity requires the use of Unit 2 macroeconomic terms and concepts to answer a microeconomics Unit 3 question, or the use of microeconomics knowledge from Unit 1 to answer a Unit 4 question.

Moving up

Much of the subject matter of Unit 3, Business economics and the distribution of income, differs significantly from the content of Unit 1, Markets and market failure. As the Unit 1 title indicates, AS microeconomics focuses on how a competitive market functions, and on the various causes of market failure. By contrast, A2 microeconomics concentrates much more on businesses and how they behave. Of course, supply and demand and the market mechanism do figure in A2 microeconomics, but in the context of labour markets rather than the product or goods markets covered in Unit 1.

Unit 4, The national and international economy, is rather different. Many of the Unit 2 National economy topics you studied a year ago at AS are equally as important at A2. These topics include macroeconomic policy objectives such as economic growth, full employment and control of inflation, together with the main types of macroeconomic policy, monetary policy, fiscal policy and supply-side policy. Most important of all is the aggregate demand/aggregate supply (*AD/AS*) macroeconomic model. This is the key theoretical model in both AS and A2 macroeconomics. You don't need to learn much more about the *AD/AS* model at A2, over and above what you learnt at AS. The main difference is that A2 exam questions, particularly essay questions, require a greater depth of analysis, together with more sophisticated evaluation of the issues posed by the question.

Both the Unit 2 and Unit 4 specifications focus on the national economy. The main add-on in Unit 4 is the international economy. This develops your understanding of the balance of payments and exchange rates that you first encountered at AS, but adds on important international topics such as trade theory and globalisation.

Background knowledge

The AQA economics specification requires candidates to 'acquire a good knowledge of trends and developments in the economy which have taken place during the past 10 years and also have an awareness of earlier events where this helps to give recent developments a longer term perspective'. With this in mind, I firmly believe that students benefit from a basic knowledge of economic history and of different schools of economic thought, such as Keynesianism and monetarism. Where I think it helps, I have adopted a historical approach, particularly in the explanation of macroeconomic topics such as theories of inflation and unemployment, and in the way monetary policy, fiscal policy and supply-side economics have developed over the years.

Exam questions

At the end of each chapter, there are a number of self-testing questions. These can be used by teachers to reinforce understanding of chapter content, or by students testing their own knowledge. The book does not provide answers to the self-testing questions, though answers are given in the *AQA A2 Economics Teacher Guide*, available from Philip Allan Updates.

Examination-style questions are not included in this book. However, data-response and essay questions relevant to the two A2 exams are available, along with summary specification coverage, in the following Student Unit Guides published by Philip Allan Updates:

AQA A2 Unit 3: Business Economics and the Distribution of Income
(ISBN: 978-0-340-94747-0)

AQA A2 Unit 4: The National and International Economy
(ISBN: 978-0-340-94746-3)

I recommend you use these to prepare for both essay and data-response questions. The Unit 1 and Unit 2 exams at AS did not include essay questions, so at the beginning of the A2 course, you may not be used to writing extended essays over 45 minutes. Essay writing requires practice, particularly in the higher-level skills of economic analysis and evaluation which account for 60% of the total marks at A2 (as against 40% at AS).

A2 data-response questions also differ from those you encountered at AS. At A2 they are context questions, which relate to the impact on the UK economy of events taking place in the European Union (the EU context) or the wider international economy (the global context).

It now remains for you to use this book to become an even better economist than you were at the end of the AS course, and to pass your A2 exams with flying colours. I wish you every success.

Ray Powell

Introduction

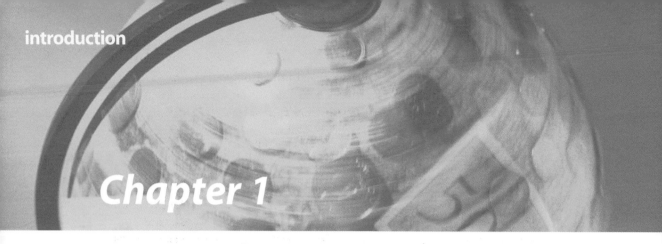

Chapter 1

How to become an even better economist

In the foreword of my AQA AS Economics textbook I stated that two of my main objectives in writing the book were for you to do well in the exams and for you to become a good economist. I want students to be capable of reading newspapers fruitfully to find out more about how economies work, and of conversing intelligently with both economists and non-economists about economic issues and government policies. This objective underlies all the chapters in this book, but as the title indicates, especially this chapter.

Learning outcomes

This chapter will:
➤ remind you of the nature and importance of economic models
➤ advise on understanding and interpreting economic statistics
➤ explain why it is important to draw graphs accurately
➤ question whether government statistics are always accurate
➤ discuss the interpretation and use of economic policy and performance indicators

Understanding and applying economic models

The AQA specification for A2 states that: 'Candidates should be able to recognise both the value and limitations of **economic models** as a means of explaining and evaluating the conduct and performance of firms in the real world. They should be able to evaluate economic models in written, numerical and graphical forms.'

Key term

An **economic model** is a small-scale replica of real-world phenomena.

Model-building is one of the most important analytical techniques used by economists. Much of the economic theory you learnt last year at AS and will continue to learn this year centres around the use of economic models. At a microeconomic level, economic models are used to try to explain the economic behaviour of the individuals and firms that make up the economy. Last year, you learnt about the **supply and demand model** of a particular market in the economy, such as the market for strawberries or the market for automobiles. This year, a large part of your microeconomic studies will focus on the **theory of the firm** in the context of **business economics**. You will also re-visit the supply and demand model, but in the context of the **labour market**.

Economic models are also at the centre of macroeconomic theory. The two main macroeconomic models you learnt last year were the **circular flow model** and the **aggregate demand/aggregate supply *(AD/AS)* model**. The *AD/AS* model is just as important at A2 as it is at AS. You won't need to learn much more about the model itself this year than you learnt last year. However, A2 exam questions are more demanding than AS questions, so your main task will be to apply what you already know in greater depth and breadth than was the case last year.

Box 1.1 The Phillips machine: a Heath Robinson economic model

Heath Robinson was a cartoonist and illustrator, who became famous for his drawings of eccentric machines. The label 'Heath Robinson' is now used to describe any quirky, complex and implausible machine or contraption. The **Phillips machine** has been described as 'a Heath Robinson device at its finest'.

A wonderful thing is a Phillips machine

In the Meade Room in the Dept of Applied Economics of Cambridge University stands a Phillips machine, a device so cunning and ingenious that it can predict the running of the national economy to within 4% accuracy. And all by means of pipes and buckets, trickling with pink-coloured water, powered by a pump scavenged from the landing gear of a Lancaster bomber. It is a hydraulic computer, invented by Bill Phillips.

Allan McRobie at CUED said 'The machine is absolutely brilliant. We all know that engineers should have a knowledge of economics, but Phillips made an enormous contribution and showed that economists could learn much from engineering.'

Issue 12 of *Enginuity*, 2003. The full article can be seen at: www-g.eng.cam.ac.uk/enginuity/issue12/index.html

Later in the A2 course, in Chapter 17 and in the context of inflation and unemployment, you will learn about an important part of macroeconomic theory called the **Phillips curve**. The curve is named after Professor Bill Phillips, a New Zealand engineer who became an economist, and later professor of statistics at the London School of Economics. Nine years before 1958 when Phillips published a paper which introduced the famous Phillips curve, he designed and built the **Phillips machine**. This machine, which is described in Box 1.1, is an example of a macro-economic model, albeit a rather unusual one. Complex modern economic models, such as the **Treasury model** used by the government to forecast changes in the UK economy, are driven by computers. However, the Phillips Machine, which pre-dated

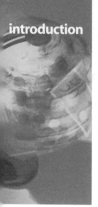

most of the developments in computer technology, was essentially a contraption of buckets and pipes around which pink fluid flowed, depicting the **circular flow of income** or money around the economy.

The essentials of an economic model

A model is a small-scale replica of real-world phenomena, often incorporating a number of simplifications. An economic model simplifies the real world in such a way that the essential features of an economic relationship or set of relationships are explained using diagrams, words and often algebra. Models are used by economists, first to understand and explain the working of the economy and second, to predict what might happen in the future. The ultimate purpose of model-building is to derive predictions about economic behaviour, such as the prediction of demand theory that demand will increase when price falls.

At AS, the main economic models you studied are listed in the top half of Table 1.1 below. In a similar way, the bottom half of the table lists models not in the AS course, but which feature strongly in the A2 course. Note that rather more new models are included in A2 microeconomics, than are in A2 macroeconomics. This does not mean there is less to learn when studying Unit 4; rather it means that much of A2 macroeconomics simply develops with greater depth the circular flow and *AD/AS* models you came across at AS.

AS models	
Micro	**Macro**
Supply and demand model	Circular-flow model
	Aggregate-demand/aggregate-supply model

A2 models	
Micro	**Macro**
Theory of the firm	• Aggregate-demand/aggregate-supply model
• Perfect competition model	• Phillips-curve model
• Monopoly model	• International-trade model
• Oligopoly model	
• Game-theory models	
Labour-market models	
• Monopsony model	

Table 1.1 Economic models at AS and at A2

Specification advice on the use of economic statistics

For AS candidates, the specification advises: 'Candidates should be familiar with the various types of statistical and other data which are commonly used by economists. For example, they should be able to interpret data presented in the form of index numbers.' Obviously, this advice is just as relevant at A2. However, the A2 specification goes on to add: 'Candidates should be able to interpret different types of economic data, such as the Human Development Index, and use them to compare the living standards of the residents of different countries. They should be able to discuss the limitations of using such data to arrive at conclusions.' And in the context of inflation, the advice is: 'Candidates should have an understanding of how index numbers are calculated and used to measure changes in the price level.' Although a detailed technical knowledge is not expected of indices such as the retail prices index (RPI) and consumer prices index (CPI), candidates should have an awareness of the underlying features, for example, the Expenditure and Food Survey, the concept of the 'average family', the basket of goods and services, and weighting.

Interpreting economic statistics

Unlike university economics, A-level economics makes few mathematical demands on its students. The main skills you will have to undertake in the context of economic data are **identification of relationships**, **description**, **comparison** and **explanation**.

The demands on your skills at A2 are no different from those you applied when answering AS questions last year. So in this sense, you don't have to become an *even better economist* at A2 in order to score more marks in your handling of economic data. Also, at the beginning of your A2 course, you should be familiar with economic data presented in index numbers, for example the retail prices index (RPI) and the consumer prices index (CPI), together with the two main measures of unemployment, the claimant count and the Labour Force Survey (LFS) measure. Likewise, your AS studies should have provided you with an understanding of the difference between data presented in real and nominal (or money) forms.

If you have forgotten some or all of the above, you will be well advised to buy, or get your school to buy, the A2 Student Unit Guides for AQA economics, also published by Philip Allan Updates, in which I explain, and give plenty of examples of, the statistical data that is likely to be in the Unit 3 and Unit 4 data-response questions.

Using government statistics

Government statistics, often drawn from the **Office for National Statistics (ONS)**, are used in most A2 (and AS) data-response questions. The ONS provides up-to-date information on a range of macroeconomic variables, including output, economic growth, employment, unemployment, wages, prices, the inflation rate and trade figures. Until quite recently, it was generally agreed that, over the years, there had been a general improvement in the quality of information about the economy available to policy-makers. In recent years, however, a number of worries have emerged about the accuracy of ONS statistics. Mervyn King, the Governor of the Bank of England has hinted that the effectiveness of monetary policy has been adversely affected by possible inaccuracy in the unemployment and population figures. In July 2004, the headline of a news story in the *Independent* was 'Government statisticians lose 60,000 people in latest ONS gaffe'. Concern has also been expressed about an alleged creeping privatisation of the production of official statistics. There has been a considerable increase in the extent to which data analyses paid for by public funds have been outsourced to private companies whose analyses are available only to those who pay. At the same time, cutbacks at the ONS led to a loss of over 700 full-time jobs between 2004 and March 2008.

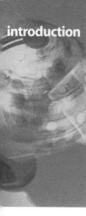

Box 1.2 Are government statistics accurate?

Politicians, newspapers and independent economists have become worried about the accuracy of official government statistics produced by a semi-independent Office for National Statistics (ONS). If we accept that official statistics are not always as accurate as they could be, a question that arises is: 'are inaccurate statistics the result of conspiracy or cock-up?' Popular newspapers (and sometimes opposition politicians) tend to favour conspiracy theories in which unwelcome information is hushed up by governments. The truth however is usually more prosaic; in the UK at least, cock-up and incompetence, rather than conspiracy, are more often than not responsible for provision of misleading and inaccurate information about economic performance. The following extract comes from an article about Gordon Brown when he was chancellor of the exchequer in 2005.

The numbers game

One of the most important figures for Gordon Brown when presenting his budget on March 16th was the current-budget balance. This is the gap between current revenues and current spending. It matters to the chancellor of the exchequer because he is committed to meeting his own golden rule of borrowing only to invest, so he has to ensure that the current budget is in balance or surplus over the economic cycle.

Mr Brown told MPs that he would meet the golden rule for the current cycle with £6 billion to spare — a respectable-sounding margin, though much less than in the past. However, the margin would have been halved but for an obscure technical change announced in February by the Office for National Statistics to the figures for road maintenance of major highways. The ONS said that the revision was necessary because it had been double-counting this spending within the current budget.

The Conservative shadow chancellor pointed out that the timing of the ONS decision was 'very convenient for the government'. If this were an isolated incident, then it might be disregarded.

But it is not the first time that the ONS has made decisions that appear rather convenient for the government. Mr Brown aims to meet another fiscal rule, namely to keep public net debt below 40% of GDP. At present he is meeting it but his comfort room would be reduced if the £21 billion borrowings of Network Rail were included as part of public debt. They are not thanks to a contro-versial decision by the ONS to classify the rail-infrastructure corporation within the private sector, even though the National Audit Office, Parliament's watchdog, said its borrowings were in fact government liabilities.

Whatever the rights and wrongs of the two decisions, they have left the ONS struggling to explain them. 'Both incidents put a question-mark over the capacity of the ONS to demonstrate its integrity and independence', says Richard Alldritt, chief executive of the Statistics Commission, an advisory body.

Gordon Brown addresses business leaders

When Labour came to power, it set a range of targets for the public sector, which include Mr Brown's fiscal rules, and hundreds more besides. As a result, its credibility is bound up with the official figures that measure how it has performed against these targets. This makes it particularly worrying that the official figures can show one thing, whereas the public experiences another.

The Economist, 23 March 2005

Follow-up questions

1 Explain the difference between a 'conspiracy theory' and a 'cock-up' theory.
2 What happened to the Labour government's 'fiscal rules' in 2008?

Practising drawing graphs at A2

At AS, you should have got plenty of practice in drawing supply and demand diagrams and marginal cost and benefit diagrams (for Unit 1) and *AD/AS* diagrams (for Unit 2). At A2, supply and demand diagrams are still needed, but largely in the context of the **labour market** (in Unit 3) and the **foreign exchange market** for a currency (in Unit 4). However, you must also learn to draw completely new graphs. For Unit 3 (Business Economics and the Distribution of Income), it is extremely important to learn and practise drawing graphs which show costs, revenues and profit in the different market structures of **perfect competition**, **monopoly** and **oligopoly**. You may also have to plot cost curves or revenue curves from a table of data presented in an exam question. Labour market diagrams are also important, particularly those relating to the supply of labour, and to perfectly competitive labour markets and monopsony labour markets. (*Monopsony* means a single *buyer* in a market, whereas *monopoly* is a single *seller* in a market.)

Fortunately, the diagrams you learnt at AS to show the market failures of negative and positive externalities, and demerit goods and merit goods, don't need adding to for Unit 3. Likewise, the *AD/AS* diagrams learnt for Unit 2 are quite sufficient for answering Unit 4 (The National and International Economy) questions. In both these cases, the diagrams you learnt at AS don't really need any further development. The main difference is that at A2, you will be applying the diagrams in a more sophisticated way, so as to display the 'higher order' skills of analysis and evaluation in answers of greater depth and breadth.

As is the case with Unit 3, new diagrams have to be learnt for Unit 4. Perhaps the most important set of new diagrams relate to **Phillips curve analysis** (see Box 1.1), which brings together relationships between unemployment and inflation at A2.

Many students who underachieve in economics exams appear to rote learn diagrams, without understanding how the graphs they draw are constructed. Usually this means that the unfortunate student makes mistakes when drawing from memory a complicated diagram in an exam answer. To prevent this happening, your teacher has probably gone through the building blocks of the diagram when first teaching you the diagram. In this situation, providing you have understood what your teacher has said, you have a greater chance of properly

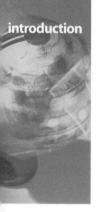

understanding the diagram and its mechanics, which in turn means you are less likely to make mistakes when drawing the diagram in exam conditions.

In the later chapters of this book, I have used the building block approach to explain how each new diagram is constructed. However, there is a danger here. It is seldom if ever relevant to explain to the examiner all of the building blocks of a diagram. If you do this your answer will drift into irrelevancy and waste valuable examination time. Instead, you should draw the finished diagram, and then get on with the job of using it as a visual aid in addressing the issue posed by the question.

Remember also the good habits you learnt at AS, namely labelling axes and curves accurately, drawing horizontal and vertical coordinates, explaining the short-hand you are using (such as *AD* for aggregate demand), and drawing diagrams of a reasonable size. If you can't remember a diagram, and if its inclusion is not necessary for your answer, then 'if in doubt, leave out'.

However, if a question explicitly requires a diagram, one must be drawn. Don't unnecessarily repeat the same diagram in an answer, but remember that relevant diagrams make it easier for examiners to read your answers. Examiners are put off by pages of turgid text, unbroken either by new paragraphs or by diagrams.

Interpreting economic policy and performance indicators

To become an *even better economist*, you should develop an understanding of the meaning of, and the difference between, economic policy indicators and economic performance indicators.

➤ A **policy indicator** (such as the money supply) provides policy makers with information about the recent success or lack of success in achieving the target set for a particular type of economic policy such as monetary policy or fiscal policy. Policy indicators also provide information about whether current policy is on course to hit the future target set for the stated policy.

Performance indicators are much the same as policy indicators, though they tend to be more general and are not necessarily focused on a particular type of economic policy such as monetary policy or fiscal policy. Performance indicators, such as information about **labour productivity** and **productivity gaps,** can also be used to compare the performance of the UK economy with that of competitor countries.

 Key terms

A **policy indicator** provides information about whether a particular policy is on course to achieve a desired policy objective.

A **performance indicator** provides information about what is happening in the economy.

A **lead indicator** provides information about the likely future state of the economy.

Performance indicators can be divided into *lead* and *lag* indicators. **Lead indicators** provide information about the future state of the economy (stemming from the way people are currently forming their expectations). Surveys of consumer and business confidence and investment intentions indicate the existence of a feel-good or feel-bad factor and provide information about the likely state of aggregate demand a few months ahead. Statistics for house-building starts and the number of people who have booked expensive summer or skiing holidays several months in advance also provide information about future spending, while data on commodity and input prices can signal future changes in retail price inflation.

By contrast, **lag indicators** provide information about *past* economic performance and the extent to which policy objectives such as economic growth and control of inflation have been achieved. Data on the level of GDP, and current and recent employment and unemployment figures provide examples of lag indicators that provide information about current and recent economic performance.

> **Key term**
>
> A **lag indicator** provides information about past events that have already taken place in the economy.

The usefulness of a performance indicator depends of course on whether it provides accurate information about the state of the economy. Likewise, a policy indicator is only useful if it provides accurate information about a variable relevant to achieving the policy's objective(s). Performance and policy indicators are, however, almost always presented in the form of statistical data, e.g. unemployment and growth figures in the case of lagged indicators, and projections about the number of house-building starts in the case of lead indicators. The accuracy of the information provided by performance and policy indicators is thus highly dependent on the accuracy of the statistics available from the government and other sources.

Box 1.3 David Smith's skip index

Every Sunday David Smith, the Economics Editor of the *Sunday Times* writes an Economic Outlook column, which I thoroughly recommend you to read if you want to become a good economist. (You don't have to buy the *Sunday Times*; the Economic Outlook column can be accessed on the *Sunday Times* website on the internet.)

A few years ago, David Smith came up with the idea of a **skip index**, as an informal **lead indicator** of what might happen to the economy in the future. David returns to this theme from time to time. I have reproduced below two extracts from David Smith's Economic Outlook columns. The first extract explains what the skip index is, while the

The refuse skip, a once common sight on Britain's streets

second extract introduces some other informal economic lead indicators, starting off with the more informal such as a crane count, and then moving to more formal indicators such as measures of business optimism and builders' house starts.

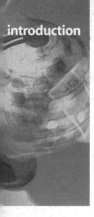

Worrying news. The skip index, one of my most reliable economic indicators, has slumped. The index, for those unfamiliar with it, is based on the number of builders' skips in my street. Four is a boom, two normal and zero tells us the economy has ground to a halt. The reading is now zero.

Sunday Times, 18 April 2004

Suggestions for alternative indicators include the 'crane count' (the number visible from the skyline), champagne sales and some of the usual suspects — the ease of getting a restaurant booking and taxi queues in the rain.

Other imaginative suggestions include sales of personalised car numbers, dumped mattresses by the roadside (when people like that replace their bedding, things must be looking up), Chinese takeaway prices — nobody is better tuned to the market than their owners, and waiting lists for car park season tickets at popular commuter stations.

The Office for National Statistics used to publish leading indicators for the economy but stopped doing so as a result of spending cutbacks.

There is no mystery about leading indicators. They are made up of freely available information which leads the economic cycle by a short time, for example consumer credit, new car registrations, consumer confidence, CBI new orders, or by a longer time — 12 months or more — for example housing starts, interest rates, business optimism and the financial surplus or deficit of firms. The virtue of leading indicators is that they combine different data to produce a coherent whole.

Sunday Times, 30 May 2004

Summary

> Understanding and applying economic models lies at the heart of becoming an *even better economist*.

> An economic model is a small-scale replica of real-world phenomena.

> At AS, you learnt about the supply and demand model, the circular flow model and the *AD/AS* model.

> AS models remain important at A2, but new models also need to be learned.

> The models of perfect competition, monopoly, oligopoly and the labour market are important A2 microeconomic models.

> The *AD/AS* model remains important at A2, and needs relatively little further development.

> The Phillips curve model and the international trade model are new macro models at A2.

> At A2 as at AS, it is important to understand and apply a range of economic statistics.

> You should not always rely on the accuracy of UK government statistics.

> Poorly-drawn graphs contribute to under-achievement in exams.

> At A2 as at AS, it is important to understand and apply economic policy and performance indicators.

Business economics and the distribution of income

Unit 3

Chapter 2

Introduction to business economics

In 1925, American President Calvin Coolidge allegedly said 'The business of America is business'. This quote, true or not, serves to introduce the notion that businesses are central to modern economies. Business economics covers some of the most important topics in the Unit 3 specification. This chapter provides an introductory survey of the different topics included in business economics.

Learning outcomes

This chapter will:
➤ provide an introduction to the theory of the firm
➤ explain the meaning of industrial policy
➤ address the question: what is a business?
➤ describe the different types of business in the UK today

The building blocks of business economics

At the heart of business economics is a body of theory that economists call the **theory of the firm**. The theory of the firm comprises a number of theoretical building blocks, which are are:
➤ Production theory
➤ Cost theory
➤ Revenue theory and market structure
➤ Profit maximisation in perfectly competitive and monopoly market structures
➤ Using efficiency and welfare criteria to evaluate the good and bad features of perfect competition and monopoly
➤ Applying these criteria to evaluate a third market structure: oligopoly

Business economics also includes a number of other topics. These are: how and why firms grow; the divorce between ownership and control; business objectives

other than profit maximisation; and the government's industrial policy in areas such as the ownership of businesses (private ownership versus public ownership), competition policy and the regulation or deregulation of industries, markets and business behaviour.

Introducing production theory

Figure 2.1 introduces the links between the first four of the building blocks that make up the theory of the firm. At the top of the chart is production theory. As I explain in the next chapter, **production** is simply a process or set of processes that convert inputs into outputs. Production theory divides into **short-run** production theory and **long-run** production theory. The key concept in short-run production theory, which is shown along the upper left-hand flow arrow in Figure 2.1, is the **law of diminishing returns** (which is also known as the **law of diminishing marginal productivity**). The law explains what happens to output when more and more labour is added to the fixed capital employed by a business.

 Key terms

Production is a process or set of processes that converts inputs into outputs.

The **short run** is the time period in which at least one factor of production is fixed.

The **long run** is the time period in which the scale of *all* factors of production can be changed.

The key concept in long-run production theory (located along the upper right-hand arrow in Figure 2.1) is **returns to scale**. Here there are three possibilities: increasing returns to scale; decreasing returns to scale; and constant returns to scale. For example, increasing returns to scale depict a situation in which output increases at a faster rate than total inputs when the scale of *all* the factors of production employed by the firm increases.

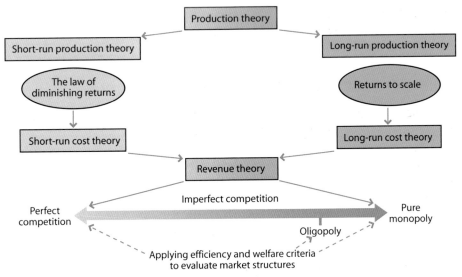

Figure 2.1 *The building blocks of the theory of the firm*

Introducing cost theory

The vertical flow lines located below the short-run and long-run production theory boxes in Figure 2.1 show how cost curves (and cost theory) are derived from short and long-run production theory. The left-hand arrow links short-run production theory (and the law of diminishing returns) to short-run cost curves. Likewise, the right-hand arrow depicts the link between long-run production theory (and returns to scale) and long-run cost curves.

> **examiner's voice**
> Make sure you don't confuse cost theory with production theory.

In examination answers, students often confuse production theory with cost theory. The important difference to note is that production theory includes no mention of the money costs that a business incurs when it changes the level of output it produces. In contrast, as the name itself indicates, cost theory is all about money costs of production.

Production theory and cost theory are however related. As I explain in the next chapter, the impact of the law of diminishing returns (short-run production theory) leads to an increase in a firm's short-run **marginal costs** of production, and thence to the 'U' shape of the **average cost** of production curve.

Likewise increasing returns to scale followed by decreasing returns to scale cause a firm's long-run average cost curve also to have a 'U' shape, though other assumptions about the nature of returns to scale lead to other shapes for the long-run average cost curve. Falling long-run average costs are known as **economies of scale**, whereas rising long-run average costs show **diseconomies of scale**.

Introducing revenue theory and market structure

Besides confusing production theory with cost theory, another common trap that students fall into when learning about the theory of the firm centres on the two words: **returns** and **revenue**. The word 'returns', as in the *law of diminishing returns* and *returns to scale*, refers to the units of production such as cars or TV sets that a firm produces. By contrast, *revenue* (or *sales* revenue) is the money a firm earns when selling its output.

> **examiner's voice**
> Make sure you don't confuse revenue with returns (as in production theory).

The nature of a firm's sales revenue depends on the competitiveness of the market structure in which the firm sells its output. Here, there are two extremes, which are shown at opposite ends of the double-headed arrow drawn towards the bottom of Figure 2.1. The two extreme market structures are **perfect competition** and **pure monopoly**. In perfect competition there are very large numbers of buyers and sellers, each of whom is a price taker, passively accepting the ruling market price determined by the interaction of all the many market participants. By contrast, a pure monopolist, who faces no competition at all, is a

> **examiner's voice**
> Perfect competition, monopoly and oligopoly are the three market structures you need to know.

price maker who uses monopoly power or market power to determine the price at which it sells. These and other conditions facing a perfectly competitive firm and a monopoly are explained in more detail in Chapter 6.

All the markets lying along the spectrum separating perfect competition and pure monopoly in Figure 2.1 are examples of **imperfect competition**. Imperfect competition varies from highly competitive markets towards the left-hand part of the spectrum to much less competitive markets that resemble pure monopoly at the other end of the range of market structures. Markets towards the right-hand end of the spectrum provide examples of **oligopoly**, or imperfect competition among the few.

Profit maximisation and the objectives of a firm

When studying AS economics, you learnt that economists usually assume that all economic agents, e.g. households, firms and the government, have an objective that they wish to maximise. For firms, economists assume that the objective is profit (though as I explain in Chapter 8, there are a number of other possible business objectives, such as maximising sales revenue and the firm's rate of growth). **Profit** is defined as sales revenue minus costs of production.

> **examiner's voice**
> You should be aware of business objectives other than profit maximisaiton.

> **Key term**
> **Profit** is revenue minus costs.

Profit in perfectly competitive and monopoly market structures

The ability of a firm to make profit depends on the competitiveness of the market in which it sells its output. In Chapter 5, I explain how perfectly competitive firms make very little profit in the long run because the absence of **barriers to entry** means that significant profits made by incumbent firms (firms already in the market) attracts new firms into the market. The market price falls, which reduces the profit made by firms that decide to stay in the market. Monopoly, by contrast, is protected by barriers to entry. As you learnt at AS, unless regulated by the government, a monopoly can use its market power to restrict output and raise the price at which it sells its output. As a result, monopoly profit is much higher than the rate of profit earned by firms producing in highly competitive markets. For similar reasons, oligopoly profits also tend to be high.

Evaluating the strengths and weaknesses of different market structures

Having surveyed the building blocks of the theory of the firm, I have arrived at the final but most important of the topics which relate to market structure and business behaviour. This is evaluation of the 'good' and 'bad' elements of perfect competition, monopoly, and oligopoly.

Economists evaluate the strengths and weaknesses of the different market structures by applying two sets of criteria to address the questions:

➤ Which market structure is 'best' and why?
➤ Is it 'best' in all circumstances?

Efficiency concepts provide the first criteria. We must ask 'Is perfect competition more efficient than monopoly and oligopoly?' At AS, you used just one measure of economic efficiency: **productive efficiency**. To this, I must add: **allocative efficiency**, **static efficiency**, and **dynamic efficiency**. Along with a recap of the meaning of productive efficiency, these are explained in Chapter 6.

Welfare concepts provide the second criteria. In Chapter 6, I explain the meaning of two measures of economic welfare, **consumer surplus** and **producer surplus**, which I then apply, along with the efficiency criteria just mentioned, to evaluate the desirable and less desirable characteristics of perfect competition and monopoly. In a similar way in Chapter 7, I evaluate the strengths and weaknesses of imperfect competition and oligopoly.

Industrial policy

During your AS studies, you learnt that monopoly can be a form of **market failure**, but that it can also be a source of economies of scale that may lead to falling average costs and prices from which consumers benefit. You also learnt that governments can intervene in markets to try to eliminate or reduce the various failures associated with monopoly, such as restricting output and raising the price that consumers pay and restricting consumer choice. At A2, you study **competition policy** in depth, evaluating the costs and benefits of monopoly and different policies governments can undertake with regard to established monopolies, mergers that might create new monopolies, and anti-competitive trading restrictive practices. Chapter 9 on **industrial policy** also analyses and evaluates state ownership of firms (**nationalisation**) and its opposite, **privatisation**, together with the **regulation** and **deregulation** of markets and industries.

> **Key terms**
>
> **Welfare** basically means human happiness.
>
> **Industrial policy** is the government's microeconomic policy.
>
> A **firm** is a business that sells its output commercially in a market.

What is a firm?

A **firm** is a business enterprise which either produces or deals in and exchanges goods or services. Unlike non-business productive organisations, for example a central government department such as HM Revenue and Customs (HMRC), firms are commercial, earning revenue to cover the production costs they incur.

Firms operate in both the private sector and the public sector of the economy. Public sector business enterprises include nationalised industries such as the Royal Mail (which may soon be partly privatised), and certain municipally-owned trading enterprises. The dividing line between private and public sector business enterprise is not always clear cut. In the past, some businesses were joint ventures, owned in part by both the private sector and by the state, whilst others were state-majority shareholdings, in which the state owned a controlling interest in a nominally private sector company. Since around 1980, these and other nationalised industries have mostly been privatised. Privatisation occurs when industries or firms are transferred from the public sector to the private sector.

The main forms of business enterprise in the UK economy are shown in Figure 2.2, though it must be stressed that some of these, such as **mutually-owned societies** such as **building societies** (in the private sector) and the various forms of public sector business enterprise have become much less important in recent years.

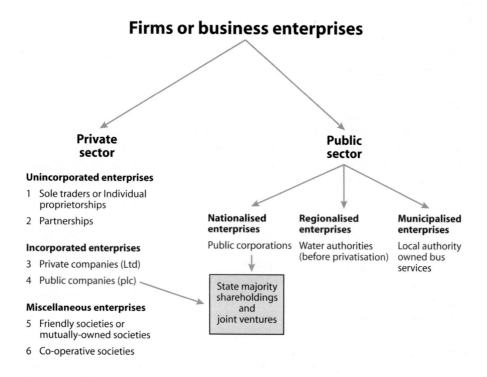

Figure 2.2 *Different forms of business enterprise in the UK economy*

Businesses and their legal status

In terms of legal status, firms in the private sector of the UK economy include sole traders (or individual proprietors), partnerships, and companies.

Sole traders

In the private sector, there are more than a million small businesses, many of which are sole traders or individual proprietorships. Sole traders are common in the labour-intensive provision of personal services, where not much capital is needed.

Along with other forms of small business such as partnerships and smaller private companies, sole traders often occupy specialised market niches, sometimes providing services to much larger companies in the same or related markets. But although there are many of them, small size means that sole traders produce only a small proportion of national output.

Partnerships

A partnership is formed whenever two or more people agree to undertake a business or trading activity together, instead of operating separately as sole traders. There are in fact two rather different kinds of partnership. On the one hand, there are many thousands of small informal partnerships, usually with just two or three partners functioning much as if they were sole traders. (See Box 2.2 on the history of Marks & Spencer.)

The second type of partnership is more formal and often much larger than the small informal partnerships just described. Formal partnerships dominate the supply of professional services, such as architects, accountants and solicitors. Some partnerships in the accountancy and legal professions are very large, with scores of partners providing funds for the business. In these and other professions, professional ethic, which requires a member of the profession to be fully liable to clients for the service provided, prevents members of the profession from forming companies. Along with sole traders, partners traditionally had unlimited liability, which meant that the partners were personally liable for any loss incurred by the firm. As Box 2.1 explains, the law was changed in 2001 and the members of large partnerships now enjoy an element of limited liability.

Box 2.1 Partnerships in the accountancy profession

A partnership is the main form of business organisation in professions such as accountancy, law and architecture. In accountancy, the 'big four' firms (PricewaterhouseCoopers (PWC), Ernst & Young, KPMG and Deloitte) are huge multinational partnerships that act as auditors, consultants, insolvency practitioners, and advisers for tax, business and corporate finance to all the leading public and private companies in the UK. The 'big four' used to be the 'big five', but in 2002 amidst the Enron scandal, the fifth firm, Andersens, collapsed.

Partnerships are private businesses owned completely by the member partners. Until quite recently each and every partner had unlimited liability. In 2001 the government created a new legal entity, the Limited Liability Partnership (LLP). Many accountancy firms changed their legal status to become Limited Liability Partnerships.

Follow-up questions
1   What is meant by limited liability and what is its main advantage?
2   Compared to companies, partnerships face difficulties in raising capital. Explain why.

Box 2.2 The growth of Marks & Spencer

Michael Marks started in business as a sole trader in Kirkgate open market in Leeds in 1884. Ten years later, Marks formed a partnership with Tom Spencer and Marks & Spencer was born. The growth of the business that followed, including the transformation of M&S into first a private company and then a public company, is portrayed in the business's 'time line' shown below.

1884 Michael Marks, a Russian born Polish refugee, opened a stall at Leeds Kirkgate Market. Goods sold included nails, screws, soap, wooden spoons and luggage labels.

1894 Michael formed a partnership with Tom Spencer, a former cashier from the wholesale company I. J. Dewhirst.

1903 Marks & Spencer Ltd was incorporated. The partnership was converted into a limited company with £30,000 in £1 ordinary shares of which 14,996 each were allotted to Marks and to Spencer.

1924–31 In 1924 Marks & Spencer's head office moved from Manchester to the City of London. In 1931 the M&S headquarters moved again to Baker Street in the West End. In 1926 the company, needing an injection of cash, was converted into a public company to raise new capital.

2004 Marks & Spencer moved its headquarters to Paddington Basin near Paddington Station. To update its image, in recent years M&S has replaced its old St Michael trade mark with brand names such as Autograph.

Follow-up questions

1 Explain why a successful business such as Marks & Spencer decided over time to change its legal status to eventually become a public limited company (plc).

2 Sometimes public companies such as Virgin change and revert to private company status. What are the disadvantages of public company status that lead to such decisions?

Marks & Spencer store, Marble Arch

Companies

Outside the professions, the owners of growing and successful small businesses usually prefer to run their businesses as **companies** rather than as sole traders or partnerships. Companies are owned by shareholders who benefit from limited liability. This limits the shareholder's financial risk to the amount invested in the company. Without limited liability, only the safest and most risk-free business ventures could attract the large-scale supply of funds or savings required to finance large-scale capital investment.

 Key *term*

A **company** is an incorporated business enterprise.

There are two main types of company: **private companies** and public companies. A private company has the word 'limited' in its business name, whereas a public company can be recognised by the letters plc in its business name. Most private companies are small or medium-sized, though a few are quite large. Some private companies are wholly-owned subsidiaries of public companies. For example, Lever Brothers Ltd is owned by Unilever plc, which is an Anglo-Dutch public company. Household-name public companies such as Tesco plc and Marks & Spencer plc are usually much larger than private companies.

Key terms

A **private company** issues shares that are not for sale on a market.

A **public company** issues shares that the general public can buy on a market or stock exchange.

Due to their large size, **public companies** are the most important form of business organisation in the UK, despite the fact that there are considerably fewer public companies than private companies. In recent years, however, there has been a move in the opposite direction, converting companies that used to be plcs back into private company ownership. The first reason for this is that a company's dominant shareholders don't want the company to be vulnerable to a hostile takeover bid. Only public companies and not private companies can be taken over against the will of major shareholders, unless of course a private company is forced out of business into receivership or liquidation. The second reason is that the company's dominant shareholders may also prefer the greater secrecy that private companies enjoy. Thirdly, the emergence of a new financial industry called **private equity finance** provides a source of capital that allows a private company to grow without the need to 'go public'.

Plants and firms

In microeconomic theory, it is often assumed that a typical firm operates a single manufacturing plant to produce a specific product within a well-defined industry. Though single plant/single product firms certainly exist, particularly amongst small businesses, large firms tend to be much more diverse. A **plant** is an individual productive unit within the firm, such as a factory, office or shop. Many big firms operate a large number of plants producing a range of products. Such multi-plant and multi-product firms, often organised as holding companies owning subsidiary companies in each of the industries they operate in, are much more typical amongst big business than the single product/single plant firm.

A BP-owned garage in Poland. This is an example of a plant.

The largest business corporations are **multinational companies** owning subsidiary enterprises throughout the world. Some multinationals such as BP and GlaxoSmithKline (GSK) are British owned, with their headquarters and most of their shareholders located in the UK. However, many of the multinational corporations operating subsidiary companies and branch factories in the UK are overseas-owned. Nissan, Toyota and Honda are Japanese-owned multinationals which have built factories in the UK in recent years, while Ford, General Motors and IBM are US multinationals that have produced in the UK for many years.

> **Key** *term*
>
> A **multinational company** is a business with headquarters in one country that owns and operates subsidiary companies in other countries.

Summary

➤ The theory of the firm is the main part of business economics.

➤ The building blocks of the theory of the firm include production theory, cost theory and revenue theory.

➤ Production and cost theory divide into short-run and long-run theory.

➤ A firm's sales revenue is influenced by the market structure in which the firm sells its output.

➤ Perfect competition, monopoly and oligopoly are the three market structures you need to know, and you must be aware of the meaning of imperfect competition.

➤ Economists usually assume that maximising profit is a firm's main business objective.

➤ Profit is total sales revenue minus total costs of production.

➤ The government uses industrial policy to promote competition and to reduce the harmful effects of monopoly and oligopoly.

➤ Competition policy, privatisation and regulation and deregulation form the main parts of industrial policy.

➤ Firms can be defined according to their legal status as sole traders, partnerships and private and public companies.

Questions

1 Define production.

2 In microeconomic theory, what is the difference between the short run and the long run?

3 What is the difference between sales revenue and profit?

4 Outline three business objectives a firm may have other than profit maximisation.

5 Distinguish between a firm and a plant.

6 Outline the main forms of business organisation in the private sector of the UK economy.

Chapter 3

Production and cost theory

Throughout this book you will be reminded that the ultimate purpose of economic activity is to increase economic welfare. (The economic welfare enjoyed by consumers is also known as utility.) For most people, most of the time, increased welfare means higher levels of demand for and consumption of consumer goods and services. But before goods and services can be consumed, they first have to be produced. This chapter explains two important parts of microeconomic theory: production theory and cost theory. Production theory centres on the relationship between inputs into the production process and the output of goods or services produced. Cost theory then links production theory to the money costs of production firms incur when purchasing labour and the other factor services necessary for production to take place.

Learning outcomes

This chapter will:
➤ explain the meaning of production
➤ compare short-run and long-run production
➤ derive short-run cost curves from short-run production theory
➤ derive long-run cost curves from long-run production theory
➤ remind you of economies of scale and diseconomies of scale

What you should already know

Unit 1 at AS introduced a number of production and cost terms and concepts. You learnt that production converts inputs, or the services of factors of production such as capital and labour, into final output. You should also understand the meanings of productivity (including labour productivity), and productive efficiency. You should be familiar with production possibility and average cost curve diagrams. However, at AS you were not expected to know the distinction between short-run and long-run cost curves or detailed explanation of the shape of cost curves.

At AS you also came across economies and diseconomies of scale and learnt how they affect average costs and the growth of firms. You should be able to give examples of types or causes of economy and diseconomy of scale.

Production and costs

Production, which is depicted in Figure 3.1, involves processes that convert inputs into outputs. The inputs into production processes (land, labour, capital and enterprise) are also called **factors of production**. The nature of production depends to a great extent on the time period in which production is taking place. In microeconomics, there are three time periods: the market period, the short run and the long run. The market period is a period so short that production cannot be changed at all. This chapter examines how firms can increase production, and thence incur **costs of production**, in the short run and in the long run.

Key term

Production is a process that converts inputs of factor services into outputs of goods.

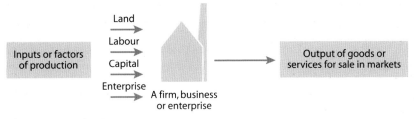

Figure 3.1 *Production*

---

examiner's voice

Economists often use the terms *short run* and *long run*. Be careful with these terms because they sometimes have a different meaning in macroeconomics to their meaning in microeconomics. In microeconomics, at least one factor of production is fixed and cannot be varied in the short run, whereas in the long run the *scale* of all inputs can be varied. By contrast, when we are looking at the future impact of government macroeconomic policies, the short run stretches ahead for about a year, the medium term lasts from about 1–3 years and the long run refers to any period longer than about 3 years.

Short-run production theory

In microeconomic theory, the **short run** is the time period in which at least one of the inputs or factors of production is fixed and cannot be changed. (By contrast, in the **long run**, the scale of all the factors of production can be changed.) As a simplification, I shall pretend that only two inputs or factors of production are needed for production to take place — capital and labour.

Key terms

The **short run** is the time period in which at least one factor of production is fixed.

The **long run** is the time period in which the scale of *all* factors of production can be changed.

I shall also assume that in the short run, capital is fixed. It follows that the only way the firm can increase output in the short run is by adding more of the variable factor of production, labour, to the fixed capital.

Table 3.1 *Short-run production with fixed capital*

Number of workers (fixed capital)	0	1	2	3	4	5	6	7	8	9
Total output, product or returns	0	1	4	9	16	25	32	35	36	34
Average output, product or returns	–	1	2	3	4	5	5.3	5	4.5	3.8
Marginal output, product or returns		1	3	5	7	9	7	3	1	–2

Table 3.1 shows what might happen to car production in a small luxury sports car factory when the number of workers employed increases from 0 to 9. The first worker employed builds one car a year, and the second and third workers respectively add three and five cars to total production. These figures measure the marginal product (or marginal returns) of the first three workers employed. **Marginal product** is the addition to total output brought about by adding one more worker to the labour force.

In Table 3.1, the first five workers benefit from increasing marginal productivity (or increasing marginal returns). An additional worker increases total output by *more* than the amount added by the previous worker. Increasing marginal productivity is indeed very likely when the labour force is small. In this situation, employing an extra worker allows the workforce to be organised more efficiently. By dividing the various tasks of production among a greater number of workers, the firm benefits from **specialisation** and the **division of labour**. Workers become better and more efficient in performing the particular tasks in which they specialise, and time is saved that otherwise would be lost as a result of workers switching between tasks.

But as the firm adds labour to fixed capital, eventually the **law of diminishing marginal productivity** (or **law of diminishing marginal returns**) sets in. In this example, the law sets in when the sixth worker is employed. The fifth worker's marginal product is nine cars, but the sixth worker adds only seven cars to total output. Diminishing marginal productivity sets in because labour is being added to fixed capital. When more and more labour is added to fixed plant and machinery, eventually the marginal product of labour must fall, though not often at a labour force as small as six workers.

 Key term

The **law of diminishing marginal returns** is a short-term law which states that as a variable factor of production is added to fixed factors, eventually the marginal returns (or marginal product) of the variable factor will begin to fall.

Note that diminishing marginal productivity does not mean that an extra worker joining the labour force is any less hardworking or motivated than his or her predecessors. (In microeconomic theory we often assume that workers and other factors of production are completely interchangeable and homogeneous.) The law sets in because the benefits resulting from any further specialisation and division of labour eventually become exhausted as more labour is added to a fixed amount of capital or machinery.

Product curves

Figure 3.2 illustrates the law of diminishing marginal returns. In the upper panel of the diagram, the law begins to operate at point *A*, where the slope of the total product curve begins to change. With increasing marginal productivity, the slope of the total product curve increases, moving from point to point up the curve. When diminishing returns set in, the total product curve continues to rise as more workers are combined with capital, but the curve becomes less steep from point to point up the curve. Point *Y* shows where *total* product begins to fall. Beyond this point, additional workers begin to get in the way of other workers, so the marginal product of labour becomes negative. However, you must avoid explaining negative marginal productivity in terms of workers' hostility or their tendency to throw a spanner in the works.

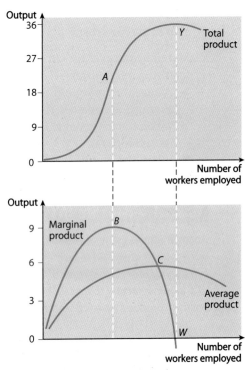

Figure 3.2 *Total, marginal and average product curves*

The total product curve in the upper panel of Figure 3.2 plots the information in the top row of Table 3.1. By contrast, the lower panel of the diagram plots the marginal product of labour (from the information in the bottom row of Table 3.1) and the average product of labour (from the information in the middle row of Table 3.1).

It is important to understand that all three curves (and all three rows in Table 3.1) contain the same information, but used differently in each curve (and row). The total product curve plots the information cumulatively, adding the marginal product of the last worker to the total product before the worker joined the labour force. By contrast, the marginal product curve plots the same information non-cumulatively, or as separate observations. Finally, at each level of employment, the average product curve shows the total product of the labour force divided by the number of workers employed.

In the lower panel of Figure 3.2, the law of diminishing marginal productivity sets in at point *B*, at the highest point on the marginal product curve. Before this point, increasing marginal productivity is shown by the rising (or positively sloped) marginal product curve, while beyond this point, diminishing marginal productivity is depicted by the falling (or negatively sloped) marginal product curve. Likewise, the point of diminishing *average* productivity sets in at the highest point of the average product curve at point *C*. Finally, marginal product becomes negative beyond point *W*.

The relationship between marginal product and average product

The relationship between the marginal productivity and the average productivity of labour is an example of a more general relationship that you need to know. Shortly, I shall provide a second example, namely marginal cost and its relationship to average cost.

Marginal and average curves plotted from the same set of data always display the following relationship:

➤ When the marginal is greater than the average, the average rises.
➤ When the marginal is less than the average, the average falls.
➤ When the marginal equals the average, the average is constant, neither rising nor falling.

> **examiner's voice**
> Make sure you understand the relationship between the marginal and average values of an economic variable.

Box 3.1 Adam Smith's pin factory

Adam Smith was an eighteenth-century Scottish philosophy professor, and later customs commissioner, who is often said to be the founder of modern economics. In his great book, *An Inquiry into the Nature and Causes of the Wealth of Nations*, which was published in 1776, Adam Smith used the example of a local pin factory to explain how the division of labour amongst workers greatly increases their ability to produce. Here is a slightly abridged version of what Adam Smith wrote:

A workman not educated in the business of pin making could scarce, perhaps, with his utmost industry, make one pin in a day, and certainly could not make twenty. But in the way in which this business is now carried on, one man draws out the wire, another straights it, a third cuts it, a fourth points it, a fifth grinds it at the top for receiving the pin head. The business of making a pin is divided into about eighteen distinct operations. Ten persons could make among them upwards of forty-eight thousand pins in a day. Each person, therefore, making a tenth part of forty-eight thousand pins, might be considered as making four thousand eight hundred pins in a day. But if they had all wrought separately and independently, and without any of them having been educated to this peculiar business, they certainly could not each of them have made twenty, perhaps not one pin in a day.

This great increase in the quantity of work is a consequence of the division of labour. There are three different aspects of this: first, the increase of dexterity in every particular workman; secondly, the saving of the time which is commonly lost in passing from one species of work to another; and lastly, the invention of a great number of machines which enable one man to do the work of many.

Follow-up questions
1 What is meant by the division of labour?
2 What effects does the division of labour have on production and costs?

Short-run costs

Cost curves measure the costs that firms have to pay to hire the inputs or factors of production needed to produce output. In the short run, when the inputs divide into fixed and variable factors of production, the costs of production can likewise be divided into fixed and variable costs. This can be written as:

total cost = total fixed cost + total variable cost

or:

$TC = TFC + TVC$

Likewise, average total cost per unit can be written as:

average total cost = average fixed cost + average variable cost

or:

$ATC = AFC + AVC$

To explain how total costs of production vary with output in the short run, I shall look first at fixed costs and then at variable costs.

Fixed costs

Fixed costs of production are overheads, such as the rent on land and the maintenance costs of buildings, which a firm must pay in the short run. Suppose, for example, that a car manufacturing company incurs overheads of £1 million a year

> **Key term**
>
> **Fixed costs** are the costs of employing the fixed factors of production in the short run.

from an assembly plant it operates. I can represent these costs both as the horizontal total fixed cost curve in Figure 3.3(a) and as the downward-sloping average fixed cost curve in Figure 3.3(b). If the plant only managed to produce one automobile a year, *AFC* per car would be £1 million – the single car would bear all the overheads. But if the company were to increase production, average fixed costs

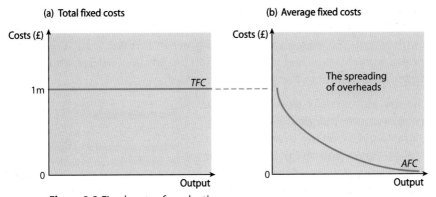

Figure 3.3 *Fixed costs of production*

would fall to £500,000 when two cars are produced, £333,333 when three cars are produced and so on. Average fixed costs per unit of output fall as output increases, since overheads are spread over a larger output.

Variable costs

Variable costs are the costs that the firm incurs when it hires variable factors of production such as labour and raw materials. For simplicity, I shall assume that labour is the only variable factor of production. The upper panel of Figure 3.4 shows the marginal and average productivity of labour. Diminishing marginal returns begin at point A. Increasing marginal productivity of labour (or increasing marginal returns) is shown by the positive (or rising) slope of the marginal product curve, while diminishing marginal returns are represented, beyond point A, by the curve's negative (or falling) slope.

When labour is the only variable factor of production, variable costs are simply wage costs. If all workers receive the same hourly wage, total wage costs rise in exact proportion to the number of workers employed. However, with increasing marginal labour productivity, the total variable cost of production rises at a slower rate than output. This causes the marginal cost (*MC*) of producing an extra unit of output to fall. In Figure 3.4, the increasing marginal productivity of labour (shown by the positive slope of the marginal product curve in the upper of the two diagrams) causes marginal cost (shown in the lower of the two diagrams) to fall.

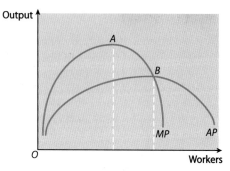

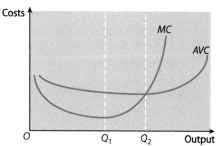

Figure 3.4 *Deriving the* MC *and* AVC *curves from short-run production theory*

Key **term**

Variable costs are the costs of employing the variable factors of production in the short run.

However, once the law of diminishing marginal productivity sets in, marginal cost rises with output. The wage cost of employing an extra worker is still the same, but each extra worker is now less productive than the previous worker. Variable costs rise faster than output, so marginal cost also rises.

Just as the *MC* curve is derived from the marginal returns or marginal productivity of the variable inputs, so the average variable cost (*AVC*) curve (illustrated in the lower panel of Figure 3.4) is explained by the average returns or productivity curve (shown

examiner's voice

Make sure you understand the relationship between marginal product curves (or marginal return curves) and marginal cost curves, in the economic short run.

AQA A2 Economics

in the upper panel). When increasing average returns are experienced, with the labour force on average becoming more efficient and productive, the *AVC* per unit of output must fall as output rises. But once diminishing average returns set in at point *B*, the *AVC* curve begins to rise with output.

Average total costs

The firm's average total cost (*ATC*) curve is obtained from the addition of the *AFC* and *AVC* curves, as shown in Figure 3.5(a). Figure 3.5(b) shows the *ATC* curve on its own, without showing its two components (*AFC* and *AVC*). You should note that the *ATC* curve is typically U-shaped, showing that average total costs per unit of output first fall and later rise as output is increased. In the short run, average total costs must eventually rise because, at high levels of output, any further spreading of fixed costs becomes insufficient to offset the impact of diminishing returns upon variable costs of production. Sooner or later, rising marginal costs (which, as we have seen, result from diminishing marginal returns) must cut through and 'pull up' the *ATC* curve.

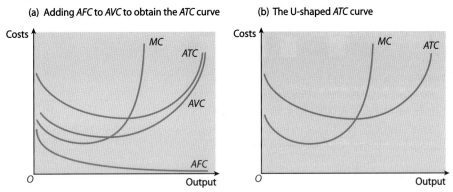

Figure 3.5 *The average total cost (ATC) curve*

examiner's voice

You must understand that in the short run, the law of diminishing returns leads to rising marginal costs, which in turn cause a firm's average total cost curve to be U-shaped. Note also that the *MC* curve cuts both the *AVC* and the *ATC* curves at their lowest points (at the bottom of the 'U').

Long-run production theory

The only way a firm can increase output in the short run is by adding more variable factors of production (such as labour) to its fixed capital. But eventually the law of diminishing productivity sets in, which causes short-run marginal costs to rise. When the *MC* curve rises through the firm's *ATC* curve, average total costs of production also rise.

To escape the adverse effect of rising short-run costs upon profit, in the economic long run a firm may decide to change the *scale* of its operations. In the long run there are no fixed factors of production. In this time period, the firm can change the

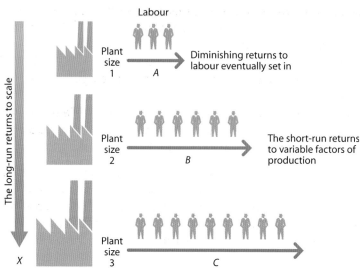

Figure 3.6 *Returns to scale*

scale of all its factors of production, including its capital or production plant, which is normally assumed to be fixed in the short run.

Returns to scale

Figure 3.6 illustrates the important distinction between returns to a variable factor of production, which occur in the short run, and **returns to scale**, which operate only in the economic long run. Suppose that initially a firm's fixed capital is represented by plant size 1 in the diagram. Initially, the firm can

Key term

Returns to scale describes how output changes when the scale of *all* the factors of production change in the long run. They divide into increasing returns to scale, decreasing returns to scale and constant returns to scale.

increase production in the short run, by moving along the horizontal arrow *A*, employing more variable factors of production such as labour. However, the only way the firm can further increase profits once the short-run profit-maximising output has been reached is to change the scale of its operations, assuming that the firm cannot operate its existing plant more efficiently. In the long run, the firm can invest in a larger production plant, such as plant size 2, shown as the move along the vertical arrow *X* in the diagram. Once plant size 2 is in operation, the firm is in a new short-run situation, able to increase output by moving along arrow *B*. But again, the impact of diminishing returns may eventually cause the firm to expand the scale of its operations to plant size 3 in the long run.

The law of diminishing marginal productivity, explained earlier in the context of short-run production, is a short-run law that does not operate in the long run when a firm increases the scale of all its inputs or factors of production. With returns to scale there are three possibilities:

> ➤ **Increasing returns to scale.** If an increase in the scale of all the factors of production causes a more than proportionate increase in output, there are increasing returns to scale.

> ➤ **Constant returns to scale.** If an increase in the scale of all the factors of production causes a proportionate increase in output, there are constant returns to scale.

> ➤ **Decreasing returns to scale.** If an increase in the scale of all the factors of production causes a less than proportionate increase in output, there are decreasing (or diminishing) returns to scale.

It is important not to confuse returns to scale, which occur in the long run when the scale of all the factors of production can be altered, with the short-run returns that occur when at least one factor is fixed. We have already seen how short-run returns affect the shape of a firm's short-run cost curves. I shall now explain how returns to scale affect the shape of a firm's long-run average costs (*LRAC*) of production.

Long-run costs

In the long run, a firm can change the scale of all its factors of production, moving from one size of plant to another. Figure 3.7 shows a number of short-run average total cost (*SRATC*) curves, each representing a particular size or scale of firm. In the long run, a firm can move from one short-run cost curve to another, with each curve associated with a different scale of capacity that is fixed in the short run. The line drawn as a tangent to the family or set of *SRATC* curves is the long-run average cost (*LRAC*) curve.

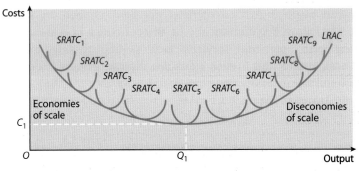

Figure 3.7
A U-shaped LRAC curve and its related SRATC curves

Economies of scale and diseconomies of scale

Just as it is important to avoid confusing short-run returns or productivity with long-run returns to scale, so **returns to scale** must be distinguished from a closely related concept: **economies and diseconomies of scale**. Returns to scale refer to the technical relationship in production between inputs and outputs measured in physical units. For example, increasing returns to scale occur if a doubling of a car firm's factory size and its labour force enables the firm to more than double its output of cars. There is no mention of money costs of production in this example of increasing returns to scale. Returns to scale are part of long-run production

theory, but economies and diseconomies of scale are part of long-run cost theory. Economies of scale occur when long-run average costs (*LRAC*) fall as output increases. Diseconomies of scale occur when *LRAC* rise as output increases.

> ### examiner's voice
>
> You must develop your understanding of economies and diseconomies of scale from the knowledge you learnt at AS. In particular, you must know that economies of scale reduce a firm's long-run average costs. At A2 you must thoroughly understand cost theory, especially the difference between short-run and long-run cost curves.

There is, however, a link between returns to scale and economies and diseconomies of scale. Increasing returns to scale lead to falling long-run average costs or **economies of scale**, and likewise decreasing returns to scale bring about rising long-run average costs or **diseconomies of scale**.

 Key terms

Economies of scale are defined as falling long-run average costs as the size or scale of the firm increases.

Diseconomies of scale mean rising long-run average costs as the size or scale of the firm increases.

The shape of the long-run average cost curve

Figure 3.7 illustrates a U-shaped long-run average cost curve in which economies of scale are eventually followed by diseconomies. An increase in all the inputs or factors of production causes *LRAC* to fall to C_1, at output Q_1, but after this point, diseconomies of scale set in.

However, the long-run average cost curve need not be U-shaped, in which economies of scale are followed symmetrically by diseconomies of scale. Some industries, including many personal services such as hairdressing, exhibit **economies of small-scale production**. In such industries, diseconomies of scale may set in at a relatively small size of production plant or fixed capacity, resulting in the rising *LRAC* curve illustrated in Figure 3.8.

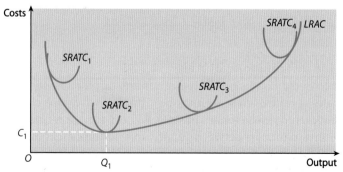

Figure 3.8
Economies of small-scale production

In other industries, which lack significant economies or diseconomies of scale, the horizontal *LRAC* curve depicted in Figure 3.9 may be more typical, allowing firms or plants of many different sizes to exist within the same industry.

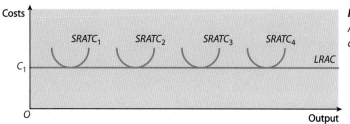

Figure 3.9
A horizontal LRAC curve

In much of the manufacturing industry, however, statistical studies suggest that the *LRAC* curve is L-shaped, as illustrated in Figure 3.10. Beyond output Q_1 the *LRAC* curve is horizontal. No further economies of scale are possible, but likewise there are no diseconomies of scale. In industries such as automobile and aircraft building, for which the L-shaped curve may be typical, size of firm is limited by market constraints rather than by the onset of diseconomies of scale.

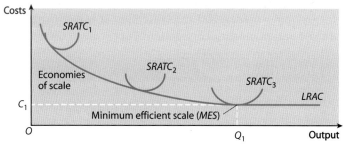

Figure 3.10
An L-shaped LRAC curve and the minimum efficient scale (MES)

The optimum size of firm and minimum efficient scale

The size of plant at the lowest point on the firm's *LRAC* curve is known as the **optimum plant size**. When the long-run average cost curve is U-shaped, as in Figure 3.7, we can identify a single optimum plant size level of output, occurring after economies of scale have been gained, but before diseconomies of scale set in.

Engine construction at a Rolls-Royce manufacturing plant

In Figure 3.7, optimum plant size is shown by the short-run cost curve $SRATC_5$, with optimum output at Q_1. In the case of the horizontal $LRAC$ curve illustrated in Figure 3.9, where there are no economies or diseconomies of scale, it is not possible to identify an optimal plant size.

However, when the $LRAC$ curve is L-shaped, as in Figure 3.10, the long-run average cost curve flattens out. Plant size 3 is therefore known as the **minimum efficient scale (MES)**, indicating the smallest size of plant that can benefit from minimum long-run average costs. Some economies of scale may still be possible, for example technical

Key term

Minimum efficient scale (MES) is the smallest size of plant that can benefit from minimum long-run average costs.

economies, but these would be offset by diseconomies of scale emerging elsewhere within the business, for example managerial diseconomies of scale. (I explain technical economies of scale and managerial diseconomies of scale in Chapter 8.)

Box 3.2 Outsourcing and economies of scale

Economics students often assume that economies of scale mean that large firms enjoy a cost advantage over smaller firms. In recent years, however, a number of developments in the organisation of production have reduced the advantages of large size. Around 1998, Peter Wells and Paul Nieuwenhuis of the Cardiff Business School came up with the idea of micro-factories assembling low volumes of cars within local markets. Their micro-factories would also act as retail distribution points. Taken to the extreme, this could see the emergence of a 'virtual' company that would

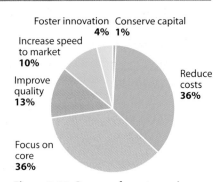

Figure 3.11 Reasons for outsourcing

outsource just about everything, from organising networks of suppliers, to manufacturing, design and delivery and service. Manufacturing would be done in small plants within separated national markets, to ensure that it took place close to the customers. Parts would be made in a network of factories in low-wage countries.

Outsourcing is a term used to describe almost any business activity that is managed by an outside firm. Outsourcing has three main advantages:

► The greater economies of scale that can be gained by a third party that is able to pool the activity of a large number of firms. It is thus frequently cheaper for a firm to outsource specialist activities (where it cannot hope to gain economies of scale on its own) than it is to carry them out itself. Some firms gain the economies of scale by taking on the activity of others, becoming an outsourcer themselves.

► The ability of a specialist outsourcing firm to keep abreast of the latest developments in its field.

► The way that it enables small firms to do things for which they could not justify hiring full-time employees.

The most commonly cited disadvantage of outsourcing is the loss of control involved in delegating responsibility for particular processes to others.

Outsourcing has grown exceptionally fast in recent years. According to one estimate, in 1946 only 20% of a typical American manufacturing company's value-added in production and operations came from outside sources; 50 years later the proportion had tripled to 60%. In the car industry in the 1990s, firms with the biggest profit per car, such as Toyota and Honda, were also the biggest outsourcers (sourcing around 70% to various suppliers). Those that outsourced the least, for example General Motors were the least profitable.

Some firms have been so taken with the idea of outsourcing that they have left themselves with little to do. An American company called Monorail Computers outsourced the manufacture of its computers as well as the ordering, delivery and the accounts receivable. Only the design was left to be handled in-house.

Source: *The Economist* 29 September 2008

Follow-up questions

1 Describe three examples of outsourcing, apart from those outlined above in the car industry.
2 Evaluate the view that outsourcing reduces rather than increases the importance of economies of scale.

Summary

➤ Production is a process or set of processes for converting inputs into outputs.

➤ The key concept in short-run production theory is the law of diminishing returns.

➤ This law is also known as the law of diminishing marginal productivity.

➤ In the short-run, the marginal cost curve and the average variable cost curve are derived from the law of diminishing marginal returns.

➤ The short-run average cost curve is 'U'-shaped.

➤ The key concept in long-run production theory is returns to scale.

➤ Increasing returns to scale, constant returns to scale and decreasing returns to scale are all possible.

> Increasing returns to scale lead to economies of scale and falling long-run average costs.
> Decreasing returns to scale lead to diseconomies of scale and rising long-run average costs.
> The long-run average cost curve may be 'U' shaped, but other shapes are possible.
> Minimum efficient scale (*MES*) are illustrated on an 'L'-shaped *LRAC* curve.

Questions

1 What are the factors of production?

2 Distinguish between a fixed factor and a variable factor of production.

3 Give two examples of fixed costs.

4 Explain the law of diminishing returns.

5 How does the law of diminishing returns affect the marginal product curve and the average product curve of labour?

6 How do marginal returns affect marginal costs?

7 Why is a short-run *ATC* curve U-shaped?

8 Distinguish between short-run returns and returns to scale.

9 What is the relationship between returns to scale and economies of scale?

10 Distinguish between economies and diseconomies of scale.

11 Must the *LRAC* curve be U-shaped?

Chapter 4

Revenue theory and market structures

Chapter 3 explains how production takes place, and how the nature of production affects a firm's costs of production, in both the short run and the long run. This chapter develops two further elements in the theory of the firm, namely the market structures in which firms sell their output, which in turn affect the sales revenue that firms earn when they increase the quantity of output they sell.

Learning outcomes

This chapter will:
➤ develop the explanation of market structures first mentioned in Chapter 2
➤ explain how the competitiveness of a market structure affects a firm's revenue curves
➤ explain the difference between average revenue and marginal revenue
➤ compare a perfectly competitive firm's revenue curves with those of a monopoly

What you should already know

At AS, you learnt very little about the subject matter of this chapter. Having studied Unit 1: Markets and Market Failure, all you are required to know at the beginning of the A2 course is that profit is the difference between revenue and cost. Prior knowledge of revenue curves in the different market structures is not expected at the beginning of the A2 course.

However, an understanding of price elasticity of demand is very useful when learning about monopoly revenue curves. Elasticity is one of the key Unit 1 topics that is tested synoptically in the Unit 3 exam at A2.

The different market structures

In Chapter 2, I briefly mentioned that the nature of a firm's sales revenue depends on the competitiveness of the **market structure** in which the firm sells its output. Figure 2.1 on page 13, introduced the main market structures covered in this and the next three chapters, namely **perfect competition**, **monopoly**, and **oligopoly**. These are shown in greater detail in Figure 4.1 below.

Key term

Market structure is the framework within which a firm sells its output.

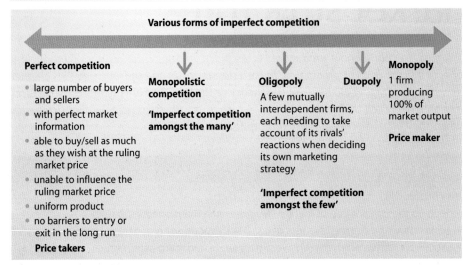

Figure 4.1 *The main market structures*

Market structures are defined by the number of firms in the market. However, this leads to other important aspects of the market, such as the competitiveness of the market, and the ways in which firms behave and conduct themselves in the market. Perfect competition and monopoly are at the opposite extremes of the spectrum of market structure shown in Figure 4.1. The market structures that lie between these extremes provide examples of **imperfect competition**.

Pure monopoly, in which a single firm produces the whole of the output of a market or industry, is the most extreme form of imperfect competition. Indeed, a pure monopolist faces no competition at all, since there are no other firms to compete against. Usually, however, monopoly is a *relative* rather than an *absolute* concept.

Key term

Pure monopoly exists where there is only one firm in a market.

Until quite recently, the British Gas Corporation was the single producer of piped gas to households and most industrial customers, but it experienced competition from other sources of energy such as electricity and oil. British Gas's monopoly power was further reduced in 1998 when other companies, including electricity companies, were allowed to sell gas to customers via the pipelines previously owned by British Gas. Monopolists do, therefore, face competitive pressures, both from substitute products and sometimes also from outside firms trying to enter the market to destroy their monopoly position.

At the other end of the spectrum, **perfect competition** is actually non-existent. It is best to regard perfect competition as an unreal or abstract economic model defined by the conditions listed in Figure 4.1. In Chapter 5, I explain that real-world markets cannot display simultaneously *all* the conditions necessary for perfect competition. Since any violation of the conditions of perfect competition immediately renders a market imperfectly competitive, even the most competitive markets in the real economy are examples of imperfect competition rather than perfect competition.

Key term

Perfect competition exists in a market containing a large number of firms and meets the six conditions that define the market structure.

But despite the lack of perfect markets in the real world, the theory of perfect competition is perhaps the most important and fundamental of all conventional economic theories. Critics of orthodox microeconomic theory strongly argue that economists pay undue attention to perfect competition as a market structure and that this encourages a false belief that a perfect market is an attainable ideal. As you read this and the next few chapters, remember at all times that perfect competition is an unrealistic market structure. (It would be clearer for students if perfect and imperfect competition were respectively called *unrealistic competition* and *realistic competition*.)

Nevertheless, perfect competition performs a very useful function. It serves as a standard or benchmark against which we may judge the desirable or undesirable properties of the imperfectly competitive market structures of the world we live in.

As I have mentioned, all markets between the polar extremes of perfect competition and monopoly are labelled as **imperfectly competitive**. There are two main imperfectly competitive market structures, **monopolistic competition** and **oligopoly**. If you use another textbook,

Key term

Oligopoly is an imperfectly competitive market containing only a few firms.

alongside this one, that covers the requirements of all the GCE examining boards, you will find a chapter there on monopolistic competition. However, monopolist competition is not in the AQA economics specification, so don't bother learning about it, at least beyond knowing that monopolistic competition is, as Figure 4.1 indicates, imperfect competition amongst the many. This means that there are a large number of firms in the market. By contrast, in oligopoly, which Figure 4.1 describes as imperfect competition amongst the few, there are generally only a handful of firms. (Indeed in **duopoly**, which is a special case of oligopoly, there are only two firms in the market.)

Almost all real world markets, certainly in developed economies such as the United Kingdom, are imperfectly competitive, and some of them, such as the video games console market, are oligopolies. Chapter 7 explains how oligopoly and concentrated markets divide into **competitive oligopoly**, in which firms compete actively against each other, and **collusive oligopoly**, in which firms cooperate with each other.

Microsoft, Sony and Nintendo form an oligopoly in the video games console market

Revenue

Revenue is the sales revenue or money that a firm earns when selling its output. As I emphasise in Chapter 2, you must not confuse a firm's *revenue* with the *returns* or output that the firm produces.

Likewise, you must not confuse **total revenue**, **average revenue** and **marginal revenue**. Total revenue is *all* the money a firm earns from selling the total output of a product. It is cumulative. Selling one more unit of a product or good usually causes total revenue to rise. By contrast, at any level of output, average revenue is calculated by dividing total revenue by the size of output:

> **examiner's voice**
>
> Make sure you don't confuse revenue with returns or with profit.

> **Key** term
>
> **Revenue** is the money income a firm receives from selling its output.

$$\text{average revenue} \ = \ \frac{\text{total revenue}}{\text{output}} \quad \text{or} \quad AR \ = \ \frac{TR}{Q}$$

where TR, AR and Q are the symbols I use for total revenue, average revenue and the level of output.

Marginal revenue is the addition to total revenue resulting from the sale of one more unit of output. Marginal revenue can be calculated by using the equation:

$$\text{marginal revenue} \ = \ \frac{\Delta \text{ total revenue}}{\Delta \text{ output}} \quad \text{or} \quad MR \ = \ \frac{\Delta TR}{\Delta Q}$$

where *MR* and Δ are the symbols used for marginal revenue and for the change in marginal revenue.

The Greek delta symbol Δ is used by mathematicians as the symbol for a change in the value of a variable over a range of observations. The word 'marginal' means the change in the value of a variable when there is one more unit of the variable, so Δ is the symbol that indicates this change. It is used in the formulae for marginal product and marginal cost, as well as marginal revenue.

How the competitiveness of a market structure affects a firm's revenue curves

Having explained the meaning of total, average and marginal revenue, in the final two sections of this chapter I shall explain how a firm's average revenue curve and its marginal revenue curve are derived, first in perfect competition and then in monopoly. (I explain oligopoly revenue curves in Chapter 7, rather than in this chapter.)

Revenue curves in perfect competition

I shall use the conditions of perfect competition, listed at the left-hand side of Figure 4.1, to derive the revenue curves facing a firm in a perfectly competitive market. The first four of the conditions of perfect competition are:

➤ a large number of buyers and sellers
➤ buyers and sellers possessing perfect information about the market
➤ possible to buy and sell as much as needed at the ruling market price set by market forces in the market as a whole
➤ individual market transactions unable to influence the ruling market price

Taken together, the four conditions I have listed tell us that a perfectly competitive firm, which is depicted in panel (a) of Figure 4.2, faces a perfectly elastic demand curve for its product. The demand curve facing the firm is located at the ruling market price, P_1, which itself is determined through the interaction of market demand and market supply in panel (b) of the diagram.

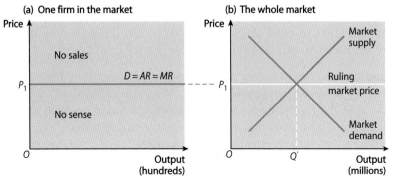

Figure 4.2
Deriving a perfectly competitive firm's average and marginal revenue curves

The assumption that a perfectly competitive firm can sell whatever quantity it wishes at the ruling market price P_1, but that it cannot influence the ruling market price by its own action, means that the firm is a passive **price-taker**.

The labels 'No sales' and 'No sense' that I have placed on Figure 4.2(a), respectively above and below the price line P_1, help to explain why a perfectly competitive firm is a price-taker. 'No sales' indicates that if the firm raises its selling price above the ruling market price, customers desert the firm to buy the identical products (perfect substitutes) available from other firms at the ruling market price. 'No sense' refers to the fact that although a perfectly competitive firm can sell its output below the price P_1, doing so is irrational. No extra sales can result, so selling below the ruling market price inevitably reduces both total sales revenue and profit. Such a pricing policy therefore conflicts with the profit-maximising objective that firms are assumed to have.

The horizontal price line facing a perfectly competitive firm is also the firm's **average revenue (AR)** and its **marginal revenue (MR)** curve. Suppose for example that the firm sells 100 units of a good, with each unit of the good priced at £1.00. The firm's total sales revenue (TR) is obviously £100.00.

Key *terms*

Average revenue equals total revenue divided by the size of output.

Marginal revenue equals the change in total revenue divided by the change in the size of output.

$$AR = \frac{TR}{Q} \text{ or } \frac{£100.00}{100} = £1.00$$

$$MR = \frac{\Delta TR}{\Delta Q} \text{ or } \frac{£1.00}{1} \text{ also} = £1.00$$

The price or average revenue is £1.00, as is the marginal revenue the firm earns when it sells one more unit.

$$Price = AR = MR$$

Revenue curves in monopoly

It is worth repeating that the demand curve facing a perfectly competitive firm, besides being located at the ruling market price, is also the firm's average revenue (AR) curve and its marginal revenue (MR) curve. By contrast, for monopoly the demand curve for the firm's output is also its AR curve, *but not* its MR curve.

This is because the demand curve facing a monopolist differs from the demand curve facing a firm in a perfectly competitive market. The industry demand curve and the demand curve for the monopolist's output are the same because the monopoly *is* the industry. This means that a monopolist faces a downward-sloping demand curve, whose elasticity is determined by the nature of consumer demand for the monopolist's product.

The downward-sloping demand curve affects the monopolist in one of two different ways. If the monopolist is a **price-maker**, choosing to set the price at which the product is sold, the demand curve dictates the maximum output that can be sold at this price. For example, if the price is set at P_1 in Figure 4.3, the maximum quantity that can be sold at this price is Q_1. And if the monopolist raises the price to P_2, sales fall to Q_2, unless the monopolist successfully uses advertising or other forms of marketing to shift the demand curve to the right. Alternatively, if the monopolist is a **quantity-setter** rather than a price-maker, the demand curve dictates the maximum price at which the chosen quantity can be sold. The fact that the demand curve is downward-sloping means that the monopolist faces a trade-off. A monopoly cannot set price and quantity independently of each other.

The demand curve is the monopolist's average revenue (AR) curve because the demand curve shows the price the monopolist charges at each level of output. However, unlike in perfect competition, marginal revenue and average revenue are *not* the same in monopoly. To explain this, I shall re-introduce the second statement in the mathematical relationship between a marginal variable and the average to which it is related:

when the marginal < the average, the average falls

(The full relationship is on page 26.)

examiner's voice

You should understand that a monopoly can be a price-maker or a quantity-setter, but not both at the same time.

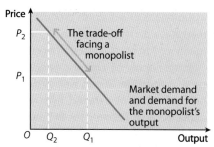

Figure 4.3 *The trade-off facing a monopolist*

examiner's voice

Questions in the Unit 3 examination on perfect competition, monopoly or oligopoly may be synoptic, testing your understanding of and ability to apply the concept of elasticity introduced in the AS course.

Since the monopolist's average revenue curve falls as output or sales rise, marginal revenue *must* be below average revenue. This relationship is shown in Figure 4.4, which depicts a monopolist's AR and MR curves, with the MR curve drawn twice as steep as the AR curve. This is always the case whenever the AR curve is a straight line or linear. (This property does not apply however, when the AR curve is non-linear, though the MR curve will always be below the AR curve as long as the AR curve is falling.)

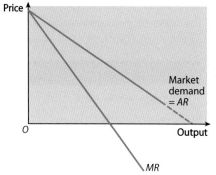

Figure 4.4 *Monopoly average revenue and marginal revenue curves*

A synoptic link: elasticity and revenue curves

Earlier in the chapter, I mentioned that the horizontal price line facing a perfectly competitive firm is also the **perfectly elastic** demand curve for the firm's output. The explanation for this lies in the word **substitutability**. In AS microeconomics you learnt that the availability of substitutes is the main determinant of price elasticity of demand. Now in perfect competition, because of the assumptions of a uniform product and perfect information, the output of every other firm in the market is a perfect substitute for the firm's own product. If the firm tries to raise its price above the ruling market price, it loses all its customers.

In monopoly by contrast, providing the demand curve is a straight line as well as downward sloping, price elasticity of demand falls moving down the demand curve. Demand for the monopolist's output is elastic in the top half of the curve, falling to be unit elastic exactly half way down the curve, and inelastic in the bottom half of the curve. This is shown in Figure 4.5. Demand is elastic between A and B, unit elastic at B, and inelastic between B and C.

I shall revisit the significance of elasticity in the next chapter, when comparing profit maximisation with revenue maximisation.

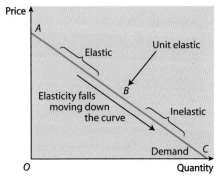

Figure 4.5 *Price elasticity of demand for a monopoly*

The next diagram, Figure 4.6, explains the relationship between a monopolist's *AR* and *MR* curves. The firm can only sell an extra unit of output by reducing the price at which *all* units of output are sold because the demand curve (or *AR* curve) facing the monopolist is downward-sloping. Total sales revenue increases by the area *k* in Figure 4.6, but decreases by the area *h*. Areas *k* and *h* respectively show the revenue gain (namely the extra unit

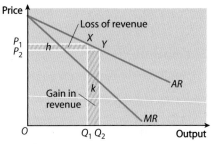

Figure 4.6 *Explaining the monopolist's* MR *curve*

sold multiplied by its price) and the revenue loss resulting from the sale of an extra unit of output. The revenue loss results from the fact that in order to sell one more unit of output, the price has to be reduced for *all* units of output, not just the extra unit sold. Marginal revenue, which is the revenue gain minus the revenue loss (or *k − h*), must be less than price or average revenue (area *k*).

Summary

➤ Market structures provide the framework in which businesses exist.

➤ Different market structures display different degrees of competitiveness.

➤ Perfect competition, monopoly and oligopoly are three main market structures.

➤ In pure monopoly there is only one firm in the market.

➤ There would be a very large number of firms (and also buyers) in a perfectly competitive market.

➤ But no real world market is perfectly competitive because not all the conditions of perfect competition can be met at the same time.

➤ Perfect competition provides a yardstick or benchmark against which the desirable and undesirable properties of real world markets can be measured.

➤ A perfectly competitive firm is a passive price-taker in the market in which it exists.

➤ A perfectly competitive firm's average and marginal revenue curve is located along the horizontal ruling market price line, determined in the market as a whole.

➤ The ruling market price in perfect competition is also the perfectly elastic demand curve facing each firm in the market.

➤ A monopolist's demand curve is the market demand curve for the industry.

➤ A monopolist can be a price-maker or a quantity-setter, but not both at the same time.

➤ A monopolist's marginal revenue curve lies below its average revenue curve.

➤ Price elasticity of demand falls moving down a (linear) demand or *AR* curve facing a monopolist.

Questions

1 Distinguish between total revenue, average revenue and marginal revenue.

2 State the formulae for average revenue and marginal revenue.

3 Why is a perfectly competitive firm's average revenue curve horizontal?

4 Explain the three parts of the mathematical relationship between the average and marginal values of an economic variable.

5 Explain the relationship between average revenue and marginal revenue in monopoly.

6 How does price elasticity of demand change when moving along a firm's average revenue curve in perfect competition and monopoly?

Chapter 5

Perfect competition and monopoly

Chapters 2 and 4 have already introduced you to the two market structures of perfect competition and monopoly. Arguably, these are the two most essential topics you need to know when answering Unit 3 exam questions on business economics, though oligopoly, covered in Chapter 7, is also very important. This chapter draws on the information about cost and revenue curves explained in Chapters 3 and 4 to explain how profit maximisation occurs in perfect competition and monopoly. Chapter 6 then evaluates the desirable and less desirable features of the two market structures.

Learning outcomes

This chapter will:
➤ explain how profit maximisation occurs
➤ analyse perfect competition equilibrium in the short run and the long run
➤ analyse monopoly equilibrium

What you should already know

At AS, there is a section of Unit 1 called 'Resource allocation in competitive markets'. However candidates are not expected to know about perfect competition at AS. This means that at the beginning of the A2 course, you should understand how a competitive market works in a supply and demand context. Chapters 2–4 introduced you to perfect competition.

Monopoly is mentioned in the AS specification in the section on market failure. You are expected to 'understand that monopolies have market power and that the basic model of monopoly suggests that higher prices, inefficiency and a misallocation of resources may result in monopoly, compared to the outcome in a competitive market'. You should also know that monopoly can provide an example of market failure, the sources or causes of monopoly power, and the possible benefits of monopoly such as economies of scale.

Profit-maximising behaviour

When I briefly mentioned how firms behave in Chapter 2, I stated that all economic agents, e.g. households, firms and the government, have an objective that they wish to maximise. I then said that for firms, economists assume that the objective is profit maximisation. This assumption is fundamental to the traditional (or neoclassical) theory of the firm. At any level of output:

total profit = total revenue − total cost

Providing we assume that it wishes to make the largest possible **profit**, a firm therefore aims to produce the level of output at which $TR − TC$ is maximised. The maximisation of $TR − TC$ is the **equilibrium condition** (or **optimising condition**) for a profit-maximising firm, for if the firm succeeds in producing and selling the output yielding the biggest possible profit, it has no incentive to change its level of output.

> **Key term**
>
> **Profit** is total sales revenue minus total costs of production.

However it is generally more convenient to state the equilibrium condition for profit maximisation as:

marginal revenue = marginal cost, or $MR = MC$

MR = MC means that a firm's profits are greatest when the addition to sales revenue received from the last unit sold (marginal revenue) equals exactly the addition to total cost incurred from the production of the last unit of output (marginal cost).

> **Key term**
>
> **MR = MC** is the marginalist condition that must be met if profits are to be maximised.

Imagine for example, a market gardener producing tomatoes for sale in a local market, but unable to influence the ruling market price of 50 pence per kilo. At any size of sales, average revenue is 50 pence, which also equals marginal revenue. Suppose that when the horticulturalist markets 300 kilos of tomatoes, the cost of producing and marketing the 300th kilo is 48 pence. If the tomato grower decides not to market the 300th kilo, 2p of profit is sacrificed. Suppose now that total costs rise by 50p and 52p respectively when a 301st kilo and a 302nd kilo are marketed. The marketing of the 302nd kilo causes profits to fall by 2p, but the 301st kilo of tomatoes leaves total profits unchanged: it represents the level of sales at which profits are exactly maximised.

To sum up, when:

$MR > MC$, profits rise when output increases

$MR < MC$, profits rise when output reduces

So only when $MR = MC$ are profits maximised.

When $MR > MC$ or $MR < MC$ the firm fails to maximise profit. These are examples of **disequilibrium**. To maximise profit the firm must change its level of output until

it reaches the point at which *MR* = *MC*. Once reached, the firm has no incentive to change output, unless some event disturbs either costs or revenues.

It is important to understand that firms in *all* market structures (perfect competition, monopoly and imperfectly competitive markets such as oligopoly) can only maximise profit when marginal revenue equals marginal cost. *MR* = *MC* is a universal equilibrium or profit-maximising condition relevant to all market structures.

Normal and supernormal profit

Before explaining the concept of the profit-maximising firm in perfect competition, I must first introduce **normal profit** and **supernormal profit**. (Supernormal profit is also known as abnormal profit and above-normal profit.) Normal profit is the minimum level of profit necessary to keep incumbent firms in the market (i.e. firms that are already in the market). However, the normal profit made by incumbent firms is insufficient to attract new firms into the market. Economists treat normal profit as a cost of production, including it in a firm's average cost curve because a firm must make normal profit to stay in production. In the long run, firms unable to make normal profit leave the market. Supernormal profit is extra profit over and above normal profit. In the long run, and in the absence of entry barriers, supernormal profit performs the important economic function of attracting new firms into the market.

The conditions of perfect competition

You first came across the conditions of **perfect competition** in Figure 4.1 in Chapter 4. To remind you, the six conditions that must be present in a perfectly competitive market are:

1 a large number of buyers and sellers
2 perfect information about what is going on in the market, including prices of goods and their costs of production
3 firms being able to sell as much as they wish to at the ruling price established by demand and supply in the whole market
4 independent action by firms will not influence the ruling market price
5 a uniform, identical or homogeneous product
6 complete freedom for firms to enter or leave the market, but only in the long run

Short-run equilibrium in perfect competition

At this stage, you should refer back to page 41 and look again at Figure 4.2. The diagrams illustrate how each firm in a perfectly competitive market passively accepts the ruling market price, which becomes each firm's average revenue (AR) and marginal revenue (MR) curve. The third condition of perfect competition tells us that a perfectly competitive firm can sell as much as it wishes at the market's ruling price. But, how much will it actually wish to produce and sell? Providing we assume that each firm's business objective is solely to maximise profit, the answer is shown in Figure 5.1.

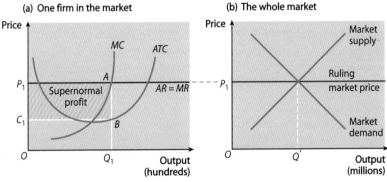

Figure 5.1 *Perfect competition short-run equilibrium*

Panel (a) of Figure 5.1 adds the perfectly competitive firm's average total cost (ATC) and its marginal cost (MC) to the revenue curves shown in Figure 4.2. Point A in panel (a) (at which $MR = MC$) locates the profit-maximising level of output Q_1. At this level of output, total sales revenue is shown by the area OQ_1AP_1. Total cost is shown by the area OQ_1BC_1. Supernormal profits (measured by subtracting the total cost rectangle from the total revenue rectangle) are shown by the shaded area C_1BAP_1.

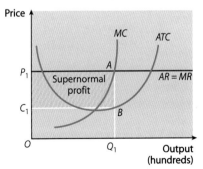

Figure 5.2 *A perfectly competitive firm in short-run equilibrium*

examiner's voice

A competitive market is in equilibrium when planned demand equals planned supply. A firm is in equilibrium when profit is maximised and $MR = MC$. True equilibrium is long-run equilibrium. By contrast, short-run equilibrium is really a constrained equilibrium which lasts only as long as new entrants are kept out of the market.

Figure 5.2 is the same as panel (a) of Figure 5.1, but presented without any information about what is going on in the market as a whole. The diagram enables you to focus on the short-run equilibrium of a perfectly competitive firm, especially the positions of the cost and revenue curves and the supernormal profit rectangle.

Long-run equilibrium in perfect competition

Referring back again to the list of the conditions of perfect competition, you will see that although firms cannot enter or leave the market in the short run, they can do so in the long run (condition 6). Suppose that in the short run, firms make supernormal profit, as illustrated in Figures 5.1 and 5.2. In this situation, the ruling market price signals to firms outside the market that supernormal profits can be made, which provides an incentive for new firms to enter the market. Figure 5.3 shows what might happen next. Initially, too many new firms enter the market, causing the supply curve to shift to the right to S_2 in panel (b) of the diagram. This causes the price line to fall to P_2, which lies below each firm's *ATC* curve. When this happens, firms make a loss (or **subnormal profit**). However, just as supernormal profit creates the incentive for new firms to enter the market, subnormal profit provides the incentive for marginal firms to leave the market. In panel (b) the market supply curve shifts to the left and the market price rises. Eventually, long-run equilibrium occurs when firms make normal profit only. For the market as a whole, this is shown at output Q''' and price P_3 in Figure 5.3.

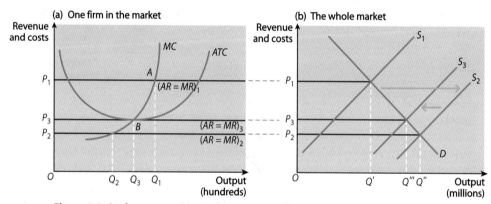

Figure 5.3 *Perfect competition in long-run equilibrium*

Panel (a) of Figure 5.3 shows a perfectly-competitive firm in long-run equilibrium. The price the firm faces is of course P_3, but its output is Q_3, which is immediately below the point at which *MR = MC*. This is shown more clearly in the next diagram, Figure 5.4, which shows the perfectly competitive firm in long-run equilibrium.

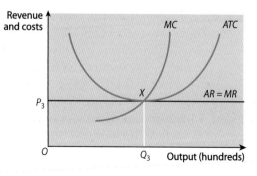

Figure 5.4 *A perfectly competitive firm in long-run equilibrium minimising average costs of production*

In Figure 5.4, the firm's total revenue and also its total cost are shown by the rectangle bounded by the points OQ_3XP_3. The entry of new firms into the market, attracted by short-run supernormal profits, has whittled away supernormal profit until in long-run equilibrium surviving firms make normal profit only. (Remember, normal profit is treated as a cost of production, and is not shown explicitly in the diagram.) For the firm, output Q_3 is the long-run or true equilibrium. Total revenue equals the total cost of production, normal profit only is made, and there are no incentives for firms to enter or leave the market.

Synoptic link: sources of monopoly power

Section 3.1.4 of the AS specification states that candidates should be aware of the various sources of monopoly power which affect the behaviour and performance of firms. These include:

➤ **Natural monopoly.** This occurs when there is only room in the market for one firm benefiting to the full from **economies of scale**. In the past, **utility industries** such as water, gas, electricity and the telephone industries were regarded as natural monopolies. Because of the nature of their product, utility industries experience a particular marketing problem. The industries produce a service that is delivered through a distribution network or grid of pipes and cables into millions of separate businesses and homes. Competition in the provision of distribution grids is extremely wasteful, since it requires the duplication of fixed capacity, therefore causing each supplier to incur unnecessarily high fixed costs.

➤ **Geographical causes of monopoly.** A pure natural monopoly can occur when, for climatic or geological reasons, a particular country or location is the only source of supply of a raw material or foodstuff. Geographical or spatial factors also give rise to another type of monopoly, for example a single grocery store in an isolated village. Entry to the market by a second store is restricted by the fact that the local market is too small. Monopoly does not exist in an absolute sense, since the villagers can travel to the nearest town to buy their groceries. Nevertheless, the grocery store can still exercise considerable market power, stemming from the fact that for many villagers it is both costly and inconvenient to shop elsewhere. Prices charged are likely to be higher than they would be if competition existed nearby.

➤ **Government-created monopoly.** Governments sometimes create monopoly in markets they believe are too important to leave to competition. 'National flag' airlines are an example and trade mark and patent legislation also create monopoly to protect intellectual copyright. Some governments also have a monopoly over broadcasting.

➤ **Advertising as a source of monopoly power.** Monopolies and other large firms can prevent small firms entering the market with devices such as **saturation advertising**. The small firms are unable to enter the industry because they cannot afford the minimum level of advertising and other forms of promotion for their goods which are necessary to persuade retailers to stock their products. The mass-advertising, brand-imaging and other marketing strategies of large established firms effectively crowd-out newcomers from market place.

Monopoly equilibrium

The profit-maximising or equilibrium level of output in monopoly is shown in Figure 5.5. As in perfect competition, the equilibrium output Q_1 is located at point A, where $MR = MC$. It is worth repeating that providing the firm is a profit maximiser, the equilibrium equation $MR = MC$ applies to *any* firm, whatever the market structure. However in monopoly, point A does *not* show the equilibrium price, which is located at point B on the demand curve or AR curve above point A. The equilibrium price is P_1, which is the *maximum* price the monopolist can charge and succeed in selling output Q_1.

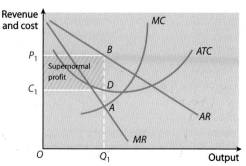

Figure 5.5 *Monopoly equilibrium*

You will notice that Figure 5.5 does not distinguish between *short-run* and *long-run* equilibrium in monopoly. This is because a monopoly is protected by barriers to entry, which prevent new firms entering the market to share in the supernormal profit made by the monopolist. Entry barriers enable the monopolist to preserve supernormal profits in the long run as well as in the short run. By contrast, in perfect competition supernormal profits are temporary, being restricted to the short-run. Indeed in monopoly, supernormal profits are often called **monopoly profit**. A monopolist has the market power to preserve profit by keeping competitors out.

Key term

Monopoly profit is the supernormal profit a monopoly or imperfectly competitive firm makes in the long run as well as in the short run.

examiner's voice

Make sure you understand and can draw this diagram, and that you can compare it to the diagram showing perfect competition long-run equilibrium.

Extension material

Profit maximisation versus revenue maximisation
Students often confuse profit maximisation with revenue maximisation, but the two concepts are different. Profit maximisation occurs at the level of output at which the difference between a firm's total sales revenue (*TR*) and its total costs of production (*TC*) is greatest. This is also the level of output at which marginal revenue equals marginal cost

($MR = MC$). By contrast, revenue maximisation occurs at the level of output at which marginal revenue is zero. The difference between profit maximisation and revenue maximisation is shown in Figure 5.6.

The profit-maximising level of output Q_1 is located below point X where $MR = MC$. By contrast, the revenue-maximising level of output Q_2 is located at point Z, where $MR = 0$. Providing the AR and MR curves slope downward to the right and are linear (straight lines), the profit-maximising level of output is *always* below the revenue-maximising level of output.

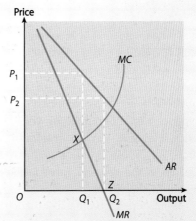

Figure 5.6 *Profit maximisation and revenue maximisation*

examiner's voice
Make sure you don't confuse profit maximisation with revenue maximisation.

Extension material

Marginal private benefit and marginal private cost
Provided that a firm's sole business objective is to maximise profit, marginal revenue can be thought of as the firm's **marginal private benefit**. Similarly, the marginal cost it incurs when producing output is its **marginal private cost**.

This is just a special case of the general proposition that all maximising economic agents, be they firms, consumers or workers, should undertake the activity they wish to maximise up to the point at which:

marginal private benefit = marginal private cost

or: $MPB = MPC$

This generalisation covers the possibility that a firm may wish to maximise an objective other than profit, such as: sales revenue, the growth of the firm or managerial objectives (e.g. status or managers' pay). These possibilities are explored further in Chapter 7.

At AS you also came across the idea of equating marginal private benefit and marginal private cost in your study of market failure and externalities. This will be revisited in Chapter 10.

Synoptic link: monopoly and elasticity of demand

It is often said that a monopolist's ability to exploit consumers is greatest when demand is price inelastic and consumers are captive in the sense that no substitutes are available. It is obviously true that a monopolist may choose to produce a level of output for which demand is price inelastic. But to maximise profit, a monopoly must produce within the *elastic* section of the demand curve facing the firm. Figure 5.7 shows why.

As in Figure 5.5, profit maximisation occurs at output Q_1, Q_1 drawn below point A on the diagram, where $MR = MC$. Now, because marginal cost is positive at point A, marginal revenue must also be positive at point A, marginal revenue must also be positive. Yet, whenever MR is positive,

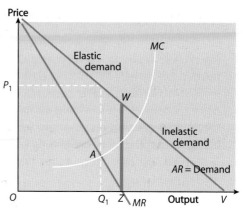

Figure 5.7 *Elasticity of demand and profit maximisation*

demand is price-elastic. When the demand curve slopes downward and is linear (a straight line), the monopolist's MR curve is twice as steep as the AR or demand curve. In the diagram, the MR curve intersects the quantity axis at point Z, which is exactly half way between the origin and point V, where the AR curve meets the quantity axis. The vertical line above point Z cuts the average revenue curve at point W, which is also half way along the AR curve. You should remember from your AS studies, that demand is elastic at all points on the top half of a linear downward-sloping demand curve, and inelastic at all points on the bottom half. Bringing all these points together, the profit-maximising level of output Q_1 must lie below the top half of the average revenue curve. If it wishes to maximise profit, the monopoly must produce within the elastic section of the demand curve, even though monopoly power may appear to be greater when demand is inelastic.

Summary

➤ Profit is total sales revenue minus total costs of production.

➤ Profit maximisation occurs at the level of output at which marginal revenue equals marginal cost ($MR = MC$).

➤ The $MR = MC$ profit-maximising condition applies to all market structures: monopoly, oligopoly, as well a perfect competition.

➤ Normal profit is just sufficient to keep incumbent firms in the market but is insufficient to attract new firms into the market.

➤ Normal profit is treated as a cost of production, and is included in a firm's cost curves.

➤ Supernormal profit is any profit over and above normal profit. On a graph it is shown by a profit rectangle

➤ In a perfectly competitive market, supernormal profit attracts new firms into the market, until it has been competed away.

➤ A perfectly competitive firm is a price taker, but a monopoly is a price maker or quantity setter.

➤ In short-run equilibrium, perfectly competitive firms can make supernormal profit, but not in long-run or true equilibrium.

➤ In monopoly, entry barriers prevent the entry of new firms from competing away supernormal profit. Supernormal profit exists in monopoly in the long run as well as in the short run.

➤ The point at which $MR = MC$ lies below the AR curve in a monopoly diagram, but not in a perfect competition diagram.

Questions

1 Explain why profit is maximised when $MR = MC$.

2 Distinguish between normal and supernormal profit.

3 Draw a diagram to show short-run equilibrium in perfect competition.

4 What happens to supernormal profit in the long run in perfect competition?

5 Outline four sources of monopoly.

6 Draw a diagram to show monopoly equilibrium.

7 How does elasticity of demand affect monopoly?

Chapter 6

Evaluating perfect competition and monopoly

Evaluation is the most demanding of the four skills tested in the Unit 3 and 4 examinations. Evaluation is tested when answering part (c) of your chosen question in the exam paper, and part (b) of the essay questions. In the context of perfect competition and monopoly, Unit 3 essay questions are likely to ask: which is the best market structure? To answer this question you need to be able to apply efficiency and welfare criteria. This chapter explains how.

Learning outcomes

This chapter will:
➤ explain the meaning of economic efficiency and of efficiency concepts such as allocative efficiency and dynamic efficiency
➤ ask whether perfect competition is more efficient than monopoly
➤ introduce two welfare criteria: consumer surplus and producer surplus
➤ use these criteria to evaluate perfect competition and monopoly

What you should already know

Monopoly, but not perfect competition, is introduced in Unit 1. This means that, although you should be able to evaluate one weakness and one strength of monopoly, you cannot at this point in the course do the same for perfect competition.

Although the idea of improving economic welfare is in the Unit 1 specification, welfare concepts such as consumer surplus and producer surplus are not in the AS specification.

How do economists evaluate perfect competition and monopoly?

Economists use two sets of concepts to answer questions such as: is perfect competition preferable to monopoly? First, they apply efficiency concepts, such as productive efficiency, X-efficiency, allocative efficiency, and static and dynamic efficiency. Second, they ask how perfect competition and monopoly affect the consumer surplus and producer surplus that households and firms respectively enjoy, and hence the effect on general economic welfare.

> **examiner's voice**
> You must learn to evaluate in order to display the skills needed to achieve an A grade.

> **examiner's voice**
> Economic efficiency is a key concept that can be used in the analysis of a wide range of economic topics, for example taxation and market failures.

Economic efficiency

I have already stated several times in previous chapters that a fundamental purpose of any economic system is to achieve the highest possible state of human happiness or welfare. Within a market economy, perfect competition and monopoly must ultimately be judged on the extent to which they contribute to improving human wellbeing, while remembering of course, that perfect competition is an abstract and unreal market structure.

> **Key term**
> **Economic efficiency**, in general terms, minimises costs incurred, with minimum undesired side effects.

In order to judge the contribution of a market structure to human welfare, we must first assess the extent to which the market structure is efficient or inefficient. In terms of private self interest, any decision made by an individual, a firm or by a government is economically efficient if it achieves the economic agent's desired objective at minimum cost to the agent itself, and with minimum undesired side effects. However, in terms of the whole community, the social costs incurred and the social benefits received need also to be considered.

Before discussing the extent to which perfect competition and monopoly can be considered efficient or inefficient, below are some of the meanings economists attach to the word efficiency.

Technical efficiency

A production process is technically efficient if it maximises the output produced from the available inputs or factors of production. Alternatively, we may say, that at any level of output, production is technically efficient if it minimises the inputs of capital and labour needed to produce that level of output.

> **Key term**
> **Technical efficiency** maximises output from the available inputs.

Productive efficiency or cost efficiency

To achieve **productive efficiency**, a firm must use the techniques and factors of production which are available, at lowest possible cost per unit of output. In the short run, the lowest point on the relevant short-run average total cost curve locates the most productively efficient level of output for the particular scale of operation. Short-run productive efficiency is shown in Figure 6.1.

However, *true* productive efficiency is a long-run rather than a short-run concept. A firm's long-run average cost curve shows the lowest unit cost of producing different levels of output at all the different possible scales of production. The most productively-efficient of all the levels of output

Key term

Productive efficiency involves minimising the average costs of production.

occurs at the lowest point on the firm's *long-run* average cost curve. This is shown at output Q_N in Figure 6.2. Output Q_1 is also productively efficient, but only for the short-run cost curve $SRATC_1$.

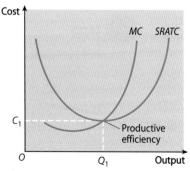

Figure 6.1 Productive efficiency in the short run

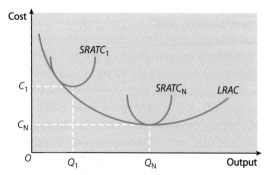

Figure 6.2 Short-run and long-run productive efficiency

Figure 6.3 illustrates another application of the concept of productive efficiency which you came across at AS. All points such as A and B on the production possibility frontier drawn for the whole economy are productively (and also technically) efficient. When the economy is on its production possibility frontier, it is only possible to increase output of capital goods by reducing output of consumer goods (and vice versa). By contrast, a point such as C inside the frontier is productively and technically inefficient. Output of capital goods could be increased by using inputs in a technically more efficient way, without reducing output of consumer goods.

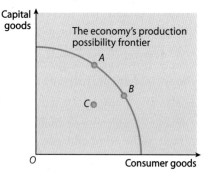

Figure 6.3 Productive and technical efficiency illustrated on a production possibility frontier

X-efficiency

In the 1960s, the American economist Liebenstein argued that, due to organisational slack resulting from the absence of competitive pressures, monopolies are always likely to be technically and productively inefficient. This happens at all levels of output. Liebenstein introduced the term X-inefficiency to explain organisational slack.

Consider the short-run average total cost curve illustrated in Figure 6.4, which shows the lowest possible unit costs of producing various levels of output, given such conditions of production as the scale of the firm's fixed capacity and the prices of the factors of production used to produce the good. According to the cost curve, it is impossible for the firm to produce output Q_1 at a level of unit costs or average costs below C_1 e.g. at a point such as A, cannot be reached, unless of course the cost curve shifts downward over time. Conversely, if factors of production are combined in a technically inefficient way, unit costs *greater* than C_1

Key term

Productive efficiency for the economy as a whole can also be defined in terms of producing on the economy's production possibility frontier.

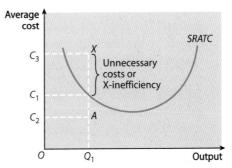

Figure 6.4 *X-inefficiency occurring when a firm incurs unnecessary costs*

examiner's voice
While X-efficiency is not in the AQA specification, it is an extremely useful concept to apply when analysing and evaluating market structures.

would be incurred when producing output Q_1. In this case, the firm would be producing off its cost curve, at a point such as X, at which average costs are C_3 rather than C_1. Point X, and indeed any point above the cost curve, is said to be X-inefficient. All points on the cost curve (including the productively-efficient point where unit cost is lowest) are X-efficient. X-inefficiency occurs whenever, for the level of output it is producing, the firm incurs unnecessary production costs i.e. if the firm wished, it could reduce its costs.

There are two main causes of X-inefficiency. First, a firm may simply be technically inefficient, for example, employing too many workers (over-manning) or investing in machines it never uses. Second, X-inefficiency can be caused by the firm paying its workers or managers unnecessarily high wages or salaries, or by buying raw materials or capital at unnecessarily high prices. X-efficiency requires that the lowest possible prices are paid for inputs or factors of production.

Allocative efficiency

This rather abstract concept is of great importance to the understanding of economic efficiency. **Allocative efficiency** occurs when $P = MC$ in all industries and

Key term

Allocative efficiency occurs when it is impossible to improve overall economic welfare by reallocating resources between industries or markets (assuming an initial distribution of income and wealth). For resource allocation in the whole economy to be allocatively efficient, price must equal marginal cost in each and every market in the economy.

markets in the economy. To explain this further, we must examine closely both P and MC. The price of a good, P, is a measure of the value in consumption placed by buyers on the last unit consumed. P indicates the utility or welfare obtained at the margin in consumption. This is the good's opportunity cost in consumption. For example, a consumer spending £1 on a bar of chocolate cannot spend the pound on other goods. At the same time, MC measures the good's opportunity cost in production; i.e. the value of the resources which go into the production of the last unit, in their best alternative uses.

Suppose that all the economy's markets divide into two categories: those in which $P > MC$ and those in which $P < MC$. In the markets where $P > MC$, households pay a price for the last unit consumed, which is greater than the cost of producing the last unit of the good. The high price discourages consumption, so we conclude that at this price the good is under-produced and under-consumed. Conversely, in the second set of markets in which $P < MC$, the value (P) placed on the last unit consumed by households is less than the MC of the resources used to produce the last unit. The price is too low, encouraging too much consumption of the good; thus at this price the good is over-produced and over-consumed.

Suppose resources can be taken from the second group of markets where $P < MC$ and re-allocated to the former group of markets in which $P > MC$. Arguably, total consumer welfare or utility will increase as re-allocation of resources takes place. As the re-allocation proceeds, prices tend to fall in those markets *into which* resources are being shifted and prices tend to increase in the markets *from which* resources are being moved. Eventually, as prices adjust, P equals MC in all markets simultaneously. Beyond the point at which $P = MC$ in all markets, no further re-allocation of resources between markets can improve consumer welfare (assuming of course that all the other factors which influence welfare such as the distribution of income, remain unchanged). The outcome in which $P = MC$ in all markets is allocatively efficient.

In summary, allocative inefficiency occurs when $P > MC$ or $P < MC$. For any given employment of resources and any initial distribution of income and wealth amongst the population, total consumer welfare can increase if resources are re-allocated from markets where $P < MC$ into those where $P > MC$, until allocative efficiency is achieved when $P = MC$ in all markets.

Box 6.1 Microsoft's pricing policy, allocative efficiency and resource allocation

Economists often judge the monopoly power of a firm by the extent to which the price of the product is above marginal cost. The greater the gap between the marginal cost of production and the price, they argue, the greater the monopoly power. They also argue that when prices exceed marginal costs, economic inefficiency and resource misallocation occur.

It can readily be conceded that the price of Windows, whether $40 or $89, is substantially above the marginal cost of producing an extra copy of Windows, and that this makes Microsoft's operating system very profitable. The marginal cost of producing and supplying one extra copy of Windows is very close to zero, but the price charged must be higher so that Microsoft can recover the very significant development cost of Windows. Much of the price of a copy of Windows is unrelated to the marginal cost of

producing an extra copy. But the price is still substantially below the price Microsoft could and would charge if it had the vast monopoly power the US Justice Department has claimed Microsoft possesses.

From *Trust on Trial* by Richard McKenzie, 2001

Microsoft's Redmond campus

Follow-up questions

1 Explain the meaning of marginal cost.
2 Explain the statement: 'Much of the price of a copy of Windows is unrelated to the marginal cost of producing an extra copy'.

Dynamic efficiency

All the forms of efficiency so far considered are examples of **static efficiency**, i.e. efficiency measured at a particular point in time. By contrast, **dynamic efficiency** measures improvements in technical and productive efficiency that occur over time. Improvements in dynamic efficiency result from the introduction of better methods of producing existing products, including firms' ability to benefit to a greater extent from economies of scale and also from developing and marketing completely new products. In both cases, invention, innovation and research and development (R&D) improve dynamic efficiency. (**Invention** refers to advancements in pure science, whereas **innovation** is the application of scientific developments to production.)

 Key terms

Static efficiency measures technical, productive, X and allocative efficiency at a particular point in time.

Dynamic efficiency measures the extent to which various forms of static efficiency improve over time.

Perfect competition and economic efficiency

Figure 6.5 shows the long-run equilibrium of a perfectly competitive firm. The diagram clearly shows that a perfectly competitive firm achieves both productive and allocative efficiency in the long run, provided there are no economies of scale. The firm is productively efficient because it produces the optimum output at the lowest point on the *ATC* curve, and it is allocatively efficient because *P* = *MC*. (Strictly, I should qualify this conclusion by stating that the firm is allocatively efficient only if *all* markets in the economy are perfectly competitive and in long-run equilibrium, which means that every firm in every market is producing where *P* = *MC*.)

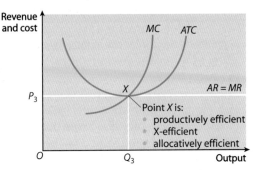

Figure 6.5 *In the long run a perfectly competitive firm is productively, allocatively and X-efficient*

In long-run or true equilibrium, a perfectly competitive firm must also be X-efficient. The reason is simple. If the firm is X-inefficient, producing at a level of unit costs above its *ATC* curve, the firm could not make normal profits in the long-run. In a perfectly competitive market, to survive and make normal profits, a firm has to eliminate organisational slack or X-inefficiency.

Monopoly and economic efficiency

In contrast to perfect competition — and once again assuming an absence of economies of scale — monopoly equilibrium is both productively and allocatively inefficient. Figure 6.6 shows that at the profit-maximising level of output Q_1, the monopolist's average costs are above the minimum level and that $P > MC$. Thus, compared to perfect competition, a monopoly produces too low an output which it sells at too high a price.

The absence of competitive pressures, which in perfect competition serve to eliminate supernormal profit, mean that a monopoly is also likely to be X-inefficient, incurring average costs at a point such as X which is above the average cost curve. A monopoly may be able to survive, perfectly happily and enjoying an 'easy life', incurring unnecessary production costs and making satisfactory rather than maximum profits. This is because **barriers to entry** protect monopolies. As a result, the absence or weakness of competitive forces means there is no mechanism in monopoly to eliminate organisational slack.

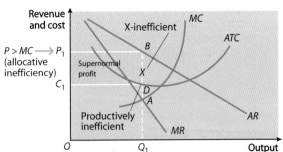

Figure 6.6 *A monopoly is productively and allocatively inefficient, and it is likely to be X-inefficient*

Natural monopoly and economies of scale

On the basis of the above analysis, it seems we can conclude that perfect competition is both productively and allocatively efficient whereas monopoly is neither. Monopoly is also likely to be X-inefficient. However, the conclusion that perfect competition is productively more efficient than monopoly depends on an assumption that there are no economies of scale. When substantial economies of scale are possible in an industry, monopoly may be more productively efficient than competition.

Figure 6.7 illustrates a natural monopoly where, because of limited market size, there is insufficient room in the market for more than one firm benefiting from full economies of scale. The monopoly may of course be producing above the lowest point on short-run average cost curve $SRATC_N$, hence exhibiting a degree of productive inefficiency. However *all* points on $SRATC_N$ incur lower unit costs — and are productively *more* efficient — than any point on $SRATC_1$, which is the relevant cost curve for each firm if the monopoly is broken into a number of smaller competitive enterprises.

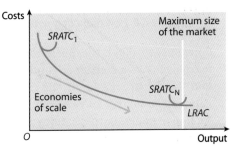

Figure 6.7 *The justification of monopoly when economies of scale are possible*

Dynamic efficiency in monopoly

Under certain circumstances, monopolies may also be more *dynamically efficient* than a perfectly competitive firm. Protected by entry barriers, a monopoly earns monopoly profit without facing the threat that the profit disappears when new firms enter the market. This allows an innovating monopoly to enjoy, in the form of monopoly profit, the fruits of successful R&D and product development. By contrast, in perfect competition, there is little or no incentive to innovate because other firms can free-ride and gain costless access to the results of any successful research. This argument justifies patent legislation, which grants a firm the right to exploit the monopoly position created by innovation for a number of years before the patent expires.

However, there is a counter-argument that monopoly reduces rather than promotes innovation and dynamic efficiency. Protected from competitive pressures, as I have noted, a monopoly may *profit-satisfice* rather than *profit-maximise*, content with satisfactory profits and an easy life.

Evaluating perfect competition and monopoly in terms of economic welfare

In order to analyse how market structures affect economic welfare, I must first explain the concepts of **consumer surplus** and **producer surplus**. These are both measures of **economic welfare**, as their names imply respectively for consumers and firms. Both are illustrated in Figure 6.8.

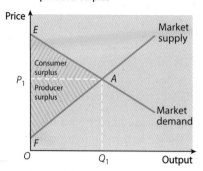

(a) Consumer surplus and producer surplus

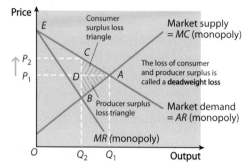

(b) How the formation of a monopoly results in a loss of economic welfare

Figure 6.8 *How monopoly reduces economic welfare*

Consumer surplus is the difference between the *maximum price* a consumer is prepared to pay and the *actual price* he or she need pay. In a competitive market such as Figure 6.8 (a), the total consumer surplus enjoyed by all the consumers in the market is measured by the triangular area P_1EA. Consumer welfare increases whenever consumer surplus increases, for example when market prices fall. Conversely, however, higher prices reduce consumer surplus and welfare.

examiner's voice

It is important to understand consumer surplus and producer surplus in order to analyse how economic welfare may be affected by events that raise or lower the price of a good. The next chapter and Chapter 20 apply the concepts in the analysis of price discrimination, free trade and the effect of tariffs.

Key terms

Consumer surplus is a measure of the economic welfare enjoyed by consumers: surplus utility received over and above the price paid for a good.

Producer surplus is a measure of the economic welfare enjoyed by firms or producers: the difference between the price a firm succeeds in charging and the minimum price it would be prepared to accept.

Economic welfare is human happiness or utility.

Producer surplus, which is a measure of producers' welfare, is the difference between the *minimum price* a firm is prepared to charge for a good and the *actual price* charged. In Figure 6.8 (a), the producer surplus enjoyed by all the firms in the market is measured by the triangular area FP_1A.

Figure 6.8 (b) illustrates what happens to economic welfare when monopoly replaces perfect competition (again, assuming there are no economies of scale). Market equilibrium in perfect competition is determined at point A; output is Q_1 and price is P_1. However, monopoly equilibrium is determined at point B where $MR = MC$. *(Note that the marginal cost curve in monopoly is the same curve as market supply in perfect competition.)* The diagram illustrates the standard case against monopoly, namely that compared to perfect competition, monopoly restricts output (to Q_2) and raises price (to P_2).

But I can take the analysis one stage further and investigate how consumer surplus and producer surplus (and hence economic welfare) are affected. If a monopoly raises the price from P_1 to P_2 it gains the consumer surplus equal to the rectangular area $P_1 P_2 CD$. This means that producer surplus (in the form of monopoly profit) increases at the expense of consumer surplus. Over and above this transfer however, there is a net loss of economic welfare caused by the fact that the amount bought and sold falls to Q_2. The welfare loss or **deadweight loss** is shown by the two shaded triangular areas in Figure 6.8 (b), which respectively depict the loss of consumer surplus (the top triangle) and the loss of producer surplus (the bottom triangle).

Consumer sovereignty and producer sovereignty

Arguably, perfect competition has the advantage of promoting **consumer sovereignty**, in the sense that the goods and services produced are those that consumers have voted for when spending the pounds in their pockets. When consumer sovereignty exists, the 'consumer is king'. (However, the extent to which consumer choice exists in a perfectly competitive world would be extremely limited. All the firms in a particular market would sell identical goods at an identical price, namely the ruling market price.) Firms and industries that produce goods other than those for which consumers are prepared to pay, do not survive in perfect competition.

By contrast, a monopoly may enjoy **producer sovereignty**. The goods and services available for consumers to buy are determined by the monopolist rather than by consumer preferences expressed in the market place. Even if producer sovereignty is not exercised on a 'take-it-or-leave-it basis' by a monopoly, the monopolist may still possess sufficient market power to manipulate consumer wants through such marketing devices as persuasive advertising. In these situations, the 'producer is king'.

Why firms like to become monopolies

Economists generally regard perfect competition as more desirable than monopoly. However, the desirable properties of perfect competition (namely economic efficiency, welfare maximisation and consumer sovereignty) do not result from any assumption that businessmen or entrepreneurs in competitive industries are more highly motivated or public-spirited than monopolists. Economic theory assumes that everyone is motivated by self-interest and by self-interest alone. This applies just as much to firms in competitive markets as it does to monopolies. Entrepreneurs in competitive industries would very much like to become monopolists, both to gain an easier life and also to make bigger profits. Indeed, from a firm's point of view, successful competition means eliminating competition and becoming a monopoly. But in perfect markets, market forces (Adam Smith referred to the *invisible hand* of the market) and the absence of barriers to entry and exit, prevent this happening.

Imagine for example, a situation in which a firm in a perfectly competitive industry makes a technical break through which reduces production costs. For a short time

the firm can make supernormal profits. But because in perfect competition, perfect market information is available to all firms, other firms within the market and new entrants attracted to the market can also enjoy the lower production costs. A new long-run equilibrium will soon be brought about — at the lower level of costs resulting from the breakthrough — with all firms once again making normal profits only.

Ultimately of course, consumers benefit from lower prices brought about by technical progress and the forces of competition, but it is market forces, and not some socially-benign motive or public spirit assumed on the part of entrepreneurs, that accounts for the optimality of perfect competition as a market structure.

How competitive is perfect competition?

Although perfect competition is an abstract and unreal market structure, it is inter-esting to consider the forms competition might take in a perfectly competitive market economy. The first point to note is that price competition, in the form of price wars or price-cutting by individual firms, would not take place. In perfect competition, all firms are passive price-takers, able to sell all the output they produce at the ruling market price determined in the market as a whole. In this situation, firms cannot gain sales or market share by price cutting. Other forms of competition, involving the use of advertising, packaging, brand-imaging or the provision of after-sales service to differentiate a firm's product from those of its competitors simply destroy the conditions of perfect competition. These are the forms of competition which are prevalent, together with price competition, in the imperfectly competitive markets of the real economy in which we live.

So the only form of competition, both available to firms and also compatible with maintaining the conditions of perfect competition, is cost-cutting competition. Cost-cutting competition is likely in perfect competition because each firm has an incentive to reduce costs in order to make supernormal profit. But even the existence of cost-cutting competition in a perfect market can be questioned. Why should firms finance research into cost-cutting technical progress when they know that other firms have instant access to all market information and that any super-normal profits resulting from successful cost-cutting can only be temporary?

Think also of the nature of competition in a perfect market, from the perspective of a typical consumer. The choice is simultaneously very broad and very narrow. The consumer has the doubtful luxury of maximum choice in terms of the number of firms or suppliers from whom to purchase a product. Yet each firm is supplying an identical good or service at exactly the same price. In this sense, there is no choice at all in perfect competition.

Summary

> Economists evaluate perfect competition and monopoly using efficiency and welfare criteria.

> The main efficiency concepts are technical efficiency, productive efficiency, X-efficiency, allocative efficiency and static and dynamic efficiency.

➤ Providing we ignore dynamic efficiency considerations, perfect competition wins over monopoly in terms of being productively and allocatively efficient, and also X-efficient.

➤ However, monopoly can be justified by dynamic considerations, particularly through its ability to reduce prices over time as a result of benefiting from economies of scale and innovation in new products and methods of production.

➤ By restricting output and raising prices, monopolies transfer consumer surplus to producer surplus, and also trigger a net welfare loss.

Questions

1 Briefly explain the main types of economic efficiency.

2 Is perfect competition efficient?

3 Is monopoly efficient?

4 How do economies of scale affect productive efficiency?

5 How does monopoly affect consumer surplus?

6 Is monopoly necessarily more dynamically efficient than perfect competition?

Chapter 7

Oligopoly and concentrated markets

Almost all real world markets are imperfectly competitive, lying between the extremes of monopoly and perfect competition. Imperfect competition is a wide ranging term, covering all market structures from duopoly (two firms only in a market) to highly competitive markets which are very close to being perfectly competitive. This chapter explains one of the most important forms of imperfect competition: oligopoly. I shall look first at competitive oligopoly, in which a relatively small number of firms compete against each other. I shall then examine conditions in which competitive oligopolists may be tempted to collude or cooperate with each other, and form cartels.

Learning outcomes

This chapter will:

➤ explain how oligopoly is a form of imperfect competition

➤ use a concentration ratio to define oligopoly in terms of market structure

➤ define oligopoly in terms of market behaviour or conduct

➤ distinguish between competitive and collusive oligopoly

➤ apply the kinked demand curve theory to illustrate competitive oligopoly

➤ explain a cartel as a form of collusive oligopoly

➤ introduce game theory as a way of modelling oligopoly

What you should already know

As oligopoly and concentrated markets are not in the AS specification, you are unlikely to be familiar with these concepts, except to the extent that brief mention of oligopoly has been made in some of the earlier chapters of this book.

Imperfect competition

I have mentioned in previous chapters that **perfect competition** does not actually exist in real world economies. The label itself is extremely misleading, since the word *perfect* suggests a state of competition that cannot be bettered. This in turn implies that any form of competition that does not meet the six conditions of perfect competition must be somehow second rate or inferior. This implication is reinforced by the fact that all market structures lying between the extremes of perfect competition and monopoly are described by economists as *imperfectly* competitive.

 Key *term*

Imperfect competition describes the range of market structures lying between perfect competition and pure monopoly.

Just as perfect competition is better described as *unrealistic* competition, so **imperfect competition,** could more accurately be called *realistic* competition. Imperfect competition covers a wide range of real world market structures. At one end of the spectrum are markets such as the stock exchange that approximate to perfect competition, without nevertheless meeting all six of the defining criteria. At the other extreme is **duopoly**, which is the market structure closest to pure monopoly. Duopoly is a special case of **oligopoly**. In a pure duopoly, there are just two firms in the market, each with considerable monopoly power. Oligopoly is a more general term, covering markets where there are several firms, which I define in more detail in the next two sections of this chapter.

Oligopoly and market structure

To recap, **market structure** is defined according to the number of firms in a market. Oligopoly, which is a market structure in which there are a relatively small number of firms, is sometimes called *imperfect competition amongst the few.* Oligopolistic firms are not pure monopolies,

 Key *terms*

Oligopoly describes a market in which there are a small number of dominant firms.
Duopoly describes a market in which there are two dominant firms.

but they possess monopoly power. You must avoid confusing *monopoly power* with *monopoly.* Pure monopoly is a precise market structure, but firms in all imperfectly competitive markets can exercise a greater or lesser degree of monopoly power, for example, by imposing **entry barriers** that enable firms to raise the price of a good. Whenever firms exercise **producer sovereignty** in this way, monopoly power exists.

Concentration ratios

Concentration ratios provide a good indicator of oligopolistic market structures. For example, a five-firm concentration ratio shows the percentage of output

 Key *term*

A **concentration ratio** measures the market share of the biggest firms in the market.

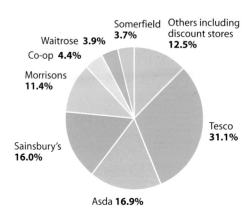

Somerfield **3.7%**

Waitrose **3.9%**

Co-op **4.4%**

Morrisons **11.4%**

Others including discount stores **12.5%**

Sainsbury's **16.0%**

Tesco **31.1%**

Asda **16.9%**

Figure 7.1 *Market shares in the UK supermarket industry, May 2008*

in an industry produced by the five largest firms in the industry. In May 2008, the five-firm concentration ratio in the UK supermarket industry can be calculated from the market share data shown in Figure 7.1. The five-firm concentration ratio of 79.8 indicates that the supermarket industry is an oligopoly.

Oligopoly and market behaviour or conduct

However, oligopoly is best defined, not by market structure or the number of firms in the market, but by **market conduct**, or the behaviour of the firms within the market. An oligopolistic firm affects its rivals through its price and output decisions, but its own profit can also be affected by how rivals behave and react to the firm's decisions. Suppose, for example, the firm reduces its price in order to increase market share and boost profit. Whether the price reduction increases the firm's profit depends on the likely reactions of the other firms. So, when deciding whether or not to lower its price, the firm must make assumptions about likely responses by other firms. Competitive oligopoly displays reactive market behaviour and *strategic interdependence* amongst firms.

> **examiner's voice**
>
> For many purposes, oligopoly is better defined by market behaviour or conduct rather than by the number of firms in the market or by concentration ratios.

Perfect and imperfect oligopoly

Perfect oligopoly exists when the oligopolists produce a uniform or homogeneous product such as petrol. One brand of petrol is really a perfect substitute for any other brand, though a petrol company such as Shell may use advertising to try to persuade motorists that Shell petrol is different from and better than other brands. By contrast, **imperfect oligopoly** occurs when the products produced by the firms are by their nature differentiated and imperfect substitutes, for example, automobiles.

Competitive oligopoly

Competitive oligopoly exists when the rival firms are *interdependent* in the sense that they must take account of the reactions of one another when forming a market strategy, but *independent* in the sense that they decide their market strategies without co-operation or collusion. The existence of uncertainty is a characteristic of competitive oligopoly; a firm can never be completely certain of how rivals will react to its marketing strategy. If the firm raises its price, will the rivals follow suit or will they hold their prices steady in the hope of gaining sales and market share?

e*xaminer's voice

Examination questions may ask you to explain why interdependence and uncertainty exist in markets dominated by a few firms. Oligopoly itself may not be mentioned in the question.

The kinked demand curve theory

The kinked demand curve theory can be used to illustrate how a competitive oligopolist may be affected by rivals' reaction to its price and output decisions. The theory was originally developed to explain alleged price rigidity and an absence of price wars in oligopolistic markets.

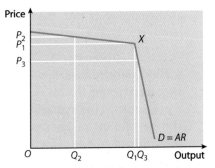

Figure 7.2 *The kinked demand curve*

Suppose an oligopolist initially produces output Q_1 in Figure 7.2, selling this output at price P_1. In order to anticipate how sales might change following a price change, firms need to know the position and shape of the demand and revenue curves for their products. But in imperfectly competitive markets, firms lack accurate information about these curves, particularly at outputs significantly different from those currently being produced. This means that the demand curve or *AR* curve in Figure 7.2 is not necessarily the correct or *actual* demand curve for the oligopolist's output. Instead, it represents the firm's *estimate* of how demand changes when the firm changes the price it is charging.

When *increasing* price from P_1 to P_2, the oligopolist expects rivals to react by keeping their own prices stable and not following suit. By holding their prices steady, rivals try to gain profit and market share at the firm's expense. This means that the oligopolist expects demand to be *relatively elastic* in response to a price increase. The rise in price from P_1 to P_2 is likely to result in a *more than proportionate fall in demand* from Q_1 to Q_2.

Conversely, when *cutting* its price from P_1 to P_3, the oligopolist expects rivals to react in a very different way, namely by following suit immediately with a matching price cut. In this situation, because the market demand curve for the products of all the firms slopes downward, each firm will benefit from *some* increase in demand. However, the oligopolist fails to gain sales from rivals *within* the market. This means the oligopolist expects demand to be less elastic, and possibly *relatively inelastic* in response to a price cut. The fall in price from P_1 to P_3 may result in a *less than proportionate increase in demand* from Q_1 to Q_3. The oligopolist therefore expects rivals to react *asymmetrically* when price is raised or lowered.

In Figure 7.2, the oligopolist's initial price and output of P_1 and Q_1 intersect at point X, or at the kink at the junction of two demand curves of different elasticity, each reflecting a different assumption about how rivals may react to a change in price. In this situation, the oligopolist fears that both a price increase and a price cut may reduce total profit. Given this fear, the best policy may be to leave price unchanged.

The theory provides a second reason why prices may tend to be stable in oligopoly. As Figure 7.3 illustrates, there is a vertical section in the MR curve at output Q_1 shown by the distance B to C. This links the marginal revenue curves associated respectively with the relatively elastic and relatively less elastic demand (or average revenue) curves.

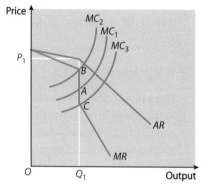

Figure 7.3 *The kinked demand curve and stable prices in oligopoly*

Suppose initially the firm's marginal cost curve is MC_1, intersecting the MR curve at point A which is positioned in the middle of the vertical section. The diagram shows that the MC curve can rise or fall within the range of the vertical section of the MR curve, without altering the profit-maximising output Q_1 or price P_1. But if marginal costs rise above MC_2 at point B or fall below MC_3 at point C, the profit-maximising output changes. In either of these circumstances, the oligopolist would have to set a different price to maximise profits, providing of course that the AR curve accurately measures demand for the firm's product at different prices. Nevertheless, the oligopolist's selling price remains stable at P_1 as long as the marginal cost curve lies between MC_2 and MC_3. The result is that the oligopolist's price remains stable, despite quite considerable changes in marginal costs.

Criticisms of the kinked demand curve theory

There are a number of weaknesses in the theory I have just described. Although on first sight attractive as a neat and apparently plausible explanation of price stability in conditions of oligopoly, few economists now accept the kinked demand theory of oligopoly pricing.

First, it is an incomplete theory, since it does not explain *how* and *why* a firm chooses in the first place to be at point X. Second, the evidence provided by the pricing decisions of real world firms gives little support to the theory. Competitive oligopolists seldom respond to price changes in the manner assumed in the kinked demand curve theory. It is more reasonable to expect a firm to test the market, i.e. raise or lower its selling price to see if rivals react in the manner expected. If rivals do not, then the firm must surely revise its estimate of the shape of the demand curve facing it.

> **examiner's voice**
> Students often wrongly believe that the kinked demand curve provides a complete theory of oligopoly. It is actually a very doubtful theory, but it does illustrate how oligopolists are interdependent and affected by uncertainty.

Research has shown fairly conclusively that oligopoly prices tend to be stable or sticky when demand conditions change in a predictable or cyclical way, but that oligopolists usually raise or lower prices quickly and by significant amounts, both when production costs change substantially, and when unexpected shifts in demand occur.

Other aspects of pricing in oligopolistic markets

The ways in which prices are set can be quite complicated in oligopolistic markets. Some of the ways in which prices are set are explained below.

Cost-plus pricing

Cost-plus pricing, also known as **mark-up pricing** and **full-cost pricing**, is the most common pricing procedure used by firms in imperfectly competitive markets. Cost-plus pricing means that a firm sets its selling price by adding a standard percentage profit margin to average or unit costs:

$$P = AFC + AVC + \text{profit margin}$$

When customers are captive and willing to pay high prices, the profit mark-up can be high; for fashionable goods that may quickly go out of style often over 100%. But when markets are more competitive, firms can find it much more difficult to charge a mark-up. Indeed in a very competitive market, the mark-up may be limited to a size which gives firms normal profit only, which then deters the entrance of new firms into the market. (See my later reference to limit pricing).

examiner's voice
Firms in real-world markets seldom use the $MR = MC$ rule when setting prices. They are much more likely to undertake cost-plus pricing. The $MR = MC$ rule is best regarded as a necessary condition for profit maximisation rather than as a decision-making rule.

Price parallelism

Price parallelism occurs when there are identical prices and price movements within an industry or market. Price parallelism can be caused by two different sets of circumstances, which make it difficult to decide whether the market is highly competitive or collusive. On the one hand, price parallelism can occur in a very competitive market, resembling perfect competition, where firms all charge a ruling market price determined by demand and supply in the market as a whole. But on the other hand, price parallelism results from price leadership in tightly oligopolistic industries, where overt or tacit price collusion occurs.

Price leadership

Because overt collusive agreements to fix the market price, such as cartel agreements, are usually illegal, imperfectly competitive firms often use less formal or tacit ways to coordinate their pricing decisions. An example of covert collusion is **price leadership**, which occurs when one firm becomes the market leader and other firms in the industry follow its pricing example.

Limit pricing

When natural barriers to market entry are low or non-existent, incumbent firms (i.e. firms already in the market) may set low prices, known as limit prices, to deter new firms from entering the market. Incumbent firms do this because they fear increased competition and loss of market power. With limit pricing, firms already in the market sacrifice short-run profit maximisation in order to maximise long-run profits, achieved through deterring the entry of new firms.

Should limit pricing be regarded as an example of a competitive pricing strategy, which reduces prices and the supernormal profits enjoyed by the established firms in the market? Or is limit pricing basically anti-competitive and best regarded as an unjustifiable restrictive practice? The answer probably depends on circumstances, but when limit pricing extends into predatory pricing, there is a much clearer case that such a pricing strategy is anti-competitive and against the consumers' interest.

Predatory pricing

Whereas limit pricing deters market entry, successful **predatory pricing** removes recent entrants to the market. Predatory pricing occurs when an established or incumbent firm deliberately sets prices below costs to force new market entrants out of business. Once the new entrants have left the market, the established firm may decide to restore prices to their previous levels.

Price discrimination

Price discrimination involves firms charging different prices to different customers based on differences in the customers' ability and willingness to pay. Those customers who are prepared to pay more are charged a higher price than those who are only willing to pay a lower price. In the main form of price discrimination, the different prices charged are not based on any differences in costs of production or supply. However in one form of price discrimination, **bulk-buying**, consumers are charged lower prices than consumers purchasing smaller quantities of the good. When this happens, different costs of supply may be involved. Bulk purchases generally have lower average costs of production than smaller purchases.

> **Key term**
>
> **Price discrimination** means charging different prices to different customers with the prices based on different willingness to pay.

> **examiner's voice**
>
> It is only usually necessary to learn about one form of price discrimination. You must also learn how to illustrate it on a diagram.

Box 7.1 Newspapers and predatory pricing

In the mid-1990s newspapers such as *The Times* and the *Sun*, which are part of Rupert Murdoch's News International stable, cut their prices aggressively in an attempt to increase market share. The owners of other newspapers, particularly the *Independent*, complained that this was a predatory pricing policy the aim of which was to put them out of business. The extract below from an article in *The Economist*, queries whether predatory pricing was actually taking place.

Nothing exercises the British press so much as the welfare of the British press. Predatory pricing, the argument goes, is endangering diversity in the newspaper market.

On 1 September 1993, Mr Murdoch's *Times* cut its cover price from 45p to 30p. Between the second half of 1993 and the second half of 1997, *The Times's* circulation rose by 92%. The *Independent* lost 20% over that period.

So is this really a case of predatory pricing? Since the price cut, *The Times* has been investigated twice by the Office of Fair Trading, Britain's competition watchdog; and twice the OFT has let it off. The OFT starts from the right point: that its job is to protect consumers, not producers. But its definition of predatory pricing is a narrow one. It requires, among other things, proof that a suspected predator intends to drive a particular competitor out of business. That might have some point in a duopolistic market such as buses, but it is irrelevant to a market such as newspapers where there are many players.

Most economists would agree on a wider definition, which would require that a predator sustain losses over a period of time, and that he should expect to be able to make monopoly profits in the long run. In other words, if a megalomaniac chooses to waste lots of money by driving some of his rivals out of business, that is fine by economists so long as there is enough competition left in the long run to keep prices down for consumers.

The Times probably does lose money. News International, which owns it, will not talk about its finances, but does not claim that it makes a profit. Industry observers reckon that it loses up to £60m a year. But it is hard to see how, facing so much competition, *The Times* could make monopoly profits even if it killed some of its weaker rivals. Its strategy, therefore, cannot be condemned as predatory pricing.

Diversity has survived the price war: the up-market newspapers like *The Times*, the *Guardian* and the *Financial Times*, continue to prosper with relatively high prices. The *Daily Telegraph* has increased its circulation, though at considerable cost to its profits. The *Independent's* troubles can be blamed on *The Times*, but also on its own bad management.

The Economist, 12 February 1998

Follow-up questions

1 Explain the difference between predatory pricing and limit pricing.
2 When firms such as News International are taken to court accused of predatory pricing, lawyers make huge amounts of money. Why do you think this is so?

Box 7.2 Perfect price discrimination

Perfect price discrimination occurs when a firm charges each customer the maximum price the customer is prepared to pay. With perfect price discrimination, which is technically known as first degree price discrimination, consumers end up with zero consumer surplus — it has all been transferred to the seller of the good as extra profit. An outcome approaching perfect price discrimination occurs when potential customers haggle with street sellers about the price they are prepared to pay for the good.

If you go online you can watch the haggle scene in the Monty Python film, *The Life of Brian*, on YouTube at : **http://uk.youtube.com/watch?v=3n3LL338aGA**

Indian bazaars provide prime examples of perfect price discrimination

Follow-up questions

1 Why do firms charge discriminatory prices?
2 Why are street sellers more likely to price discriminate than supermarket companies such as Tesco? Can you think of any ways in which supermarkets price discriminate?

A closer look at price discrimination

The case of two sub-markets or market segments

In Figure 7.4 a night club divides its market into male and female customers, each with a different elasticity of demand at each price of admission. At all the prices that could be charged for entry into the club, female demand is more elastic than male demand — indicating perhaps that women are less enthusiastic about the entertainment offered by the club. For both men and women, the downward-

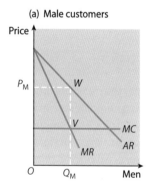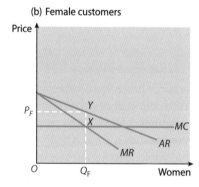

Figure 7.4
Price discrimination when a firm charges different prices to two groups of customers

sloping demand curves in Figure 7.4 show average revenue (*AR*), but not marginal revenue (*MR*). In each case, the *MR* curve is twice as steep as the *AR* curve. The diagrams also assume that the marginal cost (*MC*) incurred when an extra person enters the club is always the same. This is shown by the horizontal *MC* curve.

To maximise profit, *MR* must equal *MC* in both male and female sub-markets. As the diagrams show, this means that men pay a higher price for admission than women, namely P_M, with women paying the lower entry price of P_F. With the different prices being charged, Q_M males and Q_F females are allowed into the club. The point to note is that the different prices charged result from the different male and female price elasticities of demand. Profit is maximised when more price-sensitive female customers pay less to enter the club than the less sensitive males. Note that the *MR* received from the last man and woman admitted are the same. If this were not the case, the club could increase profit by changing the numbers of men and women admitted.

The conditions necessary for successful price discrimination

Successful price discrimination requires that the following conditions are met:

➤ It must be possible to identify different groups of customers or sub-markets for the product. This is possible when customers differ in their knowledge of the market or in their ability to shop around. Some customers may have special needs for a product and competition among oligopolists may vary in different parts of the market. In some geographical areas and for some products, a firm may face many competitors, whereas in other parts of the market the firm may be the sole supplier.

➤ At any particular price, the different groups of customers must have different elasticities of demand. Total profits can be maximised by charging a higher price in a market in which demand is less elastic.

➤ The markets must be separated to prevent **seepage**. Seepage takes place when customers buying at the lower price in one sub-market resell in another sub-market at a price which undercuts the oligopolist's own selling price in that market. In the European car market, car manufacturers have often charged higher prices for a vehicle in the UK market than in mainland Europe. Seepage has occurred when specialist car importers have bought cars on the Continent to resell in the British market, thereby undercutting the car manufacturers' recommended prices.

Why do firms price discriminate?

To understand why firms undertake price discrimination, I must reintroduce the concept of **consumer surplus** which I explained in the previous chapter. To remind you, consumer surplus, which is a measure of the economic welfare enjoyed by consumers, is the difference between the *maximum* price consumers are prepared to pay and the *actual* price they need pay. The greater the quantity of consumer surplus enjoyed by consumers, the greater their 'happiness' or economic welfare.

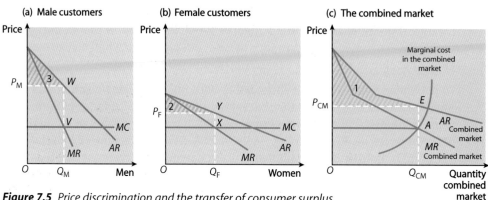

Figure 7.5 *Price discrimination and the transfer of consumer surplus*

As Figures 7.5 and 7.6 illustrate, price discrimination allows firms to increase profit by taking consumer surplus away from consumers and converting it into extra monopoly profit or supernormal profit. Figures 7.5 (a) and (b) are basically the same as Figure 7.4, but Figure 7.5 (c) has been added to show the combined market with the male and female average revenue curves added together. The male and female marginal revenue curves have also been added together. Note that for the combined market (but *not* the male and female sub-markets considered separately), the marginal cost curve slopes upwards, depicting the impact of the law of diminishing returns.

In the absence of price discrimination, all consumers pay the same price, namely P_{CM} shown in Figure 7.5 (c). Without price discrimination, consumer surplus is shown by the shaded area (labelled 1) above P_{CM} in Figure 7.5 (c). But with price discrimination, when male customers are charged price P_M and female customers P_F, consumer surplus falls to equal the shaded areas labelled 3 and 2 in Figures 7.5 (a) and (b). The firm's profit has increased by transferring consumer surplus from consumers to the producer. **Producer welfare** (or producer surplus) has increased at the expense of **consumer welfare** (or consumer surplus).

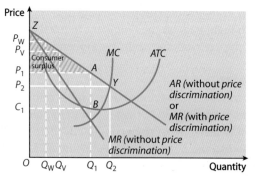

Figure 7.6
Price discrimination: the limiting case, when each consumer is charged the maximum price he or she is prepared to pay

Figure 7.6 illustrates a situation in which *all* the consumer surplus is transferred into producer surplus or producer welfare. Every customer is charged the maximum price he or she is prepared to pay. Figure 7.6 is basically the same diagram used in Chapter 5 to show monopoly equilibrium. In the absence of price discrimination, the firm produces the level of output Q_1 where $MR = MC$ and all customers are charged the price P_1. Supernormal profit is shown by the rectangle C_1P_1AB, and consumer surplus by the triangular area P_1ZA.

Now consider what happens when the firm charges each customer the maximum price he or she is prepared to pay. Customer Q_V depicted in the diagram is charged price P_V, customer Q_W is charged P_W, and so on. In this situation, there may be as many prices as there are customers. Because each customer is paying the maximum price he or she is prepared to pay, all the consumer surplus is transferred away from consumers to the firm, thereby boosting monopoly or oligopoly profit.

examiner's voice

Make sure you understand why firms price discriminate, the necessary conditions for successful price discrimination, and that you can apply the concept of consumer surplus to price discrimination. You must also be able to explain how some consumers (often the poor) as well as producers, can benefit from price discrimination.

Can consumers benefit from price discrimination?

Price discrimination leads to a loss of consumer surplus or consumer welfare. Firms exploit producer sovereignty and monopoly power, and charge *most* consumers higher prices than would be charged in the absence of price discrimination. For these reasons price discrimination is usually regarded as undesirable.

Nevertheless, *some* consumers (who may also be the poorest consumers) can benefit from price discrimination. Each time the firm sells to one more customer, total sales revenue rises by the extra units sold multiplied by the price the customer pays. Because different customers are charged different prices, charging a high (or low) price to one customer does not affect the prices charged to other customers. In the absence of price discrimination, the firm's AR curve continues to be the demand curve the firm faces, with the firm's MR curve located below the demand (and AR) curve. But when each customer is charged the maximum price he or she is prepared to pay, the demand curve now functions as the firm's MR curve. It is no longer possible to locate an AR curve. The profit-maximising level of output, where $MR = MC$, shifts to Q_2, located at Point Y in Figure 7.6. Customers who would refuse to buy the good at price P_1 buy the extra output because the prices they are charged are lower than P_1. As a result, most consumers end up paying a price which is higher than P_1 (the equilibrium price in the absence of price discrimination), but some consumers pay a lower price. The lowest of all the prices charged is P_2, which is the price charged to the marginal, and perhaps the poorest, customer.

Consider also a situation in which a firm can't make enough profit to stay in business unless some consumer surplus is taken from consumers and transferred to the producer. Market provision of healthcare by a doctor in an isolated village or very small town is an example. When charging the same price to all her patients, a doctor can't earn enough income to continue to provide the service. Without an increase in income, the doctor will move to a larger city and local medical care will no longer be available in the village. But with price discrimination, the rich pay a

higher price than the poor. Everybody gets some benefit, and a needed service is provided.

Prices involving cross-subsidy

Many students confuse *price discrimination* with *cross-subsidy*, but the two concepts are completely different. In the example of price discrimination, the marginal cost incurred by the firm was the same for all customers, but the firm charged different prices based on customers' different willingness to pay. By contrast, when cross-subsidy takes place, *all* customers pay the same price, but the marginal cost of supplying the good varies between different customers.

For example, the Royal Mail charges the same price for all first class letters of standard weight and size, whether posted to a local or to a distant part of the UK. For local letters the marginal cost incurred by the Royal Mail delivering an extra letter is less than the price charged, but for letters delivered over a long distance, MC exceeds P. Customers posting local letters (for which $P > MC$) cross-subsidise letters mailed over greater distances (for which $P < MC$). The Post Office uses profits made on the former group to subsidise losses borne on letters posted over longer distances.

As price does not equal marginal cost, cross-subsidy results in allocative inefficiency. For firms, cross-subsidy is administratively convenient and it can maximise consumer goodwill, even though it fails to maximise profits. From the public interest point of view, cross-subsidy is sometimes justified for social or regional policy reasons — for example the better off cross-subsidise the poor, or when customers in the more prosperous parts of the UK cross-subsidise those living in depressed regions. The provision of a universal service in which the same price is charged to people wherever they live in the UK also involves cross subsidy.

Marginal cost pricing and off-peak pricing

It is often argued that, to avoid cross-subsidy and to improve allocative efficiency, firms should charge customers different prices which reflect the marginal cost of providing the good or service consumed. This is called **marginal cost pricing**. In perfectly competitive markets, where firms would be passive price-takers, the market mechanism would automatically ensure that $P = MC$. But market pressures do not operate in this way in imperfectly competitive markets where $P > MC$.

Nevertheless, when demand varies on a daily, weekly or seasonal basis, firms operating in imperfect markets may charge off-peak prices, which are a special case of marginal cost pricing. Transport, energy and tourist industries provide good examples. Consider the demand for electricity, which is higher in winter than in summer. Suppose demand for electricity increases in winter months. To meet this demand, power station companies must invest in new fixed capacity. This is a long-run marginal cost. By contrast, the marginal cost involved when meeting a surge in off-peak demand in the summer months is much lower. It is the short-run marginal cost of additional raw materials or energy supplies and labour. In summer, the electricity industry meets an increase in seasonal demand by using existing fixed capacity, which would otherwise lie idle in the off-peak months.

Low off-peak prices and high peak prices are justified on the basis of differences in long-run and short-run marginal costs when providing a good or service at different times of day or year. By encouraging consumers to shift demand from the peak period of demand, off-peak pricing can achieve a better or more productively efficient utilisation of fixed capital throughout the day or year.

examiner's voice

Exam questions might ask you to explain why firms use various forms of non-price competition, and to describe and explain some of these forms, such as persuasive advertising

Non-price competition in oligopoly

As I have noted, the theory of the kinked demand curve provides a possible explanation of stable prices in oligopolistic markets. However, there is a much simpler explanation for the absence of price competition. Realising that a price-war will be self-defeating for all the firms involved, firms may tacitly agree not to indulge in aggressive price competition as a means of gaining extra profits or market share at the expense of each other. In the absence of keen price competition, oligopolistic firms are therefore likely to undertake various forms of **non-price competition**. These include:

➤ marketing competition, including obtaining exclusive outlets such as tied public houses and petrol stations through which breweries and oil companies sell their products
➤ the use of persuasive advertising, product-differentiation, brand-imaging, packaging, fashion, style and design
➤ quality competition, including the provision of point-of-sale service and after-sale service

Barriers to entry

Monopolies and firms in oligopolistic markets use **entry barriers** to protect the firm's position in the market. There are two main types of entry barrier: natural barriers and artificial or man-made barriers.

examiner's voice

Exam questions may ask how entry barriers protect oligopolists and monopolists, and influence the behaviour of firms in protected markets.

Natural barriers

Natural barriers, which are also known as **innocent barriers**, include economies of scale and indivisibilities. **Economies of scale** mean that established large firms produce at a lower long-run average cost, and are more productively efficient, than smaller new entrants, who become stranded on high-cost short-run average cost

curves. **Indivisibilities** prevent certain goods and services being produced in plant below a certain size. Indivisibilities occur in metal smelting and oil refining industries.

Artificial barriers

Artificial or man-made entry barriers, which are also known as **strategic barriers**, are the result of deliberate action by incumbent firms to prevent new firms from entering the market. Strategic entry barriers include:

➤ **Patents.** Incumbent firms acquire patents for all the variants of a product that they develop.

➤ **Limit pricing and predatory pricing.** As I have already explained, large firms often set limit prices to deter entry by new firms. Some firms also use predatory pricing to kill off small firms which have already entered the market. Predatory pricing is generally illegal, but a large firm may feel it can get away with it, as it is difficult to prove that predatory pricing has taken place.

Box 7.3 Independent schools cartel busted

In 2003, 50 top UK private schools, including Eton, Winchester and Rugby, were investigated by the UK competition authorities for restricting competition by exchanging information on the fees they charge, and in effect price fixing. The extract below is from a series of news articles published by *The Times*, the newspaper that broke the story.

Fifty schools found guilty of operating a fee-fixing cartel will pay fines and penalties totalling £3.5 million in a deal struck with the Office of Fair Trading. The schools, including Eton College, Winchester College, Harrow and Westminster, will pay fines of just £10,000 each as an acknowledgement that they broke competition law by exchanging details of proposed fee increases and other sensitive price information. The full extent of the cartel was revealed by *The Times* in September 2003. The schools breached the Competition Act 1998 by colluding against parents to fix their fees over three academic years between 2001 and 2004.

The 50 schools have until March 31 to agree the deal with the OFT and bring its 3-year inquiry to an end, but it is unlikely that any will reject it. The fines and penalties amount to an average of just £70,000 each — far below the sums that the OFT could have levied. The regulator has powers to fine organisations up to 10% of annual turnover for breaking competi-

tion law. The 50 schools charged a total of £660 million in fees last year, which could have left them facing penalties of £66 million.

The Times disclosed in 2003 that bursars at the schools routinely swapped e-mails and spreadsheets containing sensitive cost and price information as they prepared their fee recommendations to governors. One e-mail containing details of fee increases at 20 other schools was sent to Sir Andrew Large, Deputy Governor of the Bank of England and the Warden of Winchester College. Sent by Bill Organ, Winchester's then bursar, it read 'Confidential please, so we aren't accused of being a cartel.'

Jonathan Shephard, the general secretary of the Independent Schools Council (ISC), said that there was 'quite a lot of evidence that the exchange of information kept fees down'. The ISC, which represents the fee-paying sector, has said that it sees no case for compensating parents. Mr Shephard said that there was no case for compensation and that parents knew they were getting 'an outstanding education'. It has condemned the OFT's inquiry as 'a scandalous waste of public money'. Mr Shephard pleaded that the schools under investigation were charities and the charitable ethos, unlike the commercial ethos, is to exchange information. Clarissa Farr, president of the Girls' Schools Association, said she feared that the OFT ruling would inhibit schools from sharing good practice.

Source: *The Times*

Follow-up question

Why does the OFT try to persuade at least one member of an alleged cartel to become a 'whistle blower' or 'supergrass' when taking action against the cartel's other members?

Cartel agreements and collusive oligopoly

The uncertainty facing competitive oligopolists can be reduced and perhaps eliminated by the rival firms forming a **cartel agreement** or **price ring**. In Figure 7.7, five firms jointly agree to charge a price to keep Firm E, which is the least efficient firm, in the market. In a competitive market, Firm E would have to reduce costs or go out of business. Cartel agreements enable inefficient firms to stay in business, while other more efficient members of the price ring enjoy supernormal profit. By protecting

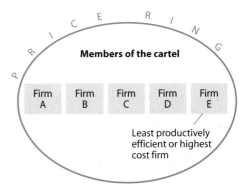

Figure 7.7 *A cartel or price ring*

the inefficient and enabling firms to enjoy an easy life protected from competition, cartels display the disadvantages of monopoly (high prices and restriction of choice). However, this is without the benefits that monopoly can sometimes bring, namely economies of scale and improvements in dynamic efficiency.

Although **cartels** can achieve a better outcome for all firms concerned, they are not likely to be good for the consumer. For this reason, cartel agreements are usually illegal and judged by governments as being anti-competitive and against the public interest. Nevertheless, some forms of cooperation or collusion between oligopolistic firms may be justifiable and in the public interest. These include joint product development (such as the multi-purpose vehicles, the Ford Galaxy, Seat Alhambra and VW Sharan, jointly developed by Ford and VW), and cooperation to improve health and safety within the industry or to

examiner's voice

Collusive or cooperative behaviour enables firms to reduce the uncertainty they face in imperfectly competitive markets. However, some forms of collusion, for example on joint product development or ensuring industry safety standards, are in the public interest.

 term

A **cartel** is a collusive agreement by firms, usually to fix prices. Sometimes output may also be fixed.

ensure that product and labour standards are maintained. Such examples of industry collaboration are normally deemed good, in contrast to price *collusion*, which is regarded as bad.

Extension material

Collusive oligopoly: joint-profit maximisation

Joint-profit maximisation, which is illustrated in Figure 7.8, occurs when a number of firms decide to act as a single monopolist, yet keeping their separate identities. The monopoly *MC* curve depicted in the right-hand side of the diagram is the sum of the identical *MC* curves of three firms (one of which is

> ℯ*xaminer's voice*
>
> Joint profit maximisation illustrates how firms can make more profit by colluding and restricting competition than by acting independently.

shown on the left of the diagram). The three firms share an output of 750 units, determined on the right of the diagram where the industry *MR* and *MC* curves intersect. Each firm charges a price of £10, which, as the diagram shows, is the maximum price consumers are prepared to pay for 750 units of the good. The monopoly output of 750 units is well below 1,000 units, which would be the output if the industry were perfectly competitive. The shaded area in the right-hand panel shows the efficiency or welfare loss caused by the cartel raising the price to £10 and restricting output to 750 units. In this example, the members of the cartel split the 750 units equally, each firm producing 250 units. The shaded area on the left of the diagram shows the supernormal profit made by each firm.

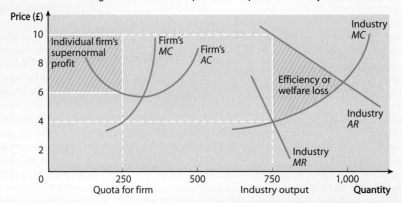

Figure 7.8 *Joint-profit maximisation by members of a cartel*

The theory of joint-profit maximisation can be used to show how each member of the cartel has an incentive to cheat on the agreement. The marginal cost of producing the 250th unit of the good is only £4, yet for the firm (but not the whole industry) the marginal revenue received from selling one more unit is £10 (that is, the price set by the cartel). One member of the cartel can increase its profit at the expense of the other firms by secretly selling an output over and above its quota of 250 units at a price less than £10, but greater than the marginal cost incurred (£4). This is an example of a divergence between individual and collective interest. The firms' collective interest is to maintain the cartel so as to keep total sales down and the price up. But each firm can benefit by cheating on the agreement — providing all the others do not cheat.

Game theory and oligopoly

Game theory provides the most interesting and fruitful method of modelling the competitive behaviour of firms in oligopolistic markets. Most examples of game theory are mathematically complicated and beyond the requirements of an A-level economics course. However, there is one example of game theory, known as the **prisoner's dilemma** game, which I shall explain in detail as it provides a useful insight into both the *interdependence* of competitive oligopolists and the *incentive to collude* or cooperate. Consider the following situation in the international arms market, in which there are just two firms, a duopoly.

Key term

Game theory is a mathematical approach to the study of conflict and decision-making which treats conflict as games with set tactics and strategies and rational players.

George W. Fixit IV is president of United States Arms Suppliers Inc. By paying bribes of $100 million to government ministers in the middle east he can be sure that they will purchase some of his weapons worth $600 million for their armed forces. However, his total sales to these governments depend on the actions of Sir Jasper Underhand, chairman of Exploitation Holdings plc, a British producer of similar weapons who is Mr Fixit's only serious rival.

If Sir Jasper Underhand also bribes the ministers responsible for the arms purchases, the deal will be shared between the two suppliers. George W. Fixit's profits will then be much less than if he alone pays bribes and gets all the business for his company. Mr Fixit thinks it a pity to pay out $100 million, but if he did not and Sir Jasper did, the British company would get all the business and he would make zero profit.

examiner's voice

You should learn a relatively simple example of game theory, for example the prisoner's dilemma game, and apply it to explaining why cartel agreements are made and sometimes broken.

What market strategies are open to the two companies and what are the likely results of each strategy? In the absence of collusion, there are two strategies available to each firm:

1 One firm pays the bribe, while the other firm does not. Outcome:
   – for the firm paying the bribe: $500 million
   – for the firm refusing to bribe: nothing
2 Both pay the bribe. Outcome:
   – the sale is shared: each firm gets $200 million

By paying the bribe, United States Arms Suppliers Inc. earns $200m if Exploitation Holdings plc also bribes. If the American company bribes, but Sir Jasper refuses to bribe, the US company's earnings rise to $500m, but Exploitation Holdings plc makes no profit at all. The same options face the British company. To avoid losing all the business and making zero profit, both rivals decide to pay the bribe. In this scenario, paying the bribe is each firm's **dominant strategy**: that is the strategy to

be pursued whatever rival firms do. Paying the bribe makes George W. Fixit better off, whatever Sir Jasper does, and vice versa.

Sir Jasper Underhand \ George W. Fixit	Pay bribe	Don't pay bribe
Pay bribe	$200m / $200m	0 / $500m
Don't pay bribe	$500m / 0	$300m / $300m

Figure 7.9
Payoff matrix for the prisoner's dilemma game

However, the dominant strategy in a competitive market *does not* deliver the best possible outcome for both firms considered together. The best outcome is illustrated in the bottom right-hand panel of the **pay-off matrix** in Figure 7.9, which shows all the possible outcomes facing the duopolists. If both firms refuse to bribe, each receives $300 million — assuming the business is shared and that the middle-east government still wants to buy the arms. This outcome is unlikely in a competitive market because each firm fears bribery by its rival. The best way to overcome this fear is agree not to pay the bribe: that is to collude or cooperate. There is always the possibility however, that one of the firms will cheat on the agreement and secretly bribe the government ministers. A collusive agreement can never completely get rid of uncertainty. If the firms really want to get rid of uncertainty, they would have to merge or be involved in a takeover.

You might be wondering how the prisoner's dilemma model obtained its name. In the original 'prisoner's dilemma', two prisoners are jointly charged with a serious crime such as armed robbery and are held in isolation from each other. The prosecutor, hoping to have his task simplified, knows that a confession from one will convict the other, but he also knows that the available evidence is insufficient to ensure a conviction. If both prisoners plead not guilty, they are likely to go free. Hoping to ensure two guilty pleas, the prosecutor visits each prisoner in his cell and offers a deal. The prosecutor informs each prisoner that he will receive one of two possible punishments, depending on how he pleads:

➤ If both prisoners plead guilty, each will go to prison for 1 year.
➤ If one prisoner pleads guilty and the other not guilty, the prisoner pleading guilty will be freed and receive a reward (if he gives evidence to convict the other prisoner) whilst the other prisoner gets a 5-year jail sentence.

I shall leave it to you to work out what each prisoner should do. Would your answer be different if both prisoners were placed in the same cell and could cooperate? Or does the offer of a reward mean that both prisoners will be tempted to cheat on any deal they agree between them, thereby ensuring that the prosecutor obtains his two convictions?

Summary

➤ Imperfect competition covers the range of market structures between perfect competition and pure monopoly.

➤ Oligopoly is a form of imperfect competition in which there are only a few firms in the market.

➤ Concentration ratios can be used to identify oligopoly market structures.

➤ Oligopoly can also be defined in terms of market conduct of behaviour.

➤ It is useful to distinguish between competitive and collusive oligopoly.

➤ The theory of the kinked demand curve is often used to model competitive oligopoly.

➤ The kinked demand curve theory illustrates uncertainty, interdependence and price stability in oligopoly, but the theory has a number of weaknesses.

➤ Oligopolies, and other firms with considerable market power, can set prices in a number of ways, which include cost-plus pricing, limit pricing, predatory pricing and discriminatory pricing.

➤ Price leadership is a common feature of oligopolistic markets.

➤ Oligopolists collude to reduce uncertainty and to increase monopoly profit.

➤ Game theory provides a fruitful way of modeling competitive and collusive oligopoly.

Questions

1 Define an oligopoly.

2 Why is there no general theory of oligopoly?

3 Distinguish between perfect and imperfect oligopoly.

4 What forms of competition are likely in an oligopoly?

5 What does the kinked demand curve theory of oligopoly predict?

6 What is cost-plus pricing?

7 Distinguish between limit pricing and predatory pricing.

8 What are the requirements for successful price discrimination?

9 Explain the effect of price discrimination upon consumer surplus and producer surplus.

10 Why is cross-subsidy considered inefficient and marginal cost pricing efficient?

11 Why may oligopolists collude and what forms may collusion take?

12 How does the prisoner's dilemma game explain the incentive to collude?

Chapter 8

Further aspects of the growth of firms

Many of the most interesting aspects of business economics stem from how real-world firms actually behave. At university level, these topics are typically a part of a course in industrial economics. The aim of this chapter is to introduce you to some industrial economics topics, both those that are now in the AQA Unit 3 specification, and some that, though outside the specification, I consider it important for an economist to have some knowledge of.

Learning outcomes

This chapter will:
➤ remind you of the meaning of a firm
➤ explain why firms grow
➤ relate the growth of firms to different possible business objectives
➤ explain the divorce between the ownership and the control of a business
➤ distinguish between the internal and external growth of firms, and between vertical, horizontal and lateral growth
➤ relate the concepts of economies and diseconomies of scale to the growth of firms
➤ explain the role of the capital market and banks in financing firms' growth

What you should already know

At AS you were introduced briefly to the different objectives a firm may have, and also to the meaning of economies of scale. Both of these are developed in greater detail in this chapter.

What is a firm?

I first explained the meaning of a **firm** in my Introduction to Business Economics in Chapter 2. I stated that a firm is a **business enterprise** which either *produces* or *deals in* and *exchanges* goods or services. Unlike non-business productive organisations, for example many charities, firms are commercial, earning revenue to cover the production costs they incur. It is also possible to classify different types of business or firm according to their **legal status**. There is an important difference between incorporated businesses such as private and public companies, and unincorporated sole traders and partnerships.

Key term

A **firm** is a business that sells its output commercially in a market.

examiner's voice

Make sure you don't confuse *why* firms grow with *how* firms grow

Why firms grow

Firms grow for all sorts of reasons. Quite often a firm grows without any deliberate intent on behalf of its owners or managers. This happens when demand for the goods or services that the firm is producing increases, and the firm increases its output and often its productive capacity or scale, simply to keep up with demand. This type of growth is particularly likely, first if it easy and relatively cheap to acquire more productive resources, and second if one of the firm's business objectives is to keep customers happy.

This brings me to the importance and significance of business objectives. Providing a good customer service is of course an important business objective, particularly for socially-minded owners and managers of businesses. However, usually it is a means to an end, the end being achieving some other business objective. *Growth for growth's sake* is another reason why firms grow (see the alternative theories of the firm below), while in some industries, business owners such as the proprietors of newspapers and TV stations sometimes believe that growth gives them not just **monopoly power**, but political influence as well. Box 8.1 describes a latter-day example: the media mogul Silvio Berlusconi in Italy.

Box 8.1 Megalomania and political power as business objectives

Megalomania is a term for behaviour characterised by delusional fantasies of wealth, power, genius, or omnipotence, in other words delusions of grandeur. Over the last century or so, the media industry has thrown up many megalomaniac newspaper proprietors: Pulitzer and William Randolph Hearst in the USA, Lord Northcliffe, who built up the *Daily Mail* in the UK, and possibly Rupert Murdoch of Sky Television and News International, publisher of the *Sun*, the *News of the World* and *The Times* in the UK.

The following Extract has been taken from an article written by Alexander Stille, professor of journalism at Colombia University, and published at the time of a general election in Italy. The article is about Silvio Berlusconi, ex-cruise ship entertainer, media mogul, owner of AC Milan football club, and in 2008, a third-time prime minister of Italy.

Foreign observers tuning in to Italy's election campaign were flabbergasted to learn that Prime Minister Silvio Berlusconi had alternately compared himself, in the space of about a week, to Napoleon, Churchill and Jesus Christ while also vowing to give up sex until after the

April poll. But Italians and those who have followed his career closely were less surprised.

Since entering politics in 1994, Mr Berlusconi has commonly referred to himself in the third person as if he were already a historical figure: 'If Italy entrusts itself to Berlusconi, it's the country's good fortune,' he said at one point. He has perfected a personal style that is a bizarre mix of megalomania, sexual braggadocio, off-colour jokes and outrageous claims, including, among his memorable antics: giving the sign of the horns over the head of the Spanish foreign minister in a group photograph of European leaders and calling a German member of the European parliament a concentration camp *kapo*. But distant observers should not be fooled by this apparent buffoonery. There is much method in Mr. Berlusconi's madness. By traditional political standards, these would seem to be mistakes. But in Mr. Berlusconi's world of celebrity politics, there is no such thing as bad publicity — it all translates into audience and ratings. And his performance in recent weeks has helped

him slash his centre-left opponent's lead from 8% to close to zero.

By dominating the media — he owns the three largest private television networks and indirectly controls the three main public networks — he controls the political discourse and silences his critics, thereby diminishing his opponents. Mr Berlusconi, like President George W Bush, is a master of rightwing populism, using the body language of the common man while pushing policies that have mainly benefited those in the upper income brackets.

Financial Times, 16 February 2006

Silvio Berlusconi (r), chairman of AC Milan

Follow-up question

Using the example of Silvio Berlusconi in Italy, discuss why media moguls are particularly likely to have business objectives other than profit maximisation.

As the last few chapters have shown, in the traditional (and neoclassical) theory of the firm, economists assume that profit maximisation is a firm's ultimate business objective. If this is the case, then firms grow because their owners believe that growth leads to higher profits. Conversely, if the owners believe that growth reduces profits or indeed leads to losses, they will resist the temptation to pursue growth.

A complication that should be introduced at this point is the possible conflict between short-run and long-run profit maximisation. Long-run profits may require substantial investment in research and new capital. If a firm has a short time horizon, if it is worried about finance or about future risk and uncertainty, or if it fears that a lack of immediate profit will lower its share price and render it

> **Key term**
>
> **Profit maximisation** occurs when total sales revenue is furthest above total cost, which is when $MR = MC$.

> **xaminer's voice**
>
> Knowledge of the traditional profit-maximising theory is more important than knowledge of alternative theories of the firm.

vulnerable to a hostile takeover raid, the firm may decide not to grow, even though it thinks that large profits could be made in the long run.

Alternative theories of the firm

In real life, the people who own and run firms may have business objectives other than to make the biggest possible profit. There are two alternative theories of the firm: **managerial theories** and **organisational** or **behavioural theories**. Both claim to be more realistic in their assumptions, and hence better at explaining the actual behaviour of firms in the real economy, than the traditional profit-maximising theory of the firm.

Managerial theories

Managerial theories of the firm assume that a firm has a maximising objective, but they focus on a managerial objective rather than shareholders' profit. Managerial theories often take as their starting point the **principal/agent problem**, which stems from the split in a large public company between shareholders as owners, and managers as decision-makers. Shareholders own companies, but they employ salaried managers or executives to make business decisions. In this situation, managers or business executives, who possess a monopoly of technical knowledge about the actual running of the company, concentrate on achieving managerial objectives such as sales maximisation, growth maximisation and maximising managerial career prospects or creature comforts.

Organisational or behavioural theories

Organisationalists or behaviouralists see the firm as an organisation comprising coalitions of different groups within the firm, each possessing different group objectives. These days, such coalitions are also regarded as company **stakeholders**: that is, groups of people with a vested interest in how the business performs.

Different stakeholders have different views on what the company should be doing. Managers form one coalition or stakeholder group, seeking prestige, power and high salaries. Other coalitions include production workers wanting higher wages and improved job security and working conditions, and shareholders desiring higher profits. Differing goals or aspirations can result in group conflict. Because of this, management may try to resolve conflict between the different interest groups within the organisation. However, attempting to satisfy the aspirations of as many groups within the organisation as possible means compromise and the possible setting of minimum rather than maximum targets.

> **Key** **term**
>
> **Managerial theory** assumes that firms wish to maximise managerial objectives rather than profit.
>
> **Organisational theory** assumes that a firm is a coalition of different groups such as shareholders, managers and workers.
>
> The **principal/agent problem** recognises that the principals (shareholders) have a different objective from that of the agents (managers).

For this reason, organisationalists introduce the concept of **satisficing** to replace the assumption of a maximising objective. Satisficing, or achieving a satisfactory outcome rather than the best possible outcome, is particularly likely for monopolies and firms in imperfectly competitive markets protected by entry barriers. In these circumstances, in seeking an easy life, a firm's managers may content themselves with satisfactory profit, combined with a degree of X-inefficiency (or unnecessary costs).

 Key *term*

Satisficing means achieving a satisfactory objective acceptable to all the competing member groups of the coalition that makes up the firm.

Satisficing also helps to resolve the conflict between managers' and shareholders' objectives. While trying to maximise executive creature-comforts such as managerial status, salaries, fringe benefits and career structures, a company's board of directors must keep shareholders happy. According to this theory, managers maximise their own objectives, subject to the constraint of delivering a satisfactory level of profit for shareholders.

Extension material

The theory of economic natural selection

The theory of economic natural selection, which is an example of **social Darwinism**, has provided a reason for supporting the traditional profit-maximising theory of the firm. Natural selection theory operates in two ways: through the economy's goods or **product markets** and through the **capital market** (described later in this chapter).

In the product market version of the theory, firms are assumed to sell their output in highly competitive goods markets. If managers make price and output decisions for reasons other than profit maximisation, they inevitably incur unnecessary production costs. But if goods or product markets are sufficiently competitive (perhaps approximating to perfect competition), the firms that stray from the profit-maximising path must mend their ways by reducing costs or go out of business. Whatever the conscious or deliberate aim of decision-makers, the 'invisible hand' of the market means that only profit-maximising firms survive. To put it another way, decision-makers who behave as if they are profit-maximisers survive, the rest fail to make normal profit and leave the market.

However, in many real-world goods markets, the forces of competition are not strong enough to allow this selection process to operate. Barriers to entry allow inefficient high-cost firms to survive. For large firms in imperfectly competitive goods markets, the second version of the theory of economic natural selection may be more significant. According to this theory, non-profit-maximising behaviour by firms is disciplined by competition in the capital market rather than by competition in the goods or product market. As I explain later in this chapter, the capital market is the financial market in which a modern large business corporation raises funds to finance investment by selling shares or ownership in the business. The **stock exchange** is an important part of the capital market.

When a firm's managers make decisions that are inconsistent with profit maximisation, the resulting low level of profit causes the company's share price to fall. This makes the company vulnerable to takeover on the stock exchange by a new owner (or **corporate raider**) who believes the company's assets can be managed better and more profitably. Even if the company is not taken over, fear of a possible takeover may prevent the corporate board and its managers from straying too far from the profit-maximising path.

The role of the entrepreneur and the divorce between ownership and control

In a firm, the **entrepreneur** is the decision maker and financial risk taker, providing answers to such standard economic questions as *what*, *how*, *how much*, *where* and *when* to produce. In many small firms, the owner of the business is the entrepreneur, so ownership and control lie in the same person. But this is not true for public companies, where ownership and control are almost always split. Medium-sized and large public companies are owned by thousands of shareholders, though the majority of shares are usually owned by a relatively small number of financial institutions such as pension funds and insurance companies. However, management decisions are made by executive directors, who are members of the company's corporate board, and by the salaried managers or executives whom the board employ.

Key term

An **entrepreneur** is a risk taker and decision maker within a firm.

In theory, the directors of a public company who exercise the entrepreneurial function are answerable to the shareholders. This means that, in the event of bad performance, the directors can be voted out of office. In practice, this seldom happens, although as I explained in the last section, institutional shareholders sometimes back hostile takeover bids, which, if successful, remove the incumbent board of directors.

examiner's voice

Remember from your AS studies the functions of the four factors of production, including that of the entrepreneur.

Perhaps the most important problem resulting from the **divorce between ownership and control** is the possibility that directors and managers will pursue an agenda of their own, which is not in the interests of the shareholders as a body. This is an example of the principal/agent problem.

How firms grow

How firms grow involves issues such as the difference between internal and external growth, vertical, horizontal and lateral growth paths, and the pursuit of economies of scale.

Internal and external growth of firms

Internal growth (which is also known as **organic growth**) occurs when a business expands by investing in new capacity (for example, a new factory, office block or retail store) which it builds from scratch. By contrast, **external growth** involves **takeover** of, **merger** with, and **acquisition** of another, previously independent firm.

Whichever growth path a business follows — internal, external or a mix of the two — its growth may be vertical, horizontal or lateral, or again a mix of all three.

Key terms

Internal growth occurs when a firm invests from scratch in new capacity such as factories and offices, also known as organic growth.

External growth is growth via acquisition, either takeover or merger.

The vertical growth of firms

Vertical growth occurs when a firm grows backward along its supply chain, or forward along its distribution chain. The vertical line drawn above and below firm X in Figure 8.1 on page 95 illustrates both processes. Backward vertical growth (illustrated by arrow 1) takes place when firm X (a car assembly firm) decides to produce for itself the engines, gear boxes and other components needed

Key term

Vertical growth occurs when a firm grows by expanding back up its supply chain or forward along its distribution chain.

to make a car. Without such vertical growth, firm X would have to buy components from independent suppliers. Arrow 2 illustrates forward growth, namely firm X owning the distribution chain through which the company sells the cars that it manufactures. (For the opposite process of outsourcing, see Box 3.2, page 34.)

In theory, vertical growth enables a firm to exercise greater control over its supply chain and/or its distribution chain: for example, in controlling the quality of components and the timing of their delivery. Often, however, it may be better to outsource component supply to independent suppliers, and to sell through independent retailers. Such a strategy can enhance competition, which in turn improves quality and drives down costs. These days, many large firms outsource a varied range of activities previously undertaken in-house. For example, ICT-provided customer service and other back office activities are increasingly being outsourced to countries with cheap labour, such as India.

In some circumstances, vertical growth creates monopoly power. A firm may deny competitors access to the supply of raw materials it has acquired. Likewise, by investing in market outlets, such as public houses and petrol stations, breweries and oil companies can prevent competitors selling through these outlets.

All the forms of growth illustrated in Figure 8.1 can be internal or external. For example, vertical internal growth could be illustrated by the car manufacturer investing from scratch in its own engine factory. By contrast, acquiring a previously independent engine manufacturer through takeover or merger illustrates vertical external growth.

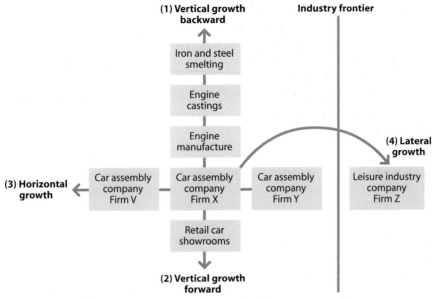

Figure 8.1 *Vertical, horizontal and lateral growth of firms*

Horizontal growth

Besides growing vertically, a firm can grow horizontally and laterally. **Horizontal growth** takes place when a firm expands by building or acquiring more plants at the same stage of production in the same industry. The possibility of achieving multi-plant economies of scale is an obvious motive for horizontal growth. A less benign motive might be to eliminate competitors

> **Key term**
>
> **Horizontal growth** occurs when a firm undertakes more of the activities it is already involved in, which can lead to economies of scale.

so as to build up and exploit a monopoly position. Firm X acquiring firms V and Y in Figure 8.1 illustrates horizontal external growth. In the motor industry, Volkswagen's acquisition of Audi and the alliance between Peugeot and Citroën have both been successful. The newly merged companies were able to rationalise their production plant and product lines, and to exploit scale economies more fully. By contrast, BMW's takeover of the Rover Group was less successful, leading to eventual demerger of the German company's UK acquisition and the creation of a new UK company. This in turn was unsuccessful. In 2005 MG Rover went bankrupt and the business was sold to a Chinese company which closed down most of the UK productive capacity.

Lateral growth

Lateral growth occurs when a firm diversifies into completely different industries. Figure 8.1 provides an example of lateral external growth, or **conglomeration**, when firm X acquires firm Z, a leisure industry firm operating cinemas and theme parks. Firms diversify in order to gain the

> **Key term**
>
> **Lateral growth** occurs when a firm diversifies into new types of production.

scale economies of massed resources and risk spreading. Lateral external growth may also allow the firm to benefit from financial and managerial economies. Lateral mergers, such as those undertaken by tobacco companies, can involve diversifying out of a declining market into what the firm believes to be markets with growth potential. However, managerial and organisational *diseconomies* may also result from the fact that the diversifying company lacks expertise in the fields into which it is expanding.

Economies of scale

Microeconomic theory generally assumes that a firm seeks to grow in order to enable more profit to be made. Profit depends on both demand conditions and supply conditions, with the latter depending, in the long run, on whether average costs of production fall or rise as the firm's scale of operations increases. In Chapter 3, I explained economies and diseconomies of scale in terms of a firm's long-run average cost curve. In this chapter I examine the causes of the different types of economy of scale.

Internal and external economies of scale

Economies of scale are of two types: internal and external. **Internal economies of scale** occur when a firm's long-run average costs or unit costs fall as a result of an increase in the size of the firm itself, or of an increase in the size of a plant or various sites operated by the firm. By contrast, a firm benefits from **external economies of scale** when unit production costs fall because of the growth of the scale of the whole industry or market, rather than from the growth of the firm itself.

> **Key term**
>
> **Internal economies of scale** mean lower long-run average production costs resulting from an increase in the size or scale of the firm in the long run.

Internal economies of scale

Sometimes firms grow larger but the plant sites they operate do not generally grow significantly in size. For this reason, it is useful to distinguish between those internal economies of scale that occur at the level of a single plant or establishment owned by a firm and those occurring at the level of the whole firm. In recent years, continued opportunities for further firm-level economies of scale have contributed to the growth of larger firms, but expansion of plant size has been less significant.

> *examiner's voice*
>
> You don't need to rote learn all this information about economies and diseconomies of scale, but make sure you can explain at least two examples of each type of economy and diseconomy.

Plant-level economies of scale

Economies of scale that occur at the level of a single plant such as a factory or supermarket operated by a firm are largely technical economies of scale, though some management economies are also possible at plant level.

Technical economies of scale. Chapter 3 explains how some economies of scale are simply the translation of increasing returns to scale into money costs of production. Increasing returns to scale mean that as plant size increases, a firm can combine its inputs in a technically more efficient way. The resulting economies are called technical economies of scale. Increasing returns to scale therefore explain technical economies of scale. Technical economies affect the size of the typical plant or establishment, rather than the overall size of the firm, which may own and control several different plant sites. Where technical economies of scale are great, the typical plant or establishment is also large in size. The main types of technical economy of scale are as follows:

➤ **Indivisibilities.** Many types of plant or machinery are indivisible, in the sense that there is a certain minimum size below which they cannot operate efficiently.

➤ **The spreading of research and development costs.** With large plants, reseach and development (R&D) costs can be spread over a much longer production run, reducing unit costs in the long run.

➤ **Volume economies.** These are also known as **economies of increased dimensions**. With many types of capital equipment (for example, metal smelters, transport containers, storage tanks and warehouses), costs increase less rapidly than capacity. When a storage tank or boiler is doubled in dimension, its storage capacity actually increases eightfold. A large smelter or boiler is technically more efficient than a small one. Volume economies are thus very important in industries such as transport, storage and warehousing, as well as in metal and chemical industries.

➤ **Economies of massed resources.** The operation of a number of identical machines in a large plant means that proportionately fewer spare parts need be kept than when fewer machines are involved. This is an application of the **law of large numbers**, since we can assume that not all the machines will develop a fault at the same time.

➤ **Economies of vertically linked processes.** Much manufacturing activity involves a large number of vertically related tasks and processes, from the initial purchase of raw materials, components and energy, through to the completion and sale of the finished product. Within a single firm, these processes may be integrated through the links between the various plants owned by the firm. The linking of processes in a single plant can lead to a saving in time, transport costs and energy.

Managerial economies of scale. Managerial economies of scale can be achieved both by increasing the size of an individual plant or, at the level of the firm, by grouping a large number of establishments under one management. Both methods of expansion allow for increased managerial specialisation and the division of labour. This involves the delegation of detail to junior managers and supervisors and a 'functional division of labour', namely the employment of specialist managers (for example, in the fields of production, personnel and sales).

Multi-plant economies of scale

Multi-plant economies of scale occur when long-run average costs fall as a result of operating more than one plant.

Firm-level economies of scale

It is obviously in a firm's interest to benefit as much as possible from plant-level economies of scale. Firms will also try to take advantage of any scale economies associated with the growth of the enterprise that are largely independent of plant size. Economies of scale at the firm level arise from the firm itself being large rather than from operating a single big plant or a number of large sites. As well as covering some of the R&D economies, massed resources economies and managerial economies already described, firm-level economies of scale also include marketing, financial and risk-bearing economies.

➤ **Marketing economies.** These are of two types: bulk buying and bulk marketing economies.

➤ **Financial or capital-raising economies of scale.** These are similar to the bulk-buying economies, except that they relate to the bulk buying or the bulk borrowing of funds required to finance the business's expansion. Large firms can often borrow from banks and other financial institutions at a lower rate of interest and on better terms than those available to small firms.

➤ **Risk-bearing economies of scale.** Large firms are usually less exposed to risk than small firms because risks can be grouped and spread. A bank can predict with some confidence the number of customers who will turn out to be bad debtors, but it is unlikely to know in advance which customers they will be. But because it knows that for each bad debt there will be many other solvent customers whose business is profitable for the bank, risks are spread and uncertainty is reduced.

Learning effects

When a firm increases the scale of its plant, it is quite likely that a new technology or new methods of working an old technology will be adopted. But if the firm's workers and managers are initially unfamiliar with the new methods, production is likely to be inefficient. A learning effect occurs when managers and workers learn from experience how to operate particular technologies and methods of production more effectively. Learning effects are usually associated with a change in the scale of a firm's operations, but they can also occur as a result of the reorganisation of existing capacity.

External economies of scale

As I have noted earlier, **external economies of scale** are shared by a number of firms (or indeed by a number of industries) when the scale of production of the whole industry (or group of industries) increases. External economies are conferred on a firm, not as a result of its own growth, but because other firms have grown larger (although, of course, the firm's own growth may also contribute to the

 Key term

External economies of scale mean lower long-run average production costs resulting from the growth of the industry of which the firm is a part.

other firms benefiting from external economies). Indeed, if the firms were to merge, external economies enjoyed by previously independent firms would become internal economies within the plants and subsidiaries of the combined enterprise. Thus takeovers and mergers internalise external economies (and diseconomies) of scale.

As with internal scale economies, it is possible to identify a number of different types of external economy of scale.

➤ **Economies of concentration.** When a number of firms in the same or related industries locate close together, they are able to gain mutual advantages through better transport facilities, the training of a pool of skilled labour and supplying each other with sources of components and market outlets. This is called a 'cluster effect'.

➤ **Economies of information.** In a large industry, it is worthwhile for specialist firms and for public bodies such as universities to undertake research and to provide information (for example, through technical and trade journals), from which all firms can benefit.

➤ **Economies of disintegration.** Although firms can often benefit from internal economies that result from linking processes internally, there may be circumstances when vertically linked production processes can be provided more efficiently by independent specialist firms. An obvious example occurs in the case of indivisibilities. If a firm is too small to use continuously plant or machinery that cannot be built on a smaller scale, it makes sense to buy supplies from an independent firm that can use the plant efficiently because it supplies a number of firms within the industry.

Box 8.2 Does size matter? Economies and diseconomies of scale in the water industry

In January 2004, Ofwat, the government's regulatory agency for the water and sewage disposal industries, published a report entitled 'Investigation into evidence for economies of scale in the water and sewerage industry in England and Wales'. The extract below is from the journal *Utility Week*.

The objective of the study was to provide answers to three key questions:

➤ Whether the process of consolidation in the industry has resulted in an industry structure consistent with the least cost production of water services in England and Wales.

➤ Whether the evidence on economies of scale presents a case for further horizontal integration in the industry.

➤ Whether there are opportunities for a more efficient industry structure through different types of restructuring (e.g. vertical separation).

The report was eagerly awaited by many in the UK water industry with the hope that it would conclude that there were economies of scale in the water industry. This would have helped pave the way for future merger activity in the sector following a long period where Ofwat have sought to, and succeeded in, blocking mergers between a number of water companies.

To the surprise of some, however, the report concluded amongst other things that there were significant diseconomies of scale for water and sewerage companies (WaSCs), i.e. the biggest water companies appear to be too big. The

report also concluded that there was likely to be constant returns to scale for the water-only companies, i.e. they are about the right size.

Maybe, however, the findings of the study are not so surprising after all. Water is, as some argue, a localised industry – and water is heavy and expensive to move around. So having utilities based around urban areas is likely to be an efficient means of operating the sector. And optimal size will be determined by the characteristics of those urban areas.

Ofwat also concluded that the results were not hugely surprising to them: 'The conclusions do not surprise us – we regulate an industry that is a conglomerate of activities each with an optimum minimum scale that is related to human and physical geography. Beyond this level we see costs rising steadily.'

So does the report's finding spell the death knell for future merger activity in the sector? It appears so and many companies will probably not have the stomach to pursue an expensive and potentially distracting process that is unlikely to succeed through the Competition Commission.

Utility Week, March 2004

Follow-up questions

1 Why might evidence of economies of scale be used to justify further horizontal integration in an industry?

2 For a utility industry such as water, what is meant by 'vertical separation'?

3 Why might the 'localised' nature of the water industry lead to diseconomies of scale?

Internal and external diseconomies of scale

In many industries, particularly in manufacturing and in tertiary activities such as the provision of financial services, firms grow large in order to benefit from the falling long-run production costs brought about by economies of scale. However, a firm may eventually reach a size beyond which higher costs that result from **diseconomies of scale** exceed any further benefits that can be squeezed out of economies of scale.

For large firms, **managerial diseconomies** are probably the most significant type of **internal diseconomy of scale**. Managerial diseconomies can result from communication failure, which occurs when there are many layers of management between the top managers and ordinary production workers. In this situation, decision making and the ability to respond to customers'

Key term

Internal diseconomies of scale mean higher long-run average production costs resulting from an increase in the size or scale of the firm in the long run.

needs or to problems arising in the course of production, both suffer. As a result, the resources the business uses are not allocated as effectively as they could be. Top management loses touch with junior managers and employees, and with the problems facing the business.

External diseconomies of scale occur when a firm's long-run average costs of production increase, not because of the growth of the firm itself, but because of the growth of the industry or market of which the firm is a part. The firm may suffer from a 'negative cluster effect', for example when the close proximity of many firms increases the cost of negative externalities such as road congestion and pollution, which each firm dumps on its market co-members. Close geographical proximity can also lead to labour shortages caused by industry firms competing for labour, and higher resulting wage costs.

> **Key term**
>
> **External diseconomies of scale** mean higher long-run average production costs resulting from the growth of the industry of which the firm is a part.

The capital market, banks and the growth of firms

All firms require finance to enable them to grow and to undertake production. Short-term finance is used to pay for the purchase of raw materials (circulating or working capital) and to pay wages. Long-term sources of funds are used to finance the internal or external growth of the firm via direct investment in new fixed plant, or through a process of takeover and merger. For all types of business enterprise, self-finance or the ploughing back in of profits (**internal finance**) is by far the most important source of finance, although the ability to engage successfully in self-finance depends upon profitability.

> **examiner's voice**
> The information provided in this and the next section is background information to provide depth to your understanding of business economics.

The main sources of **external finance** divide into borrowing (or debt) and the raising of capital by share issue. For public companies, this involves the capital market. Because private companies cannot generally raise funds on the capital market, the most important reason for private companies 'going public' (that is, becoming public companies) is to raise funds by selling new issues of shares and corporate bonds to whoever wishes to buy them. The government also raises funds on the capital market to finance its budget deficit and its borrowing requirement. The government does this by selling new issues of government bonds (called **gilt-edged securities** or **gilts**) to the general public.

Many students confuse the **capital market** with the **stock exchange**. The stock exchange is indeed an important part of the capital market, but it is only a part, and the capital market and stock exchange are not interchangeable terms. The capital market can be understood as comprising two elements: a new issues market or primary market; and a secondary market on which previously issued shares and bonds can be sold second-hand. The stock exchange is the most important part of the secondary or 'second-hand' market.

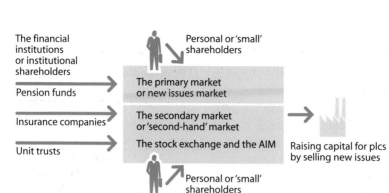

The financial institutions or institutional shareholders

Pension funds

Insurance companies

Unit trusts

Personal or 'small' shareholders

The primary market or new issues market

The secondary market or 'second-hand' market

The stock exchange and the AIM

Raising capital for plcs by selling new issues

Personal or 'small' shareholders

Figure 8.2 *The role of capital markets in financing investment in British industry*

The relationship between the primary and the secondary parts of the main capital market is illustrated in Figure 8.2. The actual raising of new capital or long-term finance takes place in the primary market when public companies (in the private sector of the economy) or the government (in the public sector) decide to issue and sell new marketable securities. Companies can borrow long-term by selling **corporate bonds**, or they may sell an ownership stake in the company by issuing **shares** or **equity**. When selling corporate bonds, the company extends its debt, and the purchaser of the bond becomes a creditor of the company.

By contrast, new issues of shares are sold when a company 'goes public' for the first time, or when an existing public company decides to raise extra capital with a new equity issue. In the latter case, the new share issue is most often a **rights issue**, in which the company's existing shareholders are given the right to buy the new issue of shares at a discount.

New issues of shares are seldom sold directly on the stock exchange. Instead, the direct sale of new issues to the general public takes place in the primary market, usually being arranged by specialised banks called **investment banks** via newspaper advertisements and the post. Nevertheless, by providing **liquidity** to the capital market, the stock exchange has an important role. Shares in private companies are illiquid and difficult to exchange for cash. By contrast, shares in listed public companies can be sold second-hand on the stock exchange. The stock exchange enables shares to be converted quickly into cash. Without the stock exchange, the general public would be reluctant to buy shares that could not easily be resold. An important source of funds necessary to finance the growth of a firm would be denied to public companies.

Extension material

The growth of venture capital or private equity finance

Until quite recently, it was not usually possible for a private company to finance expansion by extending significantly its share capital or equity, while still remaining a private company. When an ambitious private company wanted to raise a large capital sum, there were normally only two options. The company could either borrow and increase its debt or

extend its share capital by going public with a flotation on the stock exchange. However, the 1980 Companies Act introduced a significant change in the financing of private companies which has led to the growth of the modern venture capital industry. The Act allows private companies to take on new shareholders who invest considerable stakes in the business without the necessity of converting to a plc.

Venture capital is finance provided, usually to young private companies and unquoted public companies, through the sale of shares or an equity ownership stake to specialist private equity finance institutions. In the boom years and enterprise culture of the 1980s, banks and other financial institutions such as insurance companies set up specialist venture capital subsidiaries. Typically, a venture capital firm invests a large sum of money in a private company, in return for an equity stake that is highly illiquid as long as the company remains private.

Part of the deal might be that the company — having successfully grown as a result of the capital injection provided by the venture capital firm — eventually goes public, either on the 'junior stock market' known as the **alternative investment market (AIM)**, or on the main stock exchange. Going public provides an exit route for the venture capital firm. The private equity finance provider could then sell its stake in the client company and take its profit. The funds released may be used by the venture capital firm to invest in another start-up private company needing long-term funding.

The late 1990s and the early 2000s witnessed a massive growth of private equity finance in the USA and the UK. Most of this growth was fuelled by an activity very different from using venture capital to promote the growth of small start-up private companies. Instead, the private equity companies borrowed money from institutional investors and used the borrowed funds to finance leveraged (and often hostile) takeovers of established public companies. Once ownership had been transferred to the private equity company, the victim company might be broken up. Its assets would be sold and its workers sacked, to release the funds needed to pay back the borrowed funds that had financed the takeover.

For some, this represented asset-stripping, short-termism and the pursuit of private greed. But for others, private equity finance was simply a new and more efficient vehicle for engineering the restructuring of capitalism, that is: shifting productive assets from a less efficient to a more efficient use. Either way, the heyday of private equity finance was over by 2008 (at least for the time being), as a result of the credit crunch, which decimated financial businesses that had relied for their success on borrowed funds.

The trade-off facing public companies

Except in a few special circumstances such as insolvency and boardroom disputes, the directors of an independent private company generally have complete control of the business. The directors own all the shares issued by the company. Complete control means, however,

examiner's voice

Understanding the trade-off facing public companies is useful for understanding how victim companies may face hostile takeover bids.

that no capital has been raised by selling shares on the capital market. Figure 8.3 illustrates what may happen when the directors decide to go public by converting the company into a plc.

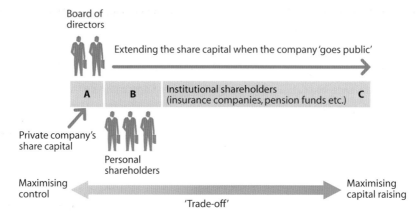

Figure 8.3 *The trade-off facing a company's board of directors*

The left-hand box (labeled A) in Figure 8.3 is the private company's share capital, all of which is owned by the directors. When the company goes public, new shares (shown by boxes B and C in Figure 8.3) are sold on the capital market. The people buying these shares comprise two very different groups of shareholders, namely small shareholders (or personal shareholders) and institutional shareholders. Small shareholders (shown by box B in Figure 8.3) are generally in the minority, particularly after selling the new issue 'second hand' to the institutions on the stock exchange. As a result of these sales, insurance companies, pension funds and other financial institutions end up owning most of the shares of plcs listed on the stock exchange. Institutional shareholdings are shown in box C in Figure 8.3.

Controlling most of the shares in public companies, the fund managers employed by pension funds and insurance companies can decide who runs these companies. The financial institutions are best regarded as sleeping owners of the companies in which they hold shares. Lacking specialised management expertise, fund managers prefer not to take an active entrepreneurial role in running the companies that their institutions effectively own. When a company's board does a good job, the financial institutions generally support the directors. However, if the board makes bad management decisions which reduce the company's profit and share price, fund managers may lose confidence in the directors. In these circumstances, fund managers can quickly switch allegiance and support a hostile takeover bid for the company.

Summary

➤ Firms grow in order to achieve their business objectives.

➤ Profit maximisation is the assumed business objective in the traditional neoclassical theory of the firm.

➤ Alternative (managerial and organisational) theories assume different business objectives, including a satisficing objective.

➤ A divorce between ownership and control may occur in large public companies when the managers who make day-to-day decisions pursue business objectives which are not in the interests of the shareholders who own the company.

➤ This is an example of the principal/agent problem.

➤ You must avoid confusing *why* firms grow with *how* firms grow.

➤ Firms may grow internally (organically) or externally via takeover and merger.

➤ Growth may also be vertical, horizontal or lateral.

➤ Vertical and horizontal growth may lead to economies of scale, but lateral growth may be more likely to result in diseconomies of scale.

➤ Internal economies of scale divide into plant-level, multi plant-level and firm-level scale economies.

➤ External economies and diseconomies of scale result from the growth of the whole market or industry, rather than from the growth of the firm itself.

➤ Avoid confusing internal and external growth with internal and external sources of finance which fund a firm's growth.

➤ Internally financed growth involves ploughing back profit, whereas external finance may be raised by borrowing from banks or selling a new share issue on the capital market.

➤ However, a new share issue may render a public company vulnerable to a hostile takeover bid.

Questions

1 Why may the traditional theory of the firm be unrealistic?

2 Name two managerial theories of the firm.

3 Distinguish between maximising and satisficing.

4 What is meant by economic natural selection?

5 Explain how the divorce between ownership and control may affect a firm.

6 Distinguish between the internal and the external growth of a firm.

7 Explain the differences between the vertical, horizontal and lateral growth of firms.

8 Explain the difference between internal and external economies of scale.

9 Explain three examples of internal economy of scale.

10 Describe how the capital market and the stock exchange may assist the growth of firms.

11 What is private equity finance, and how do venture capital firms provide finance for private companies?

Chapter 9

Industrial policy

Government economic policy divides into microeconomic policy and macroeconomic policy. In this and the next two chapters I explain microeconomic policy, which aims to make markets, industries and firms function more efficiently, more competitively, and in the public or national interest. Macroeconomic policy is, of course, covered in the third and final section of the book.

This chapter examines the meaning of industrial policy, describes its main elements, and assesses the effectiveness of the industrial policy implemented by UK governments in recent years. The three main elements of industrial policy are: competition policy; private versus public ownership of industry; and the regulation and deregulation of the UK economy.

Learning outcomes

This chapter will:
➤ provide a short history of industrial policy
➤ outline the main elements of competition policy directed at monopoly, mergers and restrictive trading practices
➤ examine nationalisation and privatisation
➤ explain policies related to privatisation such as contractualisation and the private finance initiative
➤ distinguish between regulation and deregulation
➤ analyse policies such as price caps imposed by regulatory agencies such as Ofwat

What you should already know

Although Unit 1 covers government microeconomic policy with respect to issues such as the reduction of market failures, industrial policy is not in the AS specification. The elements of industrial policy which I explain in this chapter should therefore be completely new to you.

A short history of UK industrial policy

Industrial policy is part of the government's microeconomic policy. It aims to improve the economic performance of individual economic agents, firms and industries on the supply side of the economy. Since the 1930s, when industrial policy first began as a response to the Great Depression, all UK governments have had some sort of industrial policy. However, significant changes have occurred in the nature of the policy, and also in the importance attached by different governments to industrial policy in comparison to other aspects of economic policy. Far-reaching changes occurred in UK industrial policy when, from the late 1970s until quite recently at least, free-market **supply-side economics** replaced **Keynesianism** as the prevailing economic orthodoxy.

Before this, for much of the period from 1945 until 1979, successive UK governments pursued an **interventionist** industrial policy. This reflected the Keynesian view that economic problems result from a failure of market forces, and that the problems can be cured (or at least reduced) by appropriate government intervention. During the Keynesian era (roughly the 1950s, 1960s and most of the 1970s), industrial policy in particular (and Keynesian economic policy in general) extended the roles of government and state planning in the economy. By contrast, the industrial policy pursued by governments since 1979 has mostly been **anti-interventionist** and based on the belief that the correct role of government is not to reduce the role of market forces, but to create the conditions in which market forces can work effectively and efficiently.

However, although recent governments have generally replaced interventionist industrial policy with a more free-market policy, the importance attached to industrial policy in the overall economic strategy has increased in one important way. During the Keynesian era, industrial policy and microeconomic policy were subordinate and subservient to macroeconomic policy. Keynesian macroeconomic policy was aimed overwhelmingly at the demand side of the economy, attempting to influence and control output and employment by managing the level of aggregate demand in the economy. But free-market economists believe that Keynesian demand management policies led to inflation rather than to full employment and economic growth. They also believe that the almost exclusive Keynesian concern with demand management served to divert attention away from the **supply side of the economy**, where the real problems that stand in the way of increased output and employment must be tackled. In recent years, therefore, industrial policy has been used to try to increase economic efficiency, productivity and competitiveness in goods markets and labour markets on the supply side of the UK economy.

Competition policy

For over 60 years, since its inception in 1948, competition policy has formed an important part of the UK government's wider industrial policy. **Competition policy** is the part of industrial policy that covers

 Key *term*

Competition policy aims to make goods markets more competitive. It comprises policy toward monopoly, mergers and restrictive trading practices.

monopolies, mergers and restrictive trading practices, which shall now be looked at in turn.

Monopoly policy

The USA was the first industrialised country to introduce a monopoly policy (anti-trust policy), with the 1890 Sherman Anti-Trust Act. (In the USA, monopolies are known as *trusts*.) Several decades then passed before the UK government decided that the problem of monopoly deserved special policy attention. Nevertheless, of the three main elements of competition policy I examine in this chapter, monopoly policy is the one with the longest history, dating back over half a century to the establishment of the Monopolies Commission in 1948. The role of the **Competition Commission (CC)**, as the commission is now called, is not restricted solely to the investigation of *pure* monopoly. The commission investigates mergers that might create a new monopoly as well as established monopolies. But more generally, it investigates monopoly power in oligopolistic industries that are dominated by a few large firms.

 Key term

The **Competition Commission** along with the Office of Fair Trading (OFT) implements UK competition policy.

examiner's voice

The label 'monopoly policy' is slightly misleading as very often the policy is aimed at oligopolies or concentrated markets rather than at pure monopoly.

Statutory monopoly

The UK government currently identifies two types of monopoly, known as **scale monopoly** and **complex monopoly**, which taken together are sometimes known as **statutory monopoly** (that is, monopoly as defined in law). A statutory monopoly exists in law if:

➤ one firm has at least 25% of the market for the supply or acquisition of particular goods or services (scale monopoly)

➤ a number of firms that together have a 25% share conduct their affairs so as to restrict competition (complex monopoly)

examiner's voice

Don't confuse scale monopoly and complex monopoly with the definition of a pure monopoly, i.e. one firm producing 100% of market output.

The theoretical background to monopoly policy

At this stage you should refer back to Chapter 6 and read through the sections that compare perfect competition and monopoly. The main points to note are:

➤ In the absence of economies of scale, perfect competition is more productively and allocatively efficient than monopoly, and it is also likely to be more X-efficient.

➤ In perfect competition, the 'consumer is king' and consumer sovereignty rules, whereas monopoly leads to the manipulation of consumers and the exploitation of producer sovereignty. By restricting output and raising prices, monopoly results in a net welfare loss as well as a transfer of consumer surplus into producer surplus and monopoly profit.

The model of perfect competition provides the theoretical justification for UK competition policy. However, there are two main circumstances in which monopoly may be preferable to small firms producing in a competitive market.

First, when the size of the market is limited but economies of scale are possible, monopolies can produce at a lower average cost than smaller, more competitive firms.

Second, under certain circumstances, firms with monopoly power may be more innovative than firms that are not protected by entry barriers. When this is the case, monopoly may be more dynamically efficient than a more competitive market.

Cartels versus fully-integrated monopolies

Whether a monopoly promotes or reduces dynamic efficiency, and generally 'behaves itself', depends to a large extent upon the type of monopoly and upon the circumstances in which the monopoly power was created. With this in mind, it is useful to distinguish between two very different types of monopoly: cartels and fully-integrated monopolies.

➤ **Cartels.** As I explained in Chapter 7, a cartel is usually regarded as the worst form of monopoly from the public interest point of view, since it is likely to exhibit most of the disadvantages of monopoly with few, if any, of the benefits. A cartel is a price ring formed when independent firms make a collective restrictive trading agreement to charge the same price, and possibly to limit output. A cartel acts as a monopoly in the marketing of goods, but the benefits of economies of scale are unlikely to occur because the physical or technical integration of the productive capacity of the members of the cartel does not take place. Consumer choice is restricted, and cartels tend to keep inefficient firms in business while the more efficient members of the cartel make monopoly profit. In these circumstances, it is probable that the incentive to innovate by developing new products and methods of production will be lacking. Cartels are thus likely to be dynamically inefficient. For all these reasons, cartels are generally made illegal.

➤ **Fully-integrated monopoly.** A fully-integrated monopoly (or fully-unified monopoly) may result from accident rather than design. A dynamic firm grows and benefits from economies of scale, becoming a monopoly as the reward for successful competition. Monopoly is the end result of the firm's success in innovating, reducing costs and introducing new products — which are all factors indicating that the firm is dynamically efficient. A fully-integrated monopoly may be the unintended spin-off of essentially benign motives for the firm's growth. Once established as a monopoly, the firm may continue to behave virtuously, retaining its

examiner's voice
The influential Austrian-American economist Joseph Schumpeter argued that through a process he called **creative destruction**, monopolies are more dynamically efficient than firms unprotected by barriers to entry. This is one of the two main arguments used to justify monopoly, the other being related to economies of scale from which large firms benefit.

innovating habits and using monopoly profit to finance new developments, though government regulation may be necessary to ensure continued good behaviour.

A cost–benefit approach to monopoly policy

Because economists recognise that monopoly can be either good or bad depending upon circumstances, UK policy has always been based on the view that each case must be judged on its merits. If the likely costs resulting from the reduction of competition exceed the benefits, monopoly should be prevented, but if the likely benefits exceed the costs, monopoly should be permitted. Ongoing regulation is needed to make sure the monopoly continues to act in the public interest.

The Competition Commission and the Office of Fair Trading

UK monopoly policy is implemented by two governmental agencies, the **Office of Fair Trading (OFT)** and the **Competition Commission (CC)**, which are responsible to a government ministry, the **Department for Business Enterprise and Regulatory Reform (BERR)**. BERR used to be called the Department of Trade and Industry (DTI).

> ***examiner's voice***
>
> You must understand the roles of the Competition Commission and of the Office of Fair Trading.

The OFT uses market structure, conduct and performance indicators to scan or screen the UK economy on a systematic basis for evidence of monopoly abuse. Concentration ratios provide evidence of monopolistic market structures. Market conduct indicators such as consumer and trade complaints allow the OFT to monitor anti-competitive business behaviour.

> ***examiner's voice***
>
> Evidence provided by market structure, conduct and performance indicators can be used to analyse and evaluate the costs and benefits of monopoly.

When the OFT discovers evidence of statutory monopoly that it believes is likely to be against the public interest, it refers the firms involved to the Competition Commission for further investigation. Until recently, the OFT asked the Competition Commission to decide the relatively narrow issue of whether particular trading practices undertaken by the investigated firm(s) were in the **public interest**. The public interest was fairly vaguely defined.

> ***examiner's voice***
>
> You must be able to define and interpret the term 'public interest'.

The 2002 Enterprise Act changed this, introducing **competition-based tests** to replace the public interest test. The tests centre on whether any features of the market (which include structural features and conduct by firms or customers in the market) prevent, restrict or distort competition.

Before the Enterprise Act was implemented, the Competition Commission lacked direct power to implement or enforce its recommendations. It was criticised for lacking teeth. This has changed and the commission's role is now *determinative* rather than just *advisory*. It can order firms to cease particular trading practices.

Indeed, virtually all the decisions on markets or firms to be investigated and on policy enforcement are now taken by the Competition Commission and the OFT. In practice, recommendations don't need to be forced through very often. The Competition Commission and the OFT will talk with the firms involved to persuade them to alter business behaviour voluntarily. Typically, firms will be asked to drop undesirable trading practices and to give undertakings about future conduct.

Alternative approaches to the problem of monopoly

Ever since the initial establishment of the Monopolies Commission, the UK has adopted a regulatory and investigatory approach to the problem of monopoly. Relatively few firms and takeover bids are actually investigated. The policy rationale is that the possibility of a Competition Commission investigation creates sufficient incentive for most large firms to behave well and to resist the temptation to exploit monopoly power.

However, although the Competition Commission has adopted a 'watchdog investigatory/regulatory' role, a number of other strategic approaches could, in principle, be used to deal with the problem of monopoly. These include:

➤ **Compulsory breaking up of all monopolies ('monopoly busting').** Many free-market economists believe that the advantages of a free market economy, namely economic efficiency and consumer sovereignty, can be achieved only when the economy is as close as possible to perfect competition. In itself, monopoly is bad and impossible to justify. The government should adopt an automatic policy rule to break up monopolies wherever they are found to exist. UK policy-makers have never adopted a monopoly-busting approach, although, as I have explained, powers do exist that allow the government to order the break-up of an established monopoly. By contrast, US anti-trust policy does require the break-up of firms with a very large share of the US market. However, the huge size of the US market has meant that most US firms can grow to a very large size by UK standards, without dominating the domestic market and running the risk of being broken up by the courts.

> ***e*xaminer's voice**
> Exam questions may ask for an evaluation of government intervention to deal with the problems posed by monopoly. At least two or three alternative policies should be used to evaluate the effects of monopoly.

➤ **Use of price controls to restrict monopoly abuse.** Although price controls have been used by UK governments at various times to restrict the freedom of UK firms to set their own prices, this has been part of an interventionist policy to control inflation, rather than a policy to control monopoly abuse. Under the influence of free-market economic theory, price controls have generally been abandoned in the UK in recent years. Nevertheless, as I explain later in this

The BT Tower, London

chapter, regulatory agencies have required privatised monopolies such as British Telecom (BT) to keep price rises below the rate of inflation.

➤ **Taxing monopoly profits.** As well as controlling prices directly, the government can tax monopoly profit to punish monopolistic firms for making excess profit. Monopoly taxes have not generally been used in the UK, except on a few occasions — for example, on the 'windfall' gain that landlords receive when the land they own is made available for property development. Similarly, windfall profits received by banks from high interest rates have been subject to a special tax. Also, in the late 1990s, the incoming Labour government imposed a windfall profit tax on the privatised utilities.

➤ **Rate of return regulation.** In the USA, the regulators have imposed maximum rates of return on the capital that the utility companies employ. In principle, these act as a price cap, as the utilities are fined if they set prices too high and earn excessive rates of return. However, in practice, instead of increasing productive efficiency, rate of return regulation often has the opposite effect. This type of intervention has the *unintended consequence* of encouraging utility companies to raise costs (knowing they are protected by entry barriers), rather than to cut prices to comply with the rate of return regulation.

➤ **The public ownership of monopoly.** In the past, UK Labour governments have sometimes regarded the problem of monopoly as resulting solely from private ownership and the pursuit of private profit. At its most simplistic, this view leads to the conclusion that the problem of monopoly disappears when the firms are nationalised or taken into public ownership. Once in public ownership, the monopolies are assumed to act solely in the public interest.

➤ **Privatising monopolies**. Opposing public ownership, past Conservative governments argued that state ownership produces particular forms of abuse that would not be experienced if the industries were privately owned. These include a general inefficiency and resistance to change, which stem from the belief by workers and management in the state-run monopolies that they will always be baled out by government in the event of a loss. According to the Conservative view, monopoly abuse occurs in nationalised industries, not from the pursuit of private profit, but because the industries are run in the interest of a feather-bedded workforce that is protected from any form of market discipline. The Conservatives believe that the privatisation of state-owned monopolies should improve efficiency and commercial performance, because privatisation exposes the industry to the threat of takeover and the discipline of the capital market.

➤ **Deregulation and the removal of barriers to entry.** Most economists believe that privatisation alone cannot eliminate the problem of monopoly abuse; it merely changes the nature of the problem to private monopoly and the commercial exploitation of a monopoly position. The privatisation of the telecommunication and gas monopolies was accompanied by the setting up of regulatory bodies (originally known as Oftel and Ofgas). This source of regulation, additional to that available from the Competition Commission and the OFT, was a recognition of this problem. One method of exposing monopolies — including the privatised utility industries — to increased competition is to use deregulatory policies to remove artificial barriers to entry. I explain deregulation in greater detail later in the chapter.

Contestable market theory

In recent years, much of the debate about the best way of dealing with monopoly abuse and regulating monopoly has centred upon the need to deregulate and remove barriers to market entry. This debate reflects the growing influence of **contestable market theory**. Before the free-market revival (of which the theory of contestable markets is a part), industrial policy involved an ever-increasing extension of regulation by government into the activities of private sector firms. Increased intervention was justified by the belief that regulatory powers must be strong enough, first, to countervail the growing power of large business organisations and, second, to make monopolies behave in a more competitive fashion.

examiner's voice

Contestable market theory can be applied to a wide range of exam questions on competition policy and on monopoly and other market structures. Good answers will reflect this.

At this time, monopoly was normally defined by the number of firms in the market and by the share of the leading firms, measured by a concentration ratio. The basic dilemma facing the policy-makers centred on how to reconcile the potential gains in large-scale productive efficiency, with the fact that lack of competitive pressure can lead to monopoly abuse and consumer exploitation. But in contestable market theory, monopoly is defined neither by the number of firms in the market nor by concentration ratios, but rather by the potential ease or difficulty with which new firms may enter the market. Industrial concentration is not a problem, providing that an absence of barriers to entry and exit creates the potential for new firms to enter and contest the market. *Actual* competition in a market is not essential. The threat of entry by new firms or *potential* competition is quite enough, according to contestable market theory, to ensure efficient and non-exploitative behaviour by existing firms within the market.

For a market to be perfectly contestable, there must be no barriers to entry and no **sunk costs**. Sunk costs are costs incurred when entering a market that are irrecoverable should the firm decide to leave the market. *Sunk costs* must not be confused with *fixed costs*, although some sunk costs are also fixed costs. Suppose a firm invests in new machinery when it enters the market. This is a fixed cost, but if the machinery can be sold at a good price to another firm, it is not a sunk cost. In this situation, the cost can be recovered if the firm decides to leave the market. By contrast, if the machinery has no alternative use and a cost of disposal rather than a second-hand value, investment in the fixed capital is also a sunk cost. Another sunk cost might be expenditure on advertising to establish the firm in the market. If market entry is unsuccessful and the firm decides to leave, the expenditure cannot be recovered.

In recent years, contestable market theory has had a major impact upon UK monopoly policy. The theory implies that, providing there is adequate *potential* for competition, a conventional regulatory policy is superfluous. Instead of interfering with firms' pricing and output policies, the government should restrict the role of

monopoly policy to discovering which industries and markets are potentially contestable. Deregulatory policies should be used to develop conditions in which there are no barriers to entry and exit, to ensure that reasonable contestability is possible. Appropriate policies suggested by the theory of contestable markets include:

➤ removal of licensing regimes for public transport and television and radio transmissions
➤ removal of controls over ownership, such as exclusive public ownership
➤ removal of pricing controls that act as a barrier to entry, such as those previously practised in the aviation industry

Merger policy

Whereas a government's monopoly policy deals with established monopoly, or markets already dominated by large firms, **merger policy** is concerned with takeovers and mergers that might create a *new* monopoly. Strictly, a **merger** involves the voluntary coming together of two or more firms, whereas a **takeover** is usually involuntary, at least for the victim being acquired through a **hostile takeover**. However, the term *merger policy* is used to cover all types of acquisition of firms, friendly or hostile, willing or unwilling.

Until recently, the government rather than the OFT decided on whether to make merger references. This laid government open to the criticism that, when deciding against a merger reference, it was bending to the lobbying power of big business and engaging in political opportunism. However, recent competition policy legislation gives the OFT power to make virtually all merger references. The Office keeps itself informed of all merger situations that might be eligible for investigation on public interest grounds by the Competition Commission. Currently, a takeover or merger is eligible for reference to the Competition Commission if it is expected to lead to a **substantial lessening of competition (SLC)**.

In the 1990s, barely 100 mergers (out of a total of over 3,000) were in fact referred to the Competition Commission for investigation. Of these, only a minority were found to be against the public interest and banned. These figures give some support to the argument that UK governments were not serious in their attitude to mergers and the problem of growing industrial concentration. Governments tended to assume that all mergers were beneficial unless it could clearly be shown that the effects were likely to be adverse.

One effect of current legislation is that horizontal mergers are far more likely to be investigated than lateral mergers. This may be unfortunate because lateral mergers may produce managerial diseconomies of scale. By contrast, horizontal mergers, which tend to fall foul of current merger policy, may be **synergetic**. In this context, synergy means that when two firms merge the sum is greater than the two parts. However, lateral mergers may have the opposite result, with the sum being less than the two parts.

*e*xaminer's voice
Mergers and takeovers, which occur when a firm grows *externally*, can be analysed in terms of the vertical, horizontal and lateral growth of firms.

Box 9.1 Overruling merger policy? Lloyds TSB's takeover of HBOS

In October 2008 the UK's banking system was in deep trouble in the financial meltdown triggered by the credit crunch. Halifax Bank of Scotland (HBOS) nearly went bankrupt. To rescue HBOS, the government waived through a takeover by another large bank, Lloyds TSB, without referring the takeover to the Competition Commission as the OFT recommended. The extract below is from a leader article in *The Economist*.

Lloyds TSB took over HBOS

Letting Lloyds TSB proceed with its takeover of HBOS is a mistake

It was a desperate attempt to stem financial panic, and it worked a treat. As banks, house prices and stockmarkets all tumbled in mid-September, news that Britain's government had brokered a rescue of its biggest mortgage lender, troubled HBOS, by the relatively sturdy Lloyds TSB revived spirits no end. No matter that the deal would weld the country's fourth and fifth biggest banks, by assets, into its biggest retail-banking outfit: ministers argued correctly that saving the financial system was more important than fussing about competition.

Six weeks on, things look different. The government has slung a £400 billion safety net under all the banks. HBOS, which was formed from the merger of the Halifax, a former building society, with the Bank of Scotland, would presumably be as entitled to government support on its own as is, say, the wounded Royal Bank of Scotland (RBS). Yet the £17 billion earmarked for HBOS and Lloyds TSB is said to be dependent on their merger. On October 31st the business secretary disregarded the recommendations of the official competition watchdog, the Office of Fair Trading (OFT), and waved through the deal. He made the wrong call.

There is a world of difference between rescuing a stand-alone HBOS and rescuing it as a subset of Lloyds TSB. A new banking behemoth would reduce competition significantly. The OFT made this clear on October 31st, when it published a sober analysis of a merged Lloyds and HBOS. The combined banks would have around 30% of personal current accounts, about the same share of mortgages and 40–50% of small-business services in Scotland – strengthening a duopoly with RBS that already exists there. So far the only clear advantage of the deal to consumers is the knowledge that HBOS will not go bust – and that is something now covered by the government's new bail-out arrangements. It is a shame that the bid was not referred, as the OFT urged, to the Competition Commission for more study. The point of controlling mergers at the outset is that, once consummated, they cannot easily be undone, nor behaviour changed. When goals conflict, competition is the surest lodestar.

The Economist, 6 November 2008

Follow-up questions

1 Why might Lloyd TSB's takeover of HBOS be deemed anti-competitive?

2 Do you agree that the takeover was anti-competitive and that the government should have referred the takeover to the Competition Commission for investigation? Justify your answer.

European Union merger policy

The **European Commission**, which is the executive body of the European Union (EU), has long had powers to prevent and control mergers in member countries of the EU, but before 1990, the commission did not apply these powers systematically. However, in 1990 a new EU merger policy came into operation to control the growing number of mergers involving companies active in more than one member country. The EU policy is based on the principle of **subsidiarity**, which delegates policy as much as possible to national governments. Member countries will continue to use national policy to deal with smaller mergers, but the European Commission will adjudicate on larger mergers with a community dimension. As with UK merger policy, nearly all the commission's criteria for assessing whether a merger is justified are competition related, showing again the influence of contestable market theory.

examiner's voice

The Unit 3 specification states that candidates should know the general features of both UK and EU competition policy. This is a fruitful topic for a data-response question on the impact of the EU upon the UK economy.

The European Commission justifies its policy as providing a one-stop regulatory system for mergers, in which the borderline between national and EU jurisdiction is clear-cut. However, many commentators believe that the opposite is the case. They criticise EU merger policy as an unclear, time-consuming lawyers' paradise. UK firms contemplating a merger or takeover bid have to register their plans with both UK and EU authorities to minimise the chance of falling foul of either.

Restrictive trading practice policy

Restrictive trading practices undertaken by firms in imperfect product markets can be divided into two broad kinds: those undertaken independently by a single firm, and collective restrictive practices that involve either a written or an implied agreement among two or more firms.

Key term

A **restrictive trading practice** is undertaken by a firm on its own or in collusion with other firms that restricts competition and is anti-competitive.

Independent restrictive trading practices

Cases of independent restrictive practices are initially considered by the OFT, which decides whether or not to refer firms to the Competition Commission for further investigation. Independently undertaken restrictive practices include:

examiner's voice

Avoid confusing *trading* restrictive practices with *labour* restrictive practices, which are mentioned in Chapter 12.

➤ decisions to charge discriminatory prices
➤ the refusal to supply a particular resale outlet
➤ full-line forcing, whereby a supplier forces a distributor who wishes to sell one of its products to stock its full range of products

Collective restrictive trading practices

Collective restrictive agreements and practices can be referred by the OFT to a court of law, the Restrictive Practice Court (RPC). Arguably, policy towards collective restrictive practices is more effective than other aspects of competition policy because the policy is enforced by a court. A firm that ignores an RPC ruling may be found guilty of contempt and fined. Nevertheless, the punishments that the RPC can hand out are quite weak — usually a fine of just a few thousand pounds. Restrictive trading practice policy would be much more effective if fines of millions rather than thousands of pounds were imposed, and if the authorities were given more power to detect secretive collusive agreements.

However, most agreements registered with the RPC are voluntarily dropped by the firms concerned because the firms realise that the legality of the agreements will not be upheld by the court. A collective agreement, such as a cartel agreement, is illegal unless the firms involved persuade the court that it is in the public interest — for example, to protect the public from injury.

Private versus public ownership of industry

Nationalised industries

A **nationalised industry** or business is one that is owned by the state. The history of nationalisation in the UK extends back to the middle of the nineteenth century, when the Post Office was established as a civil service department. Several nationalisations occurred in the 1920s when the Central Electricity Board, the London Passenger Transport Board and the BBC were established as public corporations (usually during

Conservative governments) by Acts of Parliament. Most of the early public corporations represented what has been called *gas and water socialism*. This describes the regulation through public ownership of an essential utility or service regarded as too important to be left to the vagaries of private ownership and market forces.

In the mid-twentieth century, industries were nationalised in the UK by Labour governments for two main reasons: as an instrument of socialist planning and control of the economy; and as a method of regulating the problem of monopoly — in particular, the problem of natural monopoly in the utility industries.

The 1950s to the 1970s were the decades of the **mixed economy**, when the major political parties agreed that the mix of public and private enterprise worked and was 'right' for the UK. But with the election of a radical free-market-orientated administration under Margaret Thatcher in 1979, this consensus broke down. The Conservative governments of the 1980s and 1990s set about the task of breaking up the mixed economy and moving the UK economy closer to a pure market economy.

Privatisation

Privatisation involves the transfer of publicly owned assets to the private sector. In the UK this has usually involved the sale to private ownership of nationalised industries and businesses that were previously owned by the state and accountable to central government. The main privatisations are shown in Table 9.1. Although the main privatisations have involved the sale of nationalised industries, other state-owned assets such as land and council houses have also been privatised.

Before privatisation some state-owned industries, such as electricity, gas and the railways, were vertically integrated. When selling these industries to the private sector, their privatisation involved significant vertical disintegration. The industries were split into horizontal layers, with different companies in each layer buying or selling from companies above or below them in the supply or distribution chain. However, the gas industry was initially privatised in fully, vertically integrated form, with British Gas owning all the stages of production from purchasing natural gas to selling through regional marketing boards to the customer. The industry was split into separate layers a few years after the initial privatisation in order to weaken natural monopoly and promote competition.

For gas and electricity, this strategy has generally been successful. Consumers now choose between competing electricity and gas marketing companies, and the prices of electricity and gas fell in real terms, at least for a number of years. However, as Box 9.2 on page 126 explains, by 2008 rapidly rising prices led to calls for the reintroduction of controls on gas and electricity prices.

Privatisation and the free-market revival

The general case for privatisation can only be properly understood when seen as part of the revolution (or counter-revolution) in economic thinking known as the **free-market revival**. In the past, socialists often regarded nationalisation as an end in itself, apparently believing that by taking an industry into public ownership, efficiency and equity would automatically improve and the public interest be served.

Table 9.1 *The main privatisations in the UK*

British Aerospace	1981
National Freight Corporation	1982
British Leyland (Rover)	1984
British Telecom (BT)	1984
British Shipbuilders	1985
National Bus Company	1985
British Gas	1986
British Airports Authority	1987
British Airways	1987
British Steel	1989
Water authorities	1989
Electricity distribution (regional electricity boards — RECs)	1990
Electricity generation (the PowerGen and National Power duopoly)	1991
British Coal	1994–95
British Rail	1995–96

examiner's voice

Several years ago, exam questions were set on the *reasons* for privatisation and on the *advantages* and *disadvantages* of privatisation. While such questions are still possible, modern questions are more likely to be set on evaluating the success or failure of a privatisation, for example that of the gas industry, on its *track record*.

In much the same way, supporters of the free-market revival at the opposite end of the political and economic spectrum believe that private ownership and capitalism are always superior to public ownership. Whatever the circumstances, they believe that the privatisation of state-run industries must inevitably improve economic performance.

The advantages of privatisation

Specific arguments used to justify privatisation include:

➤ **Revenue raising.** Privatisation, or the sale of state-owned assets, provides the government with a short-term source of revenue, which at the height of privatisation was at least £3–4 billion a year. But obviously an asset cannot be sold twice.

➤ **Reducing public spending and the government's borrowing requirement**. After 1979, Conservative governments aimed to reduce public spending and government borrowing. By classifying the moneys received from asset sales as negative expenditure rather than as revenue, governments were able, from an accounting point of view, to reduce the level of public spending as well as government borrowing. In addition, when the state successfully sold loss-making industries such as the Rover Group, public spending on subsidies sometimes fell. Government borrowing can also fall if private ownership returns the industries to profitability, since corporation tax revenue is boosted and the state earns dividend income from any shares that it retains in the privatised company.

➤ **The promotion of competition.** Privatisation has been justified on the ground that it promotes competition through the break-up of monopoly. At the time of their privatisation, industries such as gas and electricity were natural monopolies. But as I explain later in the chapter, the growth of technology-driven competition, together with the removal of barriers to entry by regulating agencies such as Ofgem, has significantly increased competition.

➤ **The promotion of efficiency.** For free-market economists, this is perhaps the most important justification of privatisation. Supporters of privatisation believe that public ownership gives rise to special forms of inefficiency which disappear once an industry moves into the private sector — even if the industry remains a monopoly. The culture of public ownership makes nationalised industries resistant to change. Through exposure to the threat of takeover and the discipline of the capital market, the privatisation of a state-owned monopoly should improve the business's efficiency and commercial performance.

➤ **Popular capitalism.** The promotion of an **enterprise culture** was an important reason for privatisation in the UK. Privatisation extended share ownership to employees and other individuals who had not previously owned shares, and thus added to the incentive for the electorate to support the private enterprise economy. Privatisation has generally proved popular with voters, so governments, both Conservative and then Labour, saw no point in abandoning a winning programme.

unit 3

The disadvantages of privatisation

Privatisation has the following possible disadvantages:

➤ **Monopoly abuse.** Opponents of privatisation have argued that, far from promoting competition and efficiency, privatisation increases monopoly abuse by transferring socially owned and accountable public monopolies into weakly regulated and less accountable private monopolies.

➤ **Short-termism wins over long-termism.** Many of the investments that need to be undertaken by the previously nationalised industries can only be profitable in the long term. There is a danger that under private ownership, such investments will not be made because company boards concentrate on the short-termism of delivering dividends to keep shareholders and financial institutions happy. Under-investment in maintaining the rail track and in technically advanced trains by the privatised railway companies provides an example. However, there is a counter-argument: that under public ownership, the government starved the nationalised industries of investment funds in order to keep government borrowing down.

➤ **Selling the family silver.** Opponents of privatisation also argue that if a private sector business were to sell its capital assets simply in order to raise revenue to pay for current expenditure, it would rightly incur the wrath of its shareholders. The same should be true of the government and the sale of state-owned assets. Taxpayers should not sanction the sale of capital assets owned on their behalf by the UK government to raise revenue to finance current spending on items such as wages and salaries. In reply, supporters of the privatisation programme argue that, far from selling the family silver, privatisation merely returns the family's assets to the family: that is, from the custody of the state to direct ownership by private individuals.

➤ **The free-lunch syndrome.** Opponents of privatisation also claim that state-owned assets have been sold too cheaply, encouraging the belief among first-time share buyers that there is such a thing as a free lunch. This is because the offer-price of shares in newly privatised industries was normally pitched at a level which has guaranteed a risk-free capital gain or one-way bet at the taxpayer's expense. This encourages the very opposite of an enterprise economy.

Economic liberalisation

So far, I have defined privatisation in a strictly narrow sense, as the transfer of assets from the public sector to the private sector. Some commentators extend the definition of privatisation to include other aspects of the programme of economic liberalisation pursued by UK governments since 1979. Policies that are closely related to privatisation include:

➤ contractualisation
➤ marketisation
➤ public-private partnerships (PPP) and the private finance initiative (PFI)
➤ deregulation

AQA A2 Economics

Contractualisation

Contractualisation or **contracting out** takes place when services such as road cleaning and refuse collection are put to private sector tender, although the taxpayer still ultimately pays for the service. To try to get value for money for the taxpayer, services that were previously provided *in house* by public sector workers are provided *out of house* through **competitive tendering**.

Marketisation

Whereas privatisation (narrowly defined) involves transferring assets from the public sector to the private sector, **marketisation** (or **commercialisation**) shifts the provision of services from the non-market sector into the market sector. A price is charged for a service that consumers previously enjoyed 'free'. Governments have also experimented in creating internal markets, whereby one part of a state-owned enterprise charges a price to another part of the same enterprise for the service it provides within the organisation. This is a form of transfer pricing.

Public–private partnerships and the private finance initiative

As the name suggests, **public–private partnerships (PPPs)** are partnerships between the private and public sectors to provide public services. They include the contractualisation of services that I have already described, but also cover activities such as the transfer of council homes to housing associations using private loans. PPP has been particularly important in the provision of health services, but private sector providers are running prisons, local authority revenue and benefit services, the majority of residential homes for the elderly, and schools.

The **private finance initiative (PFI)**, which was introduced by the Conservative government in 1993 and enthusiastically taken up by the subsequent Labour government, is closely related to PPP. Before PFI, the government was involved in all stages of planning, building and then running a public investment project such as a new school. Under PFI, the government's role is restricted to deciding the service it requires and then seeking tenders from the private sector for designing, building, financing and running the project. The government becomes an *enabler* rather than a *provider*.

Recent governments have favoured PFI because public sector services can be provided, but government borrowing (or at least on-balance sheet borrowing) does not increase, at least in the short run. The capital costs of the project are paid for by the private sector provider, but the taxpayer pays if a subsidy is required if the project is not self-financing. Taxpayers also contribute towards the profit made by the private provider. The government hopes, however, that efficiency gains resulting from private sector provision will more than offset the payment of taxpayers' funds into private sector profits. Public service trade unions oppose PPPs, and especially the PFI, because they see them as the creeping privatisation

of public services. By contrast, governments argue that PPPs can provide the public sector with the cultural values of the private sector, injecting a fresh, innovative and entrepreneurial 'can-do'. approach. They believe that without PPP, public services have a tendency to be entrenched, reactive and conservative.

Deregulation

The nature of economic regulation

Economic regulation involves the imposition of rules, controls and constraints, which restrict freedom of economic action in the marketplace. There are two types of regulation: external regulation and self-regulation.

> **External regulation**, as the name suggests, involves an external agency laying down and enforcing rules and restraints. The external agency may be a government department such as the BERR, or a special regulatory body or agency set up by government, for example the Competition Commission or the OFT.
> By contrast, **self-regulation** or **voluntary regulation** involves a group of individuals or firms regulating themselves, for example through a professional association such as the Law Society or the British Medical Association.

Regulation and market failure

Competition can sometimes bring about a situation in which social costs and benefits are not the same as the private costs and benefits incurred and received by the people actually undertaking the market activity. As I explain in Chapter 10, the over-production of externalities such as environmental pollution, and the under-consumption of education, healthcare and other merit goods, provide familiar examples of divergence between private and social costs and benefits. Governments use regulation to try to correct such market failures and to achieve a socially optimal level of production and consumption. Monopoly is also a form of market failure, and regulation is used to limit and deter monopoly exploitation of consumers.

Other examples of government regulation aimed largely at reducing the social costs of market activity include health and safety at work, anti-discrimination and safeguards of workers' rights, and consumer protection legislation. Much of this regulation is concerned with the adequate provision of information for customers and workers, and the setting of quality standards for the production of goods. Such regulation may affect advertising standards, consumers' rights of redress when purchasing faulty goods, and workers' rights in the event of discrimination or unfair dismissal.

examiner's voice

Exam questions may require a justification for removing or keeping government regulation of markets and businesses. While there is a strong case for removing regulations that protect incumbent firms or which raise business's costs unnecessarily, many regulations can be justified on the ground that they protect people from the abuse of monopoly power and from harmful externalities.

Deregulation

Deregulation involves the removal of any previously imposed regulations that have adversely restricted competition and freedom of market activity. During the last

30 years, significant deregulation has taken place in the UK and the USA. Systems of regulation built up during the Keynesian era have on occasion been completely abandoned, while in other cases they have been watered down or modified. The UK government has removed the protected legal monopoly status enjoyed, for example, by bus companies, airlines and commercial television and radio companies. Access to BT's distribution network of land lines has been given to competitors in the telecommunications industry, and private power companies have been allowed to rent the services of the national electricity and gas distribution grids.

There are two main justifications of deregulation:
➤ the promotion of competition and market contestability through the removal of artificial barriers to market entry
➤ the removal of red tape and bureaucracy which imposes unnecessary costs on economic agents, particularly businesses

Deregulation and the free-market revival

The switch away from the imposition of ever more stringent rules and regulations upon private sector economic activity, and towards the opposite policy of deregulation, reflects the decline of Keynesianism and the resurgence of free-market economics. Deregulation should be regarded as a part of an overall policy of economic liberalisation, which, as already explained, also involved the policies of privatisation, contractualisation and marketisation (or commercialisation). In recent years, governments in most industrialised countries, including most recently those in the formerly centrally planned economies of eastern Europe, have begun this process of economic liberalisation and rolling back the economic functions of the state. However, as the recent history of the financial services and banking industries shows, 'light-touch' regulation arguably was a major cause of the financial melt-down that began in 2007. Since then, there have been calls for much tougher regulation of banking and financial services.

Deregulation and the theory of contestable markets

Much of the justification for the policies of deregulation and economic liberalisation that have been pursued in recent years has been provided by the **theory of contestable markets**, which I explained earlier in the chapter. Contestable market theory argues that the most effective way to promote competitive behaviour within markets is not to impose ever more regulation upon firms and industries, but to carry out the opposite process of deregulation.

According to this view, the main function of deregulation is to remove barriers to entry, thereby creating incentives both for new firms to enter and contest the market and for established firms to behave in a more competitive way so as to deter new market entrants. Under the influence of the theory of contestable markets, governments have sought to remove or loosen all regulations whose main effect has been to reduce competition and to promote unnecessary barriers to market entry.

Regulatory capture

Another theory that has had some influence upon the trend towards deregulation is the **theory of regulatory capture**. This theory argues that regulatory agencies created by government can be 'captured' by the industries or firms they are intended to oversee and regulate. Following capture, the regulatory agencies begin to operate in the industry's interest rather than on behalf of the consumers whom they are supposed to protect.

Even if regulatory capture does not take place, the supporters of deregulation argue that much regulatory activity is unnecessary and ultimately burdensome upon industry and consumers. Once established, the regulators have an incentive to extend their role by introducing ever more rules and regulations, since in this way they justify their pay and their jobs. Regulation acts both as an informal tax upon the regulated, raising production costs and consumer prices, and also as an extra barrier to market entry, restricting competition within the regulated industry.

The regulation of the privatised utility industries

As I have explained, deregulatory policies have been implemented alongside privatisation in liberalising the UK economy. In the 1980s and 1990s, UK governments realised that once industries such as telecommunications, gas, water and electricity were privatised, there was a danger they might abuse their monopoly position and exploit the consumer. For this reason, special regulatory bodies such as **Ofgem**, which now regulates the gas and electricity industries, were set up at the time of privatisation to act as watchdogs over the performance of the utilities in the private sector. At the time of privatisation, industry-specific regulatory bodies were created. Some of these agencies have recently been merged and now cover more than one industry. For example, in the energy industry, Ofgem has replaced Ofgas and Offer, which used to regulate the gas and electricity industries respectively.

The paradox of deregulation

The establishment of regulatory agencies such as Ofgem at a time when governments have actively been pursuing a policy of deregulation and economic liberalisation has created a rather strange paradox and a source of possible conflict. On the one hand, by setting markets free, deregulation reduces the role of the state; on the other hand, new watchdog bodies such as Ofgem have extended the regulatory role of government and its agencies.

However, successive governments have argued that there need be no conflict between regulation and deregulation. This is because the regulatory bodies are themselves actively involved in deregulating the industries they oversee — for example, by enforcing the removal of barriers that prevent the entry of new firms. Recent technical progress has made it increasingly possible for new firms to enter the utility industries, particularly in the telecommunications industry. By contesting the market away from established companies such as BT and British Gas, new market entrants have eroded the natural monopoly position previously enjoyed by the privatised utilities.

Supporters of the liberalisation programme hope that the new watchdog agencies will prove so successful that eventually the new regulatory bodies can wither away, when the markets they oversee have become sufficiently competitive. However, this is likely to be a long process. Although new firms are beginning to compete in the markets previously completely dominated by state-owned utilities, established companies like British Gas are still dominant. Their continuing market power means that, certainly for the next few years, the regulatory bodies set up at the time of privatisation must continue as a surrogate for competition. Some commentators argue that, far from withering away, the new regulatory agencies may gradually extend their powers and functions. Free-market critics of economic regulation believe that the UK regulatory system provides a classic example of a growing bureaucracy.

Price-capping and the RPI minus X price formula

At the time of the state sell-off of the telecommunications, electricity and gas industries, it was realised that the newly privatised companies might use their monopoly power to raise the prices they charged and to exploit consumers. To prevent this, some form of price control was deemed necessary. The UK government decided against rate of return regulation (the system of price control used in the USA) for the reason I mentioned earlier in the chapter; namely that it raises costs and increases productive inefficiency. Instead, the UK government imposed **price caps** based on the **RPI minus X** formula. The formula limited a privatised utility's freedom to raise its prices, but encouraged it to reduce costs.

Average price increases were limited to X percentage points below the rate of inflation, as measured by the retail price index. For example, a price cap of 'RPI minus 5', set when the rate of inflation was 4%, meant that the privatised company would actually have to reduce its average prices by 1%.

*e*xaminer's voice
Exam questions may ask for an evaluation of price controls imposed on firms.

The X factor reflected the improvements in productive efficiency that the regulator believed the privatised utility could make and share with its consumers each year. Suppose, for example, that with an inflation rate of 4%, Ofgem believes that gas companies can cut costs by 10% a year. If factor X were to be set at 0%, the gas companies can raise prices by 4%, even though their costs are falling by 10%. This means that only the gas companies and their shareholders benefit from the efficiency gain, while consumers gain nothing. At the other extreme, if factor X is set at 10%, consumers rather than the gas companies benefit. This might destroy the incentive for gas companies to invest in new technology. Hence the case for pitching factor X somewhere between 0% and 10%. If set at 5%, the efficiency benefits are shared equally between consumers and producers. Consumers gain from lower prices, yet gas companies still have an incentive to invest and to increase productive efficiency. By improving efficiency by more than the factor X set by the regulator, utility companies can further increase their profits.

unit 3

Extension material

The regulatory bargain and other issues

Two significant problems emerged with the RPI minus X price formula after the price cap was first imposed on BT in 1984.

➤ Initially, the utilities believed that, as a part of a **regulatory bargain**, they would be left alone for 5 years after factor X was set, to get on with the task of running their businesses. They also believed that, if they achieved an efficiency gain during that 5-year period over and above the factor X set by the regulator, they would not be punished when the regulator reset factor X at the end of 5 years. In practice, however, the regulators intervened throughout the 5-year licence period, and in the early years, they generally raised X every time they reviewed it. Critics of the way RPI minus X was implemented believed that this reduced a utility's incentive to improve efficiency and reduce costs. This is because the regulator clawed back the utility's share of any produc-tivity gain by increasing factor X, on the ground that the utility was making excess profits.

➤ The RPI minus X pricing formula could only work properly if the regulator had a good idea of how efficient the privatised utility was, and of how efficient it might become. In order to set the X factor for 5 years ahead, the regulators needed to possess consider-able technical information about the industries they oversaw. A regulator who failed to foresee the direction that technical progress was likely to take over the next 5 years might have to reset X before the 5 years was up, thus triggering the disadvantage I mentioned above. A regulator was most likely to set X accurately if the technology in the industry was fairly mature and not subject to sudden change. In these circum-stances, the rate at which the regulator could learn about the industry was faster than the rate at which technology changed.

With the privatisation of gas and water, the RPI − X formula was modified to RPI − X + Y, and RPI + K. This was to allow unavoidable service improvement costs (such as infrastruc-ture upgrades) to be passed through to customers. These unavoidable costs included new investment demanded by the government to upgrade the gas network and improve the quality of drinking water and wastewater treatment.

Box 9.2 Whatever has happened to gas and electricity price caps?

In recent years, gas and electricity prices more than doubled at the same time as Ofgem was supposedly imposing the RPI minus X formula on both energy industries. Consumers might well have asked 'Whatever has happened to gas and electricity price caps?'. The answer is that the caps still exist, but only with regard to the transport of gas and electricity from one part of the country to another.

To make sense of this, you must understand that gas and electricity are **vertically-disintegrated** industries. Import prices of natural gas and coal, over which the UK regulator has no control, are the result of the first stage of production. The gas and electricity we then use at home are then 'manu-factured' or processed, before being transported to the consuming regions. The final stage of production is distributing gas and electricity locally to the consumer. The different stages of

AQA A2 Economics

production are undertaken by different firms. As stated, Ofgem has little or no control over import prices, and therein lies the most important reason for escalating prices. And as the extract below reveals, the UK government has removed price controls previously imposed on the energy distributing companies, from whom we buy our gas and electricity. The RPI minus X price cap is imposed on the middle transporting stage of production (e.g. the National Grid) and this has little effect on retail gas and electricity prices.

Protecting consumers? Removing price controls

When competition in a market is weak, price controls can help to protect consumers from the risk that companies might take advantage of their position to set excessive prices. Ofcom, Ofgem and Postcomm have statutory objectives requiring them to protect consumers through the introduction of competition, where appropriate. Between 2002 and 2006, Ofgem removed retail price controls from gas and electricity supply. The regulator felt that the market was sufficiently well developed for consumers to be protected by competition.

Once price controls have been removed, regulators rely on consumers to switch suppliers, thereby rewarding companies who offer good service and competitive prices, and punishing the inefficient. For this to work, consumers need to have good information about different suppliers, be able to switch supplier easily, have

sufficient confidence in the market to believe that changing supplier can make a difference, and to be able to obtain redress where a company behaves anti-competitively.

Prices of gas and electricity have risen rapidly in the recent past, and almost doubled since the start of the decade. Businesses and consumers need to be confident that markets without price controls are being effectively regulated and working well, especially at a time of rapidly rising prices. Regulators should regularly monitor business and consumer confidence in the market and its regulation so that they can respond quickly if confidence falls.

Report of the House of Commons Public Accounts Committee, November 2008
(www.publications.parliament.uk/pa/cm200708/cmselect/cmpubacc/571/571.pdf)

Follow-up questions

1 Why did gas and electricity prices rise so rapidly in 2007 and 2008?
2 Should price caps be reintroduced on retail gas and electricity prices? Justify your answer.

Technology-driven competition

Regulatory agencies have been able to lower and sometimes to remove barriers to market entry by promoting **technology-driven competition**. This type of competition occurs when technical progress enables new firms to enter markets that were previously natural monopolies. In the telecommunications industry, developments such as mobile telephony, satellite technology and the falling real cost of laying fibre-optic land lines have meant that new market entrants such as Vodafone and the cable television companies can invest in their own distribution networks. BT's distribution network is no longer a natural monopoly.

In the gas, water and electricity industries, new firms have entered the market by renting the services of the existing distribution network or grid. New electronic information and recording systems allow customers living, for example, in Manchester to buy electricity from a distribution company located in another

region. These developments make it possible for customers to shop around and find the distributor that offers the most attractive price.

Technology-driven competition can be thwarted if the distribution network through which the service is delivered into people's homes is owned by an established utility company, which is a major producer of the good or service transported through the system. In this situation, there is an obvious danger that the vertically-integrated company owning the network might prevent new market entrants from using the distribution grid. For example, a vertically-integrated British Gas Corporation could charge new gas suppliers artificially high prices for using its distribution grid, to prevent the new firms gaining market share.

This explains why government and the regulators have forced previously vertically integrated utility companies to disintegrate. Separate companies now own different layers of the gas and electricity industries. This means that the distribution layer (owned by National Grid Gas plc) is free to carry the electricity or gas of as many suppliers as it wishes, and not just the energy supplied by Powergen or British Gas.

Yardstick competition

The telecommunications industry offers the greatest scope for technology-driven competition, with new market entrants able to bypass BT's distribution network or pay fair rents for its use. However, at the other end of the spectrum, the water industry possesses the least scope for technology-driven competition to remove barriers to entry and break up the natural monopoly.

For this reason, the Office of Water Services (Ofwat) uses **yardstick competition** as the main regulatory device to promote efficient and competitive behaviour by the water companies. After comparing the performance and costs of all the water companies, Ofwat sets prices so that all the water companies have to match the standards achieved by the best in the industry. If and when the other utility watchdogs run up against the realistic limits to technology-driven competition in the industries they regulate, they may turn to yardstick competition to assess the efficiency of the companies they oversee.

> **examiner's voice**
>
> Technology-driven competition and yardstick competition provide examples of methods of competition firms can use in addition to, or in place of, price competition.

Summary

➤ Industrial policy is an important part of the government's microeconomic policy.

➤ Competition policy, policy toward private and public ownership and regulatory and deregulatory policy are the three main elements of industrial policy.

➤ The three elements of competition policy are monopoly policy, merger policy and policy toward restrictive trading practices.

➤ UK monopoly policy is based on a cost–benefit approach to large firms.

➤ Mergers are most likely to be prevented if they are viewed as potentially anti-competitive.

➤ Collective trading practices such as cartel agreements are deemed against the public interest and made illegal.

➤ From the 1980s onwards, UK governments have privatised rather than nationalised industries, though from 2007 onwards, some UK banks were effectively nationalised, at least on a temporary basis.

➤ Governments have established regulatory agencies such as Ofcom to regulate the privatised industries.

➤ Regulatory agencies also try to deregulate. If successful, the agencies can wither away.

➤ Regulatory agencies have imposed 'RPI minus X' price caps, but these have not prevented rapid price rises for goods such as electricity and gas in recent years.

Questions

1 Define industrial policy.

2 What are the three main elements of competition policy?

3 Distinguish between a scale monopoly and a complex monopoly.

4 What is a natural monopoly?

5 Distinguish between a cartel and a fully-integrated monopoly.

6 Briefly explain the possible costs and benefits of monopoly.

7 What are the roles of the Competition Commission and the Office of Fair Trading?

8 Outline possible approaches to the problem of monopoly.

9 What is the theory of contestable markets?

10 How does UK merger policy operate?

11 What is meant by privatisation?

12 State three arguments in favour of privatisation.

13 What are the disadvantages of privatisation?

14 Explain the difference between regulation and deregulation.

15 What is regulatory capture?

16 Explain the RPI minus X pricing rule for privatised industries.

17 Distinguish between technology-driven competition and yardstick competition.

Chapter 10

Market failure

Market failure occurs whenever the market mechanism or price mechanism performs unsatisfactorily. There are two main ways in which markets fail. Markets can function inequitably or they can function inefficiently. It is also useful to distinguish between complete market failure, when the market simply does not exist, and partial market failure, when the market functions but produces the wrong quantity of a good or service. In the former case, there is a missing market. In the latter case, the good or service may be provided too cheaply, in which case it is over-produced and over-consumed. Alternatively, as in monopoly, the good may be too expensive, in which case under-production and under-consumption result.

Learning outcomes

This chapter will:
➤ contrast A2 and AS coverage of market failure
➤ explain the different ways of classifying market failure
➤ summarise the main market failures you learnt at AS
➤ examine a number of case studies of market failure

What you should already know

The section of the A2 specification that covers market failure and government failure starts with the statement: 'Candidates will be expected to develop the models of market failure introduced in Unit 1'. Thus, unlike Chapters 2–9 which introduce topics not included at AS, this chapter covers topics you studied a year ago in the AS course. To avoid undue repetition, parts of this chapter summarise the coverage of market failures included in my *AQA AS Economics* textbook, without providing detail. For example, many of the diagrams included in my AS textbook on marginal private, external and social cost and benefit have been omitted from this book. You should refer back to my AS textbook, or to the notes you made last year, to remind yourself of these diagrams.

Building on your AS knowledge of market failure

Given that 'Markets and Market Failure' is the title of AS Unit 1, it is not surprising that about half of your study of microeconomics last year focused on **market failure**. Indeed, if you used my *AQA AS Economics* textbook in your AS studies, four out of the eleven chapters on Unit 1 were devoted to market failures, together with a chapter on government intervention in markets that explained how government policies attempt to correct market failures.

> **Market failure** occurs when a market functions badly, unsatisfactorily, or not at all.

In this book by contrast, only this chapter focuses specifically on market failure. However, you should appreciate that earlier chapters on monopoly and oligopoly, and the chapters that follow on from this chapter on cost–benefit analysis, poverty and income inequalities, also touch on market failure.

In this chapter, I have resisted the temptation simply to repeat what you learnt last year. Instead below is a summary of what you should already know in order for you to *develop* your knowledge and understanding, particularly by using the concept of **allocative efficiency** to analyse market failures.

> **Allocative inefficiency** occurs when it is impossible to improve overall economic welfare by reallocating resources between industries or markets.

Inequity and market failure

In this chapter, I use the word **equity** to mean fairness or justice (though in other contexts, such as the housing market, equity has the very different meaning of

> **Inequitable** means unfair or unjust.

wealth). As soon as considerations of equity are introduced into economic analysis, **normative** or **value judgements** are being made about, for example, 'socially fair' distributions of income and wealth.

As the experience of many poor countries shows, unregulated market forces tend to produce highly unequal distributions of income and wealth. Some economists, usually of a free-market persuasion, dispute whether this is a market failure. They argue that people who end up rich deserve to be rich, and people who end up poor deserve to be poor. According to this view, the market does not fail, it simply creates incentives, which, if followed, cause people to generate income and wealth which end up benefiting most of the population.

However, most economists reject as too extreme the view that the market contains its own morality with regard to the distributions of income and wealth. They argue markets are essentially 'value-neutral' with regard to income and wealth distribution. When unregulated markets produce gross inequalities that cannot be

justified on social fairness grounds, the state should intervene to limit market freedom.

Nevertheless, few economists who accept this view believe that markets should be abolished and replaced with the command mechanism. Rather, governments should modify the market so that it operates in a way more equitable than would be the case in the absence of state intervention. Taxing the better-off and redistributing tax revenues as transfers to the less well-off is the obvious way of correcting market failure to ensure an equitable distribution of income and wealth. However, as I explain in Chapters 12 and 13, the redistributive policies of **progressive taxation** and **transfers** to the poor may promote new types of inefficiency and distortion within the economy.

Markets functioning inefficiently

As I have explained in earlier chapters, monopoly and other forms of imperfect competition provide examples of market failure resulting from markets performing inefficiently. The 'wrong' quantity is produced in monopoly, particularly when there are no economies of scale, and the 'wrong' price is charged. Too little is produced and is sold at too high a price, and the market outcome is both allocatively and productively inefficient.

Complete versus partial market failure

When studying the AS course a few months ago, you learnt about **pure public goods** and **externalities**. Both of these can lead to complete market failure. In a market economy, markets may fail to provide any quantity at all of a pure public good such as national defence and they also fail to provide or encourage production of a positive externality such as a beautiful view. This leads to the emergence of **missing markets**.

 Key term

Missing markets occur when the incentive function of prices completely breaks down and a market fails to come into existence or disappears completely.

To understand a missing market, we have to return to the functions that prices perform in markets and in a market economy. The following **synoptic link** should remind you of the three functions of prices you learnt about at AS.

A synoptic link: market failure and the three functions of prices

The signalling function. Prices provide information that allows all the traders in the market to plan and coordinate their economic activities. Let me provide one example. In Chapter 5 of my AS textbook, I described how on most Friday afternoons, I visit my local street market to buy fruit and vegetables, including tomatoes and lettuce. The prices, which are shown on white plastic tabs stuck into each tray of produce, help me to decide what to buy. Of course, information about prices alone is not enough. I also need information about the quality of the goods on sale, which I try to get by looking carefully at the size of the produce and for blemishes such as bruising on apples or pears.

The incentive function. The information *signalled* by *relative prices*, such as the price of tomatoes relative to the price of lettuce, creates incentives for people to alter their economic behaviour. Suppose for example, I go to my local market intending to buy, along with other vegetables, a kilo of tomatoes and one lettuce. Being Friday afternoon, by the time I arrive at the market, the street traders have cut the price of tomatoes by 50% to try to prevent unsold stock accumulating, whose quality might deteriorate overnight. A fall in the price of tomatoes, *relative* to the price of other goods that I could buy, creates an incentive for me to buy more tomatoes, provided of course I believe the quality hasn't deteriorated.

The rationing or allocative function of prices. Suppose I respond to a fall in the relative price of tomatoes by buying more, say 2 kilos rather than the single kilo I had intended to buy as I made my way to market. Because my income is limited, spending more on one good usually means I spend less on other goods. Prices, together with income, ration the way people spend their money. Suppose tomato prices fall, not only in my local street market on a Friday afternoon, but throughout the economy for a sustained period of time. Tomatoes are now cheaper *relative* to other goods in the economy. On the one hand, the lower relative price causes households to increase their demand for tomatoes, substituting tomatoes in place of other vegetables. But, on the other hand, a lower relative price may indicate that growing tomatoes is not a very profitable activity. In response, farmers grow fewer tomatoes. If these events happen, the information signalled by changing relative prices creates incentives for economic agents to alter their market behaviour, and changes the way scarce resources are **rationed** and **allocated** between competing uses.

When explaining the nature of a missing market, we need to focus on the second function of prices, the **incentive function**. As I have explained, prices create incentives for people to behave in certain ways. In a market economy, entrepreneurs are generally unwilling to produce goods unless the goods can be sold at a profit. But with public goods and externalities, **non-excludability** and the absence of enforceable property rights create a situation in which profit can't be made within a market. The result is a **missing market**.

With partial market failure, markets do exist but they end up providing an **allocatively inefficient** quantity of the good, either too much (in the case of **demerit goods** such as narcotic drugs), or too little (in the case of a **merit good** such as healthcare).

In the next sections, I provide a brief summary of market failures and expand on what you learnt last year.

Public and private goods

Most goods are **private goods**, possessing two important characteristics. The owners can exercise private property rights, preventing other people from using the good or consuming its benefits. This is called **excludability**. The second characteristic possessed by a private good is **rivalry** or **diminish-**

Key *term*

A **private good** is a good which exhibits the characteristics of **excludability** and **rivalry**.

ability. When one person consumes a private good, less of its benefits are available for other people. Private goods also have a third characteristic: **rejectability**. People can opt out and refuse to purchase private goods.

In contrast, pure **public goods** exhibit the opposite characteristics of **non-exclud-ability**, **non-rivalry** and **non-rejectability**. It is particularly the first two of these which lead to market failure.

Key term

A **public good** is a good which exhibits the characteristics of **non-excludability** and **non-rivalry**.

Non-excludability and public goods

The best example of a pure public good is nuclear defence. If prices are charged for the benefits provided by the ring of nuclear missiles protecting Britain, then, without coercion, people could refuse to pay but still

Key term

A **free-rider** is somebody who benefits without paying.

enjoy the benefits. Any attempt by the private provider to retaliate by preventing those who do not pay from receiving the service, will not work. Withdrawing the benefits from one person means withdrawing them from all. Nevertheless, all individuals face the temptation to consume without paying, or to **free-ride**. If enough people choose to free-ride, market provision of nuclear defence breaks down. The incentive to provide the service through the market disappears. Assuming that the majority of the country's inhabitants believe nuclear defence to be necessary (that is, a 'good' rather than a 'bad'), the market fails because it fails to provide a service for which there is a need.

Non-pure public goods or quasi-public goods

Most public goods are **non-pure public goods** or **quasi-public goods** rather than pure public goods. This is because various methods can be used to exclude free-riders. Non-pure public goods include roads, television and radio broadcasts, street lighting and lighthouses. In principle, roads can be converted into private goods, provided for profit through the market. This could be done by limiting points of access, by constructing toll gates or by introducing a scheme of electronic road pricing. But even though non-pure public goods such as roads

Key term

A **non-pure public good** is a good for which it may be possible to exclude free-riders, but for which there is a case for not doing so.

examiner's voice

Make sure you understand the difference between a private good and a public good, and can give examples of both.

can be provided through the market, the second characteristic of a public good, **non-rivalry**, creates a strong case for non-market provision. Such provision will normally be made by the state at zero price to the consumer, being financed collectively out of general taxation.

Non-rivalry and public goods

Non-rivalry (also known as non-diminishability and non-exhaustibility) means that when an extra person benefits from a public good, the benefits available to other people are not reduced. In turn, this means that the marginal cost incurred by the provider of the public good when an extra person benefits from the good is zero ($MC = 0$). For example, when a person switches on a television set, the availability and benefits of the broadcast programme are not diminished for people viewing the programme on other television sets. Equally, the broadcasting company incurs no extra cost.

Box 10.1 Allocative efficiency and rail fares

The following passage has been adapted from a journal article published by British Rail in 1973. At the time, British Rail was a nationalised industry with monopoly control over the UK railway industry. Although the rail industry has since been privatised, the issue discussed in the passage is just as relevant today. The case study uses the concept of allocative efficiency to analyse the prices charged for road and rail use. Were 'correct' prices being charged?

Road users in cities pay substantially less than the costs they occasion. The greater the congestion, the truer this is. The extra cost or, as economists would call it, the marginal social cost, of an extra vehicle coming onto a road is quantifiable. Wherever there is congestion, the marginal social cost will be greater than the actual cost to the individual road user (often called the marginal road user) since the cost to the motorist of using the road are vehicle costs and time. The motorist does not have to take into account the costs imposed on other road users and on pedestrians.

On the other hand, if rail transport in cities is required to cover costs, it will then be over-priced relative to users of urban roads, since rail users will be required to cover all the real costs they give rise to, while road users will not. The effect of this difference in pricing policy is an inefficient distribution of traffic between road and rail. Less traffic travels by rail, especially in the peak, than is efficient.

One way of getting prices right would be to raise the price of urban road use until both public and private road transport covered its real costs. But if we accept it is politically imprudent or undesirable to raise the cost of using roads to a level where marginal social costs are covered, one can attempt to get the allocatively-efficient relationship between road and rail by the opposite course of action: by keeping rail fares lower than they would be if the railways charged what the market would bear rather than by raising real prices. This is the essence of the case for rail subsidies.

The essential case, if proven, must be that the traffic the railways divert from the roads reduces congestion by an amount sufficient to justify the rail subsidies required. Underlying this is the proposition that users of city roads pay less through taxation for using them than covers the real cost of their use.

Foster, C. D. (1973) *Social cost–benefit study of two suburban surface rail passenger services*

Follow-up questions

1 Define the term 'marginal social cost'.
2 The author states that subsidising rail fares can establish the 'allocatively-efficient relationship' between the prices paid for road and rail use. How may the relationship between travel prices and the prices of other goods in the economy be affected?
3 Outline the case against subsidising rail fares.

Public goods and allocative efficiency

The allocatively efficient or 'correct' quantity of any good produced and consumed is the quantity that people choose to consume when $P = MC$. But as just noted, assuming a public good is already being provided, the MC of providing the good to an extra consumer is zero. Allocative efficiency therefore occurs when $P = 0$ and the good is free for consumers. But private entrepreneurs only willingly provide goods if profits can be made, and for this to happen, the price must be above zero ($P > 0$). In the case of public goods, this means that markets can only provide the goods, assuming free-riders have been excluded, if the price is set above the marginal cost of supply ($P > MC$). This reduces consumption of the public good to below the allocatively efficient level. Market provision thus results in under-production and under-consumption of the good.

Government provision of public goods

Because markets either fail to provide or under-provide public goods, there is a strong case for the state providing the goods at zero price. Charities such as Trinity House, which is responsible for lighthouses in the UK, can also provide public goods. In theory, free provision achieves the allocatively efficient level of consumption of the public good: that is, the quantity that people wish to consume when the good is free.

Public goods and government goods

Students often wrongly define a public good as a good that is provided by the government. This is confusing *cause* with *effect*. The word *public* in public good refers to the fact that members of the general public cannot be excluded from enjoying the good's benefits. It is this that *causes* market failure. To correct the market failure, governments provide public goods. This is the *effect*. Government goods include public goods such as defence, police and roads, but they also include merit goods such as education and healthcare, which I explain later in this chapter.

Public bads

A **bad** is the opposite of a **good**. People are prepared to pay a price to gain the benefits of a good such as a bar of chocolate. Equally, they are prepared to pay a price to avoid consuming a bad such as the household sewage they produce. In this case, this is the price of the sanitation equipment installed in their houses, together with the water and sewage rates households pay to the water authority that removes the sewage from their homes.

But in the case of many bads, known as **public bads**, people can free-ride by dumping the bads they produce on others. Examples are the emission of pollution into the atmosphere and fly-tipping rubbish in public parks or in other people's gardens. If a private sector company tries to charge a price for rubbish removal, house-holds may avoid paying the price by dumping their garbage. This is why local author-ities empty dustbins for free, financing rubbish removal through local taxation.

Externalities

An **externality** is a special type of public good or public bad, which is dumped by those who produce it on other people who receive or consume it, whether or not they choose to. (These people are known as **third parties**, and the externality is sometimes called a **spin-off effect**.) Because externalities are generated and received outside the market, they also provide examples of **missing markets**.

> **Key terms**
>
> An **externality** is a public good, in the case of an external benefit, or a public bad, in the case of an external cost, and is dumped on third parties outside the market.

Externalities also exhibit the **free-rider problem**. The provider of an external benefit such as a beautiful view cannot charge a market price to any willing free-riders who enjoy it. Conversely, the unwilling free-riders who receive or consume external costs such as pollution and noise cannot charge a price to the polluter for the bad that they reluctantly consume.

Externalities are classified in two main ways:
➤ as external costs and external benefits, also known as negative externalities and positive externalities
➤ as pure production externalities, pure consumption externalities and external-ities involving a mix of production and consumption

Suppose for example that brick dust infiltrates houses and a laundry located near a brick works emitting the pollution. The pollution that soils newly-washed laundry and is breathed in by local householders is emitted in the course of production. For the laundry, brick-dust pollution is a pure production externality, emitted in the course of production and received by other producers. But for the households, the pollution is a mixed externality, generated in production and received in consumption. I shall leave it to you to think of examples of pure consumption externalities and mixed consumption externalities. If in doubt, refer back to page 109 of my *AQA AS Economics* textbook.

> **examiner's voice**
>
> Candidates often fail to understand that externalities are generated and received outside the market. Remember that both public goods and externalities provide examples of 'missing markets'.

Divergence between private and social cost and benefit

At the heart of microeconomic theory lies the assumption that, in a market situation, an economic agent considers only the private

> **Key terms**
>
> **Private benefit maximisation** occurs when $MPB = MPC$.

costs and benefits resulting from its market actions, ignoring any costs and benefits imposed on others. For the agent, **private benefit maximisation** occurs when:

marginal private benefit = marginal private cost

or:

$MPB = MPC$

However, **social benefit maximisation**, which maximises the public interest or the welfare of the whole community, occurs when:

marginal social benefit = marginal social cost

or:

$MSB = MSC$

 Key terms

Social benefit maximisation occurs when $MSB = MSC$.

Households and firms seek to maximise private benefit or private self-interest, and not the wider social interest of the whole community. They ignore the effects of their actions on other people. However, when externalities are generated, costs and benefits are inevitably imposed on others, so private benefit maximisation no longer coincides with social benefit maximisation.

Social benefit is defined as private benefit plus external benefit. As a result:

$$\text{marginal social benefit} = \text{marginal private benefit} + \text{marginal external benefit}$$

or:

$MSB = MPB + MEB$

Likewise, social cost is defined as private cost plus external cost, which means that:

$$\text{marginal social cost} = \text{marginal private cost} + \text{marginal external cost}$$

or:

$MSC = MPC + MEC$

Negative externalities and allocative inefficiency

When the production of a good causes pollution, external costs are generated, with the result that $MSC > MPC$. I shall now explain how this results in allocative inefficiency. In Chapter 6, I explained how a perfectly competitive economy can achieve a state of allocative efficiency when $P = MC$ in all markets. However, allocative efficiency occurs only if:

➤ there are competitive markets for all goods and services, including future markets
➤ there are no economies of scale
➤ markets are simultaneously in equilibrium

I can now add a fourth requirement for allocative efficiency: there must be no externalities, negative or positive. Long-run equilibrium occurs in a perfect market at the price at which $P = MPC$, which, in the absence of externalities, means also that $P = MSC$. But if negative production externalities are present, $P < MSC$ when $P = MPC$. To achieve allocative efficiency, price must equal the true marginal cost of production: that is, the marginal social cost and not just the marginal private cost. But in a market situation, profit-maximising firms are assumed only to take account of private costs and benefits. When externalities exist therefore, the market mechanism fails to achieve an allocatively-efficient equilibrium.

To put it another way, firms evade part of the true or real cost of production by dumping the externality on third parties. The price that the consumer pays for the good reflects only the private cost of production, and not the true cost, which includes the external cost. In a market situation, the firm's output is thus under-priced, encouraging too much consumption. A misallocation of resources results because the wrong price is charged. Too much consumption, and hence too much production, means that too many scarce resources are being used by the industry that is producing the negative externalities.

Government policy and negative externalities

There are two main ways in which a government can intervene to try to correct the market failure caused by negative externalities. It can use quantity controls (or regulation) or it can use taxation. Regulation directly influences the quantity of the externality that a firm or household can generate. By contrast, taxation adjusts the market price at which a good is sold and creates an incentive for less of the negative externality to be generated.

Regulation or quantity controls

In its most extreme form, regulation can be used to ban completely, or criminalise, the discharge of negative externalities such as pollution and noise. It may be impossible to produce a good or service such as electricity in a coal-burning power station without generating at least some negative externality. In this situation, banning the externality has the perverse effect of preventing production of a *good* (for example, electricity) as well as the *bad* (pollution). Because of this, quantity controls rather than a complete ban may be more appropriate. These include **maximum emission limits**, and restrictions on the time of day or year during which the negative externality can legally be emitted.

Taxation

Completely banning a negative externality such as pollution is a form of market *replacement* rather than market *adjustment*. By contrast, because taxes placed on goods affect incentives that consumers and firms face, they provide a market-orientated solution to the problem of externalities. Taxation compensates for the fact that there is a missing market in the externality. In the case of pollution, the government calculates the money value of the negative externality and imposes this on the firm as a **pollution tax**. This is known as the **polluter must pay** principle. The pollution tax creates an incentive, which was previously lacking, for less of the bad to be dumped on others. By so doing, the tax **internalises the externality**. The polluting firm must now cover all the costs of production, including the cost of

negative externalities, and include these in the price charged to customers. By setting the tax so that the price the consumer pays equals the marginal social cost of production ($P = MSC$), an allocatively efficient level of production and consumption could in theory be achieved.

Box 10.2 The introduction of the London congestion charge

In February 2003, amid much fanfare, the London congestion charge was introduced. At the time many economists believed that this marked the triumph of economic common sense over narrow self-interest and the refusal on the part of newspapers like the *Daily Mail* to accept the consequences of

ever more cars on urban roads. Economists confidently believed that many other cities, both in the UK and abroad, would rush to adopt London-style road pricing. In the outcome, this has not happened, partly because of the alleged ill-design of the London congestion charge. In November 2008, Manchester voters were asked to approve the introduction of a city centre congestion charge and they voted against it. The following article was published the week before the London congestion charge came into operation.

Congestion in central London

For 200 years, travel has been getting easier, cheaper and quicker. But many transport systems in industrial countries are now reaching full capacity. Urban roads are a particular problem. So forget science fiction visions of personal flying machines; the next big change in the way we get about is a charge for the congestion we cause. It is coming soon to cities near you. The most ambitious experiment yet starts on the streets of central London on Monday.

Vehicles in central London move no faster today than horse-drawn omnibuses did 100 years ago. Even though only 15% of city-centre travel is by car, the gridlock is endured by residents, commuters and business. Estimates of the economic costs — in lost time, wasted fuel, increased vehicle operating costs — tend to be in the range of 2–4% of gross domestic product. Because the costs of congestion rise steeply when usage is close to a road's capacity, a small reduction in traffic at peak times can bring disproportionate benefits.

The solution, most economists and transport planners agree, is to charge for the use of roads

at times of high demand. Such charges are common in other network industries: no one bats an eyelid about paying more for daytime telephone or mobile phone calls; night-time electricity is cheaper in many countries; and rail and aircraft tickets are dearer at peak times. But until recently, roads have been viewed as different: politicians and the public have rejected the idea of paying to use the Queen's highway.

To an economist, the problem of road congestion has been understood for decades. The underlying theory dates back to Arthur Pigou's 1920 book, *The Economics of Welfare*. While a driver on an empty rural road causes few problems to others, once traffic levels rise, each additional road user lowers the speed of all other drivers on the road. No driver bears this cost; so too many people drive for the capacity of each road; it becomes congested and everyone is worse off.

Pigou's theoretical solution is to levy a charge that reflects the additional cost each driver imposes on other road users. This would mean that only those who value travel more than the

charge would take to the roads, which would be less congested. Everyone else would drive at another time, take the bus, or stay at home.

Financial Times, February 2003

Follow-up questions

1 The extract states that road transport, along with the telephone and electricity industries, is a network industry. How do network industries differ from other industries?

2 Do you agree that road use should be priced? Justify your answer.

Note, however, that we can only be certain that the firm or industry is allocatively efficient if every other market in the economy is simultaneously setting price equal to *MSC*. This is an impossible requirement. We should also note that the pollution tax, like any tax, will itself introduce new inefficiencies and distortions into the market, associated with the costs of collecting the tax and with incentives created to *avoid* the tax within the law or to *evade* the tax illegally. For example, firms may dump waste at night to escape detection.

Until recently, governments have been much more likely to use regulation rather than taxation to reduce negative externalities such as pollution and congestion. Indeed, in the past, it has been difficult to find examples of pollution taxes outside the pages of economics textbooks, possibly because politicians have feared that pollution taxes would be too unpopular. But in recent years, governments have become more prepared to use pollution and congestion taxes. This reflects growing concern, among governments and the public alike, of environmental issues such as global warming and the problems posed by fossil fuel emissions and other pollutants. It may also reflect the growing influence of green or environmental pressure groups such as Friends of the Earth and a growing preference to tackle environmental problems with market solutions rather than through regulation.

Box 10.3 The European Union Directive on Carbon Emissions and the European Union Emission Trading System

In 2002 the **Kyoto Protocol** committed the UK and other EU countries to reduce greenhouse gas emissions by 12.5%, from their 1990 levels, between 2008 and 2012. To achieve this goal, the European Commission has issued a *Directive on Carbon Emissions*. Each member government has to impose tough regulations on carbon emissions for energy, steel, cement, glass, brick making, paper and cardboard industries. Once the regulatory framework was established, a market in traded pollution permits took over, creating market-orientated incentives for industries to reduce pollution because they can make money out of it. The market, which is called the **European Union Emission Trading System (EU ETS)**, is a major pillar of EU climate policy. In 2008, the EU ETS was the largest multi-national, emissions trading scheme in the world.

In 2003, as a first stage in complying with the EU directive, the UK government announced its intension to cut carbon-dioxide emissions by a fifth by 2010. This was followed in January 2004 by a more detailed plan which sets targets for reducing pollution that are tougher than those required by the Kyoto Protocol. Over the next decade the UK government intends to force power generators and heavy industry to reduce their emissions of carbon dioxide. The plan will apply to a wide range

of industries, including electricity generation, cement manufacture, paper making, refineries, metal processing and steel manufacture. However, households and transport are responsible for two thirds of carbon dioxide emissions, yet the policy does not apply to them. Critics argue that, to avoid losing votes at the ballot box, the government is unwilling to upset voters, particularly car-owning voters.

Not surprisingly, British-based manufacturing companies were alarmed, and continue to be alarmed, by the policy. They argue that industry is taking an unfair share of the burden required to reduce pollution. Given the fact that other countries have adopted lower pollution control targets, and that before 2009, the USA had still refused to ratify the Kyoto agreement, it was argued that Britain's international competitiveness would be adversely affected. Unless other countries make similar commitments, manufacturing plants located in the UK will become even less competitive than they are now.

The EU ETS covers carbon dioxide emissions from energy-intensive industrial sectors. These include electricity generation, cement, iron and steel, chemicals, and pulp and paper. The scheme has had two operating phases:

➤ phase 1 from 1 January 2005 to 31 December 2007
➤ phase 2 from 1 January 2008 to 31 December 2012

Phase 1 was strongly criticised, because emission allowances were over-allocated, causing the carbon price to collapse. In response, caps were tightened substantially for phase 2. In 2008, the EU undertook a Directive Review. Political agreement on a revised directive was expected by the end of 2008. According to an article published in the *Guardian* on 20 October 2008:

> The emerging pressure from different member states to scale back EU climate policy in the face of economic downturn is a major blow, both to the environment and to the EU economy. The French presidency appears to be driving for an agreement based on the lowest common denominator, effectively giving every member state the possibility to beg for special treatment. The aim is clearly to bully the European parliament into accepting an agreement at any cost.

Follow-up question
Research details of the revised Directive that was ratified after this case study was written, and find out up-to-date details of the EU ETS.

Pollution permits

Again until recently, the main choice of policy for dealing with the problem of pollution was between regulation and taxation. As I have explained, the former is an interventionist solution, whereas taxation, based on the principle that the polluter must pay, has been seen as a more market-orientated solution. But nevertheless it is a solution which requires the government to levy and collect the pollution tax.

In the 1990s, another market-orientated solution started in the USA, based on a trading market in **permits** or **licences to pollute**. This still involves regulation, namely imposing maximum limits on the amount of pollution that coal-burning power stations are allowed to emit, followed by a steady reduction in each subsequent year (say, by 5%) of the maximum amount. But once this regulatory framework has been established, a market in **traded pollution permits** takes over, creating market-orientated incentives for the power station companies to reduce pollution because they can make money out of it.

A tradable market in permits to pollute works in the following way. Energy companies able to reduce pollution by more than the law requires sell their spare permits to other power stations, which, for technical or other reasons, decide not to, or cannot, reduce pollution below the maximum limit. The latter still comply with the law, even when exceeding the maximum emission limit, because they buy the spare permits sold by the former group of power stations. But in the long run, even power stations that find it difficult to comply with the law have an incentive to reduce pollution. By doing so, they avoid the extra costs that otherwise result from the requirement to buy pollution permits.

> **Key term**
>
> **Traded pollution permits** allow governments to give companies licenses to pollute at a certain level. Companies can buy, sell, and trade these permits on a market.

Establishing markets for trading private property rights

In 1960, Professor Ronald Coase argued that if markets can be created for private property rights, government intervention to correct market failures may not be necessary. Coase used the example of wood-burning locomotives, which in nineteenth-century America frequently set fire to farmers' fields. If farmers possess the property right to prevent crops being destroyed, they can sell the rights to the railway companies. By contrast, if the railway companies possess the property right to emit sparks, farmers could pay the companies to reduce emissions.

Coase argued that in both cases the outcome might be the same. If farmers have a right to stop the sparks, but emitting sparks is worth more to the railway than stopping the sparks is worth to the farmers, the railway will buy the right to emit sparks from the farmers, and the damage continues. But if the railway companies have the right to emit sparks, and this right is worth more to them than to the farmers, the right will not be sold, and the damage again continues. In this example, initial ownership of property rights has no effect on the amount of resources devoted to suppressing sparks. Trading of property rights ensures the same outcome in either case.

This theory, which is known as the **Coase theorem**, has greatly influenced the free-market approach to market failures. Indeed, most economists now accept that governments should try to work *with the market* rather than *against the market* through regulation.

Extension material

Road pricing
Box 10.2 highlights that the issue of whether or not to charge motorists for the use of roads has entered public debate. The issue centres largely on road *congestion*, rather than on pollution, because fuel taxes are a better way of reducing the environmental pollution caused by vehicles burning fossil fuels. Motorists are now charged for driving in central

London during business hours, and a private sector firm owns and runs a section of toll motorway north of Birmingham. Electronic pricing has become technically possible and is likely to be used in future road charging schemes.

The case for and against road pricing brings together issues concerning both public goods and negative externalities. Roads are a good example of a quasi-public good, since toll booths or electronic pricing can be used to exclude free-riders. Road use also results in the discharge of negative externalities. The extent to which negative externalities are produced depends upon whether the road is congested or

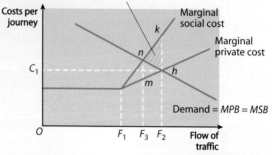

Figure 10.1 *The benefits and costs of using an uncongested and a congested road*

uncongested. The two situations are shown in Figure 10.1, which measures the flow of traffic (for example, the number of cars travelling on the road per hour) on the horizontal axis and the cost per journey on the vertical axis.

When the traffic flow is less than F_1, an extra motorist driving along the road imposes no negative externalities or external costs upon other road users — if we ignore the pollution emitted by cars. In this situation, road use should be free, to encourage the allocatively efficient or socially-optimal level of use. For levels of traffic flow between zero and F_1, the marginal social cost of road use equals the marginal private cost borne by motorists ($MSC = MPC$). But once the road becomes congested (at flows of traffic greater than F_1), this is no longer the case, and there is a case for road pricing to provide the incentive to reduce road use.

For traffic flows above F_1, each motorist who drives on the road adds to traffic congestion, which all motorists using the road then suffer. Beyond F_1, the marginal social cost of motoring is greater than the marginal private cost incurred by the motorist ($MSC > MPC$). But in the absence of road pricing, when deciding whether or not to drive on the road, motorists consider only the private cost of motoring and not the external cost dumped on other road users. Providing there is no charge for road use, motorists use their cars up to traffic flow F_2 (at point h). At F_2, the marginal private benefit of motoring equals the marginal private cost ($MPB = MPC$). At this point, the private cost incurred by the marginal motorist is C_1, but this is less than the social cost of the marginal journey, which includes the marginal cost of congestion caused by the marginal motorist but suffered by other road users. At traffic flow F_2, the marginal external cost of congestion imposed on other road users is shown by the distance ($k - h$).

Resource misallocation results. Motorists make more journeys than they would, had they to bear the full social cost resulting from the use of their cars. The shaded triangle bounded by

the points n, k and h measures the welfare loss suffered by society at the privately-optimal traffic flow F_2, at which $MPB = MPC$.

Arguably, there is a case for road pricing when roads become congested. Allocative efficiency is improved when a motorist is charged a price equal to the marginal external cost imposed on other road users, as a result of the journey. The optimal congestion charge would be $(n - m)$, which measures the marginal external cost of a journey at the socially-optimal level of road use, F_3. Some congestion still occurs at F_3, but it is less than at F_2, and motorists pay for the congestion they generate. The congestion charge or road price internalises the externality. Journeys that are worth undertaking in the absence of a congestion charge are not worthwhile once the appropriate charge is imposed.

Government policy and positive externalities

Just as governments *discourage* the production of negative externalities, in much the same way they try to *encourage* the production of positive externalities. As with negative externalities, the government can choose to regulate and/or try to change the prices of goods and activities that yield external benefits. In the latter case, subsidies rather than taxes are used to encourage production and consumption.

Regulation

Just as regulations can ban the omission of negative externalities, so the generation of positive externalities may be made compulsory. In this situation, it is illegal not to provide external benefits for others. For example, local authority bylaws can require households to maintain the appearance of properties, and the state may order landowners to plant trees.

Subsidies

A subsidy is the opposite of a tax: that is, money paid by the government to people or firms undertaking certain activities. **Producer subsidies**, given to firms, shift a good's supply curve rightward, increasing both the quantity produced of the good and the quantity of positive externalities generated from the production of the good. By contrast, a **consumer subsidy**, which is paid directly to consumers for spending on a particular good, shifts the demand curve for the good rightward. For example, a government can use both types of subsidy to encourage use of public transport. It can give money to railway or bus companies, or it can provide subsidised travel passes for passengers.

Demerit goods

Cigarettes, alcoholic drinks and narcotic drugs such as heroin are examples of **demerit goods**. People who consume these goods do so for the pleasure the goods yield. But demerit goods are often addictive, leading to

 Key term

A **demerit good** is a good, such as tobacco, for which the social costs of consumption exceed the private costs.

an outcome in which short-term pleasure eventually turns into long-term health problems. However, the short-term pleasure that consumption yields means that a *demerit good* such as a cigarette should not be confused with a *bad* such as pollution. A bad yields displeasure, dissatisfaction or nastiness to the person unwillingly 'consuming' it. As a result, people are prepared to pay to get rid of a bad, though as I explained earlier in this chapter, public bads such as rubbish and pollution can be dumped on others so that the person or firm that creates the bad avoids paying for its removal.

Examples, of course, are not the same as definitions. There are two ways of defining a demerit good, and both are acceptable in an examination answer. The first definition centres on negative externalities, whereas the second definition focuses on **information problems** that affect consumption of demerit

> **Key term**
>
> The **information problem** occurs when people make poor decisions because they don't possess, or ignore, the relevant information.

goods. In the case of the first definition, the marginal social costs suffered by the wider community are greater than the marginal private costs incurred by a smoker or drinker. By contrast, the second definition ignores externalities, but distinguishes between the short-term and long-term *private* costs incurred by the person consuming the demerit good.

> ➤ **Demerit goods and negative externalities.** When a person consumes a demerit good such as tobacco, negative externalities are generated which are unpleasant or harmful for other people. People unwillingly breathe in the fumes the smoker discharges, with eventual harmful effects on their health. (This is the problem of passive smoking.) Smelly clothing is a more trivial example of a negative externality caused by smoking.

> ➤ **Demerit goods and information problems.** When teenagers first get the 'habit' of smoking, drinking or drug-taking, they may either ignore the long-term private costs they are likely to suffer later in life, or they downplay the significance of these costs. Either way, young people tend to be myopic or short sighted with respect to the costs of consuming demerit goods. A person who started drinking as a teenager may regret the decision later in life when suffering an alcohol-related illness. But when he or she started to drink, the private costs that only emerge many years later are ignored or undervalued.

Demerit goods and allocative inefficiency

Earlier in this chapter, when discussing negative externalities, I explained that price must equal the marginal social cost of production ($P = MSC$) if the level of output in a market is to be allocatively-efficient. From this it follows that the allocatively-efficient level of production and consumption of a demerit good occurs when $P = MSC$. But when a demerit good is bought and sold in a free market, unaffected by taxes or regulation to discourage consumption, too much of the good is consumed. The privately-optimal level of consumption occurs where $P = MPC$, but at this level of consumption $P < MSC$. The good is too cheap. The result is allocatively-inefficient, with the demerit good ending up being over-consumed.

Merit goods

Education and healthcare provide examples of **merit goods**, which, as I stated earlier, must not be confused with public goods. (I also mentioned that both are examples of government goods, which leads to the possible confusion.) As is the case with demerit goods, merit goods can be defined in two ways: in terms of externalities (in this case *positive* externalities) and in relation to information problems.

> **Merit goods and positive externalities.** When a person consumes a merit good such as healthcare, the resulting positive externalities benefit other people. An obvious example is that healthy people seldom spread diseases. The social benefit enjoyed by the wider community is greater than the private benefit enjoyed by the healthy person.

> **Merit goods and information problems.** For a merit good such as healthcare, the *long-term* private benefit of consumption exceeds the *short-term* private benefit of consumption. But when deciding how much to consume, individuals take account of short-term costs and benefits, ignoring or undervaluing the long-term private costs and benefits. For many years, I taught in the Open University, where students' ages range from 22 to over 70. On numerous occasions adult students said to me: 'If only I had got my qualifications when I was younger; unfortunately I did not value education when I was at school.'

Key term

A **merit good** is a good, such as health care, for which the social benefits of consumption exceed the private benefits.

examiner's voice

Students often confuse *merit goods* with *public goods*. Like public goods, merit goods such as education are often provided by the state, but the reason for doing so is different. Students also confuse demerit goods with bads or nuisance goods. A bad, such as rubbish, yields only disutility to any unlucky individual consuming it. By contrast, a demerit good such as tobacco certainly fulfils a need and provides satisfaction (in the short run at least) to an addicted smoker.

Merit goods and allocative inefficiency

In a market situation, and given the absence of subsidies or regulations designed to encourage consumption, people under-consume a merit good such as education.

Suppose that in Figure 10.2, the price of education is set at P_1. This is the price at which $P = MPC$, but it is not the price at which $P = MSC$. At P_1, education is too expensive, too little is consumed, and the outcome is allocatively-inefficient. To achieve the allocatively-efficient level of consumption, Q_2, the price must be reduced to P_2. At P_2, $P = MSC$; hence the outcome is allocatively-efficient. The distance between Q_2 and Q_1 shows under-consumption of education at the higher price P_1.

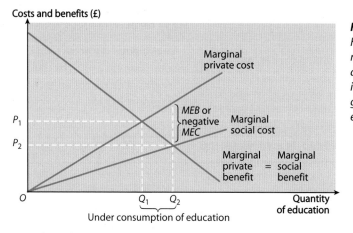

Costs and benefits (£)

Figure 10.2
How charging a market price leads to allocative inefficiency in the case of a merit good such as education

You may be rather puzzled both by Figure 10.2 and also by my explanation of the diagram. To sort out the puzzle, it is necessary to realise that a (positive) marginal external benefit can also be treated as a (negative) marginal external cost (*MEC*). This is the way that *MPB* is displayed in Figure 10.2. As a result, the marginal social cost (*MSC*) curve lies below the marginal private cost (*MPC*) curve. If we treat the externality in this way, it follows that when $P = MPC$, $P > MSC$ — the difference between the two being the (positive) marginal external benefit or the (negative) marginal external cost.

Government policy and demerit goods

I explained earlier in this chapter how regulation, taxation and subsidies can be used to limit the production of negative externalities. Similar policies can be used to discourage consumption of demerit goods. Governments can use regulation (including making consumption illegal), taxation or both to prevent or limit consumption of a good such as tobacco or alcohol.

Regulation directly influences the level of consumption of a demerit good such as tobacco. By contrast, taxation adjusts the market price of the demerit good. In its most extreme form, regulation can be used to ban completely the sale and consumption of a demerit good such as heroin. However, this may have the perverse effect of driving consumption underground into a criminalised market in which, arguably, the social costs of consumption are greater than in a legal 'above-ground' market. Rather, for 'milder' demerit goods such as tobacco and alcoholic drink, smoking and drinking can be banned in public places, while shops can be banned from selling tobacco and alcohol to younger teenagers.

Completely banning consumption and/or production of demerit goods is a form of market replacement rather than market adjustment. By contrast, because taxes placed on goods affect incentives which consumers and firms face, they provide a market-orientated solution to the problems posed by demerit goods.

Government policy and merit goods

As with other examples of positive externalities, governments can use regulation, subsidy or both to enforce or encourage consumption of merit goods. For merit goods such as car seat belts and motorcycle crash helmets, which are

infrequently purchased by road users, the UK government uses regulation but not subsidy. Consumption is compulsory, but road users must pay a market price for the merit good. In these cases, the government has decided that, as spending on a seat belt or crash helmet forms only a small part of total consumer spending, road users can afford to pay. By contrast, other merit goods, such as vaccination against contagious diseases, are completely subsidised and provided free, but in the UK consumption is not compulsory.

In the UK, education and healthcare are provided by the state and form an important part of public spending. Nevertheless, private sector provision also exists, and was growing, at least before the 2008 recession. One reason for growing private sector provision of merit goods lay in the fact that free state provision does not necessarily mean good-quality provision.

Merit goods and uncertainty, moral hazard and adverse selection

Uncertainty about future long-term benefits and costs contributes to under-consumption of merit goods. For example, a person does not know in advance when, if ever, the services of a specialist surgeon might be needed. Sudden illness may lead to a situation in which a person cannot afford to pay for costly surgery, if provided solely through a conventional market. One market-orientated solution is for private medical insurance to pay for the cost of treatment at the time when it is needed. However, private medical insurance often fails to pay for treatment for the chronically ill or for the poor. Private insurance may also fail to provide medical care for risk-takers in society who decide not to buy insurance, as distinct from risk-averters, who are always the most ready customers for insurance.

Like all private insurance schemes, healthcare insurance suffers from two further problems, both of which lead to market failure. These are the problems of moral hazard and adverse selection. **Moral hazard** is demonstrated by the tendency of people covered by health insurance to be less careful about their health because they know that, in the event of accident or illness, the insurance company will pick up the

 Key term

Moral hazard describes the tendency of individuals and firms, once insured against some contingency, to behave so as to make that contingency more likely.

bill. **Adverse selection** relates to the fact that people whose health risks are greatest are also the people most likely to try to buy insurance policies. Insurance companies react by refusing to sell health policies to those who most need private health insurance. For those to whom they do sell policies, premium levels are set sufficiently high to enable the companies to remain profitable when settling the claims of customers facing moral hazard or who have been adversely selected.

> **Key term**
>
> **Adverse selection** describes a situation in which people who buy insurance often have a better idea of the risks they face than do the sellers of insurance. People who know they face large risks are more likely to buy insurance than people who face small risks.

Public collective provision, perhaps organised by private sector companies but guaranteed by the state and funded by compulsory insurance, may be a better solution. Both private and public collective-provision schemes are a response to the fact that the demand or need for medical care is much more predictable for a large group of people than for an individual.

Value judgements and merit and demerit goods

Many people believe that an external authority, such as the state or a religious body, is a better judge than individuals of what is good for them. The state and religious bodies should therefore encourage the consumption of merit goods and discourage and sometimes completely ban the consumption of demerit goods.

Whether one agrees with this rather paternalistic view depends on one's own personal value judgement. Indeed, whether a good is regarded in the first place as a merit good or as a demerit good depends upon similar personal value judgements. Goods regarded by some people as merit goods are regarded by others as demerit goods. Examples include birth control, sterilisation and abortion, which, depending on ethical or religious standpoints, are regarded by some people as good for society, but by others as bad. The question of deciding whether, and to what extent, a good is a merit or a demerit good, or indeed neither, depends on value judgements that are likely to vary greatly from individual to individual, and between societies.

> **examiner's voice**
>
> Make sure you don't confuse a demerit good with an economic bad. When consumed, a bad yields disutility, whereas a demerit good provides utility to the consumer, at least in the short run.

Box 10.4 Should narcotic drugs be legalised?

Exasperated by the seemingly endless deaths, crime and corruption generated by the world's illicit drug trade, a growing number of public officials and scholars in recent weeks have begun to call for debate on what for years was politically unspeakable: making drugs legal.

The argument rests on the assumption that drug laws, not drugs themselves, cause the most damage to society. If drugs were legal, drug black markets worth billions of dollars would evaporate, the empires of drug gangsters would collapse, addicts would stop committing street crimes to support their habit, and the courts would no longer be overwhelmed by a problem they cannot hope to defeat.

On April 25, Mayor Schmoke of Baltimore shocked a meeting of the United States Conference of Mayors by saying illegal drug consumption should be treated as a health concern rather than a criminal justice problem.

Legalisation would eliminate most drug-related crime: the crimes of producing, selling and possessing drugs, the crimes committed by addicts to support their habits, and crimes committed by drug traffickers as they attempt to expand or protect their trade. The types of crime that might not be eliminated would be the crimes committed by people because they are under the influence of drugs, such as child abuse and assaults by people experiencing drug-induced psychosis.

Legalisation would save the federal, state and local governments more than $8 billion a year from the costs for the police, courts and prisons. The Government could reap billions in tax revenue that could be applied to drug rehabilitation and education programs.

New York Times, 15 May 1988

Follow-up questions

1   Explain why a narcotic drug such as heroin is usually viewed to be a demerit good.

2   Should the problem of drugs be treated as a health concern rather than a criminal justice problem?

3   Do you agree that narcotic drugs should be legalised? Justify your argument.

Summary

➤   Markets can fail because they function inequitably or because they function inefficiently.

➤   A highly unequal distribution of income may result from a market functioning inequitably.

➤   Allocative inefficiency provides evidence of a market functioning inefficiently.

➤   Monopoly, public goods (and public bads), externalities, merit goods and demerit goods all lead to market failure and allocative inefficiency.

➤   Complete market failure leads to missing markets.

➤   Partial market failure results in too much, or too little, of a good being provided and/or consumed.

➤   Market failure is associated with resource misallocation.

➤   Regulation, taxation and markets in permits to pollute are used to reduce negative externalities and the consumption of demerit goods.

➤   Regulation and subsidies are used to encourage the production of positive externalities and consumption of merit goods.

➤   Extending the legal entitlement to property rights is another method of reducing negative externalities and encouraging production of positive externalities.

➤   Uncertainty, moral hazard and adverse selection all contribute to under-consumption of merit goods.

➤ Lack of accurate information about what might happen in the future, or down-playing of known information, contribute to under-consumption of merit goods and over-consumption of demerit goods.

Questions

1 Distinguish between market failures resulting from inefficiency and those resulting from inequity.

2 Provide an example of a missing market.

3 Define a public good and explain the free-rider problem.

4 Distinguish between external costs and external benefits.

5 Why do externalities create allocative inefficiency?

6 How does a market in tradable pollution permits function?

7 Distinguish between a demerit good and a bad.

8 Explain how subsidies and taxes may be used to promote the allocatively efficient level of consumption of merit goods and demerit goods.

9 How can legal allocation of property rights reduce market failures?

Chapter 11

Government failure and cost–benefit analysis

One of the main functions of government microeconomic policy is to correct market failure. Often, however, such intervention leads to government failure. Government failure occurs whenever government intervention in markets or the direct provision by government of goods or services leads to an unsatisfactory outcome.

Governments often try to pre-empt and minimise the possibility of government failure by considering the costs and benefits for society as a whole that might result from government intervention in the economy. But cost–benefit analysis (CBA) need not be restricted to analysing the effects of government policy and intervention in the economy. It can be applied to private sector investment decisions, and indeed to any decision, however grand or trivial, made by an ordinary member of society such as you or me.

Learning outcomes

This chapter will:
- ➤ link government failure to attempts to correct market failures
- ➤ relate government failure to public interest theory and public choice theory
- ➤ distinguish between cost–benefit analysis and private sector investment appraisal
- ➤ discuss the problems that arise when undertaking a cost–benefit analysis

What you should already know

At AS you learnt that government failure occurs when government intervention in the economy leads to a misallocation of resources. You also learnt that government intervention in the economy, for example to try to correct market failure, does not necessarily result in an improvement in economic welfare. The Unit 1 AS specification states: 'Governments may create, rather than remove, market distortions and inadequate information, conflicting objectives and administrative costs should be recognised as possible sources of government failure.'

Cost–benefit analysis is not mentioned in the AS specification. However, you may have come across the concept when evaluating at AS the various ways in which government intervention affects the economy, particularly with respect to attempting to correct market failures.

The possibility of government failure

Economics students sometimes assume that once a government intervenes to reduce or to eliminate a market failure, the policy is immediately effective, and that everyone can then live happily ever after. But there is another possibility. When the government intervenes to try to deal with a problem, far from curing or ameliorating the problem, intervention actually makes matters worse. When this happens, the problem of **government failure** replaces the problem of market failure.

Key term

Government failure occurs when government intervention in the economy is ineffective, or wasteful or damaging.

Government failure and the law of unintended consequences

The **law of unintended consequences**, which applies in almost all fields of human behaviour, predicts that, whenever the government intervenes in the market economy, effects will be unleashed which the policy makers had not foreseen or intended. Sometimes of course, the unintended effects may be advantageous to the economy, while in other instances they may be harmful but relatively innocuous. In either of these circumstances, government intervention can be justified on the ground that the social benefits of intervention exceed the social costs and therefore contribute to a net gain in economic welfare. But if government activity – however well intentioned – triggers harmful consequences, which are greater than the benefits that the government intervention is supposed to promote, government failure will result.

examiner's voice

Merit goods, demerit goods and externalities provide a link between market failure and government failure.

Public choice theory and government failure

Economists of a free-market persuasion argue that governments should be wary of intervening to try to correct any alleged market failures, including those related to the environment. This approach to markets and market failure is associated with a wider body of theory about the role of government in the economy, known as **public choice theory**.

examiner's voice

Government failure often results from the failure of interventionist policies to correct market failure.

The free-market advocates of public choice theory regard a market economy as a calm and orderly place in which the price mechanism, working through the incentives signalled by price changes in competitive markets, achieves a more optimal and efficient outcome than could result from a policy of government intervention. They believe that risk-taking businessmen or entrepreneurs, who lose or gain through the correctness of their decisions in the market place, know better what to produce than civil servants and planners employed by the government on risk-free salaries with secured pensions. Providing that markets are sufficiently competitive, what is produced is ultimately determined by consumer sovereignty, with consumers knowing better than governments what is good for them.

According to the free-market philosophy, the correct function of government is to reduce to a minimum its economic activities and interference with private economic agents. Thus government should be restricted to a **night watchman** role, maintaining law and order, providing public goods and possibly offering other minor corrections when markets fail. Generally, government is there to ensure a suitable

Houses of Parliament

environment in which wealth creating entrepreneurship can function in competitive markets subject to minimum regulation. This philosophy of the correct role of markets and of government leads free-market economists to reject government intervention in the economy, including policies that aim to correct alleged market failures. They believe that, at best such intervention will be ineffective, at worst it will be damaging, destabilising and inefficient.

Public interest theory and government failure

Public interest theory is very different to the public choice theory I have just explained. Public interest theory is favoured by Keynesian economists who generally support government intervention in a market economy. They believe that governments intervene in a benevolent fashion in the economy in order to eliminate waste and to achieve an efficient and socially desirable resource allocation. Public interest theory, applied at the *microeconomic* level in the economy to correct market failure, is matched at the *macroeconomic* level by Keynesian economic management of the economy. Keynesians believe that government intervention at the macro level, can anticipate and counter the destabilising forces existent in the market economy, achieving a better outcome than could be achieved in an economy subject to unregulated market forces. Keynesians justify discretionary government intervention in the economy on the ground that provided the intervention is smart and sensible, government activity stabilises an otherwise inherently unstable market economy.

Government failure and cost–benefit analysis

Governments, of course, want to prevent their policies, both those currently in progress, and those they are considering undertaking in the future, being cast as government failures. To prevent or at least to minimise the possibility of

examiner's voice

CBA is used by governments to try to prevent future government failures.

government failure, governments use cost–benefit analysis (CBA). However, CBA contains its own problems, and the large amounts of taxpayers' money governments spend on CBA may themselves be regarded as a form of government failure.

examiner's voice

CBA is usually associated with investigations, commissioned by government, into large and expensive infrastructure projects. However, in recent years such examples of CBA have been thin on the ground. Governments appear to have decided that the costs of large CBA investigations are greater than any likely benefits. Nevertheless many smaller cost–benefit analyses are undertaken in-house within government departments such as DEFRA, and the Freedom of Information Act makes them accessible on the internet.

What is cost–benefit analysis?

Cost–benefit analysis (CBA) is a method of decision making that takes account of external as well as private costs and benefits. CBA undertaken by a government usually assesses whether a particular decision, for example an investment project, is socially optimal and in the public interest, and not just privately optimal and in the interest of the economic agent undertaking the activity.

Cost–benefit analysis is a technique for assessing *all* the costs and benefits likely to result from an economic decision, i.e. the social costs and benefits and not just the private costs and benefits.

In the past, CBA has most often been used by governments to help decide whether to invest in a major public project such as a motorway, an airport, or a major investment by a nationalised industry. However, there is no reason in principle why a private sector investment such as the Channel Tunnel, or indeed any action by a private economic agent or by the government (e.g. a tax change), cannot be examined by CBA. For example, a cost–benefit analysis of the proposed decision to extend Stansted Airport would take into account costs such as building and maintenance costs of the extension and of improved road and train links, compensation paid to local landowners and households, and environmental damage caused by the extension and by additional flights that will use the airport. Benefits would include any time saved by travellers, possible reductions in congestion near other airports, and the additional jobs created by the expansion.

Box 11.1 The ABC of cost–benefit analysis

A very good introductory article explaining cost–benefit analysis was written by E. J. Mishan, Professor of Economics at the LSE. The extract below is from the introduction and conclusion of Mishan's article.

Cost–benefit analyses are in high fashion. Scarcely a week goes by without an authorita- tive voice asserting that, in connection with some proposed project or other, a thorough cost–benefit study is needed. No matter how heated a controversy, a government can still the protests of the critics and be assured of a respectful silence simply by announcing that a cost–benefit analysis is in progress. The popular belief is that this novel technique provides a scientific assessment of the social value of a project, or at least an objective assessment.

True, if every benefit and every cost associated with a proposed project of investment is properly evaluated and brought into the calculus in a systematic way, the resulting sum – whether an excess of benefit over cost or the other way round – can hardly be challenged. Yet such a statement is not much more than a tautology. The fact is that evaluating 'properly' all relevant data is a guiding ideal, not a current practice. For although the procedure used in cost–benefit analysis follows certain conventions, the outcome may vary according to the economist in charge of the study, because of differences in judgement with respect both to *what* is to be included and *how* it is to be evaluated. In the absence of consensus, the individual judgement of whoever is in charge is an important factor in the outcome.

Judgements differ in the choice of which items are to be valued at market prices and which are to be valued at shadow prices; in the range of intangibles to be included in the study; in the methods used to evaluate these intangibles; in the choice of an investment criterion; and in the devices used to make allowances for future uncertainty. It is well to bear in mind that, in the present stage of its development, cost–benefit analysis is an imperfect calculus, as much an art as a matter of science, or more precisely, as much a matter of judgement as a technique.

Lloyds Bank Review, July 1971

Follow-up questions

1 Do you agree that cost–benefit analysis is more of an 'art' than a 'science'? Justify your answer.

2 What is meant by a 'shadow price', and what 'investment criterion' might be applied in a cost–benefit analysis? (Hint: read the Extension material that follows shortly.)

Why cost–benefit analysis is needed

Suppose the economy in which we live displayed the following conditions:

➤ perfect competition in all economic activities
➤ all effects relevant to the welfare of individuals are priced through the market
➤ no economies of scale and no externalities

Over 200 years ago, using the *invisible hand* metaphor, the great classical economist Adam Smith described such an economy. If such an economy actually existed, cost–benefit analysis would not be needed. Individuals pursuing private greed to maximise self interest would at the same time ensure that the social benefit of the whole community was also achieved.

But, for good or for bad, real world economies are not like this. As we have seen in previous chapters, market imperfections, economies of scale, missing markets and externalities mean that instead of maximising the social welfare of the whole community, the price mechanism misallocates resources and produces unjustifiable inequality in the distributions of income and wealth. Cost–benefit analysis is a technique for evaluating all the costs and benefits of any economic action or

decision, that is: the *social costs and benefits* to the whole community and not just the *private costs and benefits* accruing to the economic agent undertaking the action.

The differences between private sector investment appraisal and CBA

Social cost–benefit analysis is really just an extension of private sector investment appraisal in that CBA assesses *all* the costs and benefits (*external* as well as *private*), for society as a whole, of making particular economic decisions. A private sector business deciding whether or not to invest in new capacity has to estimate the initial cost of the investment, the size, shape and length of its future income stream, and to how to place monetary values on future private costs and benefits.

However, social cost–benefit analysis has to go further, calculating expected future *external* costs and benefits. Many of the social costs and benefits resulting in the future from an action undertaken now take the form of externalities that are difficult to quantify. How does one put a monetary value on the saving of a human life resulting from fewer accidents on a proposed motorway? What is the social cost of

examiner's voice

Exam questions will not be set on the techniques of private sector investment appraisal, but knowledge of the topic helps to build up an understanding of CBA.

the destruction of a beautiful view? It is extremely difficult to decide on all the likely costs and benefits, to draw a line on which to include and exclude, to put monetary values to all the chosen costs and benefits accruing immediately with those which will only be received in the distant future.

Extension material

How a business makes investment decisions

Investment in fixed capital projects, such as building a new factory, involves calculating all the future costs the project will incur and all the future benefits it will yield. A business has to put a monetary value on the project's expected net future income stream (i.e. future benefits minus future costs).

The central problem is guessing and putting money values to an unknown and uncertain future. If a firm is to maximise profit after investing in a capital project, the following condition must be met:

the rate of return per year expected over the life of the investment	>	the expected rate of interest per year which must be paid on borrowed funds to finance the investment

This requires the firm to estimate the initial fixed cost of the investment, together with details of its expected future income stream. The firm may be reasonably sure of the initial fixed cost of an investment. It also knows the current rate of interest or cost of borrowing which has to be paid to raise the funds to finance the investment. However, some of the most important features of an investment are not known, and these have to be estimated or guessed. The firm must estimate the expected life of the investment, together with the size and shape of the income stream which the investment is expected to yield over the years of its life.

Figure 11.1 illustrates some of the problems facing a business when deciding whether or not to invest in particular fixed capital projects. The diagram assumes that, because of a shortage of investment funds, the business is choosing between two investment projects. These are a fleet of trucks to transport the firm's goods to customers, and a computer system for organising business activities such as customer orders, payments to suppliers and the company's wage bill.

Estimating the size and shape of the expected income stream (future revenues less future costs) is fraught with uncertainty. Not only must the investment's physical output be calculated for each year in the asset's expected economic life, so also must the prices at which the output is sold and the running costs of the investment. This includes future interest rates or borrowing costs, and future prices of other inputs such as labour and raw materials.

For the sake of simplicity, Figure 11.1 assumes both investment projects are identical in all respects except one. Each investment costs £1 million and takes a year to complete (Year 0 in the diagram), before the investment can be used by the firm. Each investment has an expected economic life of 10 years (Years 1–10 in the diagram), and the business expects each investment to deliver exactly the same total income stream over the 10-year period. Expected income is shown by the wedge-shaped area drawn for each investment project. Finally, at the end of ten years, neither investment has a second-hand or scrap value, but equally, no disposal costs are incurred.

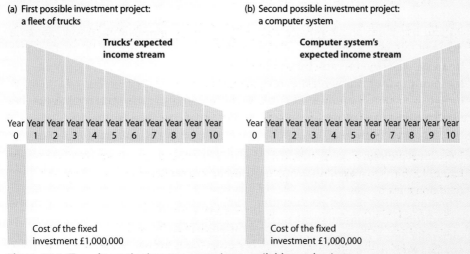

(a) First possible investment project: a fleet of trucks

Trucks' expected income stream

Year Year Year Year Year Year Year Year Year Year Year
0   1   2   3   4   5   6   7   8   9   10

Cost of the fixed investment £1,000,000

(b) Second possible investment project: a computer system

Computer system's expected income stream

Year Year Year Year Year Year Year Year Year Year Year
0   1   2   3   4   5   6   7   8   9   10

Cost of the fixed investment £1,000,000

Figure 11.1 *Two alternative investment projects available to a business*

Although both investment projects are expected to earn exactly the same *total* income, the key difference between the two projects lies in the *shape* of the expected income streams, which are mirror images of each other. The business expects the trucks to suffer breakdown and mechanical problems as they get older. This means the trucks earn most of their income early in the 10-year period. However, the computer system is expected to

yield most of its income late in the 10-year period. A possible reason for this lies in the fact that it takes time for a business to make full use of an ICT system.

Given all the information about the two competing projects, which project should be chosen by a profit-maximising business? The answer is the fleet of trucks. Two reasons justify this decision. First, the future is always uncertain, and the further we go into the future, the greater the uncertainty. Businesses must face the possibility that an investment's *economic life* (or *business life*) will be much shorter than its *technical life*. The development of new technologies, or changes in the price of labour or energy, may render an investment productively inefficient long before it actually wears out or permanently breaks down. This is particularly true in the case of computer systems. The firm may have to write off the computer system long before the 10 years are up, and replace it with a new system that was not around at the time of the initial investment.

Second, and even more importantly, income received early in a project's life can be reinvested, either in another project, or to earn the rate of interest when deposited in a bank or financial institution. This is true for all projects, but projects that earn most of their income early in life have much more potential for earning income in this way than projects earning income mostly late in life. Because the trucks deliver most of their income early in the 10-year period, they have a greater scope for earning such income.

The techniques used in cost–benefit analysis

Cost–benefit analysis is really an extension of methods that are used by private sector businesses to decide whether particular investment projects are worthwhile. To find out more about **private sector investment appraisal** read the Extension material included above. Two of the techniques used in both social cost–benefit analysis and by private businesses when choosing whether to invest are: discounting the future and shadow pricing.

Discounting the future

An important feature of both private sector investment appraisal and of social cost–benefit analysis is the method of placing monetary values, not only on current and expected future private costs and benefits, but on external costs and benefits as well. Costs and benefits occurring many years ahead must have lower monetary values placed on them than similar costs and benefits occurring in the near future. A mathematical technique known as **discounting the future** is generally used to place appropriate monetary values on costs and benefits expected in the future. Discounting the future enables both firms appraising their own investments, and the government undertaking a social cost–benefit analysis, to calculate the monetary value *now* of costs and benefits *expected in the future*. The further we go into the future, the lower the *current value* of expected future costs and benefits.

> ### examiner's voice
> Unit 3 examination questions may ask for an explanation and an evaluation of problems encountered when undertaking a cost–benefit analysis.

Shadow pricing

The prices charged for traded goods and services do not always reflect the true social marginal cost of resources in alternative uses. Market failure may produce this result, as may taxes and subsidies that do not reflect the correction of market failure. For these reasons, cost–benefit analysis sometimes uses prices which are different from the prices actually charged for goods and services. The artificial set of prices used in CBA are known as **shadow prices**. Shadow prices are *imputed prices* designed to reflect the true social costs and benefits of a particular course of action. For example, the extra journey time spent by people travelling from central London to Stansted rather than Heathrow might be valued at an appropriate hourly wage rate, as would the time saved by travellers living closer to Stansted.

> **examiner's voice**
> The Unit 3 specification states: 'candidates are not expected to have a detailed knowledge of techniques such as discounting and shadow pricing, but they should understand that money in the future is worth less than money now and that prices have to be put on economic activities where there is no market price. Candidates are expected to relate cost–benefit analysis to the problems caused by externalities and to market failure and government failure.'

Some difficulties involved in CBA

I have already mentioned some of the problems involved when undertaking a cost–benefit analysis. These include the problem of placing a monetary value on externalities, which by their nature are delivered and received outside the market; the problem of choosing an appropriate rate at which to discount the future; and the problem of setting shadow prices accurately. In addition to these problems, CBA also suffers from the following difficulties and limitations:

Forecasting

It is difficult to forecast all the costs and benefits that might occur in the future. Supply and demand patterns must be predicted, together with the development of completely new technologies that at the time of the CBA can only be guessed. Population distributions may change, and different rates of inflation can have different impacts on future costs and benefits.

Objectives

CBA helps policy makers to choose between different ways of achieving a particular objective, but it cannot be used to choose between alternative objectives. For example, CBA can be used to choose between expanding, or not expanding, Stansted, Gatwick and Heathrow airports, but it cannot be used to choose between investing more in transport or investing in hospitals, schools and universities.

Social welfare

The value of CBA is limited by a definition of an increase in social welfare, which is implicitly included in cost–benefit analysis. In CBA, an increase in social welfare

is defined according to the Hicks-Kaldor test. In this test, devised about 60 years ago by two eminent UK economists, Sir John Hicks and Lord Kaldor, social welfare improves if the welfare gain enjoyed by the 'winners' from a policy measure is greater than the welfare loss suffered by the 'losers'. To put it another way, if part of the welfare gain is paid by the 'winners' to compensate the 'losers', there is still a net welfare gain, even though in practice, such compensation is seldom paid. CBA has often justified a particular project on the grounds that, when all costs and benefits have been evaluated, there is a net welfare gain using the Hicks-Kaldor test. However, a cost–benefit analysis can reach this conclusion by effectively bypassing the distributional consequences of the project. In the case of some projects, most of the 'winners' are the already better-off, and most of the 'losers' are the already disadvantaged.

Box 11.2 Would a CBA have rejected Concorde?

In the autumn of 2003, Concorde, the supersonic airline developed jointly by the British and the French, and flown in service only by the national flag-carrying airlines, British Airways and Air France, flew its last flight. Arguably, as the extract below indicates, Concorde would never have been developed had a proper cost–benefit analysis of the commercially-doomed project been undertaken and listened to by the British and French governments.

Concorde

Back in the mid-1950s, Whitehall had an idea. Over the past few decades, planes had been becoming steadily faster, with speeds rising from 200 mph to 300 then 500 mph. The Ministry of Aviation had seen the future and it was called supersonic flight.

Concorde was a wonderful piece of kit. But the fact that it was technically superb cannot disguise that it was commercially unviable. The flaw was not in its beautiful ground-breaking design but in the belief that what the aviation market wanted was a sleek aircraft that could travel at twice the speed of sound. It didn't.

What the market was looking for was a lumbering workhorse that could satisfy the urge of the post-war consumer generation for travel and tourism. Concorde was essentially the last gasp of an era in which the image of air travel was of a cruise in the sky, with big seats, martinis and couples dressing for dinner.

An opportunity to cut losses was spurned in the early 1970s when it was clear there were no customers for the plane outside the captive markets in Britain and France, and that the small fuselage meant the 100 passengers would have to pay exorbitant fares. As such, Concorde was viable, but only if Britain and France wrote off the development costs and were prepared to accept that Concorde would serve only a tiny elite. The Chancellor the Exchequer wanted the plane scrapped, noting in his memoirs that it was 'an aircraft which is used by wealthy people on their expense accounts, whose fares are subsidised by much poorer taxpayers'.

The fact is that it was a colossal white elephant. It was the product of a system that preferred grandiose projects — missiles, super-sonic jets, nuclear power plants — to investment in the less glamorous consumer goods such as family cars, fridges, washing

machines, cameras, which people actually wanted.

The price of air travel, down by 50%, means that the demand is for flying buses which are cramped and uncomfortable, but cheap. Put simply, given the choice between 40 trips across the Atlantic at £200 a throw or one round trip on Concorde at £8,000, most of us plump for the former. The British and French governments tried to second-guess the market and got it wrong, which is why only 14 Concordes, as opposed to wild estimates of 300, entered service.

The *Guardian*, 27 October 2003

Follow-up questions

1 Before Concorde came into service, the British and French governments wrote off the aircraft's development costs. They then claimed that Concorde was commercially viable. Why might an economist still want to reject investment in Concorde?

2 Should governments invest in 'flag-waving' projects such as Concorde and space travel? Justify your argument.

A final criticism of cost–benefit analysis

Critics argue that CBA is pseudo-scientific. By this, they mean that CBA appears to be a scientific technique of evaluating projects, undertaken by impartial 'experts'. In practice, however, CBA is loaded with value judgments and arbitrary decisions disguised as objectivity. For example, different decisions on how to value an hour of a business executive's time, or for that matter a tourist's time, when travelling from London to Standsted, might lead to different results from an analysis of the proposed airport extension. At best, CBA simply may be a costly waste of time and money, or to put it another way, a job-creation scheme for economists and planners. At worst, CBA may reach the wrong decisions. Some critics also argue that CBA is a cynical method whereby politicians distance themselves from, and induce delay in, unpopular decisions, deflecting the wrath of local communities away from themselves and onto the 'impartial experts' undertaking the CBA.

Supporters of CBA reject these arguments and counter that, for all its defects it remains the best method of appraising public investment decisions because all the likely costs and benefits are exposed to public discussion. Whatever one's view, in recent years, UK governments have largely abandoned officially undertaken CBAs, tending instead to evaluate public investment projects largely on commercial or private profit criteria.

Summary

➤ Government failure occurs when governments intervene in markets, often when attempting to cure market failure, but actually making matters worse.

➤ In some instances, the adverse effects of government intervention are relatively trivial and are less than the benefits of intervention.

➤ On other occasions government intervention may be extremely damaging, with the costs exceeding any benefits resulting from the intervention.

➤ Government intervention provides many examples of the effect of the law of unintended consequences.

➤ Public choice theory and public interest theory can both be used to analyse the effects of government intervention in markets.

➤ Cost–benefit analysis provides a method of assessing whether for the whole community, the benefits of government intervention exceed the costs.

➤ Cost–benefit analysis takes account of external and social costs and benefits that might result from an investment decision or from any type of government policy.

➤ In principle, there is no reason why any decision, however great or small, or made by any economic agent such as a household or individual, cannot be subject to a cost–benefit analysis.

➤ Cost–benefit analysis must take account of future as well as current costs and benefits and quantify them.

➤ Discounting the future and using shadow prices are techniques used in cost–benefit analysis.

➤ One problem is knowing where to draw the line on which costs and benefits to include and exclude, and on how far into the future to go.

➤ Choice of discount rate is also critical to the result of an analysis.

➤ Cost–benefit analysis is more of an art than a science, and it provides a way for government ministers to put themselves at arm's length from potentially unpopular decisions.

Questions

1 Distinguish between government failure and market failure.

2 What is the law of unintended consequences?

3 In the light of the possibility of government failure, should governments intervene in markets to try to correct market failures?

4 Distinguish between private and social costs and benefits.

5 Explain the difference between investment appraisal and social cost–benefit analysis.

6 What sort of prospective policy decisions might a government subject to cost–benefit analysis?

7 Explain how problems of quantification affect cost–benefit analysis.

8 Outline problems that may arise when identifying and evaluating *future* costs and benefits.

9 What is meant by discounting the future?

10 Why is shadow pricing important in cost–benefit analysis?

11 Is cost–benefit analysis scientific or pseudo-scientific?

Chapter 12

Labour markets

In earlier chapters I explained and analysed the behaviour of households and firms in the economy's product markets. When explaining the price of a good, I assumed that the prices of inputs or factor services necessary for production to take place are generally given. This chapter reverses this assumption. When studying how wage rates and levels of employment are determined in the economy's labour markets, we generally assume that the prices of the goods that labour produces are given.

Learning outcomes

This chapter will:
- ➤ discuss role reversal in labour markets and goods markets
- ➤ compare a perfectly competitive labour market with a perfectly competitive goods market
- ➤ explain the supply of labour, both for a worker and the market supply of labour in a perfectly competitive labour market
- ➤ explain the demand for labour, both for a firm and the market demand for labour in a perfectly competitive labour market
- ➤ compare a monopsony labour market with a monopoly goods market
- ➤ analyse wage discrimination and other forms of discrimination in labour markets
- ➤ examine the impact of trade unions and the national minimum wage on wage rates and employment

What you should already know

Because there is no mention of labour markets in the AS specification, it is more than likely that you started your A2 studies having undertaken no formal analysis of the markets for factors of production, including the economy's labour markets.

I am assuming, however, that at the start of your reading of this chapter, you know little or nothing about the functioning of labour markets at the microeconomic level in the economy.

Role reversal and labour markets

Much of the theory I explain in this chapter is really just the price theory you have already studied in the **goods market** (or **product markets**) of an economy, operating in the **labour market**. A labour market is an example of a **factor market**, i.e. a market in which the services of a factor of production are bought and sold. Markets for land, capital goods and entrepreneurial skill are the other factor markets.

As Figure 12.1 shows, households and firms function simultaneously in both sets of markets, but their roles are reversed. Whereas firms are the source of supply in a goods market, in a factor market firms exercise demand for factor services supplied by households. The incomes received by households from the sale and supply of factor services contribute, of course, in large measure to the households' ability to demand the output supplied by firms in the goods market. To exercise **demand**, which requires an *ability* to pay as well as a *willingness* to pay, households need an income, which for most people requires the sale of labour in a labour market.

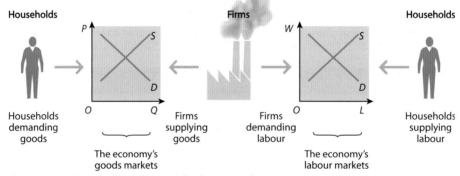

Figure 12.1 *The goods market and the factor market*

Indeed, the relationship between households and firms in the two markets is essentially circular, resembling the **circular flow of income** that you learnt at AS. In goods markets, finished goods and services flow from firms to households, who spend their incomes on the goods. In labour markets, members of households earn the incomes they spend on goods by selling labour to their employers.

Extension material

Marxist theory and labour markets

In this chapter, I use standard **price theory**, developed over 100 years ago by **neoclassical** economists such as Alfred Marshall, to explain how wage rates and levels of employment are determined.

There is, however, an alternative theory, which was developed by Karl Marx, one of the great nineteenth-century classical economists. **Marxist theory** argues that a class struggle between capitalists and workers determines the level of wages. By treating labour as a commodity and forcing their workers' wages down, capitalists extract **surplus value** from them. This chapter provides no further explanation of Marxist theory, but it does explain how, in imperfectly competitive labour markets without trade unions or minimum-wage legislation, monopsonistic employers can use market power to exploit the labour force.

Perfectly competitive labour markets

As in a perfectly competitive goods market, a perfectly competitive labour market contains a large number of buyers and sellers, each unable to influence the ruling market price (in this case the ruling market *wage*), and operating in conditions of perfect market information. Employers and workers are free to enter the market in the long run, but an individual employer or firm cannot influence the ruling market wage through its independent action.

In Chapter 4, I explained how a firm in a perfectly competitive goods market can sell as much as it wants at the ruling market price, which is also the perfectly elastic demand curve facing the firm and the firm's average and marginal revenue curve. Each firm is a passive price-taker at the ruling price determined in the market as a whole, choosing the quantity to sell, but not the price.

A very similar situation exists when a firm takes on workers in a perfectly competitive labour market, except that now the firm can buy as much labour as it wants at the ruling market wage. To state this another way, each employer faces a perfectly elastic supply of labour in a perfectly competitive labour market. Figure 12.2 illustrates why.

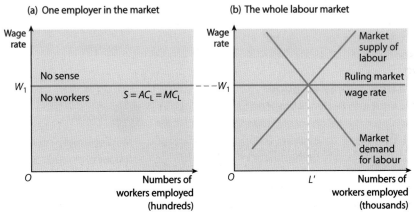

Figure 12.2 *The supply curve of labour facing each firm in a perfectly competitive labour market*

Figure 12.2 (b) shows demand and supply conditions in the whole of the labour market. The ruling market wage facing all employers and workers is W_1. Each firm, depicted in Figure 12.2 (a) could pay a wage higher than W_1, but there is no need to, since as many workers as the firm plans to employ are available at the ruling

wage. In any case, such a course of action means that the firm incurs unnecessary production costs, leading to X-inefficiency and a failure to maximise profits. Hence the label 'no sense' positioned above W_1.

Conversely, any firm offering a wage below W_1 would lose all its workers. In a perfectly competitive labour market, workers regard all employers as perfect substitutes for each other. Why work for a firm paying below the market wage when work is available from employers offering the market wage?

> ### *e*xaminer's voice
> Economic theory is easier to understand when you see how the same reasoning and way of thinking applies in different contexts. Compare Figure 12.2 with Figure 4.2 on page 41. The diagrams show perfect competition in a labour market and in a goods market. In Figure 12.2, the wage rate lies along the perfectly elastic *supply* curve of labour facing each employer. By contrast, in Figure 4.2 the price that each firm charges lies along the perfectly elastic *demand* curve for the firm's output.

Indeed, in a perfectly competitive labour market, each employer is just one among many in the market, able to hire whatever number of workers it wishes, providing only that the ruling market wage is offered to all employees taken on. This also means that W_1 (the ruling market wage rate) is each firm's **average cost of labour curve (AC_L)** and its **marginal cost of labour curve (MC_L)**. Average costs of labour are calculated by dividing total wage costs by the number of workers employed. Likewise, marginal costs of labour are measured by the growth of the total wage bill whenever an extra worker is hired.

Key terms

The **marginal cost of labour** is the addition to a firm's total cost of production resulting from employing one more worker.

The **average cost of labour** is total wage costs divided by the number of workers employed.

The market supply of labour
I shall return to perfect competition in the labour market later in the chapter. However, before I do this, I first need to explain the supply curve of labour, and then the demand curve for labour.

If we add together the labour supply curves of all the workers in the labour market, we arrive at the **market supply curve of labour** illustrated in Figure 12.2 (b). To explain this curve, I must first explain an **individual worker's supply curve of labour**. This curve shows how many hours of labour the worker plans to supply at different hourly wage rates.

Key terms

Market supply curve of labour is planned supply of labour by all the workers in a labour market.

Individual worker's supply curve of labour is planned supply of labour by one worker.

My starting point is the assumption that a worker supplies more labour to increase personal economic welfare: that is, to maximise private benefit. The welfare that a worker derives from the supply of labour divides into two parts, which taken together are sometimes called **net advantage**.

Net advantage includes:

➤ welfare derived from the wage (or strictly from the goods and services bought with the money wage)
➤ welfare derived from work (popularly known as job satisfaction, or if negative, job dissatisfaction)

Different types of work yield different amounts of positive or negative welfare (job satisfaction and dissatisfaction). When a worker enjoys the job, the net advantage of work is greater than the welfare of the wage. In this situation, the worker is willing to work for a money wage lower than the wage that would be acceptable if there were no satisfaction from the work itself. But for some workers, work such as routine assembly-line work in factories and heavy manual labour is unpleasant, yielding job dissatisfaction. The supply of labour for this type of employment reflects the fact that the hourly wage rate must be high enough to compensate for the unpleasantness (or sometimes the danger) of the job.

> ### examiner's voice
>
> Exam questions may ask for explanations of why some workers, say brain surgeons, are paid more than other workers such as supermarket cashiers. You must use theory to answer this type of question and not just common sense.

Box 12.1 Who should be paid more, MPs or news readers?

An essay question in a recent AQA exam paper asked for an explanation of why workers employed in pleasant occupations, such as television celebrities, are paid more than those in disagreeable occupations, such as road sweepers. A good answer to the question might have argued that if job satisfaction or dissatisfaction were to be the only factor determining wages, the road sweeper would be paid more. However, the answer would then go on to argue that other factors, related to supply and demand, productivity, learned skills and inate ability tend to override the job satisfaction factor and explain why television celebrities are paid more than road sweepers.

In April 2008, the Labour government minister Jack Straw asked a rather similar question: should MPs (such as himself) be paid more than television newsreaders? The passage below is from an article which asked for readers' views on the issue. Three readers' views follow the article extract.

Jack Straw has derided BBC newsreaders for raking in inflated salaries while 'prancing around the studio' instead of soberly delivering news bulletins. While Huw Edwards is reported to earn £250,000 a year for presenting the Ten O'clock News on BBC1, MPs must content themselves with a meagre £60,000 a year.

One politician questioned whether the salary would be enough to attract able new MPs, claiming it was 20% behind comparable groups outside Parliament. The *Telegraph* has suggested that MPs should settle for the average national wage, which is about £22,000.

Do you think this is enough for an MP's duties? Should newsreaders be paid more or less? Do you think state-funded salaries should be closely matched to the equivalent wage in the private sector? Or are public sector employees compensated in other ways? Many City bankers pocketed record multi-million pound Christmas bonuses last year, while

Newsreader Sophie Rayworth

nurses still struggle to earn enough to buy their own homes. Which professions do you think are overpaid, and which underpaid? Are you happy with your own salary?

Daily Telegraph, 20 April 2008

Readers' views

➤ Politics has been described as 'show business for the unattractive' so it follows that the pay should be lower than in show-biz.

➤ Newsreaders have an important function in public life, but a salary of £1 million per annum even for a journalist of such theatrical and argumentative talents as Jeremy Paxman, coupled with a remarkable ability to raise a devastating eyebrow, is blatantly wrong. Not every MP deserves their seat in the House, but most of them work immensely hard and we should treat the House and our ministers, of whichever party, with more respect.

➤ I believe that *both* are overpaid. Politicians should be made to exist on the average wage, including cabinet members. It would keep their feet on the ground and help them realise the effects of their decisions. After all they keep telling us that they are spending our money wisely.

Follow-up question

Do you believe that **both** MPs and TV newsreaders are paid too much? Use economic theory to justify your argument.

The upward-sloping supply curve of labour

As a simplification, I shall now assume that work yields neither job satisfaction nor dissatisfaction, and that a worker's net advantage derives solely from the wage. The worker must choose whether to supply an extra hour of labour time in order to earn money or whether to enjoy an extra hour of leisure time. The choice is illustrated in Figure 12.3.

*e*xaminer's voice

It is important to understand what upward-sloping and backward-bending supply curves of labour show. However, AQA exam questions are more likely to test understanding of the implications of the different shapes rather than a theoretical explanation of the different shapes. The shape of the supply curve of labour is significant for fiscal policy and for supply-side policy. Supply-side economists argue that higher rates of income tax reduce the incentive to supply labour.

There is an **opportunity cost** whenever a person decides to work. The opportunity cost of supplying one more hour of labour time (in order to earn money) is the hour of leisure time sacrificed. Because of the time constraint (there are only 24 hours in a day) a decision to supply one more hour of labour time means that the worker chooses 1 hour less of leisure time. Labour time and leisure time are substitutes for each other, and working longer hours eats into leisure time.

Figure 12.3 *The choice between supplying labour and enjoying leisure time*

But both the money wage and leisure time yield less and less extra welfare, the greater the quantity a person has. As more labour time is supplied at a particular hourly wage rate, the extra income yields less and less extra satisfaction. However, the decision to supply more labour simultaneously also means the decision to enjoy less leisure time. In this situation, each extra hour of leisure sacrificed is accompanied by an increasing loss of economic welfare. At the margin, to maximise personal welfare, a worker must supply labour up to the point at which:

$$\frac{\text{welfare from the last}}{\text{unit of money earned}} = \frac{\text{welfare from the last unit}}{\text{of leisure time sacrificed}}$$

In this situation, the marginal private benefit received by a worker from supplying labour equals the marginal private cost incurred from giving up leisure time. Providing personal preferences remain stable, there is no incentive for the worker to supply more labour at the going hourly wage rate.

However, a higher hourly wage disturbs this equilibrium. With a higher wage rate, at the margin, the welfare derived from the wage becomes greater than the welfare derived from the last unit of leisure time enjoyed. To maximise personal welfare at the higher wage rate, the worker must supply more labour and enjoy less leisure

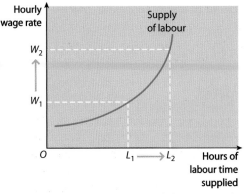

Figure 12.4 *The upward-sloping supply curve of labour*

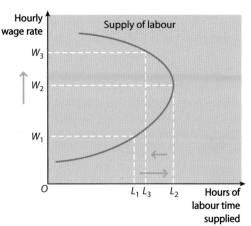

Figure 12.5
The backward-bending supply curve of labour

time. The result is the upward-sloping individual supply curve of labour shown in Figure 12.4. An increase in the hourly wage rate from W_1 to W_2 means that the worker increases the hours of labour time supplied from L_1 to L_2.

The backward-bending supply curve of labour

Under some circumstances, however, a worker's labour supply curve may be backward bending, regressive or 'perverse', showing that as the wage rises, less labour is supplied. This is illustrated in Figure 12.5. When the wage rate rises from W_1 to W_2, the worker responds by working longer. The supply of labour increases from L_1 to L_2. But in Figure 12.5, the supply curve is upward-sloping for only part of the curve. At hourly wage rates higher than W_2, the supply curve bends back towards the vertical axis of the graph, and the curve's slope is negative rather than positive. Following an increase in the hourly wage rate from W_2 to W_3, a worker reduces the number of hours of labour supplied from L_2 to L_3.

To explain the possibility of a backward-bending supply curve of labour, I must introduce two new concepts: the *substitution effect* of a change in the hourly wage rate; and the *income effect* of such a change.

➤ **The substitution effect of an increase in the hourly wage rate**. To understand the idea of a substitution effect, think of the hourly wage rate as the price of an hour of leisure time. For example, at an hourly wage rate of £10, the price of an hour of leisure time is also £10, rising to £11 if the wage rate is increased by a pound. As the wage rate rises, an hour of leisure time becomes more expensive compared to the goods that the money wage can buy. Acting rationally, a worker responds to the rise in the hourly wage rate (and the price of leisure time) by substituting more labour time in place of leisure time.

➤ **The income effect of an increase in the hourly wage rate**. If the substitution effect is the only effect operating, a worker's supply curve slopes upwards, showing labour time being substituted for leisure time as the hourly wage rate increases. However, matters can be complicated by the existence of an income

AQA A2 Economics

effect resulting from the price change. The income effect of a wage-rate increase results from the fact that, for most people, leisure time is a normal good and not an inferior good. A rise in the hourly wage rate increases the worker's real income, and as real income rises, so does the demand for the normal good, leisure time.

Up to a wage rate of W_2 in Figure 12.5, the substitution effect of any wage increase exceeds the income effect. As a result, a worker chooses to work longer hours and to enjoy less leisure time. But when the wage rate rises above W_2, the income effect of a higher wage rate becomes more powerful than the substitution effect. As a result, a worker chooses to work fewer hours so as to enjoy more leisure time – and the worker's supply curve of labour slopes backwards. Total money income may not fall. Given freedom of choice, a worker may, for example, decide to work 40 hours a week when the wage rate is £10 an hour, for a weekly income of £400. When the wage rate rises to £11, the worker may respond by working for only 38 hours, with a weekly income of £418.

A simpler approach to the backward-bending supply curve is to assume that a worker aspires to a target standard of living measured in the goods and services that the money wage can buy. When the money wage rate rises, a worker can meet the target and fulfil aspirations by working fewer hours, choosing more leisure time rather than more material goods and services. Workers are especially likely to behave in this way when the work itself is highly unpleasant or dangerous, yielding negative job satisfaction.

The shape of the supply curve of labour and government policy

Whether an individual's supply curve of labour is upward sloping as in Figure 12.4, or backward bending as depicted in Figure 12.5, is important for a government's tax and fiscal policies (and also for supply-side policy). An increase in the rate of income tax is equivalent to a fall in the hourly wage rate. With an upward-sloping supply curve of labour, a rise in income tax is a disincentive to work. When, however, the supply curve bends backwards, a rise in income tax increases the supply of labour. The tax increase has an incentive effect – a worker must now work longer to maintain a target material standard of living.

In real life, a tax increase may create an even greater need for laws to deal with tax avoidance and illegal tax evasion. In the second scenario, people may decide to supply their labour untaxed in the informal, underground economy, rather than formally, but subject to taxation.

Whatever the shape of an individual's supply curve of labour, the market supply curve of labour will probably slope upwards. The explanation lies in the fact that more workers enter the labour market in response to a wage rise, attracted both from other labour markets and from unemployment.

A perfectly competitive firm's demand curve for labour

Just as the market supply curve of labour in a perfectly competitive labour market is the sum of the supply curves of all the individual workers in the labour market,

so the market demand curve for labour is obtained by adding together each firm's demand curve for labour at different wage rates. We must therefore derive a perfectly competitive firm's demand curve for labour in order to understand the market demand curve for labour.

A firm demands labour only if profits can be increased by employing more workers. But this assumes that households in goods markets demand the goods and services that workers are employed to produce. This means that a firm's demand for labour is a **derived demand** – derived from the demand for goods. Assuming a profit-maximising objective on the part of firms, there can be no demand for labour in the long run unless the firms employing labour sell the outputs produced for at least a normal profit in the goods market. I shall now show that, in a perfectly competitive labour market, a firm's demand curve for labour is the **marginal revenue product** of labour (*MRP*) curve facing the firm.

Key term

Marginal revenue product is the monetary value of the addition to a firm's total output brought about by employing one more worker.

When deciding whether it is worthwhile employing one more worker, a firm needs to know the answers to three questions:
➤ how far will total output rise?
➤ how far will total sales revenue rise when the extra output is sold in the goods market?
➤ how far will total costs of production rise as a result of paying the worker a wage?

In a perfectly competitive labour market, a firm's demand curve for labour is derived from the answers to the first two of these questions. The answer to the third question is provided by the horizontal ruling market wage, illustrated earlier in Figure 12.2.

examiner's voice

Exam questions on the demand for labour require knowledge of marginal productivity theory. However, marginal productivity theory cannot in itself explain different wage rates. Labour supply theory is also required, together with an appreciation that different labour markets differ in their competitiveness.

The marginal physical product of labour

When answering the first of the three questions posed above, a firm has to calculate the value of the **marginal physical product** of labour (MPP). The marginal physical product or MPP of labour is (rather confusingly) just another name for the **marginal returns** (or **marginal product**) of labour, which I explained in Chapter 3. *MPP* measures the amount by which a firm's total output rises in the short run (holding capital fixed), as a result of employing one more worker. In Chapter 3, I explained how the law of diminishing returns or diminishing marginal productivity operates as a firm employs more labour when capital is held fixed. In the context of labour market theory, it is usual to assume that the law of diminishing returns begins to operate as soon as a second worker is added to the labour force. This means that the possibility of increasing marginal returns at low levels of employment is ignored.

Given this simplifying assumption, the impact of the law of diminishing returns is illustrated in Figure 12.6 (a), which shows the marginal product of labour falling as additional workers are hired by the firm.

Key term

Marginal physical product is the addition to a firm's total output brought about by employing one more worker.

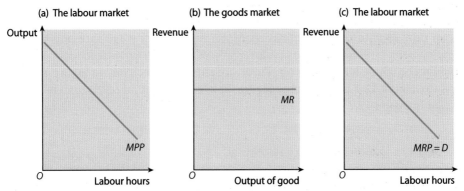

Figure 12.6 *Deriving the* MRP *curve from the* MPP *curve*

The marginal revenue product of labour

The falling *MPP* curve provides the answer to the first of the three questions I posed, showing how much total output will rise when an additional worker is employed. But as its name indicates, the *MPP* curve only shows the *physical* output produced by an extra worker — measured, for example, in automobiles or loaves of bread, or whatever goods the firm produces. To convert the marginal physical product of labour into a money value, the *MPP* of labour has to be multiplied by the addition to the firm's total sales revenue resulting from the sale in the goods market of the extra output produced by labour. We therefore multiply *MPP* by marginal revenue (*MR*) to answer the second of the three questions. When the economy's goods market is perfectly competitive, *MR* is identical to the good's price or average revenue, and is shown by the horizontal *MR* curve in Figure 12.6 (b).

Figure 12.6 (c), which shows the marginal revenue product curve of labour, can be explained with the use of the following equation:

$$\text{marginal physical product} \times \text{marginal revenue} = \text{marginal revenue product}$$

or:

$$MPP \times MR = MRP$$

As the equation shows, the marginal revenue product of labour is calculated by multiplying the *MPP* of labour in Figure 12.6 (a) by the horizontal *MR* curve in Figure 12.6 (b). When a firm sells its output in a perfectly competitive goods market, the

falling diminishing marginal revenue productivity of labour is explained solely by the diminishing marginal physical product: that is, by the law of diminishing returns.

However, if output is sold in an imperfectly competitive goods market, marginal revenue product of labour declines faster than in a perfectly competitive goods market. This is because in imperfectly competitive goods markets, the marginal revenue earned from selling an extra worker's output also falls as output increases. In this situation, there are *two* reasons for the *MRP* curve to fall as employment increases.

The equilibrium wage rate and level of employment in a perfectly competitive labour market

I can now explain the determination of the equilibrium wage rate and level of employment, both for a single employer in a perfectly competitive labour market and for the whole labour market. These are shown respectively in Figure 12.7 (a) and (b). Figure 12.7 is identical to Figure 12.2, except that an *MRP* curve has been added in Figure 12.7 (a).

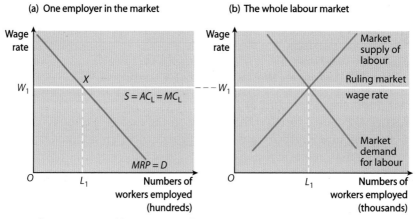

Figure 12.7 Equilibrium in a perfectly competitive labour market

A perfectly competitive firm's demand curve for labour

In a perfectly competitive labour market, each employer passively accepts the ruling market wage. At this wage, it is a passive price-taker. The ruling wage, determined in Figure 12.7 (b), is also the perfectly elastic supply curve of labour facing the firm, and the firm's AC_L and MC_L curve. Each firm can hire as many workers as it wishes at the ruling market wage, but cannot influence the ruling wage by its own actions. To maximise profit when selling the output produced by labour, the firm must choose the level of employment at which:

the addition to sales revenue resulting from the employment of an extra worker	=	the addition to production costs resulting from hiring the services of an extra worker

or:

$$MRP = MC_L$$

The marginal revenue product of labour is the **marginal private benefit** accruing to the employer when hiring an extra worker. Likewise, the **marginal cost of labour** or MC_L is the marginal private cost incurred by the firm. Since, in a perfectly competitive labour market, the marginal cost of labour always equals the wage paid to the workers, the perfectly competitive firm's level of employment is where:

$MRP = W$

Point X in Figure 12.7 (a) shows the number of workers that a firm is willing to employ at the ruling wage of W_1. Consider what happens if the firm employs a labour force larger than L_1. Additional workers add more to total cost than to total revenue, and profit falls. Conversely, with a workforce below L_1, the MRP of the last worker is greater than the wage, and the profits that a larger labour force would generate are not made.

Summarising:

If $MRP > W$: more workers should be hired

If $MRP < W$: fewer workers should be employed

If $MRP = W$: the firm is employing the number of workers consistent with profit maximisation

The market demand for labour in a perfectly competitive labour market

Earlier in the chapter, I explained that the market supply curve of labour is obtained by adding the individual supply curves of all the workers in the market at different possible wages. In a similar way, we add the demand curves for labour of all the firms in the market to obtain the market demand curve for labour shown in Figure 12.7 (b). Since each employer's demand for labour is shown by the MRP curve, the market demand curve for labour is the horizontal sum of the MRP curves.

Monopsony labour markets

Monopsony means a single buyer, just as **monopoly** means a single seller. In a monopsony labour market, workers cannot choose between alternative employers, since there is only one firm or employer available to hire them.

Key term

Monopsony means there is only one buyer in a market

Although in some ways a monopsony labour market resembles a monopoly goods market, there are also significant differences. In much the same way that the market demand curve facing a monopoly supplier of a good is the monopolist's average revenue curve, so in a monopsony labour market, the market supply curve of labour is the firm's average cost of labour curve (AC_L). The AC_L curve shows the different wage rates that the monopsonist must pay to attract labour forces of different sizes. For example, Figure 12.8 shows a monopsony employer hiring five workers at an hourly wage rate or AC_L of £10. As the diagram shows, the hourly wage per week must rise to £11 to attract a sixth worker into the firm's labour force.

unit 3

The supply or AC_L curve facing the monopsonist shows the wage that has to be paid to all workers at each size of the labour force, to persuade the workers to supply their services. However, in a monopsony labour market, the AC_L curve is not the marginal cost of labour curve (MC_L). To attract an extra worker, the monopsonist must raise the hourly wage rate and pay the higher wage to all the workers. In this situation, the marginal cost of labour incurred by employing an extra worker includes the total amount by which the wage bill rises, and not just the wage rate paid to the additional worker hired. The MC_L curve of labour illustrated in Figure 12.8 is positioned above the AC_L (or supply curve). Similarly, in the goods market, a monopolist's MR curve is below its AR curve. In Figure 12.8, the MC_L incurred per hour by employing the sixth worker is £16, made up of the £11 wage rate paid to the sixth worker, plus the £1 extra paid to each of the five workers already employed before the sixth worker joined the labour force.

examiner's voice

It is important to realise that *all* real world labour markets are imperfectly competitive to some extent. Perfect competition is as much a theoretical abstraction in labour markets as it is in goods markets.

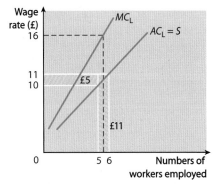

Figure 12.8 *In a monopsony labour market, the MC_L curve lies above the AC_L or supply of labour curve*

The equilibrium wage rate and level of employment

Figure 12.9 shows how the equilibrium wage and the equilibrium level of employment are determined in a monopsony labour market. As in the case of a perfectly competitive employer in the labour market, the monopsonist's level of employment is determined by the point where $MRP = MC_L$. This occurs at point A in Figure 12.9, at which L_1 workers are employed.

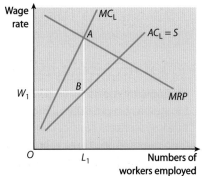

Figure 12.9 *Equilibrium in a monopsony labour market*

However, in a monopsony labour market, the equilibrium wage rate is determined at point B, which lies below A. The wage rate paid by the monopsonist (W_1 in Figure 12.9) is less than the value of the marginal revenue product of labour. Point B is positioned on the supply curve of labour facing the monopsonist. The supply curve shows that L_1 workers are willing to work for an hourly wage rate of W_1. Although the firm could pay a wage rate higher than W_1, the monopsonist has no need to pay a higher wage rate. Why pay more, when W_1 attracts all the workers the monopsonist requires? Indeed, if the monopsonist were to pay a wage higher than W_1, it would inevitably incur unnecessary production costs and end up being X-inefficient. It would fail to maximise profits when selling its output in the goods market. Profit maximisation requires that a wage no higher than W_1 is paid.

Wage equalisation in a perfectly competitive market economy

If all labour markets in the economy were perfectly competitive, there would be no barriers preventing workers moving between labour markets. In this situation, the forces of competition would reduce many of the differences in wages between different occupations. Some differences would probably remain because different types of work have different skill requirements, and innate abilities and skills would still vary between workers. Nevertheless, higher wages in one occupation would attract workers from other labour markets, causing the supply curve of labour to shift to the right in the high-wage labour market and to the left in the low-wage market.

At the same time, wage differentials would create incentives for firms in the high-wage market to reduce their demand for labour by substituting capital for labour, and for firms in the low-wage labour markets to adopt more **labour-intensive methods of production.** Demand and supply curves and wages would continue to adjust until there was no further incentive for firms to change their method of production or for workers to shift between labour markets. Wage differentials would diminish throughout the economy, but would not completely disappear.

Explanations of different wage levels

Wage differences in competitive labour markets

Even in highly competitive labour markets, wage differences exist, largely because labour demand and supply curves are in different positions in different labour markets, reflecting factors such as different labour productivities, abilities and required skills. We might also expect wage differentials to exist in highly competitive labour markets for two further reasons:

- ➤ **Different jobs have different non-monetary characteristics.** I have already explained how the net advantage of any type of work includes job satisfaction or dissatisfaction as well as economic welfare gained from the wage. Other things being equal, a firm must pay a worker a higher wage to compensate for any relative unpleasantness in the job. An equalising wage differential is the payment that must be made to compensate a worker for the different non-monetary characteristics of jobs. Following such a payment, there is no incentive for a worker to switch between jobs or labour markets.
- ➤ **Disequilibrium trading.** Economies are subject to constant change, such as the development of new goods and services and improved methods of production or technical progress. Patterns of demand also change. Because market conditions are always changing, labour markets — like other markets — are usually in disequilibrium rather than in equilibrium. Although market forces tend to equalise wages in competitive labour markets, at any point in time disparities exist, reflecting the disequilibrium conditions existent at the time.

Wage differences in imperfectly competitive labour markets

In imperfectly competitive labour markets, including monopsony labour markets, there are a number of other reasons why differences in wages occur. These include:

➤ immobility of labour
➤ different elasticities of demand for, and supply of, labour
➤ wage discrimination
➤ differences in pay between women and men
➤ the effect of trade unions
➤ the effect of different methods of pay determination, such as collective bargaining

Immobility of labour

There are two main types of labour immobility: **occupational immobility** and **geographical immobility**.

➤ **Occupational immobility of labour.** This occurs when workers are prevented, by either natural or artificial barriers, from moving between different types of job. Workers are obviously not homogeneous or uniform, so differences in natural ability may prevent or restrict movement between jobs. Some types of work require an innate ability, such as physical strength or perfect eyesight, which prevents a worker immediately switching between labour markets. Examples of artificial barriers include membership qualifications imposed by professional bodies such as accountancy associations, and trade union restrictive practices such as pre-entry closed shops, which restrict employment to those already belonging to the union. Various forms of racial, religious, age and gender discrimination are also artificial causes of occupational immobility of labour.

Key terms

Occupational immobility of labour describes the difficulty of moving from one occupation to another.

Geographical immobility of labour describes the difficulty of moving from one location to another.

➤ **Geographical immobility of labour.** This occurs when factors, such as ignorance of job opportunities, family and cultural ties, and the financial costs of moving or travel, prevent a worker from filling a job vacancy located at a distance from his or her present place of residence. Perhaps the most significant cause of geographical immobility in the UK in recent years has been the state of the housing market, which itself reflects imperfections in other factor markets. During house price booms, low-paid and unemployed workers in the northern half of the UK have found it difficult or impossible to move south to fill job vacancies in the more prosperous southeast of England. The prices of owner-occupied housing have soared and there has been very little housing available at affordable rents in either the private or the public sectors. At the same time, workers living in their own houses in the southeast may be reluctant to apply for jobs elsewhere in the country, for fear that they will never be able to afford to move back to southern England.

Different elasticities of demand for, and supply of, labour

Both the mobility of labour and wage rates in different labour markets are affected by the elasticities of the supply of, and the demand for, labour. I shall now look briefly at factors affecting labour market elasticities.

Determinants of the wage elasticity of labour demand. If the wage rate increases, but nothing else that might affect the demand for labour changes, by how much will employment fall? The answer is affected by firms' elasticity of demand for labour. The demand for a particular type of labour is likely to be relatively inelastic:

➤ when the relevant wage cost forms only a small part of total production costs (this has been called the importance of being unimportant)
➤ when the demand for the good or service being produced by the labour is inelastic
➤ when it is difficult to substitute other factors of production, or other types of labour, for the labour currently employed
➤ in the short run, rather than the long run, since it often takes time for employers to adjust their production process

Determinants of the wage elasticity of labour supply. The supply of unskilled labour is usually more elastic than the supply of a particular type of skilled labour. The training period of unskilled labour is usually very short, and any innate abilities required are unlikely to

> *examiner's voice*
> Unit 3 exam questions are likely to require synoptic application of elasticity theory, learnt in the context of goods markets in Unit 1, to the demand for, and the supply of, labour.

be restricted to a small proportion of the total population. All the factors reducing the occupational and geographical mobility of labour tend to reduce the elasticity of labour supply. The supply of labour is also likely to be more elastic in the long run than in the short run. Finally, the availability of a pool of unemployed labour increases the elasticity of supply of labour, while full employment has the opposite effect.

Wage discrimination

In imperfectly competitive labour markets, employers often possess sufficient market power to reduce the total wage bill through **wage discrimination**.

> **Key term**
> **Wage discrimination** means paying different workers different wages for doing the same job.

Figure 12.10 illustrates the effect of wage discrimination introduced into a previously competitive labour market. However, in real life, discrimination is more likely in imperfectly competitive labour markets. In the absence of wage discrimination, all workers are paid the same wage, W_1, determined by supply and demand. Employers' total wage costs are shown by the rectangle OW_1AL_1.

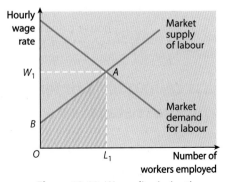

Figure 12.10 Wage discrimination

But if, instead of paying W_1 to all workers, employers pay each worker the minimum he or she is prepared to work for, the total wage bill falls to equal the shaded area $OBAL_1$. Employers thus gain at the expense of workers, which is why firms pay, and trade unions resist, discriminatory wages whenever possible.

examiner's voice

You should understand the similarity between wage discrimination in the labour market where a firm hires its labour and price discrimination in the goods market where the firm sells its output.

Extension material

Bringing together wage discrimination and price discrimination

In the case of perfect price discrimination (first degree price discrimination), a firm charges different prices to different customers for the same good, with the same marginal cost of production, so that each customer pays the maximum price he or she is prepared to pay. All the consumer surplus customers would otherwise enjoy is transferred to the firm, enlarging the firm's profit.

With perfect wage discrimination, the firm pays each worker the minimum wage the worker is prepared to accept, without transferring his or her employment elsewhere. All of the wage that the workers would otherwise get is transferred to the firm, once again boosting profit.

From an imperfectly competitive firm's point of view, the best possible outcome is simultaneous price discrimination in the goods market in which it sells its output and wage discrimination in the labour markets in which it hires its workers. Profit is boosted from two directions at once.

Can you think of reasons why such simultaneous exploitation seldom takes place?

Box 12.2 Discrimination against women in labour markets

The Unit 3 specification advises that candidates should be able to discuss the impact of gender, ethnic, age and other forms of discrimination on wages, levels and types of employment. The passage below argues that too little has been done to get rid of gender discrimination and **glass ceilings** that prevent women from rising to occupy top jobs.

Glass ceiling for women replaced by reinforced concrete as progress stalls

The so-called glass ceiling that prevents women progressing in the workplace is more like 'reinforced concrete', the chief executive of the Equality and Human Rights Commission (EHRC) has warned. Nicola Brewer, the Chief Executive of the Equality and Human Rights Commission, said:

'We always speak of a glass ceiling. These figures reveal that in some cases it appears to be made of reinforced concrete. We need radical change to support those who are doing great work and help those who want to work better and release talent.'

Young women's aspiration is in danger of giving way to frustration. Many of them are now excelling at school and are achieving great things in higher education. And they are keen to balance a family with a rewarding career. But workplaces forged in an era of stay-at-home mums and breadwinner dads are putting too many barriers in the way — resulting in an avoidable loss of talent at the top.

There are fewer women MPs in Westminster, where they make up just 19.3% of all MPs. Women's representation among FTSE 100 directors has improved slightly from 10.4 to 11.0%.

The Commission has likened women's progress to a snail's pace. A snail could crawl:

➤ nine times round the M25 in the 55 years it will take women to achieve equality in the senior judiciary

➤ from Land's End to John O'Groats and halfway back again in the 73 years it will take for equal numbers of women to become directors of FTSE 100 companies

➤ the entire length of the Great Wall of China in 212 years, only slightly longer than the 200 years it will take for women to be equally represented in Parliament

The Commission's report argues that its findings are not just a 'women's issue' but are a powerful symptom of a wider failure. The report asks in what other ways are old-fashioned, inflexible ways of working preventing Britain from tapping into talent — whether that of women or other under-represented groups such as disabled people, ethnic minorities or those with caring responsibilities. Britain cannot afford to go on marginalising or rejecting talented people who fail to fit into traditional work patterns.

Source: Equality and Human Rights Commission, September 2008

Follow-up questions

1 What is meant by a 'glass ceiling'?
2 Do 'glass ceilings' affect adversely other groups in society, such as ethnic and religious minorities and old people, or does discrimination take different forms against these groups of people?

Differences in earnings between men and women

In recent years, although women have accounted for an increasing share of total employment in the UK, women's pay often continues to be lower than men's pay, despite the fact that equal pay legislation has been in place since 1972.

According to a poll undertaken by the Equal Opportunities Commission (EOC) in 2004, 88% of women expect to earn the same as a man with the same qualifications, rising to 94% among women under 25. According to the EOC report, however, these women are 'heading for disappointment' because the latest data showed that the difference in average pay between men and women working full time is just over £6,700 a year — about 18%. The poll also found that 29% of women did not know what their colleagues earned, compared with 20% of men. As a result, women were more likely than men to be unaware of pay discrimination. More people in professional and managerial positions than in clerical and manual jobs knew what most of their colleagues earned. The EOC concluded, rather depressingly, that 'discrimination flourishes in this culture of secrecy when people cannot be sure they are rewarded fairly'.

There are two main reasons why women earn less than men:

➤ women work predominantly in low-paid industries and occupations
➤ in many occupational groups, women are paid less than men. This is often because women are under-represented in the higher-paid posts within an occupation, rather than because women are paid less for doing the same job.

Discrimination against women in labour markets may contribute to both these sets of circumstances. In addition, women are disproportionately represented in industries where the average size of firm and plant is small. These industries tend to pay lower wages and offer fewer promotional prospects than large firms and large industries. Such industries are also seldom unionised. Indeed, within all industries, women workers traditionally have been less unionised than men.

This relates to another reason why women earn less than men: on average, their attachment to the labour force is weaker. Each year of work experience raises the pay of both men and women by an average 3%. Yet when women leave the labour force, usually to look after young children, their potential pay falls by 3% for each year involved. For example, a man and woman enter employment with equal potential and after 8 years the woman leaves the work force in order to raise a family. If she re-enters the labour force 8 years later she would be 16 years, in pay terms, behind the man.

The higher labour turnover of women also imposes costs on the employer — for example, the costs of training replacement workers. This may reduce the incentive for employers to train female workers. Similarly, women may have less incentive to spend time and money on their own education and training if they expect the benefits that they will eventually receive to be less than the costs initially incurred.

The effect of introducing a trade union into a perfectly competitive market

A **trade union** is an association of workers formed to protect and promote the interests of its members. A major function of a union is to bargain with employers to improve wages and other conditions of work. Many UK employers are now reluctant to recognise and bargain with the unions to which their employees belong. However, in my analysis, I shall regard

Key term

A **trade union** is a collective association of workers whose aim is to improve the pay and other conditions of work of it members.

a trade union as a monopoly supplier of labour, which is able to keep non-members out of the labour market and also to prevent its members from supplying labour at below the union wage rate. Of course, in real life a union may not necessarily have the objectives specified above, and even if it does, it may not be able to achieve them. I shall make one other increasingly unrealistic assumption, namely that a union can fix any wage rate it chooses, and that employment is then determined by the amount of labour that employers will hire at this wage.

Given these assumptions, Figure 12.11 shows the possible effects resulting from workers organising a trade union in a labour market that had previously been perfectly competitive. Without a trade union, the competitive wage rate is W_1. The workers join a trade union, which raises the minimum wage rate acceptable to union members to W_2. Without the union, the market supply of labour curve is the upward-sloping line labelled $S = AC_L$. With the union, the market supply of labour curve is the kinked line W_2XS. For all sizes of labour force to the left of, or below, L_3, the supply curve of labour is horizontal or perfectly elastic, lying along the wage W_2 set by the trade union. If employers wish to hire a labour force larger than L_3 (and to the right of point X), a wage higher than W_2 has to be offered. Beyond L_3, the supply curve of labour slopes upwards because higher wage rates are needed to attract more workers.

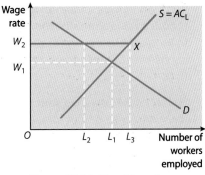

Figure 12.11 *The effect of introducing a trade union into a previously perfectly competitive labour market*

At the wage level set by the union, employers only wish to hire L_2 workers. However, L_3 workers are willing to work at this wage rate. This means there is excess supply of labour and unemployment in the labour market. More workers wish to work than there are jobs available. The resulting unemployment, called **classical unemployment**, is shown by the distance $L_3 - L_2$.

The effect described above is sometimes used to justify the argument that any attempt by a union to raise wages must inevitably be at the expense of jobs, and that if unions are really interested in reducing unemployment, they should accept wage cuts. However, many

economists — especially those of a Keynesian and left-of-centre persuasion — dispute this conclusion. They argue, first, that it is unrealistic to assume that conditions of demand for labour are unchanged. By agreeing to accept technical progress, by working with new capital equipment and new methods of organising work and by improving the skills of their members, a union can ensure (with the co-operation of management) that the *MRP* curve of labour shifts to the right. In these circumstances, increased productivity creates scope for both increased wages and increased employment.

Second, both wages and employment can rise when a union negotiates for higher wages to be paid by firms producing in an expanding goods market. In these condi-

tions, increased demand for output creates increased demand for labour to produce the output. Indeed, rising real wages throughout the economy are likely to increase the aggregate demand for the output of all firms producing consumer goods because wages are the most important source of consumption expenditure in the economy.

So far, I have assumed that trade unions try to increase pay by preventing union members supplying labour at wage rates below the rate set by the union. Figure 12.12 illustrates a second way in which much the same result can be achieved. In this case, the trade union establishes a **closed shop**, which keeps non-union workers out of the labour market. The union-controlled entry barrier shifts the supply curve of labour leftward, and increases the inelasticity of the curve. Employment falls from L_1 to L_2, and the wage rate is hiked up to W_2.

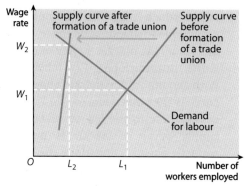

Figure 12.12 *A trade union shifting the market supply curve of labour*

The word *shop* in the term closed shop refers to the workshop or the shop floor, where manufacturing firms undertake the tasks involved in production. A closed shop is an example of a **labour restrictive practice**. There are two types of closed shop, both of which have been made illegal in the UK. Figure 12.12 illustrates the effect of a *pre-entry* closed shop, which requires workers to join the union before starting employment. By imposing a quota or ceiling on the number of union members, a union uses a pre-entry closed shop to shift the supply curve of labour to the left. By contrast, a *post-entry* closed shop permits non-members to get jobs, but all workers have to join the union to keep their jobs. Post-entry closed shops have little effect on entry barriers, but they are a means of dealing with the free-rider problem in labour markets.

Free-riding occurs when workers decline to join a union while accepting pay rises that the union negotiates. Free-riders benefit from the union 'mark-up' — that is, the generally higher pay in unionised rather than non-unionised places of work — but save themselves the cost of paying union membership fees.

How a trade union can increase both the wage rate and employment in a monopsonistic labour market

The assertion that unions raise wages at the expense of jobs is heavily dependent on the assumption that, before the union was formed, the labour market was perfectly competitive. In the case of a monopsony labour market, it is possible for a union to raise *both* the wage rate and employment, even without the *MRP* curve shifting rightward. This is illustrated in Figure 12.13. If the labour market is non-unionised, the equilibrium wage rate is W_1 and the level of employment is L_1.

The introduction of a trade union into a monopsony labour market has the same effect on the labour supply curve as in perfect competition. In Figure 12.13, the kinked line W_2XS is the labour supply curve and the average cost of labour curve (AC_L) when the union sets the wage rate at W_2. But in monopsony, W_2XS is not the marginal cost of labour curve (MC_L). The MC_L curve is the double-kinked line W_2XZV. The double kink is explained in the following way. Providing the monopsonist employs a labour force smaller than or equal to L_2, the MC_L of employing an extra worker equals both the AC_L and the union-determined wage of W_2. But beyond L_2 and point X, the monopsonist must

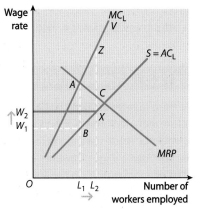

Figure 12.13 *The effect of introducing a trade union into a monopsony labour market*

offer a higher wage in order to persuade additional workers to supply labour. In this situation, with all the workers now being paid the higher wage, the MC_L curve lies above the supply curve or AC_L curve. The upward-sloping line ZV drawn in Figure 12.13 shows the MC_L of increasing employment above L_2.

This means there is a vertical gap between the horizontal section of the MC_L curve (for levels of employment at or below L_2 and point X) and the upward-sloping section of the curve (ZV). In the absence of a union, the level of employment is L_1, determined at point A (with point B determining the wage rate W_1). But when the union sets the wage rate at W_2,

examiner's voice

Exam questions may ask if trade unions (or a national minimum wage) can raise the level of employment as well as the wage rate. The answer depends on the competitiveness of the labour market.

employment rises to L_2, which is the level of employment at which the MRP curve intersects the vertical section of the MC_L curve at point C, between X and Z. The union has managed to increase both the wage rate and the level of employment.

The national minimum wage

The explanation in the previous section, of how a trade union can increase both the wage rate and the level of employment, can also be used to analyse the effect of a **national minimum wage** set by the government. Under the unrealistic assumption that labour markets are perfectly competitive, Figure 12.11 can be

Key term

A **national minimum wage** is a minimum wage or wage rate that must by law be paid to employees.

adapted to show how a national minimum wage set above the market-clearing wage rate leads to a loss of jobs and unemployment. But if, more realistically, labour markets are imperfectly competitive, Figure 12.13 should be used. This figure can be adapted to show how a national minimum wage can increase both the wage rate and the level of employment.

From 1979 until 1997, UK Conservative governments opposed the introduction of a minimum legal wage, believing that its main effect would be to increase unemployment.

Box 12.3 A trade union accepting a wage cut

In the third quarter of 2008, the UK economy entered recession. Many UK companies, including the plant manufacturers JCB, had already begun to sack workers, and those still in jobs feared they would be made redundant. To try to prevent further lay-offs, union members at JCB offered to work for lower wages. However, wage reductions didn't work. As the passage below indicates, JCB sacked more workers in the autumn of 2008, as orders for bulldozers and other construction plant dried up.

15 July 2008: JCB job cuts could hit 700

Likely job cuts at the plant and bulldozer manufacturer JCB are likely to be worse than originally feared, with up to an eighth of the workforce now facing redundancy. Last night JCB confirmed that it would cut 500 manufacturing jobs and possibly 200 office jobs. If all those posts are made redundant, it will bring the total number of job losses at the plant manufacturer to 790 since April last year – 13% of its 5,900-strong UK workforce.

23 October 2008: JCB workers take pay cut to avoid layoffs

Thousands of workers at the manufacturing firm JCB have voted to accept a pay cut of £50 a week to prevent the loss of 350 jobs, it was announced today. The GMB trade union said around 2,500 of its members had agreed to work a 4-day week for the next 13 weeks to help the company weather the economic downturn.

Despite recording pre-tax profits of £187m last year, the company has been badly hit by the downturn in property and construction. In July this year, it warned of a 'rapid decline' in demand. JCB, which employs more than 8,000 people, operates in more than 150 countries and is the world's third largest manufacturer of construction equipment. The 62-year-old company has 10 plants in the UK.

14 November 2008: JCB announces 400 more job cuts

GMB has announced that 297 shop floor jobs and 101 staff posts are to go. The firm originally proposed 510 job losses but fewer were agreed after union members voted in favour of a shorter and lower-paid working week. Works convenor Gordon Richardson said he recognised the news came as a major blow to members after the working week was reduced.

'Unfortunately, more of our members will lose their jobs than was originally expected but we can all rest assured that the selfless commitment shown in voting for the shorter working week has, without doubt, saved jobs', he said.

JCB chief executive Matthew Taylor said there had been a significant deterioration in business levels over the year and particularly during the last 2 months. He said it was not just a UK issue, markets all around the world were affected. Confidence in the market was at such a low point he did not think it could get any lower.

Source: various news reports

Follow-up questions

1 Why are companies such as JCB, whose clients are building companies, especially likely to lay off workers in a recession?

2 Track what has happened to JCB in the months and years following these news reports.

By contrast, the Labour Party and the trade union movement were both committed to the introduction of a national minimum wage, arguing that evidence from other European countries suggests that the benefits in terms of social fairness exceed any costs involved. The national minimum wage (NMW) introduced in April 1999 was set at a level of £3.60 per hour throughout the UK, or 45% of median earnings. But young workers below the age of 18 were excluded from its protection.

> ℓ**xaminer's voice**
> Exam questions may be set on different methods of pay determination and on reasons for the decline of *collective bargaining* as a method of pay determination.

The government decides the level of the national minimum wage, taking advice from the Low Pay Commission. The government does not guarantee to increase the NMW each year, although in recent years the NMW has been raised annually. There are three levels of minimum wage, and the rates from 1 October 2008 were:

➤ £5.73 per hour for workers aged 22 years and older

➤ a development rate of £4.77 per hour for workers aged 18–21 inclusive

➤ £3.53 per hour for all workers under the age of 18, who are no longer of compulsory school age

Extension material

Support for a legal minimum wage

In the 1970s and 1980s, many economists accepted that when government forces businesses to pay higher wages, businesses in turn hire fewer employees. It is a powerful argument against the minimum wage since it suggests that private businesses as a group, along with teenagers and low-wage employees, will be penalised by a mandatory raise.

This view came under attack in the mid-1990s following some work done by two Princeton economists, David Card and Alan Krueger. In 1992, New Jersey increased the state minimum wage to $5.05 an hour (applicable to both the public and the private sectors), which gave the two young professors an opportunity to study the comparative effects of that raise on fast-food restaurants and low-wage employment in New Jersey and Pennsylvania, where the minimum wage remained at the federal level of $4.25 an hour. Card and Krueger agreed that the hypothesis that a rise in wages would destroy jobs was one of the clearest and most widely appreciated in the field of economics. Both believed, at the start, that their work would reinforce that hypothesis. But in 1995, and again in 2000, the two academics effectively shredded the conventional wisdom. Their data demonstrated that a modest increase in wages did not appear to cause any significant harm to employment; in some cases, a rise in the minimum wage even resulted in a slight increase in employment.

Source: *New York Times*, 15 January 2006

Summary

➤ The price mechanism operates in the labour market in a similar way to how it operates in the goods market, but the roles of firms and households are reversed.

➤ In their role as employers, firms demand labour in the labour market.

➤ The demand for labour is a derived demand.

➤ Members of households supply labour to earn an income which then provides an effective demand for goods.

➤ A worker supplies labour to maximise net advantage, which may include job satisfaction.

➤ The opportunity cost of working is the leisure time foregone.

➤ An individual's supply curve of labour may slope upward or bend backward.

➤ The shape of the supply curve of labour affects labour market incentives.

➤ In a perfectly competitive labour market, the marginal revenue product (MRP) curve facing an employer is the employer's demand curve for labour.

➤ The supply curve of labour facing a firm in a perfectly competitive labour market is the perfectly elastic line determined by the interaction of market supply and demand.

➤ For a firm, this horizontal line is also the average cost of labour (AC_L) and the marginal cost of labour (MC_L).

➤ A monopsony is the only buyer of labour in a labour market.

➤ In monopsony, the wage rate and the level of employment are likely to be lower than in a perfectly competitive labour market.

➤ In monopsony, a trade union may be able to increase both the wage rate and the level of employment toward the perfectly competitive levels. A national minimum wage can have the same effect.

➤ wage discrimination occurs if employers exert their power to pay workers the minimum wage rates they are prepared to accept.

➤ Gender discrimination means that women often earn less than men.

Questions

1 Distinguish between the average cost of labour (AC_L) and the marginal cost of labour (MC_L).

2 When may a worker's net advantage be less than the utility of the worker's wage?

3 Why may a worker's supply curve of labour bend backwards?

4 Explain three factors significant in determining a firm's demand for labour.

5 What is meant by marginal revenue product (MRP)?

6 In what sense is a firm a passive price-taker in a perfectly competitive labour market?

7 Explain two reasons for differences in wage rates.

8 How is the equilibrium wage rate determined in a monopsony labour market?

9   How may a trade union affect the equilibrium level of employment and the wage rate in a perfectly competitive labour market and in a monopsony labour market?

10 State two determinants of the elasticity of supply of labour with respect to the wage rate.

11 Distinguish between occupational and geographical immobility of labour.

12 State two determinants of the elasticity of demand for labour with respect to the wage rate.

13 Describe two of the social determinants of wages.

14 Why are women often paid less than men?

15 Use a supply and demand diagram to analyse the national minimum wage as a price floor.

Chapter 13

Poverty and the distribution of income and wealth

As the experience of many poor countries shows, unregulated market forces tend to produce highly unequal distributions of income and wealth, which is itself a form of market failure. Of course, not all economists agree. Extreme free-market economists seem to think that people who end up poor deserve to be poor. According to this view the market does not fail; it simply creates incentives that cause people to generate income and wealth which end up benefiting most of the population. They also believe that attempts by governments to redistribute income and wealth from the rich to the poor usually end up, through the distortion of personal incentives, in government failure which harms national economic performance.

Learning outcomes

This chapter will:
➤ discuss the meaning of poverty
➤ distinguish between absolute poverty and relative poverty
➤ explain the main causes of poverty in the UK
➤ examine inequalities in the distribution of income and wealth in the UK
➤ summarise how government policies such as progressive taxation, transfers and the national minimum wage attempt to reduce poverty and make the distribution of income more equal
➤ relate progressive taxation to fiscal drag and to the poverty and unemployment traps

chapter *13*

Poverty is not mentioned in the AS specification, though the concept is implicit in the Unit 1 requirement that candidates should understand that inequalities in the distribution of income and wealth can lead to market failure. Apart from advice that candidates should be able to give examples of this cause of market failure, there is no other mention of income and wealth inequalities in the AS specifications. My advice is that you treat both poverty and income and wealth inequalities as A2 topics on which exam questions are likely to be set.

What is poverty?

Poverty is caused both by a low real national income relative to a country's total population size and by inequalities in the distributions of income and wealth. The former leads to **absolute poverty** for most of a country's inhabitants, whereas the latter causes **relative poverty**.

➤ **Absolute poverty** occurs when income is below a particular level. According to the charity Barnardo's:

> Absolute poverty refers to a set standard which is consistent over time and between countries. Measuring poverty by an absolute threshold has the advantage of applying the same standard across different locations and time periods, making comparisons easier. However, it does not take into account that you need different levels of income in different places, for example, a cup of coffee is more expensive in England than it is in Brazil.

➤ **Relative poverty** is suffered by a household if its income is below a specified proportion of average income for all households (for example, less than a third of average income). Barnardo's says:

> Relative poverty defines 'poverty' as being below a relative poverty threshold. It classifies individuals or families as 'poor' not by comparing them to a fixed cut-off point, but by comparing them to others in the population under study.

 Key *terms*

Absolute poverty occurs when income is below a particular level.

Relative poverty occurs when income is below a specified proportion of average income.

Box 13.1 Barnardo's and poverty

Many UK charities try to pressure individuals to donate to their cause and governments to intervene more in the economy to reduce poverty. Shelter centres its activities on homelessness. Barnardo's is especially concerned with child poverty. The passage below is from a Barnardo's campaign sheet.

The reality of poverty

£10 a day — the reality of living in poverty

Many families living on a low income have only about £10 per day, per person. This needs to cover all of their day to day expenditure, including necessities such as food and transport. It also needs to cover occasional items such as new shoes and clothes, school trips and activities for children, and replacing broken household items such as washing machines and kitchen equipment. In addition to this, it must pay for all household bills such as electricity, gas and water, telephone bills, and TV licences.

Did you know that a family with two adults and two children needs to have £346 each week in order to be above the poverty line? How do you think that compares to what your family has?

Average weekly spend

This graph shows you how much an average family spends each week on different items, compared to a family living in the bottom 20% of the income distribution.

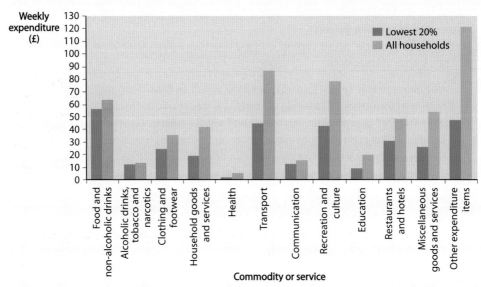

Figure 13.1 *Average household weekly expenditure for a couple household with children*

The total weekly expenditure for an average couple with children in 2007 was £630.60 per week for all households, that's equivalent to £163.50 per person. However, a family with an income in the lowest 20% spent just £371.60 each week, equivalent to £87.50 per person. That's almost half what the average family spends.

Source: www.barnardos.org.uk/childpoverty/pov-whatispoverty.htm

Follow-up questions

1 Suppose you have to live on £10 a day. After finding out about prices, and assuming you have a partner and two children, what would you spend the £10 on?
2 With the help of the graph, compare the expenditure pattern of the lowest 20% of households compared to all households taken together.

The gap between rich and poor is an issue in the UK

When all incomes grow, *absolute* poverty falls, however, *relative* poverty only falls if low incomes grow at a faster rate than average incomes. For the most part, the problem of poverty in the UK is one of relative poverty. Because the UK is a high-income, developed economy in which welfare benefits provide a minimum income and safety net for the poor, very few people suffer from absolute poverty.

> ***e**xaminer's voice*
> Exam questions may ask you to distinguish between absolute and relative poverty and to explain their different causes.

The main causes of poverty in the UK

Three of the main causes of poverty in the UK are old age, unemployment, and the low wages of many of those in work.

Old age and poverty

Old age causes poverty largely because many old people rely on the state pension and lack a private pension. Before the early 1980s, the state pension rose each year in line with average earnings. This meant that pensioners, albeit from a lower base, shared in the increase in national prosperity delivered by economic growth and higher real earnings. However, since the early 1980s, the state pension has risen in line with the **retail price index (RPI)** rather than with average earnings. (There are now plans to change this, reverting back to the old method of **indexation**, though the state of the UK economy may prevent this happening.) This has kept the real value or purchasing power of the state pension at its early 1980s level, while the real earnings of those in work have continued to rise. Pensioners reliant solely on the state for a source of income have become *relatively* worse off, even though the real value of the state pension has not fallen. The state pension is now regarded very much as a *poverty income*.

examiner's voice

The problem of poverty is a Unit 3 topic but candidates may be expected to apply knowledge learned when studying Units 2 and 4 to explain how fiscal policy can be used to reduce poverty.

examiner's voice

Exam questions may require an explanation of the causes of poverty and/or of the effects of poverty on the economy.

Unemployment and poverty

Unemployment benefits are also now linked to the RPI and, for similar reasons as the state pension, have fallen behind average earnings. An increase in unemployment therefore increases poverty. It follows that absolute poverty (and potentially relative poverty) can best be reduced by fast and sustained economic growth and by creating jobs. As I have suggested in my previous paragraph, economic growth can also create the wherewithal, if the electorate and state are so minded, to increase the real value of the state pension and unemployment benefits.

Low wages and poverty

When discussing the nature of both absolute and relative poverty in the UK, we must distinguish between the **low-waged** and the **un-waged**. The latter group includes pensioners and people whose only sources of income are unemployment benefits, income support or incapacity benefits.

Income support is an extra benefit paid to people on low incomes, such as the elderly who would otherwise be completely reliant on the state pension, and to families otherwise dependent solely on the unemployment benefit paid to one of the family's members. Incapacity benefit is a weekly payment for people who become incapable of work while under the state pension age.

The low-waged, unlike the un-waged, are workers with jobs, albeit jobs in which their hourly and weekly earnings are low. The low-waged include many unskilled workers, together with skilled workers who have lost jobs in the manufacturing industry and who have had to trade down to employment in more menial unskilled activity. The low-waged poor are almost always *relatively* poor rather than *absolutely* poor. In contrast, the many homeless people living on the street fall into the category of the absolutely poor. As I shall explain later, the introduction of the **national minimum wage** was an attempt to reduce the poverty of the low-waged.

Box 13.2 Fuel poverty

In recent years a supposedly new type of poverty has been identified, known as fuel poverty. In cold winters low-income households, especially pensioner households living in badly-insulated properties, are likely to experience fuel poverty. The problem is made worse by the fact that many pensioners and other low-income families live in houses equipped with inefficient heating systems.

The passage on page 197 summarises information taken from a number of news stories published in the autumn of 2008, just after many of the energy companies raised the prices of gas and electricity by up to 22%.

Fuel poverty affects many elderly people

Million more suffer fuel poverty

Fuel poverty is defined as households who spend more than 10% of their income on fuel. The number of households in fuel poverty in the UK rose to 3.5 million in 2006, 1 million more than in 2005, government figures show. The number of homes in fuel poverty in England rose from 1.5 million in 2005 to 2.4 million in 2006, including an extra 700,000 vulnerable households.

Philip Cullum from energy watchdog Consumer Focus said 'These historic figures show a significant rise in fuel poverty, but the situation today is even worse. We estimate 5.5 million households are in fuel poverty. We want to see government act now to push all energy suppliers to introduce social tariffs to help low income consumers cope with rising fuel bills. Our figures include around 2.75 million homes classed as vulnerable, i.e. containing a child, elderly person or someone with a long-term illness.'

Tony Woodley, leader of the Unite union, said thousands more people would slip into fuel poverty in the winter of 2008: 'The government cannot stand back while struggling households choose whether to heat or eat. If intervention is on hand to bail out the speculators and spivs who have caused this economic turmoil, then our government should not have to think twice about helping the frail and vulnerable heat their homes.'

The Help the Aged charity estimates one in four pensioners live in fuel poverty, which is 3 million people. Special advisor to the charity, Mervyn Kohler, said fuel poverty was escalating 'out of control' and the government's response was 'feeble'. He says that 'what is needed is a government strategy that combines both short and long-term solutions – crisis payments to help with the here and now and in the longer term improvements to the energy efficiency of our housing stock'.

Last month the government unveiled a £910m package of measures with the big energy companies, aimed at helping people with soaring gas and electricity bills. It includes half-price insulation for all households and a freeze on this year's bills for the poorest families.

Source: various news articles

Follow-up questions

1 Do you think that fuel poverty is a new type of poverty that did not exist until quite recently? Justify your answer.

2 Evaluate *two* different policies which the UK government might use to eliminate or reduce fuel poverty.

Poverty and the tax and benefits system

Poverty is seldom caused directly and immediately by taxation and the benefits system. However, through a process known as **fiscal drag** (which I explain later in the chapter) and through cuts in welfare benefits, poverty can increase. Making taxation more **progressive** and increasing **welfare benefits** reduces poverty and inequalities in the distribution of income, at least in the short run. However, free-market and supply-side economists believe that, in the drive to reduce inequality, these changes worsen labour market incentives, competitiveness and economic growth. According to this view, in the long run, low incomes may fail to grow and poverty may increase. If true, government intervention in labour markets causes government failure.

Inequalities in the distribution of income and wealth in the UK

At AS you will have learnt that income is a **flow** while wealth is a **stock**. Personal wealth is the stock, or historical accumulation, of everything you own that has value. By contrast, your income is the flow of money you receive hourly, weekly, monthly or annually, some of which (the part that you *save*) can add to your personal wealth. This is one of the links between income and wealth. A second link operates in the opposite direction — the wealthier you are, the more investment income you are likely to earn, which adds to your total income. Indeed, the rich benefit from a virtuous circle: wealth increases income, which allows the wealthy to save, and saving adds to wealth, and so on. By contrast, many of the poor suffer a vicious circle: low income means the poor have to borrow, borrowing adds to personal debt, income is then spent on debt repayment, consumption falls, and any wealth the poor possess disappears.

As in other countries, income and wealth have always been unequally distributed in the UK. Even when economic growth creates full employment, the incomes of the rich tend to increase faster than those of the poor. For this reason, though absolute poverty declines, fast economic growth may actually increase relative poverty and widen income differences.

> *e*xaminer's voice
> Exam questions may ask for an explanation of why inequalities in the distribution of income and wealth have changed in the UK economy in recent years. You are not required to know about events more than 10 years before the exam.

Inequality in the Keynesian era

Nevertheless, during the Keynesian era, from the 1950s to the late 1970s, a combination of sustained economic growth, low unemployment and state intervention reduced inequalities in the distribution of income in the UK. State intervention made the tax system more progressive and transferred the resulting tax revenue in welfare benefits paid largely to the poor.

Inequality in the 1980s and early 1990s

Free-market and supply-side economics replaced Keynesianism in the 1980s and early to mid-1990s. (Chapter 15 of my *AQA AS Economics* book explains this in some detail). These decades were marked by widening inequality in the distribution of income and wealth. The wealthy benefited from greater tax cuts than the poor and their income rose at a faster rate. Many commentators believe that in the 1980s, Margaret Thatcher's Conservative governments widened income and wealth inequalities quite deliberately. Thatcher believed that government policies such as progressive taxation and transfers to the poor destroy personal incentives, which in turn harms the economy. To make the poor better off in the long run, they must be made relatively worse off in the short run, in order to create the conditions in which hard work and the entrepreneurial spirit can deliver economic growth.

Box 13.3 UK income inequality at the present day

In May 1997 the election of a Labour government ended nearly 20 years of Conservative rule, extending back to the start of Margaret Thatcher's first administration in 1979. During Labour's first few years in office, redistributional policies, together with the effects of a fall in unemployment, raised the real incomes of the poor.

In December 2008, the ONS's *Economic and Labour Market Review* published an article on 'The distribution of household income 1977 to 2006/07'. The article showed that 11 years of Labour government had not closed the gap between the income of the richest and poorest households. In 2007, the top fifth of households had 42% of total disposable income, and the bottom fifth had only 7%.

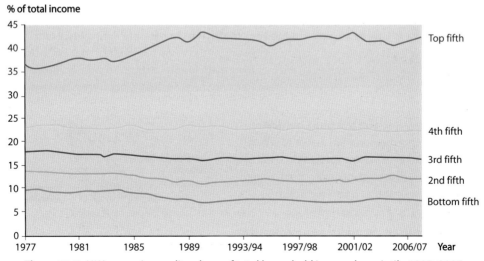

Figure 13.2 *UK income inequality: share of total household income by quintile, 1997–2007*

The lack of change was despite the government's redistributive policies that were aimed at narrowing the income gap in the UK. These policies included tax credits for working families and pensioners, and increased income support payments for young mothers.

The graph divides the UK households into income quintiles. For example, the quintile at the top of the graph shows the richest fifth of households, and the quintile at the bottom of the graph shows the poorest fifth. The quintiles between the poorest and the richest fifths of households are shown in ascending order from poorer to richer.

When the latest figures were published, Louise Bamfield, senior research fellow at the Fabian Society, said: 'You've had all these changes, but the overall effect is to end up exactly where you were, had these things not happened. You've kept income inequality at roughly the same place.'

She went on to deny that government failure had occurred, stating that inequality would have been much wider without the government's redistributive policies: 'It's like running up a down escalator, the government is trying to counter market forces. Pay at the very top has been racing away.'

She said the top 1% of the population, about 500,000 people, had enjoyed a very steep growth in pay in recent years, fuelled largely by huge bonuses paid to executives in the City. But at the same time, household income at the very bottom of the league table has suffered, because the government's tax and pensions' policies have failed to benefit the poorest, single adults who do not work.

Follow-up questions

1 Do you agree that the failure to redistribute income from rich to poor is *not* an example of government failure? Justify your answer.

2 Outline your view on whether governments should attempt to redistribute income.

Extension material

Measuring inequality

Economists use **Lorenz curves** and the **Gini coefficient** to measure inequality. Exam questions will not require use of either measure, but as exam candidates frequently use one or both of these measures, I have included them in this chapter. Be warned, however: valuable exam time is easily wasted drawing a Lorenz curve that is not necessary for the answer.

The Lorenz curve and the Gini Coefficient

A Lorenz curve measures the extent to which the distribution of income (or wealth) is equal or unequal. The degree of inequality is measured by a statistic known as a Gini coefficient.

The Lorenz curve in Figure 13.3 shows population on the horizontal axis, measured in cumulative percentages from 0% to 100%. The vertical axis shows the cumulative percentage of income received by the population. If incomes were distributed equally, the Lorenz

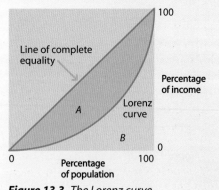

Figure 13.3 *The Lorenz curve*

curve would lie along the diagonal line in the diagram. The nearer the Lorenz curve is to the diagonal, the more equal is the distribution of income.

The Gini coefficient measures the area between the Lorenz curve and the diagonal as a ratio of the total area under the diagonal. In terms of the diagram, the Gini coefficient is calculated using the following formula:

$$\text{Gini coefficient} = \frac{\text{area } A}{\text{area } A + \text{area } B}$$

The lower the value of the Gini coefficient, the more equally household income is distributed. If the Lorenz curve were to lie along the 45-degree line in the above diagram, every household would have exactly the same income and the Gini coefficient would be zero. At the other extreme, if one person received all the income and everybody else no income, the Lorenz curve would be the reverse L-shape lying along, first the horizontal axis, and then the right-hand vertical axis in the diagram. Between these two extremes, Lorenz curves closer to the line of complete equality show greater equality (and Gini-coefficients approaching zero), while Lorenz curves further away from the diagonal display greater inequality (and Gini coefficients approaching one).

Will inequality increase in the future?

At the time of writing (April 2009), recession has hit the UK economy and unemployment has begun to grow. Assuming that the recession continues at least for a year or two, unemployment will continue to grow, reducing the incomes especially of the low paid and increasing absolute poverty. Relative poverty will probably increase too, if low incomes fall by a greater percentage than high incomes.

Government policies that aim to reduce poverty and income inequalities

The main policies UK governments have used to try to reduce poverty and to make the distribution of income and wealth more equal are progressive taxation, transfers to the poor, the tax credit system, and the national minimum wage.

Progressive taxation

In a **progressive tax** system the proportion of a person's income paid in tax *increases* as income *rises*, while in a **regressive tax** system, the proportion paid in tax *falls*. A tax is proportionate if exactly the same proportion of income is paid in tax at all levels of income. Progressivity can be defined for a single tax or for the tax system as a whole.

 Key term

Progressive taxation is a tax or tax system in which the rich pay a higher proportion of income in tax than the poor.

The word progressive is value-neutral, implying nothing about how the revenue raised by the government is spent. Nevertheless, progressive taxation has been

used by governments, particularly during the Keynesian era and to a minor extent more recently by Labour governments, to achieve the social aim of a fairer distribution of income.

It is often assumed that the UK tax system is highly progressive, and is thus used to redis-

examiner's voice

Make sure you can explain how progressive taxation and transfers have affected the economy and can evaluate whether the effects have been good or bad.

tribute income and wealth to the poor. In fact, apart from capital gains tax and inheritance tax which is quite easily avoidable, wealth (and capital) is not taxed in the UK. This means that inequalities in the distribution of *wealth* have not really been reduced by the tax system.

Nevertheless, many people believe wrongly that income taxes are strongly progressive in the UK. Personal income tax is only slightly progressive for most income groups, becoming rather more progressive for the richest fifth of households. The progressivity of income tax was significantly reduced by the abolition of all the higher marginal rates of income tax in 1988, with the exception of the 40% rate, which may soon rise (depending on the political party in power) to a top rate of 50% for those with taxable incomes over £150,000. National Insurance contributions (NICs) reduce the progressivity of the direct tax system for the top 20% of households. NICs are *regressive* on higher incomes because little or no further contributions are paid once a worker's income rises above a given ceiling. Because the council tax and indirect taxes (mostly expenditure taxes) are regressive, taking a declining proportion of the income of rich households, overall the UK tax system is at best only slightly progressive, and it may even be regressive.

 Key term

A **transfer** is an income paid by the state to benefit recipients and financed from taxation.

Transfers to the poor

Progressive taxation cannot by itself redistribute income — a policy of transfers in the government's public expenditure programme is required for this. Progressive taxation used on its own merely reduces **post-tax income differentials** compared to **pre-tax differentials**. Currently, the main transfers directed at the poor in UK public spending are the old age pension, unemployment benefits, incapacity benefit and income support. These forms of income, paid by the state to individuals who fall into the relevant category, are meant to transfer income from tax payers to people on low incomes. Income support is paid to low-waged families and the state pension can be claimed by people who stay on at work after the state retirement age. More often however, transfers are paid to the *un-waged* poor.

Tax credits

Whereas *positive* income tax is paid by people whose total yearly income is higher than their personal tax allowance, tax credits are a form of *negative* income tax, paid by the government to people in employment whose incomes are very low. Many low-paid people who work, but earn low wages, qualify for **working tax credits**.

The national minimum wage

I have already described the UK national minimum wage in Chapter 12. Read again about the national minimum wage, and assess whether the NMW has had any effect in reducing poverty and income inequalities.

Fiscal drag, poverty and low pay

The UK tax system has affected poverty partly through a process known as **fiscal drag**. Fiscal drag occurs in a progressive income tax system when the government fails to raise **tax thresholds** (or **personal tax allowances**) to keep pace with inflation. Figure 13.4 (a) shows an income pyramid with the rich at the top of the pyramid and the poor at the bottom

Key term

Fiscal drag is a failure to raise personal tax thresholds in line with inflation that brings the low-paid into the tax net.

and with the tax threshold fixed at an income of £5,000. In this example, a person with an income of £4,900 is just below the threshold and pays no income tax.

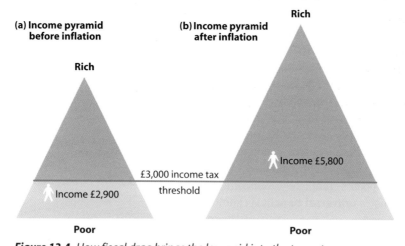

Figure 13.4 *How fiscal drag brings the low paid into the tax net*

Suppose that both prices and all money incomes exactly double. If there are no taxes, real incomes will remain unchanged, with households no better off or worse off. But if there are taxes, and the government fails to increase personal tax allowances in line with inflation (that is, to raise the tax threshold to £10,000), a doubling of the person's money income to £9,800 means that £4,800 of income is now taxable. The individual concerned is now worse off in real terms.

The new situation is shown in Figure 13.4 (b). Inflation has dragged the low-paid worker across the basic tax threshold and into the tax net. In a similar way, higher-paid workers are dragged deeper into the tax net if the higher 40% marginal tax rate remains unadjusted for inflation.

Governments can reduce relative poverty among the low paid by raising income tax thresholds by more than the rate of inflation. This takes the low paid out of the

income tax net and claws back the fiscal drag that has taken place in previous years. However, unless the government simultaneously reduces public spending (which generally benefits the low paid more than the high paid), taxes have to be raised elsewhere in the economy, which may also adversely affect the poor.

The earnings trap or poverty trap

Fiscal drag is one of the causes of the **poverty trap**. As there are a number of ways in which the poor can be trapped in poverty, this particular trap, which traps the low-waged in *relative* poverty, is better called the **earnings trap**. It affects people in employment on low rates of pay, rather than the unemployed who are un-waged. Another poverty trap contains the homeless, who are trapped in poverty because to get a job they need a home, but to get a home they first need a job.

The immediate cause of the earnings trap is the overlap, illustrated in Figure 13.5, between the income tax *threshold* (the level of income at which income tax starts to be paid) and the means-tested welfare benefits *ceiling* (the level of income at which means-tested transfer incomes cease to be paid). When **welfare benefits** are means-tested, a person's right to claim the benefit is reduced and eventually disappears completely, as income rises. By contrast, a **universal benefit** is claimed as of right and is not dependent on income, although the state can claw back universal benefits that are taxable.

A low-paid worker caught within the zone of overlap in Figure 13.5 not only pays income tax and national insurance contributions on each extra pound earned, he or she also loses part or all of the right to claim benefits. Thus low-paid workers and their families whose income falls within this zone of overlap become trapped in relative poverty, since any increase in their pay results in little or no increase (and in extreme cases a fall) in disposable income.

 Key term

The **poverty trap**, also known as the earnings trap, describes a situation in which the low paid are trapped in relative poverty by having to pay income tax and NICs at the same time as losing welfare benefits.

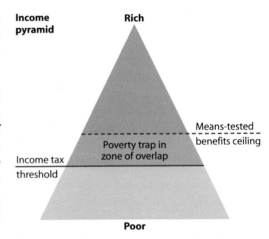

Figure 13.5 *The poverty trap or earnings trap*

*e***xaminer's voice**

Make sure you understand the difference between, but also the relationship between, the poverty trap (or earnings trap) and the unemployment trap.

*e***xaminer's voice**

See page 303 of Chapter 19 for a definition of the marginal tax rate.

The *effective* marginal rate of taxation of workers in poorly-paid occupations is high when the loss of means-tested benefits is added to deductions through income tax and NICs. Calculated in this way, the marginal tax rates of the low paid are much higher (often around 70% and in extreme cases over 100%) than the top 40% rate now paid by the better-off. Moreover, since the low paid are generally employed in occupations yielding little job satisfaction or scope for legal tax avoidance, disincentives to work imposed by the UK tax system affect the poor at the lower end of the income pyramid much more than they affect the better-off.

The poverty trap can be eliminated by getting rid of the zone of overlap in the income pyramid illustrated in Figure 13.5. The income tax threshold could be raised to take low-waged households out of the tax net. Means-tested benefits could be replaced by universal benefits, although, as taxes would have to increase to pay for any substantial increase in universal benefits, the poor might end up more heavily taxed. The national minimum wage might also reduce poverty by preventing employers paying 'poverty wages'. However, raising the NMW could be counter-productive if unemployment increases as a result.

Box 13.4 Changes to the tax and benefit system place an extra 60,000 households in the poverty trap

Through the first decade of the 2000s, UK Labour governments tried to reduce income inequalities and the impact of the poverty trap on the poor. I have already explained how for a few years, Labour succeeded in achieving the first objective in the late 1990s, though in the years immediately before 2008, when recession hit the UK economy, income differentials widened again. However, as the following passage indicates, Labour was not successful in eliminating the poverty trap.

The Government has been accused of creating a poverty trap with recent changes to the tax and benefits system which risks penalising almost two million low earners trying to boost their income.

Thousands of the lowest-paid workers choosing to work more hours will be taxed as much as 90% on their additional income because of losses in benefits and tax credits.

Those earning just above the minimum wage and receiving housing benefit are at the greatest risk of suffering from a very high 'marginal tax rate', as small increases in the amount they earn could result in the loss of the benefit.

Independent, 23 December 2008

Follow-up questions
1 Why did income differentials in the UK widen after about 2000?
2 Explain the causes of the poverty trap or earnings trap.

The unemployment trap

The poverty trap I have just described affects the low-waged in jobs rather than the unemployed or un-waged. It is important not to confuse the poverty trap or earnings trap with the **unemployment trap**. The unemployment trap is closely related to the earnings trap, since both

 Key *term*

Unemployment trap means the unemployed are trapped in unemployment as they are better off living off benefits than in a low-waged job paying income tax and NICs, while losing the ability to claim means-tested benefits.

affect the poor and result from the nature of the tax and benefits systems. But people caught in the unemployment trap are out of work — at least in terms of officially declared employment. The unemployment trap contains un-waged social security claimants who choose unemployment. This is because they decide they are better off out of work, living on benefits, than in low-paid jobs paying income tax and NICs and losing some or all of their right to claim means-tested benefits.

One link between the earnings trap and the unemployment trap is the **underground economy** — the hidden or informal economy in which people work, usually for cash payments, while failing to declare income and often fraudulently claiming social security benefits. Low-paid workers in employment can escape the earnings trap by giving up declared work in order to claim unemployment pay, while receiving income from undeclared work undertaken in the underground economy. The underground economy is sometimes called the 'black economy'.

Horizontal and vertical equity

Equity, which means fairness or justness, is a *normative* concept (a matter of opinion). The closely related but not quite identical concept of **equality** is a *positive* concept. Equality, but not equity, can be measured. Government intervention in the economy, which treats people in the same circumstances equally, obeys the principle of **horizontal equity**. Horizontal equity occurs when households with the same income and personal circumstances (for example, number of children) pay the same income tax and are eligible for the same welfare benefits. **Vertical equity** is much more controversial, since it justifies taking income from the rich (on the ground that they don't need it) and redistributing their income to the poor (on the ground that they do need it). The distribution of income *after* taxation and receipt of transfers is judged more equitable than original income before redistribution. Achieving greater vertical equity can conflict with another principle of intervention, the **benefit principle**, which argues that those who receive most benefit from government spending (for example, motorists benefiting from roads) should pay the most in taxes.

 Key terms

Horizontal equity describes households in similar circumstances paying similar taxes and receiving similar benefits.

Vertical equity redistributes income from the rich to the poor on the basis of need.

Summary

> It is important to distinguish between absolute and relative poverty.

> Absolute poverty occurs when income is below a particular specified level.

> A household is relatively poor if its income is below a specified proportion of average income for all households.

> Old age, unemployment and low wages are important causes of poverty in the UK.

> Fuel poverty is a recently identified form of poverty.

➤ Government intervention to reduce poverty may lead to government failures that may make matters worse.

➤ Inequalities in the distribution of UK income and wealth widened after 1979.

➤ After 1997, Labour governments used progressive taxation, transfers to the poor, the introduction of a national minimum wage and a tax credits system to reduce absolute poverty.

➤ However, by 2008, income inequalities and poverty relative to the richest in society widened, largely due to the rapid rise in the incomes of the well-off.

➤ Fiscal drag in the tax system has contributed to the existence of a poverty trap or earnings trap, and also to an unemployment trap.

➤ Horizontal equity occurs when households with the same income and personal circumstances pay the same income tax and are eligible for the same welfare benefits.

➤ Vertical equity increases when income taken from the rich is redistributed to the poor.

Questions

1 Explain the difference between absolute and relative poverty

2 What is fuel poverty and why has it increased?

3 Why did inequalities in the distribution of income and wealth widen in the 1980s?

4 After 1997 absolute poverty fell, but income inequalities had widened by 2008. Explain why.

5 What is fiscal drag?

6 Distinguish between the poverty trap (or earnings trap) and the unemployment trap.

7 How may vertical equity in the distribution of income be affected by progressive taxation and transfers?

The national and international economy

Unit 4

Chapter 14

Economic growth, development and standards of living

This chapter begins by explaining the difference between economic growth and economic development. Having reminded you of the difference between short-term and long-term economic growth, I shall investigate each in turn. I shall examine short-term growth in the context of the economic cycle or business cycle. Then, having surveyed the roles of investment and technical progress in causing long-term growth, I shall discuss the benefits and costs of economic growth and the issue of growth sustainability. I shall conclude the chapter by discussing whether measures of economic development such as the United Nation's Human Development Index (HDI) provide better indicators than gross domestic product (GDP) of standards of living and people's quality of life.

Learning outcomes

This chapter will:

➤ define economic growth and remind you of the difference between short-run and long-run economic growth
➤ distinguish between economic growth and economic development
➤ link economic growth to the growth of productivity in the economy
➤ relate short-run growth to the economic cycle or business cycle
➤ discuss the causes of long-run economic growth or *true* growth
➤ survey the costs and benefits of growth and possible conflicts between growth and other macroeconomic policy objectives

What you should already know

At AS you learnt that economic growth, which is one of the government's most important macroeconomic objectives, occurs when the productive capacity of the economy is increasing. You learnt to illustrate both short-run and long-run economic growth on production possibility curves and *AD/AS* diagrams. The Unit 2 specification also required the ability to analyse and evaluate the various demand-side and supply-side determinants, both of short-run growth and the long-run trend rate of economic growth. AS economics also introduced the link between short-run economic growth, the economic cycle and output gaps.

The meaning of economic growth

Economic growth can be defined as the increase, over time, of the potential level of output the economy can produce. Strictly, this is **long-run economic growth**, which is not the same as **short-run economic growth**. Long-run and short-run economic growth are both illustrated in Figure 14.1. Short-run growth is shown by the movement from point *C* inside the economy's production possibility frontier, located at *PPF*₁, to point *A* on the frontier. Long-run growth is depicted by the shift from point *A* on *PPF*₁ to point *B* on *PPF*₂.

Long-run economic growth can also be thought of as *true* growth while short-run growth is best thought of as the **economic recovery** that takes place when spare capacity or slack is taken up in the economy and production moves toward the economy's production possibility frontier.

Short-run growth or economic recovery makes use of spare capacity and takes up slack in the economy, whereas long-run growth increases total productive capacity.

In the next diagram, Figure 14.2, I illustrate the difference between long-run and short-run economic growth on an

examiner's voice

All that you learnt about economic growth at AS is equally relevant to A2 economics. This chapter adds little to what you should already know.

Key terms

Economic growth describes an increase in the potential output an economy can produce.

Long-run economic growth is shown by an outward movement of the economy's production possibility frontier, which increases the potential output the economy can produce.

Short-run economic growth is an increase in the output that results from making use of spare capacity and unemployed labour. Also known as economic recovery.

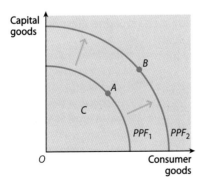

Figure 14.1 *Long-run and short-run economic growth illustrated on a production possibility frontier diagram*

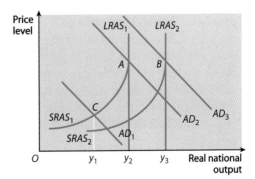

Figure 14.2 *Long-run and short-run economic growth illustrated on an AD/AS diagram*

AD/AS graph. In the diagram I initially locate macro-economic equilibrium at point *C*, where the aggregate demand curve *AD*₁ intersects the short-run aggregate supply curve *SRAS*₁. You should note that point *C* is to the left of the long-run aggregate supply curve *LRAS*₁. The level of real output y_1 lies below the full-employment level of output y_2, and there is both spare capacity and idle labour in the economy.

The initial macroeconomic equilibrium in Figure 14.2 results from deficient aggregate demand in the economy. In terms of Figure 14.1, the economy is producing *inside* its production possibility frontier. Keynesian unemployment or **cyclical unemployment** occurs as a result of this. If the government responds to this situation by using fiscal policy and/or monetary policy to increase aggregate demand (or if consumption, investment or exports increase), the aggregate demand curve may move to *AD*₂. Once again, the economy is in macroeconomic equilibrium, but at point *A* rather than point *C*, and the level of output y_2 is the full employment level of output. The economy is now producing on the **long-run aggregate supply curve** *LRAS*₁ and on production possibility frontier *PPF*₁ in Figure 14.1. Short-run economic growth has moved the economy to this position.

As there is no longer any spare capacity or idle labour in the economy, for further growth to occur, both the long-run aggregate supply curve and the production possibility frontier must shift to the right (to *LRAS*₂ in Figure 14.2 and *PPF*₁ in Figure 14.1). Among the factors that can bring about long-term growth are investment in more and better capital goods, investment in human capital through education and training, and population growth, for example through immigration. Either way, a shift to the right of the *LRAS* curve from *LRAS*₁ to *LRAS*₂, means that the full employment level of output has increased from y_2 to y_3.

Economic growth versus economic development

Economic growth does not *necessarily* improve the economic welfare of all or most of the people living in a country. On occasion, in some countries, the fruits of economic growth have allowed a rich elite to enjoy a champagne lifestyle, while the vast bulk of the population live in poverty. In such a society, growth also helps to maintain a military and police system used primarily to protect the rich and subdue the poor. Even when the benefits of economic growth are spread to all or most of the population, growth may not be sustainable. In this situation, future generations as yet unborn may eventually suffer from the profligacy of people living today and their quest for ever-faster economic growth.

Economic development is a better indicator of improved human welfare, and the ability to continue to improve welfare, than economic growth. Economic development, which includes the quality and not just the quantity of growth, is measured by:

- general improvement in living standards, which reduces poverty and human suffering
- access to resources such as food and housing that are required to satisfy basic human needs
- access to opportunities for human development (for example, through education and training)
- sustainability and regeneration, through reducing resource depletion and degradation

Resource depletion occurs when finite resources such as oil are used up, and when soil fertility or fish stocks irreversibly decline. By contrast, **resource degradation** is best illustrated by pollution of air, water and land. To benefit people in the long run, growth (and development) must be sustainable. Sustainable economic growth requires the use of *renewable* rather than *non-renewable* resources that minimise pollution and other forms of resource degradation.

The causes of long-run economic growth

The cause of short-run economic growth, which occurs when the economy moves from a point *inside* its production possibility frontier to a point *on* the frontier, is an increase in aggregate demand. By contrast, **long-run economic growth** is explained by **supply-side factors** that shift the frontier outward. However, sufficient aggregate demand has to be generated to absorb the extra output produced by the growth process. The immediate supply-side cause of long-run growth is **increased labour productivity**, which itself results from investment in, and accumulation of, capital goods and human capital, and from technical progress. **Investment**, **technical progress**, and **increased labour productivity** lie at the heart of long-run economic growth.

The importance of increasing productivity

Productivity is mentioned four or five times in the Unit 2 specification on The National Economy, but not once in the A2 Unit 4 specification on The National and International Economy. However, given the fact that the concept also surfaces in the Unit 3 specification on Business Economics and the Distribution of Income, productivity is important throughout the A-level economics course. Despite its lack of mention in the A2 macroeconomic specification, the synoptic nature of the Unit 4 exam means that you *must* know about productivity and all its implications.

To the layman, the term productivity usually means labour productivity. Labour productivity can be measured in terms of the **average product of labour**, or **output per worker**, and the **marginal product of labour**, which measures the addition to total output brought about by employing an extra worker. In general discussion, however, we usually mean average output per worker.

 Key term

Productivity means output per unit of input, e.g. labour productivity is output per worker.

These definitions are *short-run* definitions that assume capital is fixed and technical progress remains unchanged. In much the same way, the productivity of capital can be measured by adding capital to a fixed labour force, once again with a given state of technical progress. In either case, by adding labour to fixed capital, or by adding capital to fixed labour, the **law of diminishing returns** sets in, eventually reducing the average productivity of the input being changed.

To escape the impact of diminishing returns to labour or capital, labour and capital must be changed together. In this situation, when **increasing returns to scale** may operate, the key concept is **total factor productivity (TFP)**. A change in TFP measures the change in total output when *all* the factors of production are changed in the economic long run.

> **e**xaminer's voice
> Productivity is one of the most important concepts you need to understand, for Unit 3 as well as Unit 4.

Technical progress and productivity

Technical progress, or the rate of growth of technology, increases the rate of growth of total factor productivity. It measures how much more productive capital, labour and other factors of production have become in total over a period of time. There is general agreement among economists that technical progress is the main cause of economic growth, but there is considerable disagreement as to what causes technical progress itself.

Fluctuations in the level of economic activity

At AS you learnt that the level of economic activity fluctuates over a number of different time periods. These include seasonal fluctuations, taking place within a single 12-month period, and cyclical fluctuations that extend over a number of years. **Seasonal fluctuations** are largely caused by changes in climate and weather. Examples include the effect of cold winters closing down the building trade and seasonal employment in travel and tourism. Rather longer **cyclical fluctuations** divide into the short **economic cycle**, which lasts for just a few years, and **long cycles** (or long waves), which may extend over about 60 years.

The economic cycle

In an economic cycle (which is also known as a *trade cycle* or *business cycle*), the economy's growth rate fluctuates considerably from year to year. Figure 14.3 shows two complete economic cycles, together with a line showing the economy's trend growth rate or long-run growth rate. Actual growth, which is measured by the percentage change in real GDP over a 12-month period, varies in the different phases of the economic cycle. In the cycle's upswing, growth is positive, but as Figure 14.3 shows, 'growth' becomes negative if and when a recession occurs in the cyclical downturn. In

>
> **Key term**
>
> An **economic cycle** is a period of between about 4 and 10 years in which actual output fluctuates above and below the trend growth line.

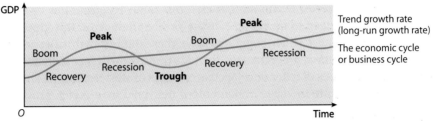

Figure 14.3 *The trend growth rate and the economic cycle*

the UK, a **recession** is defined as negative economic growth (or falling real GDP) for 6 months or more.

Before the third quarter of 2008, the UK had suffered only two recessions over the previous 30 years. The first of these was between 1979 and 1981. Then, following a period of growth sustained through the rest of the 1980s, a second recession hit the UK economy a decade later between 1990 and 1992. Both recessions (which raised unemployment to around 3 million) were followed by longer periods of recovery and boom in the rest of the 1980s and 1990s.

Economic cycles can still, however, be identified even when there are no recessions. In this situation, the annual growth rate falls in the cycle's downswing, but still remains positive. This was the situation, which is illustrated in Figure 14.4, from the end of the 1990–92 recession until 2008. There were no recessions in these years, but actual output fluctuated above and below the UK's trend growth line.

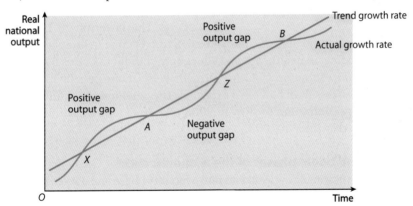

Figure 14.4 *Identifying the beginning and end of economic cycles*

The UK Treasury defines an economic cycle as starting and finishing at points when the economy is judged to be on-trend. At these points, there are no output gaps, positive or negative. In terms of Figure 14.4, an economic cycle starts at point *X* and ends at point *Z*. (Alternatively, a cycle could be dated from point *A* to point *B*.)

examiner's voice
You learnt about output gaps at AS. Your knowledge may be synoptically tested at A2.

The economy's trend (or potential) growth rate is the rate at which output can grow, on a sustained basis, without putting upward or downward pressure on inflation. The trend growth rate is measured over a period covering more than one

(and preferably several) economic cycles. Until quite recently, the UK's trend growth rate was judged to be about 2.25% a year. At first sight, this growth rate appears low, especially when compared to higher trend growth rates in newly industrialising countries. Nevertheless, the UK's trend growth rate is similar to the long-run growth rates of other developed economies in western Europe and North America. The absolute increase in real output delivered by a 2.25% growth rate may also exceed that delivered by a 10% growth rate in a much poorer country. Moreover, because of the compound interest effect, a 2.25% growth rate means that average UK living standards double every generation or so. The compound interest effect also explains why the trend growth rate line in Figure 14.3 becomes steeper from year to year, moving along the line. For example, 2.25% of £1,000 billion is a larger absolute annual increase in GDP than 2.25% of £800 billion.

ICT has improved labour productivity

In 2002, the Office for National Statistics (ONS) estimated that the trend growth rate in the UK had increased from 2.25% to about 2.75%. At the time, this was explained by the impact of new technologies such as ICT and the internet improving labour productivity and causing structural change in the economy.

The UK government accepted this estimate, but was rather more cautious, building a 2.5% projected growth rate into its financial calculations. The government hoped that faster trend growth could deliver sufficient extra tax revenue to finance increased government spending on healthcare and education, without tax rates being raised. However, by 2005 estimates of future growth were more pessimistic and tax revenues were also less than had been expected. The pessimism was fully justified, with the economy continuing to slow in 2006 and 2007, and eventually dipping into a full-blown recession in 2008.

The recovery and boom phases of the economic cycle

The upswing of an economic cycle divides into a *recovery* phase and a *boom* phase. Real output or GDP grows in both phases, but the two phases differ according to whether real output is below or above the trend growth rate line drawn in Figures 14.3 and 14.4. The recovery phase accompanies a **negative output gap**. But when real output rises above the trend growth line, recovery gives way to boom and a **positive output gap**.

Explanations of the economic cycle

In the 1930s, John Maynard Keynes argued that economic recessions are caused by fluctuations in aggregate demand. In Keynes's theory, investment and aggregate demand rise and fall as business confidence gives way to pessimism, and vice versa.

However, as Box 14.2 explains, it is now recognised that supply-side factors can also trigger economic cycles. A theory of real business cycles has recently been developed, which argues that in some circumstances, changes in technology on the supply side of the economy might be as important as changes in aggregate demand in explaining economic cycles. Among the factors that may cause or contribute to economic cycles are:

examiner's voice

You may be asked to explain three or four causes of economic cycles. Make sure you don't confuse *causes* with possible *effects* of cyclical fluctuations.

Climatic factors

The nineteenth-century neoclassical economist, Stanley Jevons, was one of the first economists to recognise the business cycle. Perhaps taking note of the Bible's reference to '7 years of plenty' followed by '7 years of famine', Jevons believed that a connection exists between the timing of economic crises and the solar cycle. Variations in sunspots affect the power of the sun's rays, influencing the quality of harvests and thus the price of grain, which, in turn, affects business confidence and gives rise to trade cycles.

Although Jevons's sunspot theory was never widely accepted, there is no doubt that climate changes do affect economic activity. The El Niño effect has renewed interest in Jevons's theory. El Niño is a severe atmospheric and oceanic disturbance in the Pacific Ocean occurring every 7–14 years. The disturbance leads to a fall in the number of plankton that upsets the entire ocean food chain, which badly damages the fishing industry. The effect leads to a complete reversal of trade winds, bringing torrential rain, flooding and mudslides to the otherwise dry Pacific coastal areas of central South America. By contrast, droughts occur in much of Asia and in areas of Africa and central North America.

Box 14.1 A new yardstick for measuring slumps is long overdue

There has been a nasty outbreak of R-worditis. Newspapers are full of stories about which of the big economies will be first to dip into recession as a result of the credit crunch. The answer depends largely on what you mean by recession. Most economists assume that it implies a fall in real GDP. But this has created a lot of confusion: the standard definition of recession needs rethinking.

To the average person, a large rise in unemployment means a recession. By contrast, the economists' rule that a recession is defined by two consecutive quarters of falling GDP is silly. If an economy grows by 2% in one quarter and then contracts by 0.5% in each of the next two quarters, it is deemed to be in recession. But if GDP contracts by 2% in one quarter, rises by 0.5% in the next, then falls by 2% in the third, it escapes, even though the economy is obviously weaker.

However, it is not just the 'two-quarter' rule that is flawed; GDP figures themselves can be misleading. The problem is that they are subject to large revisions. These are good reasons not to place too much weight on GDP in trying to spot recessions. The Business Cycle Dating Committee of the National Bureau of Economic Research (NBER), America's official arbiter of recessions, instead makes its judgments based on monthly data for industrial production, employment, real income, and wholesale and retail trade. It has not yet decided whether a recession has begun.

The Economist, 11 September 2008

Follow-up question

Compare different ways of defining a recession.

The role of speculative bubbles

Rapid economic growth leads to a rapid rise and speculative bubble in asset prices. When people realise that house prices or share prices have risen far above the assets' real values, asset selling replaces asset buying. This causes the speculative bubble to burst, which in turn destroys consumer and business confidence. People stop spending and the economy may fall into recession.

Changes in inventories

Besides investing in fixed capital, firms invest in stocks of raw materials and in stocks of finished goods waiting to be sold. This type of investment is called inventory investment or stock building. Although stock building accounts for less than 1% of GDP in a typical year, swings in inventories are often the single most important determinant of recessions. Firms hold stocks of raw materials and finished goods in order to smooth production and cope with swings in demand. But paradoxically, changes in stocks tend to trigger and exacerbate economic cycles. Stocks of unsold finished goods build up when firms over-anticipate demand for finished goods. Firms are then forced to cut production by more than the original fall in demand. The resultant de-stocking turns a slowdown into a recession. Swings in inventory investment accounted for about half of the reductions in GDP in the USA's past nine recessions. De-stocking has also made UK recessions worse.

Political business cycle theory

In democratic countries, general elections usually have to take place every 4 or 5 years. As an election approaches, the political party in power may 'buy votes' by engineering a pre-election boom. After the election, the party in power will normally then deflate aggregate demand to prevent the economy from over-heating. However, when the next general election approaches, demand is once again expanded.

Outside shocks affecting the economy

Outside shocks can be divided into *demand shocks*, which affect aggregate demand, and *supply shocks*, which impact on aggregate supply. In some cases, an outside shock hitting the economy may affect both aggregate demand and aggregate supply. Thus the outbreak of a war in the Middle East may affect demand by causing a sudden collapse in consumer and business confidence and also aggregate supply through its effects on the supply of crude oil.

*e*xaminer's voice
Unit 4 (and Unit 2) exam questions from June 2010 onward may reflect the fact that the UK economy entered recession in 2008. Earlier exam questions are unlikely to reflect this fact as they were set before the onset of recession.

Supply-side causes of recessions

Until quite recently, it was generally agreed that recessions are caused by a collapse of aggregate demand that shifts the *AD* curve to the left. However, as I explain in Box 14.2, it is now recognised that a fall in aggregate supply can also cause a recession.

AQA A2 Economics

Box 14.2 Can supply-side factors cause recessions?

Economic ups and downs have always been a fact of human life. Only in the past 50 years or so, however, have economists used technical mathematical models to explain macroeconomic fluctuations. The 2004 Nobel prize was awarded to an American, Edward Prescott, of Arizona State University, and a Norwegian, Finn Kydland, of Carnegie Mellon University. Their research has helped improve economists' understanding of booms and busts.

The two professors' work is based on a reconsideration of some of the ideas of John Maynard Keynes, whose *General Theory of Employment, Interest and Money* laid out themes that were heavily informed by the Great Depression of the 1930s. One was that economic recessions are caused in large part by a lack of aggregate demand, thanks perhaps to infectious bouts of mass pessimism.

Rather than chalking up booms and busts to the vagaries of demand, as Keynes had done, they asked whether changes in technology, or other supply shocks such as a rise in oil prices, might be as important. Might lulls in innovation be a prime cause of recessions, and surges a source of booms? This theory of 'real business cycles' remains controversial. Many economists doubt that a deep recession like that of the 1930s could be explained mostly by variations in the pace of innovation. Yet all economists now give more weight to things like technology, productivity and oil prices in explaining recessions.

The Economist, 14 October 2004

Follow-up questions

1 Using an *AD/AS* diagram, explain how changes in aggregate demand may cause a recession.

2 Using an *AD/AS* diagram, explain how supply-side factors may cause a recession.

Marxist theory

Marxist economists explain economic cycles as part of a restructuring process that increases the rate of profit in capitalist economies. Under normal production conditions, a fall in the rate of profit caused by competitive pressure threatens to bankrupt weaker capitalist firms. Marxists believe that recessions create conditions in which stronger firms either take over weaker competitors, or buy at rock-bottom prices the assets of rivals forced out of business. Either way, restructuring by takeover or bankruptcy means that the 'fittest' capitalist firms survive. (Note how this process is similar to the theory of economic natural selection explained in Chapter 8.) In Marxist analysis, business cycles are deemed necessary for the regeneration and survival of capitalism.

Marxists also argue that, in the upswing of a cycle, high employment generates wage inflation. Labour's share of output increases, but at the expense of capitalists' profits and future investment and output. The reduction in output in turn reduces demand for labour and employment, leading to lower wage inflation or wage deflation, which reduces labour's share of output. As the workers' wage share declines, profits and investment increase. This increases the demand for labour, which improves workers' bargaining power. Wages once again rise at the expense of profit, and the cycle repeats itself.

Multiplier/accelerator interaction

Keynesian economists have argued that economic cycles may be caused by the interaction of two dynamic processes: the multiplier and the accelerator. You came across the multiplier and the accelerator at AS, though I shall be examining the multiplier in more detail in the next chapter. In short, via an increase in investment, the multiplier process leads to an increase in national income. The change in income then leads, via the accelerator, to a further change in investment, and the process then repeats itself.

Stabilising the economic cycle

From the early 1950s to the 1970s, Keynesian-inspired governments attempted to manage the level of aggregate demand in the UK in order to stabilise the economic cycle. In the downswing, fiscal policy and monetary policy were used to increase or reflate aggregate demand. Conversely, in the upswing, governments contracted or deflated aggregate demand, before the economy overheated in the cycle's boom phase.

However, stable and milder business cycles may result more from the role of **automatic stabilisers** (which I explain in Chapter 19) than from demand-management policies. Demand management led to the stop–go problem. In successive economic cycles, periods of slow growth became longer, while periods of 'go' were quickly brought to a halt by the economy running into higher rates of inflation, or a balance of payments crisis.

Some economists argue that in the Keynesian era, government intervention actually destabilised business cycles, widening rather than reducing cyclical fluctuations and possibly reducing the economy's trend growth rate. There are three reasons why Keynesian demand-management policies may have done this. In the first place, the success of demand management depends on correct timing. By responding to changes in unemployment rather than to changes in output or GDP, governments may have got their timing wrong. (Changes in employment and unemployment often occur several months after changes in output.) Instead of expanding demand when the growth of output slowed, governments intervened too late, after output had already begun to recover. Likewise, governments contracted demand after the peak of the business cycle, thus worsening the downturn. Second, the timing of intervention may have resulted from the government's need to win votes rather than to manage the economy properly. Third, by causing the public sector to grow in size, expansionary fiscal policies may have crowded out the private sector, thereby reducing the economy's trend growth rate.

In the monetarist era in the early 1980s, stabilising the business cycle through the use of demand management policies went out of fashion. But since the early 1990s, managing aggregate demand has been back in fashion. Monetary policy but not fiscal policy was used for this purpose up until the onset of recession in 2008. However, this changed as soon as recession set in, and at the time of writing (April 2009), fiscal policy and the use of a huge budget deficit has supplemented monetary policy as an anti-recessionary weapon.

Using national income statistics to measure welfare and standards of living

examiner's voice

At AS, you learnt about the meaning and measurement of national income, and other measures of national output such as GNP and GDP. Make sure you revise these concepts thoroughly.

Because GNP, GDP and other national income statistics are the main source of data on what has happened and what is happening in the economy, they are often used as indicators of economic growth, economic and social welfare, and changing living standards, and for comparison with other countries.

To see how living standards change over time, we must look at real per capita GNP figures (real GNP divided by the number of people living in the country). Rising real GNP per capita gives a general indication that living standards are rising, but it may conceal great and sometimes growing disparities in income *distribution* (see Box 14.3). This is especially significant in developing countries, where the income distribution is typically extremely unequal and where only a small fraction of the population may benefit materially from economic growth.

Besides the problem of income distribution, a number of other problems surface when using national income statistics to measure living standards.

The non-monetised economy

National income statistics underestimate the true level of economic activity because the non-monetised economy is under-represented. In the UK, housework and 'do-it-yourself' home improvement take place without money incomes being generated. When measuring national income, a decision has to be made on whether to estimate or to ignore the value of this production. The UK accounts can be criticised for estimating the value of some but not all of the non-monetised economy.

Imputed rents are estimated for the housing services delivered to owner-occupiers by the houses they live in, based on an estimate of the rent that would be paid if the house-owners were tenants of the same properties. But housekeeping allowances paid within households are not estimated, implying that housework — most of which is undertaken by women — is unproductive. Judgments such as these lead to the anomaly that national income appears to fall when a man marries his housekeeper or paints his own house, having previously employed a decorator.

The hidden economy

Economic activity undertaken illegally in the hidden economy may be omitted. The hidden economy (which is also known as the informal economy, the underground economy and the black economy) refers to all the economic transactions conducted in cash that are not recorded in the national income figures because of tax evasion. It is impossible to make a completely accurate estimate of the size of the hidden economy, but it can be approximated by the gap between the GNP total obtained by the income and expenditure methods of measurement. The hidden economy probably equals about 10% of the UK's measured GNP, while countries such as Greece, Spain and Portugal have hidden economies equal to 20% of GNP.

The quality of goods and services

Over time, the quality of goods changes for better or worse, presenting a particularly difficult problem in the construction and interpretation of national income figures. This is also true of services. When services such as public transport and healthcare deteriorate, GNP may rise even though welfare and real living standards decline.

Negative externalities

National income statistics overestimate living standards because of the effects of negative externalities such as pollution and congestion, and of activities such as crime. What is, in effect, a welfare loss may be shown as an increase in national output, falsely indicating an apparent welfare gain. For example, the stresses and strains of producing an ever-higher national output lead to a loss of leisure time and people become ill more often. Loss of leisure and poorer health cause welfare to fall. However in the national accounts, these show up as extra production and as extra consumption of healthcare, both of which imply a welfare gain. Traffic congestion increases the cost of motoring, and hence the value of national income. Motorists would prefer uncongested roads and less spending on petrol and vehicle wear and tear.

Likewise, installing *regrettables* such as burglar alarms raises national income, but most people would prefer a crime-free environment and no burglar alarms. Along with the effects of divorce and other elements of social breakdown, national income statistics treat the effect of crime on economic activity as a welfare gain.

Comparing national income between countries

Comparisons of national income per head between countries are misleading if the relative importance of the non-monetised economy differs significantly. There are also differences in the degree of statistical sophistication in data collection, particularly between developed and developing countries, and a lack of international uniformity in methods of classifying and categorising the national accounts.

There are further problems in making comparisons when different commodities are consumed. Expenditure on fuel, clothing and building materials for cold winters is usually greater in developed countries than in much warmer developing economies. However, greater expenditure on these goods may not indicate higher real incomes and living standards.

Standards of living and the quality of life

For the national economy, the average standard of living can be defined as consumption per head of population of purchased goods and services. But because it focuses solely on material goods and services bought largely in the shops, this definition is really too narrow. More widely defined, the standard of living includes quality of life factors and general economic welfare, as well as narrow GNP-related consumption. A wider definition of living standards might include the three elements shown in the following equation:

$$
\begin{array}{l}
\text{standard} \\
\text{of living}
\end{array}
=
\begin{array}{l}
\text{economic} \\
\text{welfare derived} \\
\text{from goods and} \\
\text{services} \\
\text{purchased in the} \\
\text{market economy}
\end{array}
+
\begin{array}{l}
\text{economic welfare} \\
\text{derived from} \\
\text{public goods and} \\
\text{merit goods} \\
\text{collectively} \\
\text{provided by the} \\
\text{state}
\end{array}
+
\begin{array}{l}
\text{economic welfare} \\
\text{derived from quality of} \\
\text{life factors, including} \\
\text{external benefits and} \\
\text{intangibles minus} \\
\text{external costs and} \\
\text{intangibles}
\end{array}
$$

If used carefully, national income figures can provide a reasonable estimate of economic welfare derived from the first two of these three elements, both of which relate to the direct consumption of material goods and services. However, national income figures fail to estimate how externalities and other quality of life factors affect economic welfare and living standards.

Education can be used as a measure of standard of living

Additionally, national income fails to reflect the effect of resource depletion and environmental degradation resulting from producing *current* income on humankind's ability to produce *future* income. This means that national income and GDP do not address the issue of sustainability.

Box 14.3 What's wrong with GNP as a measure of economic welfare?

The gross national product includes air pollution and advertising for cigarettes, and ambulances to clear our highways of carnage. It counts special locks for our doors, and jails for the people who break them. GNP includes the destruction of the redwoods and the death of Lake Superior. It grows with the production of napalm and missiles and nuclear warheads... And if GNP includes all this, there is much that it does not comprehend. It does not allow for the health of our families, the quality of their education, or the joy of their play. It is indifferent to the decency of our factories and the safety of our streets alike. It does not include the beauty of our poetry or the strength of our marriages, or the intelligence of our public debate or the integrity of our public officials... GNP measures neither our wit nor our courage, neither our wisdom nor our learning, neither our compassion nor our devotion to our country. It measures everything, in short, except that which makes life worthwhile; and it can tell us everything about America — except whether we are proud to be Americans.

US Senator Robert Kennedy, 1967

Follow-up question
Compare alternative measures of economic welfare.

Alternative measures of economic welfare

The environmental pressure group Friends of the Earth argues that measures of national income such as GDP were never intended to be indicators of progress or welfare. Indeed, over 70 years ago, Simon Kuznets, the inventor of the GDP concept, argued that 'The welfare of a nation can scarcely be inferred from a measurement of national income'. Not surprisingly, therefore, other measures that are less dependent on raw GNP or GDP are increasingly used to place a value on economic and social progress.

One of the earliest of these was the **Measure of Economic Welfare (MEW)**, developed by Nordhaus and Tobin in 1972. The MEW showed that welfare in the USA grew, but at a slower rate than GDP, between 1950 and 1965. More recent attempts to adjust conventional national income figures include the **United Nations Human Development Index (HDI)**, the **Index of Sustainable Economic Welfare (ISEW)** and the **Genuine Progress Indicator**.

The United Nations Human Development Index (HDI)

The HDI is the average of three indicators:
➤ standard of living, measured by real GNP per capita, valued at US$ purchasing power parity
➤ life expectancy at birth, in years
➤ educational attainment, as measured by a weighted average of adult literacy and enrolment ratio in schools and colleges

The maximum value of the HDI is one (or unity). The closer a country's HDI is to one, then the greater its human development, measured in terms of the three indicators specified in the Index.

The HDI is by no means a perfect index of economic welfare and human development, since it ignores the distribution of income and expenditure on healthcare.

In 2009, the most recent statistics available for the HDI were for 2006. Out of the 179 countries in the Index, Iceland, Norway, Canada, Australia and Ireland were ranked in the top five (though this was well before the financial crash of 2007–08, which particularly hit the Iceland economy). By contrast the sub-Saharan African countries of Mozambique, Liberia, the Democratic Republic of Congo, and Sierra Leone languished in the bottom five places.

The Index of Sustainable Economic Welfare (ISEW)

The ISEW attempts to capture the effects of externalities and other intangibles upon human happiness and welfare. According to Friends of the Earth, the Index of Sustainable Economic Welfare is significantly better than GDP for looking at how sustainable welfare changes over time. Although starting from the method of measuring consumer expenditure used in the construction of GDP, the ISEW adjusts GDP figures to account for a number of aspects of economic life that GDP ignores. These include pollution, noise, commuting costs, capital growth, health and education spending, urbanisation, and the loss of natural resources.

The Genuine Progress Indicator (GPI)

GPI attempts to measure whether a country's growth (increased production of goods and expanding services) has actually resulted in the improvement in the economic welfare of the inhabitants of a country. GPI is claimed to be a more accurate measure of economic progress as it distinguishes between 'good' or 'worthwhile' growth and 'bad' or 'uneconomic' growth. The latter is economic growth that reflects or creates a decline in the quality of life.

Is economic growth sustainable?

Sustainable growth meets the needs of people living today without compromising the ability of future generations to meet their own needs. Environmentalists, ecologists and some economists predict that the pursuit of ever-growing GNP is unsustainable, arguing that growth will eventually lead to the depletion of non-renewable resources. However, many, although certainly not all, economists believe this is too simplistic. They question the environmentalists' assumptions of an ever-faster rate of resource usage accompanied by an ever-faster rate of decline of resource reserves.

You learnt at AS that prices perform three main functions in a market economy: signalling, creating incentives and allocating scarce resources between competing uses. Other things being equal, an increase in the rate of resource usage causes resource prices to rise. In their turn, rising resource prices create incentives for consumers and producers to alter economic behaviour — literally, to economise. Consumers buy less of goods and services whose relative prices are rising. Producers, meanwhile, respond to the changing relative prices of their inputs or factors of production. First they do this by altering methods of production. Second, producers explore the earth's crust for new supplies of minerals and fossil fuels, which would be uneconomic to search for and extract at a lower resource price.

Nevertheless, most economists have taken on board the environmentalists' belief that governments should aim for sustainable economic growth and development. R. K. Turner has defined an optimal sustainable growth policy as one that maintains 'an acceptable rate of growth in per capita incomes without depleting the national capital asset stock or the natural environment asset stock'.

The benefits and costs of economic growth

For many people and most economists, achieving a satisfactory and sustained rate of economic growth is arguably the most important of all the macroeconomic objectives that governments wish to achieve. Without growth, other objectives, particularly full employment and competitive export industries, may be impossible to attain. And when growth becomes negative, as in the recession that started in the UK in 2008, people become all too aware of the rapid disappearance of the fruits of growth. For most people, standards of living fall, with the most unfortunate losing their jobs as the industries that used to employ them collapse or slim down.

However, as I hinted at in earlier parts of the chapter, including the last section, in the long run, *sustained* economic growth may not be *sustainable*. With countries in the developing world, particularly the 'emerging market' countries, recently growing at a far faster rate than richer developed economies, maintaining global growth rates may not be sustainable. The rapid using-up of finite resources and the pollution and global warming that spin-off from economic growth will result increasingly in desertification, water shortages, declining crop yields, famines and wars.

Some economists argue an opposite effect, namely that one of the benefits of growth, at least as far as advanced developed countries are concerned, is the development of environmentally-friendly technologies. These reduce the ratio of energy consumption to GDP. Nevertheless, rich developed economies, especially the USA, continue to be, at least for the time being, the world's biggest consumers of energy and the biggest polluters.

Benefits of economic growth
➤ Economic growth increases standards of living and people's welfare.
➤ Growth leads to more civilised communities who take action to improve the environment.
➤ Growth provides new more environmentally-friendly technologies.
➤ Economic growth has increased the length of people's lives and has provided the means to reduce disease.
➤ Economic growth provides a route out of poverty for much of the world's population.
➤ Economic growth produces a 'fiscal dividend', namely the tax revenues that growth generates. Tax revenues can be used to correct market failures, to provide infrastructure, thereby increasing the economic welfare of the whole community.
➤ For a particular country, economic growth can generate a 'virtuous circle' of greater business confidence, increased investment in state-of-the-art technology, greater international competitiveness, higher profits, even more growth, and so on.

Costs of economic growth
➤ Economic growth uses up finite resources such as oil and minerals that cannot be replaced.
➤ Economic growth leads to pollution and other forms of environmental degradation, with the earth eventually reaching a tipping point, beyond which it cannot recover.
➤ Growth can destroy local cultures and communities and widen inequalities in the distribution of income and wealth.
➤ Economic growth leads to urbanisation and the spread of huge cities, which swallow up good agricultural land.
➤ In its early phases, economic growth leads to a rapid growth in population, more mouths to feed, and more people actually poor.
➤ Growth produces losers as well as winners. Countries suffering low growth may enter a vicious circle of declining business confidence, low profits, low investment, a lack of international competitiveness, even lower profits, zero growth, and so on.

Summary

➤ Economic growth is the increase, over time, of the potential level of output the economy can produce.

➤ Short-run economic growth makes use of spare capacity and labour in the economy.

➤ Short-run economic growth is also known as economic recovery.

➤ Long-run economic growth shifts the economy's production possibility frontier outward.

➤ Economic growth should not be confused with economic development.

➤ Technical progress, investment and increased labour productivity are important causes of economic growth.

➤ Fluctuations in economic activity, known as the economic cycle, accompany short-run economic growth.

➤ Economic cycles are usually caused by fluctuations in aggregate demand, though supply-side factors can also lead to cycles.

➤ Changes in national income or GDP can be used to measure changes in living standards.

➤ Other measures, such as the United Nations Human Development Index (HDI) provide better measures.

➤ Sustainable economic growth should not be confused with sustained economic growth.

➤ There are a number of benefits and costs of economic growth.

Questions

1 Define economic growth.

2 Illustrate short-term and long-term economic growth on a *PPF* diagram.

3 State three ways in which economic activity fluctuates.

4 Briefly explain three possible causes of economic cycles.

5 What is a recession?

6 Explain how the multiplier and the accelerator affect economic cycles.

7 Outline the determinants of long-term economic growth.

8 Outline two problems that occur when using national income or GDP to measure living standards.

9 Distinguish between narrow and broad definitions of standards of living.

10 How is the United Nations Human Development Index (HDI) constructed?

11 What are the differences between the Index of Sustainable Economic Welfare (ISEW) and GDP as measures of economic welfare?

12 What is meant by sustainable economic growth?

13 State two benefits and two costs of economic growth.

Chapter *15*

Developing the aggregate demand and aggregate supply macroeconomic model

In this chapter, I start by reminding you of the meaning of aggregate demand (AD) and aggregate supply (AS) and by drawing the AD and AS curves that illustrate these important macroeconomic concepts.

In the last 30 years, the AD/AS model has become the preferred theoretical framework that many economists use for investigating macroeconomic issues. The model is particularly useful for analysing the effect of an increase in aggregate demand upon the economy. This addresses a key issue: will expansionary fiscal policy and/or monetary policy increase real output and jobs (i.e. will it be reflationary), or will the price level increase instead (i.e. will it be inflationary)? As this chapter explains, the answer to this key macroeconomic question depends on the shape of the AS curve, both in the short run and long run.

Learning outcomes

This chapter will:
- ➤ provide a brief summary and reminder of the main features of the *AD/AS* model
- ➤ explain the nature of aggregate demand and short-run aggregate supply
- ➤ remind you of the meaning of macroeconomic equilibrium
- ➤ distinguish between short-run and long-run aggregate supply
- ➤ use an *AD/AS* diagram to illustrate output gaps
- ➤ revisit the Keynesian long-run aggregate supply curve
- ➤ develop your AS knowledge of the multiplier theory

What you should already know

At A2, you don't really need to know much more about aggregate demand and aggregate supply than you learnt a year ago at AS. To prepare for the Unit 4 data-response and essay questions, you must practise your skills in shifting *AD* curves to illustrate the effects of changes in any of the components of aggregate demand. You must also identify supply-side factors that influence the positions of the *SRAS* and *LRAS* curves, and understand how monetary and fiscal policy affect aggregate demand and supply.

The meaning of aggregate demand

Aggregate demand must not be confused with the national income concept of national expenditure. Aggregate demand is the total *planned* spending on the goods and services produced *within* the economy in a particular time period, for example a year. Aggregate demand measures *planned* spending, whereas national expenditure measures realised or actual spending, which has already taken place.

> **Key term**
>
> **Aggregate demand** is total planned spending on the goods and services produced within the economy in a particular time period.

Four sources of spending are included in aggregate demand; each originating in a different sector of the economy: households, firms, the government sector and the overseas sector. These are shown in the following equation:

> **examiner's voice**
>
> At A2, as at AS, exam questions seldom instruct you to draw an *AD/AS* diagram, or to apply *AD/AS* analysis. Nevertheless, these are the key skills needed for answering many data-response and essay questions in the Unit 4 exam.

$$\text{aggregate demand} = \text{consumption} + \text{investment} + \text{government spending} + \text{exports (net of imports) or:}$$

$$AD = C + I + G + (X - M)$$

where *C*, *I*, *G*, *X* and *M* are the symbols used respectively for planned consumption, investment, government spending, exports and imports.

> **examiner's voice**
>
> Make sure you understand and can apply the aggregate demand equation:
>
> $$AD = C + I + G + (X - M)$$
>
> It is useful in a number of different contexts, such as monetary and fiscal policy. You may be tested synoptically on your understanding of the components of aggregate demand, consumption, investment and exports.

The London Olympic stadium is an example of a government spending project

Key **term**

Short-run aggregate supply shows the quantities of real output businesses plan to produce and sell at different price levels, assuming there is spare capacity in the economy.

The *AD* curve

The aggregate demand curve is illustrated along with a **short-run aggregate supply** (*SRAS*) curve in Figure 15.1. This diagram shows the total quantities of real output that all economic agents plan to purchase at different price levels within the economy, when all the factors influencing aggregate demand other than the price level are held constant. If any of the determinants of aggregate demand change (apart from the price level), the *AD* curve shifts to the right

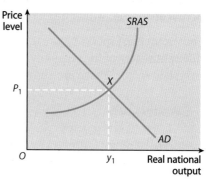

Figure 15.1 *A downward-sloping* AD *curve and an upward-sloping* SRAS *curve*

*e*xaminer's voice

The *slope* of the *AD* curve tells us what happens to aggregate demand when the price level changes. Don't make the mistake of asserting that a change in the price level *shifts* the *AD* curve.

or to the left, depending on whether there has been an increase or a decrease in aggregate demand. For example, an increase in consumer or business confidence shifts the *AD* curve to the right, via the effect on consumption or investment. An increase in net export demand (*X* – *M*) has a similar effect, as does expansionary monetary policy and expansionary fiscal policy. By contrast, an increase in imports,

contractionary monetary or fiscal policy, or a collapse in consumer or business confidence, shift the *AD* curve to the left.

Explaining the shape of the aggregate demand curve

The *AD* curve slopes downward to the right, showing that as the price level falls, aggregate demand expands. A number of factors explain the *slope* of the *AD* curve, as distinct from a *shift* of the curve.

➤ One explanation lies in a **wealth effect** or **real balance effect**. Assuming a given nominal stock of money in the economy, a decrease in the price level increases peoples' *real* money balances i.e. the same amount of money buys more goods and services. An increase in real money balances makes people wealthier because money is a part of peoples' wealth.

➤ The increase in real money balances I have just described also means that the real money supply has increased, relative to the demand to hold real money balances. Basic supply and demand analysis tells us that when the supply of *any* commodity increases relative to demand for the commodity, its price tends to fall. Now, the *rate of interest* is the price of money. The increase in the supply of real money balances relative to demand reduces real interest rates, which in turn leads to higher levels of consumption and investment.

➤ A third factor relates to exports and imports. When the domestic price level falls (and assuming the exchange rate remains unchanged), demand increases for the country's exports. At the same time, consumers buy domestically produced goods instead of imports. Aggregate demand thus increases as the price level falls.

The *SRAS* curve

Just as the *AD* curve shows the total quantities of real output that economic agents plan to purchase at different levels of domestic prices, so the *SRAS* curve shows the quantities of **real output** that businesses plan to produce and sell at different price levels.

Before explaining the shape of the *SRAS* curve, I shall first explain the factors determining the *position* of the curve. If one of these factors changes, the *SRAS* curve shifts to the right or left to a new position. The factors are indeed virtually the same as those fixing the position of a market supply curve in a particular microeconomic market. The main determinants of the position of the *SRAS* curve are:

➤ costs of production
➤ taxes firms have to pay
➤ technology
➤ productivity
➤ attitudes
➤ enterprise
➤ factor mobility
➤ economic incentives facing workers and firms
➤ the institutional structure of the economy

Explaining the shape of the short-run aggregate supply curve

Whereas the *AD* curve is almost always drawn downward sloping, different assumptions about the nature of aggregate supply lead to different shapes and slopes of the *AS* curve. A short-run aggregate supply (*SRAS*) curve is illustrated in Figure 15.2.

The shape of the upward-sloping *AS* curve is explained by two assumptions of microeconomic theory of the firm (refer to Chapter 3), which are:

> all firms aim to maximise profits
> in the short run, the law of diminishing returns or diminishing marginal productivity operates

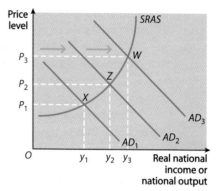

Figure 15.2 *An upward-sloping SRAS curve*

Following an increase in aggregate demand from AD_1 to AD_2 in Figure 15.2, which disturbs an initial macroeconomic equilibrium at point *X*, the price level rises to P_2 to create conditions in which profit-maximising firms are happy to supply more output.

If the prices firms could charge did not rise, it would not be profitable for firms to increase supply. The explanation for this is as follows. First, I assume that firms are already producing the profit-maximising level of output, which occurs when $MR = MC$. If firms increase output beyond this point, marginal costs rise, which leads to falling profit. This is because the marginal product of the workers needed to produce the extra output falls, which increases marginal costs. For profit-maximising firms to produce more output in the face of rising marginal costs, marginal revenues must also rise. This requires higher prices. Without a higher price level, profit-maximising firms will not voluntarily increase the supply of output.

It is important to emphasise that, because each short-run *AS* curve is drawn under the assumption that the money wage rate remains unchanged, there is a different short-run *AS* curve for each and every money wage rate. When the money wage rate rises, production costs increase and firms reduce the quantity of output they are willing to supply at the current price level. As a result, the short-run *AS* curve shifts to the left to a new position. Conversely, a fall in the money wage rate shifts the *AS* curve to the right.

Macroeconomic equilibrium

Macroeconomic equilibrium occurs when the aggregate demand for real output equals the aggregate supply of real output i.e. where:

$$AD = AS$$

Key term

Macroeconomic equilibrium occurs when $AD = AS$ and when injections into the circular flow of income equal leakages from the flow.

When $AD = AS$, households, firms, the government and the overseas sector plan to spend in real terms within the economy an amount exactly equal to the level of real output that firms are willing to produce. Referring back to Figure 15.1, macro-economic equilibrium occurs at point X, where the AD curve intersects the AS curve. The equilibrium level of real output is y_1, and the equilibrium price level is P_1.

> ### examiner's voice
> You can also explain macroeconomic equilibrium by using a circular flow diagram. Equilibrium occurs when $S + T + M = I + G + X$. Do not, however, confuse *macroeconomic* equilibrium for the *whole* economy with *microeconomic* equilibrium in a market *within* the economy.

Long-run aggregate supply

The aggregate supply curve I have considered so far in this chapter is a short-run AS curve. I shall now extend the analysis to explain the economy's **long-run aggregate supply** ($LRAS$) curve. Economists generally believe that the $LRAS$ curve is vertical, though there is an exception known as the **Keynesian $LRAS$ curve**. A vertical $LRAS$ curve, such as the curve illustrated in Figure 15.3, means that in the long run a rightward shift of aggregate demand increases the price level, but *not* real output.

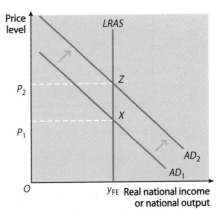

Figure 15.3 *A vertical long-run aggregate supply (LRAS) curve*

The explanation for the vertical $LRAS$ curve is quite simple. The $LRAS$ curve in Figure 15.3 is located at the full-employment level of real output y_{FE}, with production taking place on the economy's production possibility frontier. Firms cannot produce more output to meet the increase in aggregate demand depicted by the shift of the AD curve from AD_1 to AD_2. In this situation, the excess demand for real output is met by an increase in the price level, with the point of macroeconomic equilibrium moving from point X to point Z.

Supply and demand in a busy supermarket

> ### Key term
> **Long-run aggregate supply** is the real output that can be supplied when the economy is on its production possibility frontier and producing at full potential.

Long-run economic growth and a shift of the *LRAS* curve

At this point you should go back to Chapter 14 and reread the section at the beginning of the chapter on the meaning of economic growth. There you will see two diagrams, Figures 14.1 and 14.2, which show, respectively, the economy's production possibility frontier shifting outward, and the *LRAS* curve shifting to the right. Figure 15.4 shows similar diagrams.

(a) An outward movement of the economy's production possibility frontier

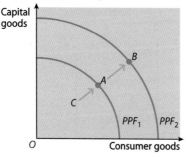

(b) A rightward shift of the *LRAS* curve

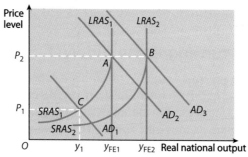

Figure 15.4 *Economic growth, the economy's production possibility frontier and the* LRAS *curve*

Suppose the economy is initially at point *C* in both panels of the diagram, producing output y_1. In this situation, an increase in aggregate demand from AD_1 to AD_2 in panel (b) takes up the slack in the economy, and short-run economic growth takes place. Output increases from y_1 to y_{FE1} in panel (b) of the diagram, and the economy moves from point *C* to point *A* in both panels. However, as I have explained, for firms to produce the extra output the price level must rise.

Once at point *A*, the economy is on production possibility frontier PPF_1, and also producing on long-run aggregate supply curve $LRAS_1$. The level of output is now y_{FE1}. Because there is no spare capacity, for output to increase on a permanent basis long-run economic growth must take place. Long-run growth shifts the economy's production possibility frontier outward from PPF_1 to PPF_2, and the *LRAS* curve rightward from $LRAS_1$ to $LRAS_2$. The economy now produces at point *B* rather than point *A* in both panels of the diagram. Note that panel (b) shows aggregate demand increasing from AD_2 to AD_3. In this situation aggregate demand increases just sufficiently to *absorb* the increase in aggregate supply without the price level rising or falling. Although output has increased to y_{FE2}, the price level has remained at P_2. If aggregate demand were to remain at AD_2, or if the *AD* curve were to shift by either more or less than is shown in panel (b), the price level would change.

The economy's natural level of output and long-run aggregate supply

For free-market, monetarist and supply-side economists, the full employment level of real output y_{FE} is also the economy's natural level of output (y_N) toward which market forces and a flexible price mechanism eventually adjust. The **natural level of output** is the

Key *term*

The **natural level of output** is the long-run equilibrium level of potential output.

long-run equilibrium level of *potential* output associated with the economy's natural levels of employment and unemployment in the economy's aggregate labour market. For free-market economists the vertical *LRAS* curve carries the message that the short-run expansionary effect on output and employment of increasing aggregate demand may be negated in the long run by the way the supply side of the economy responds to the demand stimulus.

Revisiting output gaps

You first came across **output gaps** at AS when learning, in the context of the economic cycle, how the economy's actual growth rate departs from the trend growth rate. Negative and positive output gaps are illustrated in Figure 14.4 of Chapter 14. Before proceeding any further, go back to this diagram and make sure you understand the meaning of an output gap.

Positive output gaps occur when the economy temporarily produces at a point outside its current production possibility frontier. However, because this represents overuse of capacity, such a point cannot be sustained for long. In the context of the *AD/AS* model, this means that the economy temporarily produces a level of output to the right of the *LRAS* curve, and above the full-employment level of output, for example at point *W* in Figure 15.5. Note that I have drawn the diagram so that the *SRAS* curve extends to the right of the full-employment level of output y_{FE}, without becoming vertical at point *X*. For a short period, output can rise above y_{FE} to y_1, but eventually output falls back to the full-employment level.

>
> **Key term**
>
> An **output gap** is the difference between actual output and the trend growth level of output.

> ***e*xaminer's voice**
>
> Don't confuse an *output* gap with a *productivity* gap, which is the gap between the productivity levels of two countries.

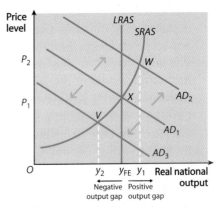

Figure 15.5 *Positive and negative output gaps and the* LRAS *curve*

By contrast, the economy suffers a **negative output gap** whenever the level of output is to the left of the *LRAS* curve and *below* the full employment level of output y_{FE}. A negative output gap occurs at point *V* in Figure 15.5, with the short-run macroeconomic equilibrium level of output at y_2.

> **Key terms**
>
> A **negative output gap** is the difference between actual output and the trend growth level of output when actual output is below trend output.
>
> A **positive output gap** is the difference between actual output and the trend growth level of output when actual output is above trend output.

Revisiting the Keynesian long-run aggregate supply curve

The vertical *LRAS* curve I have described is often called the *free market* or *supply-side LRAS* curve. This label reflects the view commonly expressed by free-market economists that, provided markets function competitively and efficiently, the economy always operates at or close to full capacity. As I explained earlier, in the short-run real output is influenced by the average price level, but in the long-run aggregate supply is determined by maximum production capacity.

Most modern Keynesians (who are often called **New Keynesians**) agree that the *LRAS* curve is vertical. However in the past some Keynesians were associated with the rather different *LRAS* curve illustrated in Figure 15.6. This curve is derived from Keynes's own views on how the economy operates.

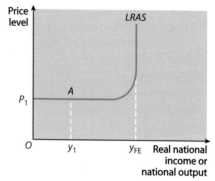

Figure 15.6 *The Keynesian LRAS curve*

The 'Keynesian' *LRAS* curve is based on Keynes's explanation of the Great Depression in the UK and US economies in the 1930s. Keynes argued that a depressed economy can settle into an under-full employment equilibrium, shown for example by point A on the horizontal section of the *LRAS* curve in Figure 15.6. At point A, the level of real national output is y_1. Keynes argued that without purposeful intervention by the government, an economy could display more or less permanent demand-deficiency. Market forces would fail to adjust automatically and achieve full employment. But if the government is able to shift the *AD* to the right along the horizontal section of the *LRAS* curve (mainly through expansionary fiscal policy), the existence of huge amounts of spare capacity would lead, in Keynes's view, to a growth in real output (and employment), without an increase in the price level.

The vertical long-run aggregate supply curve and economic policy

As I have mentioned, the vertical *LRAS* curve favoured by free-market and supply-side economists is located at the natural or equilibrium level of real output, which is the level of output consistent with the natural rate of unemployment in the labour market. Because output and employment are assumed to be at their natural or equilibrium levels, an increase of aggregate demand causes the price level to rise, but with no long-term effect upon the levels of real output and employment.

Free-market and supply-side economists therefore conclude that it is generally irresponsible for governments to use expansionary fiscal or monetary policies to try to increase national output and employment *above* their natural rates and levels.

While such policies may succeed in the short run, though at the expense of inflation, they are doomed eventually to fail. In the long run, output and employment fall back to their equilibrium or natural rates and levels, which are determined by the economy's production potential or ability to supply. Thus, instead of increasing aggregate demand to reduce unemployment *below* its natural rate, supply-side economists believe that the responsible approach is for the government to use microeconomic supply-side policies to reduce the natural rate itself.

Market-orientated supply-side policies aim to improve incentives and the performance of individual economic agents and markets. They shift the economy's production possibility frontier outward and the *LRAS* curve rightward, thereby increasing the natural levels of output and employment in the economy.

In summary, in the *extreme* supply-side or free-market view, providing output, employment and unemployment are at their natural levels, there is no case for demand management. Instead, macroeconomic policy should be subordinated to the needs of a supply-side orientated microeconomic policy aimed at increasing the economy's production potential. Policy should focus on shifting the *LRAS* curve rightward.

However, more *moderate* free-market economists do these days accept that demand can legitimately be increased if the economy is suffering recession and a negative output gap. In this situation, with output and employment below their natural levels and unemployment above its natural level, there is a case for increasing aggregate demand. Keynesians take this view further. The recession of 2008 led to many governments in the UK, the USA and elsewhere, to return to Keynesian economics by accepting the case for a fiscal stimulus and for 'spending economies out of recession'. However, France and Germany were less enthusiastic about this.

Aggregate demand and the national income multiplier

You first came across the **national income multiplier** when studying Unit 2 at AS, but at A2 it is useful to understand the multiplier process in more depth. A **multiplier** exists whenever a change in one variable induces or causes multiple and successive stages of change in a second variable. Each succeeding stage of change is usually smaller than the previous one so that the total change induced in the multiplier process comes effectively to an end when further stages of change approach zero. We can calculate the value of a multiplier by dividing the total change induced in the second variable by the size of the initial change in the first variable. For example, a multiplier of eight tells us that an increase in the first variable will cause successive stages of change in the second variable, which are eight times greater in total than the initial triggering change.

 Key *term*

The **national income multiplier** measures the relationship between a change in any of the components of aggregate demand and the resulting change in the equilibrium level of national income.

In macroeconomic theory, the national income multiplier (or Keynesian multiplier) measures the relationship between a change in aggregate demand in the economy and the resulting change in the equilibrium level of national income. The size of the national income multiplier is significant for fiscal policy.

Nested within the national income multiplier are a number of specific multipliers, each related to the particular component of aggregate demand that initially changes. These are the consumption multiplier, the investment multiplier, the government spending multiplier, and the export multiplier. There are also *negative* multipliers for changes in taxation and imports. Taken together, the government spending and tax multipliers are fiscal policy multipliers. Likewise, the export and import multipliers are foreign trade multipliers.

Fiscal policy and the multiplier

During the Keynesian era, fiscal policy rather than monetary policy was used primarily to manage the level of aggregate demand in the economy. From the 1950s to around 1979, governments used fiscal policy to increase or decrease aggregate demand to reduce demand-deficient unemployment (in a recession) and demand-pull inflation (in a boom). Using fiscal policy like this to fine-tune aggregate demand and stabilise the economic cycle often brought about a multiplier effect.

The government spending multiplier

As Figure 15.7 below illustrates, an increase in government spending (or in any component of aggregate demand) causes multiple successive changes in national income that are greater in total than the initial increase in government spending.

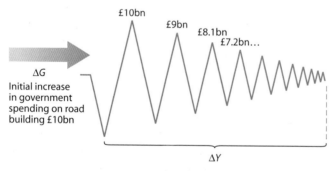

Figure 15.7
The government
spending multiplier

£10bn £9bn £8.1bn £7.2bn...

ΔG
Initial increase in government spending on road building £10bn

ΔY
Successive stages of increase in national income £100bn

---

examiner's voice

The multiplier is not mentioned explicitly in the Unit 4 specification at A2, but the synoptic nature of the specification means that good exam answers should make use of and apply the multiplier concept.

Key term

The **government spending multiplier** measures the relationship between a change in government spending and the resulting change in the equilibrium level of national income.

The multiplier process, which is essentially dynamic, taking place over time, resembles ripples spreading over a pond after a stone has been thrown in the water. However the ripples in a pond last only a few seconds, whereas the ripples spreading through the economy following a change in aggregate demand can last for months and even years. Figure 15.7 illustrates the ripple effect. The diagram, which shows the government spending multiplier, can easily be adapted to illustrate the investment multiplier or any other national income multiplier.

In order to explain the government spending multiplier, I shall assume there is demand-deficient unemployment in the economy, and that the levels of taxation and imports do not change when aggregate demand increases. To reduce demand-deficient unemployment, the government decides to spend an extra £10 billion on road building.

> In the first stage of the multiplier process, £10 billion is received as income by building workers who, like everybody in the economy, spend ninety pence of every pound of income on consumption. (I am also assuming the marginal propensity to consume (*MPC*) is 0.9 throughout the economy, which means that people plan to consume 90 pence out of an increase of income of £1.00, and save 10 pence.)
> At the second stage of the multiplier process, £9 billion of the £10 billion income is spent on consumer goods and services, with the remaining £1 billion leaking into unspent savings.
> At the next and third stage, consumer good sector employees spend £8.1 billion, or 0.9 of the £9 billion received at the second stage of income generation.
> Further stages of income generation then occur, with each successive stage being 0.9 of the previous stage. Each stage is smaller than the preceding stage due to the fact that part of income leaks into savings.

Assuming that nothing else changes in the time taken for the process to work through the economy, the eventual increase in income ΔY resulting from the initial injection of government spending is the sum of all the stages of income generation. ΔY is larger than ΔG, which triggered the initial growth in national income.

The multiplier formula

In the numerical example above, consumption is the only income-related component of aggregate demand (with saving thus being the only income-induced leakage of demand from the circular flow of income). In this case, the size of the multiplier depends on the values of the marginal propensities to consume and save. Given this assumption, the formula for the multiplier is:

$$k = \frac{1}{1 - c}$$

where c is the marginal propensity to consume (*MPC*), or:

$$k = \frac{1}{s}$$

where s is the marginal propensity to save (*MPS*).

The formula reflects the fact that at each succeeding stage of the dynamic multiplier process, a fraction of income, determined by the *MPS*, leaks into saving and is not available for consumption at the next stage of income generation. The larger the *MPC* (and the smaller the *MPS*), the larger is the value of the multiplier.

examiner's voice

At A2 as at AS, you are not required to know multiplier formulas, or to do multiplier calculations. However, knowledge of why the size of the government spending multiplier is likely to be small may be necessary.

In the example I have used, the size of the multiplier is:

$$k = \frac{1}{1 - 0.9} = 10$$

Using the equation:

$$\Delta Y = k\,(\Delta G)$$

where *k* is the symbol for the multiplier, we arrive at:

$$\Delta Y = 10 \times \pounds 10 \text{ bn}$$

which tells us that the increase in government spending causes equilibrium national income to increase by £100 bn.

The multiplier in the UK economy

However, in the case of the UK economy, the size of the multiplier is considerably less than ten. The earlier formula for the multiplier treated saving as the only income-induced leakage or withdrawal of demand from the circular flow of income. But this is not so. Taxation and imports also change as income changes. A more realistic formula for the multiplier is:

$$\frac{1}{s + t + m}$$

where *t* is the marginal tax rate, and *m* is the marginal propensity to import.

The marginal tax rate (*t*) and the marginal propensity to import (*m*) respectively measure the proportion of a change in income paid in tax and the proportion people wish to spend on imports. Once the marginal propensity to import and the marginal tax rate are included in the multiplier formula, the size of the multiplier falls significantly. In the United Kingdom, the marginal tax rate is around 0.4 and the British economy is open to trade. This means that the marginal propensity to import is also quite high. Given a marginal propensity to save (*s*) of 0.15, and setting the marginal tax rate (*t*) at 0.4 and the marginal propensity to import (*m*) at 0.35, the value of the multiplier becomes:

$$\frac{1}{0.9}$$

or 1.1. The value of the government spending multiplier in the UK economy is thus quite small. The UK economy is an economy open to imports, with a relatively high income tax rate when national insurance contributions are included in the tax rate. This means that fiscal policy, used in a Keynesian way, may not be effective in managing aggregate demand. The larger the multiplier, the more powerful fiscal policy is as a demand management instrument. Conversely, the smaller the multiplier, the less effective is fiscal policy used in this way. The main effect of an expansionary fiscal policy may be to pull imports into the economy – even when there is substantial unemployment – with relatively little increase in domestic output and employment. This is because a significant fraction of the income received from an increase in government spending leaks into taxation and imports, as well as into savings.

Extension material

The multiplier and Keynesian theory

The national income multiplier first came into prominence as a key part of Keynesian economic theory. The multiplier concept was first stated in 1931 by R.F. Kahn, a colleague and former pupil of John Maynard Keynes at Cambridge University. In its early days, the multiplier theory was an **employment multiplier** showing how a change in public sector investment, for example in road building, might trigger a subsequent multiple growth in employment. Keynes made use of Kahn's employment multiplier for the first time in 1933 when discussing the effects of an increase in government spending of £500, a sum that he assumed to be just sufficient to employ one man for 1 year in road construction. Keynes wrote:

> If the new expenditure is additional and not merely in substitution for other expenditure, the increase of employment does not stop there. The additional wages and other incomes paid out are spent on additional purchases, which in turn lead to further employment...the newly employed who supply the increased purchases of those employed on the new capital works will, in their turn, spend more, thus adding to the employment of others and so on.

By 1936, when Keynes's *General Theory* was published, the multiplier had become a part of Keynes's explanation of how unemployment might be caused by deficient aggregate demand. In his *General Theory*, Keynes explained the investment multiplier, which suggests how a collapse in investment and business confidence might cause a multiple contraction in output, leading in turn to large-scale unemployment. Keynes then went on to argue that through an active fiscal policy, the government spending multiplier might reverse this process.

The multiplier and Keynesian demand management

Despite the possibility of a low multiplier effect during the Keynesian era, governments in many industrialised mixed economies (including the UK), based macroeconomic policy on the management of aggregate demand. This became known as

discretionary fiscal policy. To achieve full employment, governments deliberately ran budget deficits (setting $G > T$). This increased aggregate demand, but sometimes too much demand 'overheated' the economy. Excess demand pulled up the price level in a demand-pull inflation or pulled imports into the country and caused a balance of payments crisis. In these circumstances, governments were forced to reverse the thrust of fiscal policy, cutting public spending or raising taxes to reduce the level of demand in the economy.

The Keynesians used fiscal policy in a discrete way, supplemented at times by monetary policy, to *fine-tune* the level of aggregate demand in the economy so as to stabilise the fluctuations in the economic cycle and to try to achieve the macro-economic objectives of full employment and economic growth without excessive inflation or an unsustainable deterioration in the balance of payments.

The decline and rebirth of demand-side fiscal policy

Whatever the size of the multiplier, the multiplier process increases *nominal* national income, and not necessarily *real* national income. You must always remember that *nominal* national income can increase in two ways: through reflation of real output, or through inflation of the price level in a demand-pull inflation. Keynesians believed, providing the economy has spare capacity, expansionary fiscal policy stimulates real output more than inflation.

By contrast, free-market and supply-side economists believe that an increase in government spending stimulates *prices* rather than *real output*, and that government spending **crowds out** private sector investment. (Crowding out is explained in Chapter 19.) They also argue that the more fiscal policy is used to increase aggregate demand, the more it injects larger and larger doses of inflation into the economy, irrespective of whether the economy is in boom or recession.

In the 1970s this argument became more and more persuasive. Keynesian economics went into decline and was replaced by the free-market revival. Fiscal policy was no longer used to manage aggregate demand. However, in 2008 the onset of recession and the introduction of a fiscal stimulus designed to tackle the recession brought about a revival in Keynesian demand management and with it renewed interest in the size of the government spending multiplier.

Using an *AD/AS* diagram to illustrate the government spending multiplier

Figure 15.8 shows the multiplier effect of an increase in government spending in an *AD/AS* diagram. The initial increase in government spending is shown by the

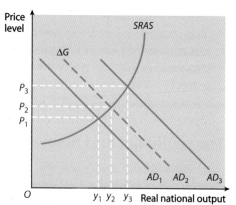

Figure 15.8 *Illustrating the government spending multiplier on an AD/AS diagram*

horizontal distance between the curves AD_1 and AD_2, labelled ΔG. If the size of the multiplier is 1, there are no further stages in the multiplier process, and the story ends here. Real income increases from y_1 to y_2, and the price level rises from P_1 to P_2. However, with a multiplier greater than 1, the aggregate demand curve now shifts further to the right from AD_2 to AD_3. The larger the government spending multiplier, the greater the distance between the two AD curves. Real national income increases to y_3 and the price level rises to P_3.

In Figure 15.8, the effect of the multiplier on *real* national income depends on the shape and slope of the AS curve. With the upward-sloping $SRAS$ curve depicted in Figure 15.8, real income increases from y_1 to y_3, but part of the multiplier effect is deflected into an increase in the price level (from P_1 to P_3). If I had drawn the diagram with a vertical $LRAS$ curve, as opposed to an upward-sloping $SRAS$ curve, an increase in government spending would not in the long run produce an increase in real output. Conversely, if the economy is in deep recession and operating on the horizontal section of the Keynesian $LRAS$ curve illustrated in Figure 15.6, all of the multiplier effect falls on real output, until the upward-sloping and vertical sections of the curve are reached.

Extension material

A recent development in *AD/AS* analysis

Students are often puzzled by a particular feature of the *AD/AS* model as taught and learnt at A-level. If you look carefully at Figure 15.9, you will see that a leftward movement of the *AD* curve from AD_1 to AD_2 results in a *fall* in the price level, i.e. deflation. However, we all know that except in a deep recession, contractionary fiscal or monetary policy that shifts the *AD* curve to the left results not in falling prices but in a slowdown in the rate of inflation, or disinflation. Average prices still rise, but at a slower annual rate of increase.

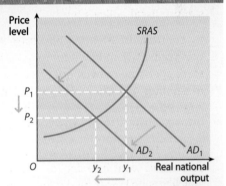

Figure 15.9 *The traditional* AD/AS *model*

This difference results from the fact that the original *AD/AS* model (i.e. the one you have learnt) is misleading. In a fairly recent development of the model, David Romer of the University of California explained why. Romer's explanation goes well beyond the requirements of A-level economics. If you are interested it is in an academic paper called *Keynesian Macroeconomics without the LM Curve*, which you can find in the *Journal of Economic Perspectives*, Volume 14, Number 2, Spring 2000. You can also find the article on the internet at:

http://elsa.berkeley.edu/~dromer/papers/JEP_Spring00.pdf

For a simpler account of Romer's *AD/AS* model, look at the Bized PowerPoint presentation on aggregate demand and aggregate supply, which can also be found on the internet at:

www.bized.co.uk/educators/16-19/economics/adas/presentation/adas.ppt

Romer's central argument is as follows. The AD/AS model learnt at A-level assumes that when a central bank such as the Bank of England implements monetary policy it does not allow the money supply to change. Given this assumption, the shift to the left of the AD curve illustrated in Figure 15.9 is indeed correct. But in recent years, monetary policy has operated in a different way, through the raising or lowering of interest rates rather than on tight control of the money supply. This leads to the outcome illustrated in Figure 15.10 and *not* in Figure 15.9. Contractionary fiscal or monetary policy, and indeed a fall in any of the components of aggregate demand, reduces the rate of inflation (shown in Figure 15.9 by the symbol $\dot{P}$), but not necessarily the price level.

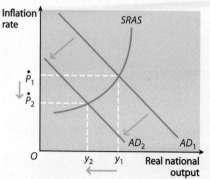

Figure 15.10 *The Romer AD/AS model*

Summary

➤ The aggregate demand/aggregate supply macroeconomic model provides the main theoretical framework for answering Unit 4 examination questions.

➤ Macroeconomic equilibrium occurs when $AD = AS$.

➤ Aggregate demand is the total planned spending on the goods and services produced within the economy, per period of time.

➤ The aggregate demand equation $AD = C + I + G + (X - M)$ includes the different components of aggregate demand.

➤ The aggregate demand curve slopes downward to the right showing that at a lower price level, more real goods and services are demanded.

➤ The short-run aggregate supply (SRAS) curve shows the quantities of real output that businesses plan to produce and sell at different price levels.

➤ SRAS curves slope upward to the right, showing that at a higher price level more real goods and services are supplied.

➤ The long-run aggregate supply (LRAS) curve is generally assumed to be vertical.

➤ The vertical slope of the LRAS curve results from the fact that the curve is located at the full capacity level of output. Firms cannot increase output in the short-run following an increase in aggregate demand.

➤ Expansionary fiscal and monetary policy shifts the *AD* curve to the right. Contractionary fiscal and monetary policy shifts the *AD* curve to the left.

➤ Supply-side policies attempt to shift the *LRAS* curve to the right.

➤ Changes in aggregate demand induce multiplier effects in which nominal or money national income changes by a multiple of the initial change in aggregate demand.

➤ The government spending multiplier is likely to be small in size. This reduces the power of fiscal policy used as a means of demand management.

➤ A new version of the *AD/AS* model has been developed in which the level of real output is a function of the rate of inflation rather than the price level.

Questions

1 Briefly explain the different components of aggregate demand.

2 What is aggregate supply?

3 Why is the slope of the aggregate supply curve significant?

4 Analyse supply-side fiscal policy using an *AD/AS* diagram.

5 Define a multiplier.

6 Explain the stages of the multiplier process.

7 Why has the multiplier concept been important for Keynesian economic policy?

8 Why is the value of the multiplier small in the UK economy?

9 What is the economy's natural level of output?

10 Must a decrease in aggregate demand lead to deflation?

Chapter 16

Employment and unemployment

On numerous occasions in recent years, when writing about employment and unemployment, I usually started by asserting that unemployment, though serious in the past, has become less and less of a problem for UK macroeconomic policy makers. The reason for such a confident assertion was simple: since the end of a deep recession in 1992, unemployment fell more or less continuously from a peak of around 3 million to half that amount by early 2008.

Unfortunately, by early 2009 the picture had radically changed. As recession hit the UK economy, unemployment climbed fast to reach 2.3 million by the end of March 2009. Indeed, throughout the months in which I have been writing this book, unemployment has grown in virtually all high-income countries such as the USA, Germany, France, Italy and Australia. Even in the good years, unemployment never disappeared in much of the developing world, where joblessness and hidden unemployment have kept billions of people in poverty. Granted, millions of new jobs have been created in emerging market economies such as China and India, but not nearly enough to absorb the tens of millions of peasants moving from rural areas to the towns.

In the UK, it is only a few months since governing politicians were promising the end of 'boom and bust' and the economic cycle. Since then, the 'R' word (recession) has returned with a vengeance, the 'D' word (depression) is now being talked about, and the problem of mass unemployment has resurfaced.

Learning outcomes

This chapter will:
> discuss the meaning of full employment
> explain equilibrium unemployment or the natural level or rate of unemployment
> describe how employment and unemployment are measured
> remind you of the types of unemployment learnt at AS

> explain the other types of unemployment you need to know at A2
> assess the costs unemployment imposes on the jobless, their families, wider society and the economy

What you should already know

At AS, you became aware of the main UK measures of unemployment: the claimant count and the Labour Force Survey measure. You developed an understanding of how employment and unemployment may be determined by both demand-side and supply-side factors. You practised using production possibility curves and *AD/AS* diagrams to analyse and evaluate demand-side and supply-side causes of unemployment. Finally, the AS specification required knowledge and understanding of cyclical, frictional, seasonal and structural unemployment.

The meaning of full employment

Along with economic growth and higher living standards, achieving **full employment** or low unemployment is a major objective of macroeconomic policy. Although economists do not have a formal definition of full employment, there are at least two definitions that are often used by economists and politicians. The first is known as the

 Key term

Full employment, according to the Beveridge definition, occurs when 3% of the labour force are unemployed.

Beveridge definition. In 1944, a famous White Paper on employment policy, inspired by Keynes but largely written by William Beveridge, effectively committed postwar governments to achieving full employment. William Beveridge was an economist at the London School of Economics and University College London who later became Lord Beveridge. In the White Paper, Beveridge defined full employment as occurring when unemployment falls to 3% of the labour force.

During the 1950s and 1960s, unemployment was always below 3%, so full employment, according to Beveridge's definition, was achieved during the post-war Keynesian decades. However, during and after the crisis in Keynesian economics in the 1970s, UK unemployment rose considerably above 3%, peaking at 11.3% (with over 3 million workers unemployed) in 1986. High unemployment in the mid-1980s was the result of recession at the beginning of the decade.

Likewise, the second recession suffered by the UK economy from 1990 to 1992 led to unemployment rising again to 9.9% (and 2.9 million unemployed) in 1993. Between 1997 and 2009, UK unemployment was always less than 5%, falling to meet Beveridge's definition of full employment (at 2.8%) in 2007. However, with the onset of a possibly long and deep recession in 2008, many if not most commentators fear that UK unemployment will once again rise above 3 million. In January 2009, the British Chambers of Commerce (BCC) predicted that by 2011 UK unemployment would rise to a peak of 3.1 million, or some 10% of the workforce.

Free-market economists generally favour a second definition of full employment, partly because they regard Beveridge's 3% definition as too arbitrary. Free-market economists define full employment in terms of the aggregate demand for and the aggregate supply of labour in the economy, as illustrated in Figure 16.1. The downward-sloping aggregate demand curve for labour (AD_L) shows that as the *real wage rate* paid to workers falls,

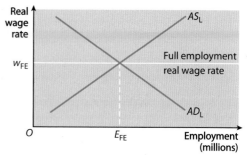

Figure 16.1 *Full employment illustrated in the economy's aggregate labour market*

employers or entrepreneurs are willing to employ more labour. There are two main reasons for this:

> In the short run, labour's diminishing marginal product means that it is unprofitable for firms to take on more workers unless the cost of hiring labour falls.
> The real wage falls relative to the cost of capital, firms substitute labour for capital and adopt more labour-intensive methods of production.

In contrast to the aggregate demand curve for labour, the aggregate supply curve for labour (AS_L) slopes upward, showing that workers are prepared to supply more labour as the real wage rate rises. Again, there are two main reasons for this:

> As the real wage rate rises, workers with jobs are prepared to work longer hours.
> People who are unwilling to join the economically active labour force at lower real wage rates, such as family members with children, decide to supply labour at a higher real wage rate.

For free-market economists, full employment occurs at the market-clearing real wage rate at which the number of workers wishing to work equals the number of workers employers wish to hire. In Figure 16.1 this is shown at the level of employment E_{FE}, at the real wage rate of w_{FE}.

PHOTODISC

Labourers working

examiner's voice

The natural rate of unemployment (NRU) is the unemployment rate when unemployment is restricted to its equilibrium level. I explain the NRU in detail in Chapter 17.

Equilibrium unemployment or the natural level of unemployment

Figure 16.1 shows the economy's aggregate labour market in a state of balance or rest, i.e. in *equilibrium*. It appears from the diagram that there is *no* unemployment at all when the labour market is in equilibrium. But as Figure 16.2 now shows, this is not the case.

For free-market economists, full employment does not necessarily mean that every single member of the working population is in work. Instead, it means a situation in which the number of people wishing to work at the going market real wage rate equals the number of workers that employers wish to hire at this real wage rate.

But even this definition needs qualifying, since in a dynamic economy change is constantly taking place, with some industries declining and others growing. Workers moving between jobs may decide to take a break between the two employments. This is called *frictional* unemployment. As new products are developed and demand and cost conditions change, firms demand more of some labour skills while the demand for other types of labour declines. This leads to

Key terms

Equilibrium unemployment is the level of unemployment when the economy's aggregate labour market is in equilibrium.

The natural rate of unemployment (NRU) is the rate of unemployment when the aggregate labour market is in equilibrium.

structural unemployment. Frictional and structural unemployment make up what is called **equilibrium unemployment**. Equilibrium unemployment exists even with the real wage rate at its market-clearing level. The equilibrium level of employment is also known as the natural level of unemployment. Expressed as a *rate* of unemployment, rather than as a *level*, this is the **natural rate of unemployment (NRU)**. I explain and examine the NRU in more detail in the next chapter on inflation.

In Figure 16.2, the AS_{LN} curve represents all the workers available for work and not just those willing to work at different real wage rates. Full employment occurs at E_{FE}, depicted where the AD_L and AS_L curves intersect at point X. In this situation equilibrium unemployment, or the natural level of unemployment, is measured by the distance from X to Z, or E_1 minus E_{FE}.

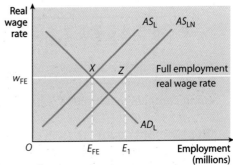

Figure 16.2 *Equilibrium unemployment*

Measuring employment and unemployment

The employment rate

Figure 16.3 shows changes in the UK employment rate for those over the school-leaving age, covering the years from 1972 to the onset of recession in 2008. The employment rate is strongly correlated with the economic cycle, rising in the recovery and boom phases of the cycle, but falling when growth slows down or becomes negative. However, the employment and unemployment cycles usually lag a few months behind the output cycle. Employers hang on to their best workers at the beginning of a downturn, until they are sure that demand for their output is actually falling. Likewise, employers tend to wait and see at the beginning of a recovery period, offering overtime to their current employees before deciding to recruit new workers.

The UK employment rate rose above 60% in the early 1970s, in the boom at the end of the 1980s, and again in 2004. The working age employment rate is rather higher than the rate shown in Figure 16.3, peaking at 74.8% at the beginning of 2008. However, both measures of the employment rate began to fall in the second half of 2008. As the economy entered recession, there was much less evidence of a lag between the fall in output and the fall in employment, possibly because people had been expecting the downturn for several months.

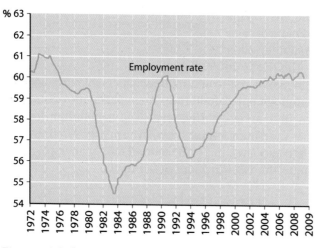

Figure 16.3 *Changes in the UK employment rate for those in paid employment above the age of 16*

Source: Government statistics

Figure 16.3 shows the employment rate, rather than the total number of people in employment. Largely due to population growth and immigration, this figure was significantly higher in 2008 than it had been at earlier peaks of employment.

The claimant count

Until quite recently the main measure of unemployment officially used in the UK was the monthly **claimant count**. This is a by-product of the administrative system for paying out unemployment-related benefits. The main benefit is currently the **jobseeker's allowance**. Many economists believe

Key term

The **claimant count** measures the number of people claiming unemployment-related benefits.

that the claimant count provides an inaccurate measure of true unemployment. Free-market economists argue that the claimant count overstates true unemployment because many claimants are either not genuinely looking for work or not genuinely unemployed because they already have undeclared jobs in the informal economy.

But in other ways, the claimant count understates true unemployment. The toughening up of eligibility requirements in the 1980s and early 1990s reduced the claimant count without actually reducing unemployment. In addition, various groups of unemployed, such as young workers on government training schemes and unemployed workers approaching retirement (who were reclassified as 'early retired') have been removed from the register even though they would like full-time jobs.

The Labour Force Survey

The government now recognises a second measure of unemployment based on the **Labour Force Survey** (LFS) of households, which uses internationally recognised definitions recommended by the International Labour Organisation (ILO). The LFS is a quarterly survey of 60,000 households, which counts people as unemployed if they are actively seeking work (that is, if they have been looking for a job in the last 4 weeks) and have not had a job in the week in question.

> **Key term**
>
> The **Labour Force Survey** estimates unemployment by surveying 60,000 households to see if they are looking for work.

Both the claimant count and the LFS measure may understate true unemployment because they ignore discouraged workers and roughly half a million people who are classified as economically inactive. Discouraged workers are people who have given up hope of finding a job even though they would take one if it were offered.

Interpreting the data

The data in Figures 16.3 and 16.4 show a more or less continuous fall in unemployment (and rise in employment) over an 11-year period from 1993 to 2004. By 2001,

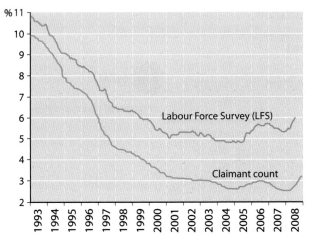

Figure 16.4
UK unemployment shown by the LFS and claimant count measures, 1993–2008

unemployment had fallen below the psychologically important level of 1 million, at least when measured by the claimant count. As I have noted, the fall in unemployment is explained by the performance of the UK economy over most of the 1990s and early 2000s. Indeed, some economists believe that the economy experienced a second golden era (the first one having been in the golden age of Keynesian economics in the 1950s and 1960s). By the early 2000s, many communities in the UK, particularly in southeast England, were fully employed. However, other regions in the north and west of the UK were not so fortunate, and there were also pockets of unemployment in parts of London, such as Hackney.

It is worth noting that much of the increase in employment in the early 2000s resulted from the growth of the public sector. Even in the good years, private sector growth was considerably weaker and did not create many jobs.

The data series in Figures 16.3 and 16.4 both come to an end around the time that the UK economy switched from positive economic growth to negative growth and recession in 2008. Compared to previous downturns, the 2008 recession has led to job cuts right across the private sector. Even before the recession began, manufacturing had ceased to be a major employer of UK labour. Major manufacturing employers had gone to the wall and shed their labour forces, either in previous recessions, or, as in the case of MG Rover, when the economy as a whole was doing well. Of the remaining car firms that are large employers of labour, Jaguar and Land Rover are in danger of closing down with their foreign owners shipping their assets overseas. The future of the Japanese-owned Honda, Nissan and Toyota plants is probably more secure, though not guaranteed, and some job shedding is already occurring. However, unlike in previous recessions, it is the previously resilient sectors such as banking and finance, and retailing, that are experiencing the greatest number of closures and mass redundancies.

Causes or types of unemployment

As I mentioned at the beginning of the chapter, you first came across frictional, seasonal, structural and cyclical unemployment last year at AS. Before explaining the other causes or types of unemployment you must now learn, I shall remind you of what you should already know.

Frictional unemployment

Frictional unemployment, which is also known as **transitional unemployment**, is unemployment that occurs as people are between jobs. As its name suggests, this type of unemployment results from frictions in the labour market that create a delay or time-lag during which a worker is unemployed when moving from one job to another. Note that the definition of frictional unemployment assumes that a job vacancy exists and that frictions in the job market prevent unemployed

Key term

Frictional unemployment is unemployment that occurs while people are between jobs.

workers from filling vacancies. It follows that the number of unfilled job vacancies is a measure of the level of frictional unemployment in the economy.

Among the causes of frictional unemployment are geographical and occupational immobilities of labour, which prevent laid-off workers from filling job vacancies immediately. Family ties, ignorance about vacancies in other parts of the country and, above all, the cost of moving and obtaining housing are responsible for the *geographical* immobility of labour. The need for training and the effects of restrictive practices and discrimination in labour markets are among the causes of *occupational* immobility.

The **search theory of unemployment** provides a further explanation of frictional unemployment. Consider the situation illustrated in Figure 16.5, in which a worker earning £1,000 a week in a skilled professional occupation loses his job. While there appear to be no vacancies in his current line of work, there are vacancies for low-skilled office workers earning around £300 a week. Suppose now that the newly unemployed worker sets his *aspirational wage* at £1,000. This means that he will choose to remain unemployed, at least to start with, rather than to fill the lower-paid vacancy. The lower weekly wage on offer, and perhaps also poorer conditions of work and status associated with the lower-paid job, render the vacancy unattractive. He also lacks accurate information about the state of the job market. All this means that he needs to search the labour market to find out whether better-paid and higher-status vacancies exist.

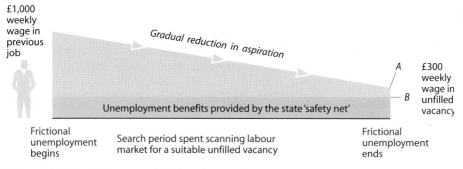

Figure 16.5 *Search theory and frictional unemployment*

Under this interpretation, frictional unemployment is a voluntary search period in which newly unemployed workers scan the labour market, searching for vacancies that are likely to meet their aspirations. There are a number of ways in which this voluntary search period can end. First, the job searcher eventually learns of a vacancy that meets his initial aspiration and for which he is qualified. Indeed, the vacancy may have been there all the time but, until he searched the job market, the worker did not know about it. Second, the vacancy may have arisen during his search period, perhaps resulting from a general improvement in the labour market. Third, he may end his voluntary unemployment as soon as he realises that his initial aspirations were unrealistically high, meaning he decides to settle for a lower-paid, less attractive job.

Skilled professionals are unlikely to want low-paid office jobs

Long search periods, which increase the amount of frictional unemployment in the economy, can be caused by the welfare benefit system. Without welfare benefits, search periods must be financed by running down stocks of savings, or through the charity of family and friends. In this situation, the threat of poverty creates incentives to search the job market more vigorously and to reduce aspirational wage levels. However, the availability of a **state safety net** of unemployment and other income-related welfare benefits, together in some cases with redundancy payments, permits unemployed workers to finance longer voluntary search periods. Because of this, free-market economists support a reduction in the real value of unemployment benefits relative to take-home pay in work, together with restricting the benefits to those who can prove they are genuinely looking for work. They believe that these policies create incentives for the unemployed to reduce aspirations quickly, which in turn shortens search periods.

The **replacement ratio** is a useful concept to use when analysing unemployment. For a relatively low-paid worker losing a job, the replacement ratio is a factor influencing the length of time searching for work while unemployed. It is given by the following formula:

$$\text{replacement ratio} = \frac{\text{disposable income out of work}}{\text{disposable income in work}}$$

The size of the replacement ratio is determined largely by the level of welfare benefits claimable when unemployed, relative to income after taxation and receipt of benefits when in work. A replacement ratio of 100% means that a worker is no better off in work than out of work, living off the state.

Even for low-paid workers, replacement ratios are seldom as high as 100%. Nonetheless, high replacement ratios approaching 100% destroy the incentive to work, at least in the formal economy. For people whose job prospects are poor, a high replacement ratio leads to the **unemployment trap**, which I briefly mentioned in Chapter 13. For the worker shown in Figure 16.5, the replacement ratio equals B/A. Point B shows the level of welfare benefit claimable out of work, while point A shows disposable income in work.

Casual and seasonal unemployment

Casual unemployment is a special case of frictional unemployment, occurring when workers are laid off on a short-term basis in trades such as tourism, agriculture, catering and building. **Seasonal unemployment** is casual unemployment resulting from seasonal fluctuations in demand, for example, building workers laid off during cold winter months.

Structural unemployment

Structural unemployment results from the structural decline of industries, unable to compete or adapt in the face of either changing demand and new products or the emergence of more efficient competitors in other countries. Structural unemployment is also caused by changing skill requirements as industries change ways of producing their products.

Key terms

Seasonal unemployment results from seasonal fluctuations in the demand for labour.

Structural unemployment results from the structural decline of industries and the inability or difficulty of workers switching to new industries.

Technological unemployment is a special case of structural unemployment, resulting from the successful growth of new industries using labour-saving technology. In contrast to **mechanisation** (workers operating machines), which has usually increased the overall demand for labour, **automation** (machines operating other machines) reduces the demand for labour. Whereas the growth of mechanised industry increases employment, automation of production can lead to the shedding of labour, even when industry output is expanding.

The growth of international competition in an increasingly globalised economy is an important cause of structural unemployment. During the Keynesian era from the 1950s to the 1970s, structural unemployment in the UK was concentrated in regions where nineteenth-century staple industries such as textiles and ship-building were suffering structural decline. Regional unemployment caused by the decline of **sunset industries** was more than offset by the growth of employment elsewhere in the UK in the **sunrise industries** that replaced them. However, in the severe recessions of the early 1980s and the early 1990s, structural unemployment affected almost all regions in the UK, as **deindustrialisation** spread across the manufacturing base. In the 2008 recession, deindustrialisation spread to service sector industries.

It is not easy to separate changes in structural unemployment from other causes of unemployment, particularly changes in aggregate demand. Manufacturing output grew in many of the years between 1993 and 2008, but manufacturing employment fell. However, during these years, there was a danger of exaggerating the growth of unemployment in manufacturing industries because many activities, ranging from cleaning to information technology maintenance, previously undertaken in-house by manufacturing firms, were out-sourced to external service-sector providers.

Structural unemployment has occured within the service sector, partly due to the increasing use of information and communication technology (ICT) and automated services. Call centre employment has grown significantly in the service sector in recent years. However, a decline has been forecast, partly due to call centres moving overseas, but also because companies employ automated communication software rather than humans to provide customer services.

Disequilibrium unemployment

As I explained earlier in the chapter, equilibrium unemployment, which is illustrated in Figure 16.2, comprises the frictional and structural unemployment occurring when the labour market is in equilibrium. By contrast, as the name indicates, disequilibrium unemployment results from the labour market being out of equilibrium. This occurs when:

> the aggregate supply of labour exceeds the aggregate demand for labour
> labour market imperfections prevent the real wage rate falling to restore labour market equilibrium (**wage stickiness**)

There are two main types of disequilibrium unemployment. These are:
> classical unemployment or real-wage unemployment
> Keynesian, cyclical or demand-deficient unemployment

Classical unemployment or real-wage unemployment

In the 1920s, large-scale persistent unemployment occurred in the United Kingdom, preceding the spread of unemployment worldwide in the Great Depression of the 1930s. Much of British unemployment in the 1920s probably resulted from the lack of competitiveness and decline of nineteenth-century staple industries such as ship-building and textiles. This problem was made worse by an overvalued exchange rate. However, the pre-Keynesians blamed a substantial part of the unemployment on excessively high wages.

Key *term*

Classical or **real-wage unemployment** is a form of disequilibrium unemployment that occurs when the aggregate labour market fails to clear. This is caused by real wage rates being too high.

Unemployment caused by excessively high wage rates is called **classical unemployment** or **real-wage unemployment**. This type of disequilibrium unemployment is illustrated in Figure 16.6. In the diagram, full employment is determined where the aggregate demand for labour equals the aggregate supply of labour, at the real wage rate w_{FE}. However, suppose wages are fixed at a higher real rate, at w_1 rather than w_{FE}. At this real wage rate, employers wish to hire E_1 workers, but E_2 workers wish to supply their labour. There is excess supply of labour in the labour market.

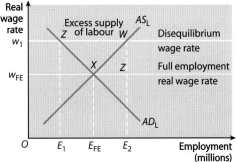

Figure 16.6 *Classical or real-wage unemployment*

As I have mentioned, the pre-Keynesians believed that, as long as the labour market remained competitive, the resulting classical or real-wage unemployment would be temporary. Competitive forces in the labour market would cure the problem, bidding down the real wage rate to w_{FE}, thereby eliminating the excess supply of labour. Full employment would quickly be restored when the number of workers willing to work equalled the number that firms wished to hire.

But suppose labour market rigidity, perhaps caused by trade unions, prevents the real wage rate falling below w_1. In this situation, the market mechanism fails to work properly, the excess supply of labour persists, and real-wage or classical unemployment occurs. Pre-Keynesian free-market economists blamed trade unions and other causes of labour market imperfection for the resulting mass unemployment. In their view, responsibility for unemployment lay with the workers in work and their trade unions who, by refusing to accept lower wages, prevented the unemployed from pricing themselves into jobs.

Cyclical, Keynesian or demand-deficient unemployment
In the inter-war years in the 1920s and 1930s, John Maynard Keynes argued that deficient aggregate demand was the main cause of persistent mass unemployment in the UK economy. Pre-Keynesian economists did not accept this explanation. They believed that although deficient demand can occur in the economy, the resulting **cyclical unemployment** (as they called it) would quickly be eliminated by the self-regulating nature of market forces.

To explain the difference between the pre-Keynesian (free-market) and Keynesian views on the existence of deficient demand in the economy, I must introduce **Say's Law**, named after an early 19th century French economist, Jean-Baptiste Say. In popular form, Say's Law states that supply creates its own demand. Whenever an output, or supply, is produced, factor incomes such as wages and profits are generated that are just sufficient, *if spent*, to purchase the output at the existing price level, thereby creating a demand for the output produced. Stated thus, there is nothing controversial about Say's Law, it is really a statement that is true by definition.

The controversial and critical issue concerns whether the *potential* demand or incomes generated are *actually* spent on the output produced. The pre-Keynesians believed that the incomes are spent and that Say's Law holds. Keynes argued that under some circumstances incomes are saved and not spent and that Say's Law breaks down and the resulting deficient demand causes unemployment.

Figure 16.7 shows how **demand-deficient unemployment** occurs. In panel (a) of the diagram, macroeconomic equilibrium is initially at point X at the full employment level of output y_{FE}. However, a significant fall in aggregate demand, caused for example by a collapse of consumer and business confidence, shifts the AD curve inward from AD_1 to AD_2. Real output falls to y_2, which is considerably below y_{FE}.

Key term

Demand-deficient unemployment, which is also known as cyclical and Keynesian unemployment is caused by deficient aggregate demand in the economy.

(a) A leftward shift of the AD curve leads to deficient aggregate demand

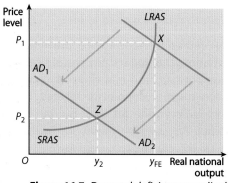

(b) The result is a shift in the employers' aggregate demand for labour curve

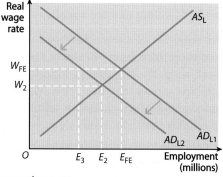

Figure 16.7 *Demand deficient or cyclical unemployment*

Panel (b) of Figure 16.7 shows what happens in the economy's aggregate labour market following the fall in the aggregate demand for output. Producing the level of output y_2 requires fewer workers than level of output y_{FE}. As a result, the curve showing employers' aggregate demand for labour shifts inward from AD_{L1} to AD_{L2}. What happens next depends on whether real wage rates are flexible and adjust to the new situation, or whether they are 'sticky' and inflexible downwards. Given wage flexibility (as assumed by free-market economists), the real wage falls from w_{FE} to w_2. Employment also falls, but only to E_2. However, if wage rates are sticky, as Keynesians assume, the real wage rate may remain at w_{FE}. Given this outcome, demand-deficient unemployment is higher, with employment at E_3.

The costs and consequences of unemployment

Unemployment is a waste of human capital. By definition, when unemployment occurs, the economy produces inside its production possibility frontier. Nevertheless, free-market economists believe that a certain amount of unemployment is necessary to make the economy function better. They believe that, by providing downward pressure on wage rates, unemployment reduces inflationary pressures. However, unemployment widens income differentials and increases absolute and relative poverty. Higher unemployment also means greater spending on unemployment and poverty-related benefits, the opportunity cost of which is less spending on the provision of hospitals, schools and other useful resources.

Unemployment is obviously bad for the unemployed themselves and for their families, largely through the way in which the low incomes that accompany unemployment lead to low standards of living. However, the costs of unemployment for the unemployed go further than this. Apart from situations in which the unemployed enjoy having 24 hours of leisure time each day and every day, or when the 'unemployed' are engaged in the black economy, unemployment destroys hope in the future. The unemployed become marginalised from normal economic and human activity and their self-esteem is reduced and sometimes shattered. Families suffer increased health risks, greater stress, a reduction in the quality of diet, an increased risk of marital break-up, and social exclusion caused by the loss of work and income. The longer the duration of unemployment, the greater is the loss of marketable skills in the labour market.

Box 16.1 The credit crunch and aggregate demand

By late 2008, the view that modern unemployment is caused primarily by supply-side factors had been overtaken by events. There is no doubt that the main cause of the massive increase in unemployment in the recession that hit the world economy was a collapse of aggregate demand on a global scale. The key event that triggered the collapse of demand was the credit crunch, which originated in the USA in August 2007, but then quickly spread to reduce aggregate demand in other countries including the United Kingdom.

Virtually all firms, large and small, require a reliable supply of credit or bank lending in order to remain in business. In normal circumstances, the banking system provides this liquidity, which businesses, consumers and governments usually take for granted. Historically, the source of this liquidity stemmed from banks borrowing household savings, which the banks then lent on for others to spend.

However, by 2007, banks throughout the world, but particularly in America, were raising the funds they lent to customers by borrowing from each other rather than from households. The funds were borrowed on the inter-bank market. In the USA, much of the borrowed funds were lent in the form of mortgages to low-income customers who were bad credit risks. These loans became known as *sub-prime* mortgages (in contrast to *prime* mortgages, which are secured loans granted to low-risk home owners).

From a bank's point of view, a mortgage granted to a customer is an *asset*. For the borrower, it is a *liability*, since the house owner must eventually pay back the loan and pay interest in the intervening months and years. By definition a sub-prime mortgage is a risky asset since there is a danger of the loan turning into a bad debt, which the bank owning the loan cannot recover. In 2007, the credit crunch developed because the banks that had created sub-prime mortgages repackaged the risky assets and sold them on to other banks as if they were prime mortgages. In essence, banks were buying 'toxic debt' from each other, without realising the repackaged assets were extremely risky. As banks realised that many of their so-called 'assets' were more or less worthless the situation quickly deteriorated and the supply of liquidity began to freeze. Banks

became unwilling to lend to each other because they distrusted each other's credit-worthiness. At the next stage, the credit crunch triggered a financial meltdown when banks either collapsed (Lehmann Brother in the USA) or were nationalised by governments (Northern Rock in the UK).

Follow-up questions

1 Why is a supply of liquidity so important for an economy to function properly?
2 How has the credit crunch affected business and consumer confidence and thence aggregate demand?

Appropriate government policies to reduce unemployment

Governments generally implement policies to try to reduce unemployment, but the appropriate policy obviously depends on identifying correctly the underlying cause of unemployment. For example, if unemployment is diagnosed incorrectly in terms of demand deficiency, when the true cause is structural, a policy of fiscal or monetary expansion to stimulate aggregate demand will be ineffective and inappropriate. Indeed, in such circumstances reflation of demand would create excess demand, which raises the price level through demand-pull inflation, with no lasting beneficial effects upon employment.

In the late 1990s and early 2000s, it was generally agreed, by Keynesians as well as by free-market economists, that the dominant cause of unemployment in countries such as the UK lay on the supply side of the economy rather than on the demand side. There was no evidence in these years of deficient aggregate demand. However, there was disagreement on the appropriate policies to improve supply-side performance. Free-market economists argue that poor supply-side performance was the legacy of the three decades of Keynesian interventionism from the 1950s to 1970s. In the free-market view, the economic role of the state must be reduced to cut frictional, structural and real-wage unemployment.

By setting markets free, encouraging competition and fostering private enterprise and the entrepreneurial spirit, an enterprise culture could be created in which the price mechanism, and not the government, delivers economic growth and reduces unemployment. Free-market economists believe that the correct role of government is to create the conditions in which the market mechanism and private enterprise function properly. This is done by controlling inflation, promoting competitive markets and maintaining the rule of law and social order. Keynesian economists disagree, believing that unemployment results from a massive market failure that can be cured only by interventionist policies to modify markets and make them function better.

Summary

> Full employment, or low unemployment, is a major macroeconomic objective.

> There is no single accepted definition of full employment, though full employment is most usually defined as occurring when the number of workers wishing to work equals the number of workers employers wish to hire.

➤ There is still some unemployment, known as the equilibrium level of unemployment, when the economy is 'fully employed'.

➤ Equilibrium unemployment, which is also known as the natural level of unemployment, comprises frictional, seasonal and structural unemployment.

➤ Disequilibrium unemployment occurs when the economy's aggregate labour market fails to clear.

➤ There are two main types of disequilibrium unemployment: classical or real-wage unemployment and demand-deficient, cyclical or Keynesian unemployment.

➤ Classical unemployment is caused by real wage rates being too high. The policy solution is wage cuts.

➤ Cyclical or Keynesian unemployment is caused by deficient aggregate demand. The policy solution is to use fiscal and/or monetary policy to increase aggregate demand.

➤ To reduce unemployment without undesirable side-effects it is important to diagnose the cause or causes of unemployment and then to implement appropriate policies.

➤ Unemployment imposes significant costs on the economy and on the unemployed themselves and their families.

Questions

1 List and briefly describe the main causes of unemployment.

2 What is equilibrium unemployment?

3 What is the natural rate of unemployment (NRU)?

4 What may be the effect of reducing unemployment below its natural rate?

5 How may the natural rate of unemployment be reduced?

6 How may reducing the replacement ratio affect unemployment?

7 Can any benefits result from unemployment?

8 What is the 'credit crunch' and how has it affected unemployment?

Chapter 17

Inflation and the Phillips curve

Forty or so years ago in the 1970s, accelerating and highly variable rates of inflation caused acute problems in the UK economy. As a result, in the monetarist decade of the 1980s, the control of inflation was elevated to pole position in the league table of government macroeconomic policy objectives. Eventually, the policy became remarkably successful. From 1993 until 2007, the UK inflation rate remained within 1% above or below the 2% inflation rate target set by the government, apart from on one occasion when it nudged over the 3% upper limit.

Until 2008, control of inflation was accompanied by arguably the longest period of continuous economic growth the UK has ever experienced, at least in modern times. However, in 2007 things started to go wrong. Along with other economies, the UK was hit by a sudden burst of cost-push inflation, mostly imported from the rest of the world via escalating oil, gas, commodity and food prices. Together with the credit crunch that began in the USA, severe cost-push inflation undermined business and consumer confidence. Then, in 2008, aggregate demand collapsed and the UK economy entered recession. Worldwide shortages of oil and commodities such as copper gave way to surpluses and the rate of inflation began to fall. At the time of writing in April 2009, many economists and politicians fear that the problem of price deflation may replace the problem of price inflation for as long as the recession lasts.

Learning outcomes

This chapter will:
> remind you of the meaning of inflation, deflation and reflation
> show how the UK rate of inflation has changed in recent decades
> describe how a price index is constructed to measure the average price level
> summarise how theories of the causes of inflation have changed over the years
> recap on the theories of demand-pull and cost-push inflation you learnt at AS
> introduce Phillips curve analysis

> use the concept of the long-run Phillips curve to develop the monetarist theory of inflation
> link the long-run Phillips curve to the natural rate of unemployment (NRU)
> explain how expectations of future inflation may affect current inflation
> assess the costs and benefits of inflation

What you should already know

At AS, you learnt how, along with other objectives such as economic growth and full employment, control of inflation is one of the government's major macroeconomic policy objectives. You also learnt about policy conflicts and policy trade-offs, for example the conflict between controlling inflation and achieving full employment. You should also understand how price indices, such as the RPI and the CPI, are used to measure the price level and the rate of inflation. The AS specification required knowledge and understanding of the basic differences between demand-pull and cost-push price inflation and of the difference between price inflation and price deflation. You also studied control of inflation as the main UK monetary policy objective.

Inflation, deflation and reflation

Key terms

Inflation is best defined as a persistent or continuous rise in the price level, or as a continuing fall in the value of money. **Deflation** is the opposite, namely a persistent tendency for the price level to fall or for the value of money to rise. However, the overall price level has seldom fallen in western industrialised countries since the 1930s, though as I have stated, in 2009, many economists fear that a deepening recession may lead to a falling average price level. The term deflation is therefore usually applied in a rather looser way to describe a reduction in aggregate demand and levels of economic activity, output and employment. A deflationary policy uses fiscal or monetary policy to reduce aggregate demand, in order to take excess demand out of the system. Likewise, **reflation** refers to an increase in economic activity and output, and a reflationary policy stimulates aggregate demand. Often, inflation is 'reflation gone wrong', stimulating the price level rather than real output and employment.

Inflation is a continuous and persistent rise in the price level and fall in the value of money.

Deflation is a continuous and persistent fall in the price level and increase in the value of money.

Reflation is an increase in real output and employment following an increase in aggregate demand.

Changes in the UK inflation rate

Key term

Until 2003, the UK government measured changes in the rate of inflation through changes in the RPIX. The **retail prices index** (RPI) measures the headline rate of inflation,

The **retail prices index** is the UK price index used for setting welfare benefit increases.

whereas RPIX measures the underlying rate of inflation: that is, the headline rate minus mortgage interest rates. The government still uses the RPI for deciding the level at which welfare benefits such as the state pension and the jobseeker's allowance should be set.

However, when setting a target inflation rate for the Bank of England to meet through monetary policy, the **consumer prices index** (CPI) has replaced RPIX. Currently, the Bank of England aims to hit a CPI target rate of 2%, rather than the old RPIX target rate of 2.5%. The CPI, which is based on the method of measuring the price level used in the European Union, is likely eventually to replace the RPI and RPIX completely.

Key terms

The **consumer prices index** is the UK price index most central to UK monetary policy.

A **price index** is an index number that measures the average price level.

Figure 17.1, which shows how the rate of CPI inflation changed in the UK between 1989 and 2008, divides into five distinct data periods. These were:

> **The late 1980s and early 1990s.** These were years when inflation increased to an unacceptably high rate of 8.5%, which prompted the introduction of inflation rate targets, which are still the centrepiece of current UK monetary policy.

> **1992–1994.** A rapid fall in the inflation rate to around 2%, the current inflation rate target.

> **1994–2006.** The so-called **nice** (non-inflationary, consistently expansionary) years, when the UK inflation rate was almost always close to the central target of 2%.

> **2007–mid-2008.** The UK economy suffered a severe bout of cost-push inflation, as rising prices of imported oil, gas and food pushed up the inflation rate to 5.2%, well above the upper 3% target ceiling. *Nice-ness* had come to an end and some economists gloomily predicted a return to 1970s-style **stagflation** of low or nonexistent growth combined with unacceptably high inflation.

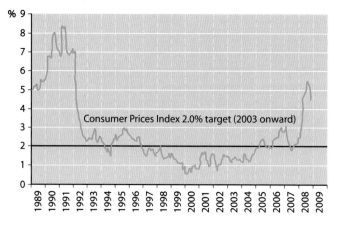

Figure 17.1
The annual rate of change in UK inflation, measured by the consumer prices index, 1989–2008

> **Mid-2008 onward.** The inflation rate began to fall, with the previous bout of cost inflation having passed through the system. The UK and other economies had now entered a severe recession, and many economists and politicians feared that deflation (falling prices) would replace inflation.

Constructing a price index to measure inflation

Two main tasks are undertaken in the construction of the CPI and the RPI. These are the choice of a representative sample of goods, and the *weighting* of each good in the sample.

> **examiner's voice**
>
> The specification advises that, although a detailed technical knowledge is not expected of indices such as the retail prices index (RPI) and consumer prices index (CPI), candidates should have an awareness of the underlying features of the index, such as the role of the Expenditure and Food Survey (EFS), the concept of the 'average family', the basket of goods and services, and the weighting.

Choice of sample

According to the **Office for National Statistics (ONS)**, the most useful way to think about both the CPI and RPI is to imagine a shopping basket containing those goods and services on which people typically spend their money. As the prices of the various items in the basket change over time, so does the total cost of the basket. Movements in the CPI and RPI indices represent the changing cost of this representative shopping basket (see Figure 17.2).

Currently, around 120,000 separate price quotations are used every month in compiling the indices, covering some 650 representative consumer goods and services for which prices are collected in around 150 areas throughout the UK. The goods and services that figure in the representative sample are derived from the annual **Expenditure and Food Survey (EFS)**, in which 7,000 households throughout the country are asked to record what they spent in a given fortnight and to give details of big purchases over a longer period. Every year the contents of the sample are revised to reflect changes in how the average family spends its income.

There are some specific differences in the commodity coverage of the CPI and RPI indices. For example, the RPI basket includes a number of items chosen to represent owner-occupier housing costs, including mortgage interest payments and depreciation costs, all of which are excluded from the CPI. Otherwise, the contents of the CPI and RPI baskets are very similar, although the precise weights attached to the individual items in each index do differ.

Weighting the goods in the sample

Each item in the sample is given a *weight* to reflect its relative importance in the expenditure pattern of a typical family.

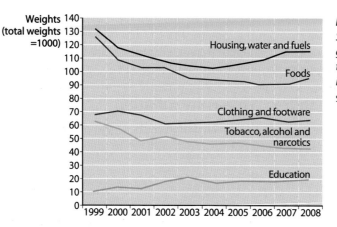

Figure 17.2
Selected weights for goods and services in the UK consumer prices index

Source: ONS

The contents of the RPI and CPI baskets of goods and services and their expenditure weights are updated each year.

Box 17.1 Changes in the national shopping baskets

Every March the Office for National Statistics revises the items in the national shopping baskets from which the CPI and the RPI are constructed. However, because of a lag effect, the annual review has gained a reputation for including an item just as it has gone out of fashion. Here is an extract from an article published in the *Guardian* commenting on some of the new items introduced into the national shopping basket in 2008.

Could Britons be getting healthier? Fruit smoothies are in, ready meals and microwaves are out.

The latest basket of goods and services used by national statisticians to monitor inflation reflects a changing attitude to food, the abandoning of camera films and CD singles, but also a tendency to buy lager in multipacks.

The 61st annual shakeup from the Office for National Statistics reflects what it calls a growing 'café culture' with muffins as well as smoothies going into the basket for the first time.

'Fruit smoothies are included as the emerging market of healthy soft drinks continues to rise in supermarkets', it said.

Smoothies are now in the national shopping basket

'Muffins are included for the first time to represent snacks such as croissants and cakes that people generally buy with a coffee in cafés around the UK.'

The *Guardian*, 17 March 2008

Follow-up question

Why is it necessary to change each year the items in the national shopping baskets used to construct the CPI and the RPI, and the weights attached to the different items?

How theories of the causes of inflation have changed over the years

Table 17.1 provides a summary of how theories of inflation have developed over the years. The following sections then explain in some detail the main theories of the causes of inflation.

Table 17.1 *A summary of how the main theories of inflation have changed over the years*

Eighteenth century to the 1930s	The old quantity theory of money is dominant.
1930s	The problem of inflation disappears. Keynes's *General Theory* explains deflation in terms of deficient aggregate demand.
1940s	Keynes develops his *General Theory* to explain how, in conditions of full employment, excess demand can pull up the price level through demand-pull inflation.
1950s	The early monetarist theory of inflation begins to develop when Milton Friedman revives the quantity theory of money (the modern quantity theory).
1950s–1960s	Many Keynesians switch away from demand-pull to the cost-push theory of inflation.
1960s	The Keynesian demand-pull versus cost-push debate is conducted with the aid of the Phillips curve.
1968	The role of expectations in the inflationary process is incorporated into the monetarist theory of inflation. The theory of adaptive expectations is built into Milton Friedman's theory of the expectations-augmented Phillips curve (or long-run Phillips curve).
1970s	The short-run Phillips curve relationship breaks down.
1980s onward	There is controversy once again between cost-push and demand-pull explanations of inflation with New-Keynesian explanations versus monetarist and new-classical (rational expectations) explanations.
2008	Once again the problem of inflation largely disappears, being replaced by the fear of deflation or falling prices. However, fears of the return of accelerating inflation remain.

examiner's voice

As at AS, you must continue to understand the difference between demand-pull and cost-push inflation and be able to use *AD/AS* diagrams to illustrate both causes of inflation. Questions set at A2 require more understanding of the theories of inflation than those at AS.

Theories on the causes of inflation

The old quantity theory of money

The **quantity theory of money** is the oldest theory of inflation, dating back at least to the eighteenth century. For two centuries until the 1930s, when it went out of fashion with the Keynesian revolution, the quantity theory was *the* theory of inflation. However, Milton Friedman's revival of the quantity theory in

Key term

The **quantity theory of money** is the theory that assumes inflation is caused by a prior increase in the money supply.

modern form in the 1950s is usually regarded as marking the beginning of the monetarist counter-revolution. In recent years, the quantity theory has once again occupied a central place in debate and controversy about the causes of both inflation and deflation.

All versions of the quantity theory, old and new, are based on a special case of **demand-pull inflation**, in which rising prices are caused by excess demand. In the quantity theory, the source of excess demand is located in *monetary* rather than *real* forces, in an excess supply of money created or condoned by the government. At its simplest, the quantity theory is sometimes described as too much money chasing too few goods. The starting point for developing the theory is the **Fisher equation of exchange**, devised by an American economist, Irving Fisher, early in the twentieth century:

$$\text{money supply (stock of money)} \times \text{velocity of circulation of money} = \text{price level} \times \text{total transactions}$$

or:

$$MV = PT$$

In the Fisher equation, for a particular time period, say a year, the stock of money in the economy (M) multiplied by the velocity of circulation of money (V) equals the price level (P) multiplied by the total number of transactions (T). A transaction occurs when a good or service is bought. T measures all the purchases of goods and services in the economy. (These days, the equation is usually written as $MV = Py$, where y is real output.)

To convert the equation of exchange ($MV = PT$) into a theory of inflation, it is necessary to make three assumptions. The first two are:

➤ The velocity of circulation or speed at which money is spent and total transactions (which are determined by the level of real national output in the economy) are both fixed, or at least stable.

➤ In the quantity theory, money is a *medium of exchange* (means of payment), but *not* a store of value. This means that people quickly spend any money they receive.

Suppose the government allows the money supply to expand faster than the rate at which real national output increases. As a result, households and firms possess money balances that are greater than those they wish to hold. According to the quantity theory, these excess money balances will quickly be spent. This brings us to the third assumption in the quantity theory: changes in the money supply are assumed to bring about changes in the price level (rather than vice versa).

In summary, the main elements of the quantity theory that you need to know are:

➤ Initially the government creates or condones an expansion of the money supply greater than the increase in real national output.

➤ As a result, households and firms hold excess money balances which, when spent, pull up the price level. It is assumed that real output cannot expand in line with the increase in spending power.

Extension material

Keynesian rejection of the quantity theory

Keynesians generally reject the quantity theory of money as an explanation of inflation, or claim that it only provides an explanation of rising prices when a number of highly restrictive assumptions hold. There are three ways in which Keynesians have attacked the quantity theory.

➤ Much of the debate between Keynesians and monetarists about the quantity theory has centred on the issue of whether the velocity of circulation of money (V) is constant. In ordinary language, V represents how often money is spent. Monetarists believe that, because money earns little or no interest, it is rational to spend quickly any extra money holdings, either on goods or on non-money financial assets such as shares. For a monetarist, it is irrational to hold idle money balances for any length of time. By contrast, Keynesians take the opposite view, arguing that under certain circumstances (particularly when share and bond prices are expected to fall), it is perfectly sensible to hold idle money balances. In this situation, to avoid capital losses they expect to suffer from falling financial asset prices, people decide to hold money instead as an idle wealth asset. They hang on to, rather than spend, their extra money holdings.

➤ Keynesians also attack the quantity theory by arguing that if there is spare capacity and unemployment in the economy, an increase of the money supply may increase real income and output (y and q) rather than the price level P.

➤ The two Keynesian attacks on the quantity theory I have so far examined accept the monetarist argument that changes in *MV can* cause changes in *Py*, but they argue that an increase in the money supply (M) does not *necessarily* result in inflation (an increase in P). Instead an increase in the money supply may be absorbed in a slowing down of the velocity of circulation of money (V), or in a reflation of real income or output, which is a good thing. The third Keynesian attack on the quantity theory is more deep seated, since it is based on the idea of *reverse causation*. Reverse causation means that, instead of changes in the money supply causing changes in the price level, the true relationship is the opposite, i.e. changes in the price level cause the money supply to change. In this interpretation, inflation is caused by cost-push institutional factors in the real economy. The money supply then passively adapts, expanding to the level required to finance the level of desired transactions that the general public undertake at the new higher price level. In essence, the money supply accommodates itself to (rather than determines) the price level. Keynesians agree with the monetarists over what they consider to be the rather trivial point that an increase in the money supply is needed to finance a higher price level and allow inflation to continue. However the reverse causation argument rejects the view that an increase in the money supply is the cause of inflation.

Keynesians argue that if a government tightly restricts the growth of money to try to stem inflation, the main effects might be that the current level of transactions cannot be financed, so real activity will fall, resulting in higher unemployment. This effect occurred in the credit crunch that started in 2007, though the cause of the credit crunch lay not in tight control of the money supply by the government, but in a sudden collapse in the supply of money or liquidity emanating from the banking system itself.

The Keynesian demand-pull theory of inflation

The quantity theory of money and the Keynesian demand-pull theory are both demand theories of inflation, which locate the cause of inflation in excess demand for goods and services. After 1945, Keynesian economists accepted the argument that inflation results from excess demand pulling up the price level, but they rejected the quantity theory view that the source of the excess demand lies solely in excess monetary growth. Instead, Keynesians located the cause of inflation firmly in the real economy, in behavioural factors that cause the planned expenditure of economic agents (households, firms, the government and the overseas sectors) to exceed the quantity of output that the economy was capable of producing. In Keynesian theory, inflation is explained by real forces determining how people behave and not by money.

In the Keynesian era, from the 1950s to the 1970s, governments were committed to achieving full employment. Arguably, this caused people to behave in an inflationary way, both as workers and as voters. Workers and their unions bargained for money wage increases in excess of any productivity increase without fear of unemployment. At the same time in the political arena, the electorate added to the pressure of demand by voting for increased public spending and budget deficits. As a result of these pressures, excess demand for output emerged.

Nonetheless, the Keynesian demand-pull theory and the quantity theory of inflation may not really be very different. In both theories, the ultimate cause of inflation may lie with the government. In the quantity theory of money, the government's budget deficit and borrowing requirement cause monetary expansion, which first triggers and then sustains **demand-pull inflation**. In the Keynesian demand-pull theory, a budget deficit leads to an injection of spending into the circular flow of income that, with full or near-full capacity, results in excess demand.

At A2, you can use exactly the same AD/AS diagrams to illustrate inflation as you used last year at AS. Figure 17.3 illustrates demand-pull inflation. Suppose aggregate demand and supply are initially represented by the curves AD_1 and $SRAS$, with macroeconomic equilibrium at point X. Real national output is y_1 and the price level is P_1. There is spare capacity in the economy, which means that demand-deficient unemployment is also present.

> ## Key term
>
> **Demand-pull inflation** is caused by excess aggregate demand for output.

> ## examiner's voice
>
> Students often fail to appreciate that the quantity theory of money and the monetarist theory of inflation assume that the price level is pulled up by excess demand. The main difference between monetarist and Keynesian demand-pull theories lies in their assumptions about the underlying cause of excess demand.

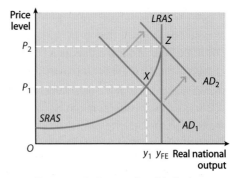

Figure 17.3 Demand-pull inflation

If aggregate demand increases to AD_2, real output and the price level both increase respectively to y_{FE} and P_2. Demand-deficient unemployment is eliminated, though at the expense of some inflation.

But once full employment arrives real output cannot increase any more, at least in the short run. The economy is now producing at its production potential on the *LRAS* curve. Since there is no spare capacity, a further shift to the right of the aggregate demand curve would lead only to inflation, with no increase in output.

The Keynesian cost-push theory of inflation

During the Keynesian era, creeping inflation continued even when there was no evidence of excess demand in the economy. Towards the end of the 1950s and during the 1960s and 1970s, this caused many Keynesians to switch away from the demand-pull theory of inflation to a new theory: the theory of **cost-push inflation**.

 Key term

Cost-push inflation is caused by rising business costs of production.

Cost theories of inflation locate the cause of inflation in structural and institutional conditions on the supply side of the economy, particularly in the labour market and the wage bargaining process. Most cost-push theories are essentially **wage-push theories**, although other variants include **profits-push** and **import cost-push theories**. The rapid cost-push inflation that occurred in the UK in 2007 and in the first half of 2008 was caused by rises in the price of imported oil, gas, commodities such as copper, and food.

Wage-push theories generally argue that the growth of monopoly power in both the labour market and the goods market is responsible for inflation. They usually assume that wages are determined in the labour market through the process of **collective bargaining**, while in the goods market, prices are formed by a *cost-plus pricing rule* in which imperfectly competitive firms add a standard profit margin to average cost when setting prices. In labour markets, growing trade union strength in the Keynesian era enabled trade unions to bargain for money wage increases in excess of any rise in labour productivity. Monopoly firms were prepared to pay these wage increases, partly because of the costs of disrupting production and partly because they believed that they could pass cost increases on to consumers through higher prices when output was sold.

The question then arises as to why trade union militancy and power grew in the Keynesian era. The guarantee of full employment by the state and the provision of a safety net of labour protection legislation and welfare benefits may have sustained the inflationary process. In the cost-push theory this created the conditions in which trade unions could successfully be more militant.

*e*xaminer's voice
You learn about cost-plus pricing, collective bargaining and the general functioning of labour markets when studying the Unit 5 specification.

Cost-push inflation is illustrated on an aggregate demand and supply diagram in Figure 17.4. Initially, macroeconomic equilibrium is at point X, with real output and the price level respectively at y_1 and P_1. Firms' money costs of production rise, for example, because money wages or the price of imported raw materials increases. This causes the SRAS curve to move upward and to the left from $SRAS_1$ to $SRAS_2$. The cost-push inflationary process increases the price level to P_2, but higher production costs have reduced the equilibrium level of output that firms are willing to produce to y_2. The new macroeconomic equilibrium is at point Z.

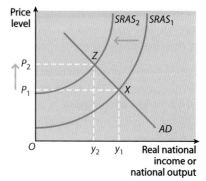

Figure 17.4 *Cost-push inflation*

The rise of the Phillips curve

Fifty years or so ago, Keynesians could be divided into demand-pull and cost-push schools in terms of the views held by members of each school on the causes of inflation. After 1958, the debate between demand-pull and cost-push Keynesians was conducted with the aid of a statistical relationship, the **Phillips curve**, which is illustrated in Figure 17.5.

Before reading further, you might refer back to Box 1.1, where I describe the Phillips machine model of the circular flow of income in the economy. When developing the Phillips curve from his analysis of the role of aggregate demand in the economy, Phillips argued that a stable inverse statistical relationship existed between the rate of change of wages (the rate of *wage* inflation)

> **Key term**
>
> The **Phillips curve** is based on evidence from the economy, showing the relationship between the rate of inflation and the level of unemployment.

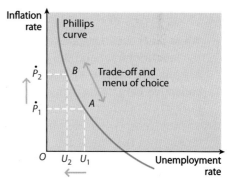

Figure 17.5 *The Phillips curve*

and the percentage of the labour force unemployed. Later versions of the Phillips curve, such as the one illustrated in Figure 17.5, measure the inverse relationship between unemployment and the rate of *price* inflation.

The Phillips curve is not a theory of inflation, but it does give support to both Keynesian theories of inflation. In the demand-pull theory, falling unemployment is associated with excess demand, which pulls up money wages in the labour market. In the cost-push theory, falling unemployment means that trade union power increases, enabling unions to use their monopoly power to push for higher wages.

Although the Phillips curve illustrates the conflict between full employment and control of inflation as policy objectives, it also suggests how the conflict can be dealt with. Suppose unemployment initially is U_1 and the rate of inflation is $\dot{P}_1$ with the economy at point A on the Phillips curve. (Note, I am using the symbol $\dot{P}$ to show the rate of price inflation.) By increasing aggregate demand, the government can move the economy to point B. Unemployment falls to U_2, but at the cost of a higher rate of inflation at $\dot{P}_2$. By using demand management policies, it appears possible for governments to trade off between increasing the number of jobs in the economy and reducing inflation. Points such as A and B on the Phillips curve represent a menu of choice for governments when deciding an acceptable combination of unemployment and inflation.

The monetarist theory of inflation

To understand the monetarist theory of inflation, it is useful to divide its development into three stages:

> the revival in 1956 by Milton Friedman of the **quantity theory of money**
> the development, also by Milton Friedman, of the theory of the **expectations-augmented Phillips curve**, which gave rise to gradualist monetarism
> the incorporation of the theory of **rational expectations** into the explanation of the inflationary process, which became known as new-classical monetarism

In order to understand how the monetarist theory of inflation has developed through these three stages, I need first to take a look at the breakdown of the Phillips curve relationship that occurred in the 1970s.

The breakdown of the Phillips relationship

In the 1970s, the Phillips relationship broke down when accelerating inflation and growing unemployment occurred together. The nicknames **stagflation** and **slumpflation** were given to the combination of these two evils. Out of stagflation and the breakdown of the Phillips relationship developed the second and third stages in the monetarist explanation of inflation, in which theories on the role of expectations in the inflationary process were tacked on to the quantity theory of money. First, in 1968 Milton Friedman developed the theory of the expectations-augmented Phillips curve and in the 1970s and 1980s the new-classical school of monetarists explained inflation in terms of the theory of rational expectations.

The theory of the expectations-augmented Phillips curve and the natural rate of unemployment (NRU)

The word *augment* means *to add*. The rather clumsy term 'expectations-augmented Phillips curve' reflects the fact that expectations of future inflation came to be viewed as a determinant of current inflation.

Economists now generally recognise that the Phillips curve in Figure 17.5 is a **short-run Phillips curve** (*SRPC*), representing the short-run relationship between inflation and unemployment. In

> **Key term**
>
> The **short-run Phillips curve** is a downward-sloping Phillips curve showing a trade-off between reducing inflation and reducing unemployment.

Key terms

The **long-run Phillips curve** is a vertical Phillips curve along which trade-offs between reducing inflation and reducing unemployment are not possible.

The **natural rate of unemployment** is located where the *LRAS* curve intersects the unemployment axis on a Phillips curve diagram. It is the equilibrium level of unemployment.

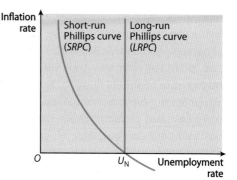

Figure 17.6 *The long-run Phillips curve and the natural rate of unemployment*

Figure 17.6, a vertical **long-run Phillips curve** (*LRPC*) has been added to the diagram, intersecting the short-run Phillips curve where the rate of inflation is zero. The rate of unemployment at this point is called the **natural rate of unemployment** (NRU), depicted by the symbol U_N. (As I explained in Chapter 16, when expressed as the number of workers unemployed, it is called the natural *level* of unemployment.)

Free-market economists argue that it is impossible to reduce unemployment below the NRU, except at the cost of suffering an ever-accelerating unanticipated inflation. This is likely to accelerate into a hyperinflation, which in any case eventually destroys the economy. The explanation for this lies in the fact that the original Keynesian explanation of the (short-run) Phillips curve wrongly took into account only the current rate of inflation and ignored the important influence of the expected rate of inflation.

The theory of the expectations-augmented Phillips curve brings together two important theories supported by modern free-market economists:
> the free-market theory of the labour market
> the theory of the role of expectations in the inflationary process

The free-market theory of the labour market assumes that the natural levels of employment and unemployment are determined at the equilibrium real wage at which workers voluntarily supply exactly the amount of labour that firms voluntarily employ.

I shall now use Figure 17.7 to introduce the role of expectations into the inflationary process. As a simplification, I shall assume that the rate of growth of labour productivity is zero and that the rate of increase of prices (price inflation) equals

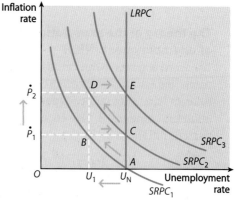

Figure 17.7 *Long-run and short-run Phillips curves*

AQA A2 Economics

the rate of increase of wages (wage inflation). The economy is initially at point A, with unemployment at the natural rate U_N. At point A, the rate of inflation is zero, as is the rate of increase of money wages. I shall also assume that people form expectations of future inflation in the next time period solely on the basis of the current rate of inflation. Thus at point A, current inflation is zero, so workers expect the future rate of inflation to also be zero.

examiner's voice

You must understand the difference between, but also the relationship between, short-run and long-run Phillips curves. However, exam questions are unlikely to ask for a detailed explanation of how the long-run Phillips curve is derived from short-run Phillips curves.

Suppose the government increases aggregate demand, to trade off along Phillips curve $SRPC_1$ to a point such as B, where unemployment at U_1 is below the natural rate, U_N. Inflation initially rises to $\dot{P}_1$ or 5%. But a point such as B is unsustainable. For workers to supply more labour, the real wage must rise, yet a rising real wage causes employers to demand less labour. In the short run, more workers may indeed enter the labour market in the false belief that a 5% increase in money wages is also a real wage increase. (This false belief is an example of **money illusion**.) Similarly, firms may be willing to employ more labour if they also suffer money illusion, falsely believing that rising prices mean that sales revenues are rising faster than labour costs.

This means that, to sustain an increase in employment above the natural rate, workers and employers must suffer money illusion in equal but opposite directions, thereby keeping expectations of inflation, formed in the previous time period, consistently below the actual rate to which inflation has risen. However, as workers continuously adjust their expectations of future inflation to the rising actual rate and bargain for ever-higher money wages to restore the real wage to the level necessary to reduce unemployment below U_N, the short-run Phillips curve shifts outward from $SRPC_1$ to $SRPC_2$ and so on. There is indeed a separate short-run Phillips curve for each expected rate of inflation. Further out short-run Phillips curves such as $SRPC_2$ and $SRPC_3$ are associated with higher expected rates of future inflation. Conversely, the short-run Phillips curve shifts inward when the expected rate of inflation falls.

Free-market economists argue that, in the long run, the only way to keep unemployment below the NRU is to permit the money supply to expand and finance an ever-accelerating inflation. Actual inflation always has to be above the expected rate for workers and firms to be willing respectively to supply and to demand more labour. But, as I noted earlier, accelerating inflation will eventually create a hyper-inflation, which, in the resulting breakdown of economic activity, is likely to increase the NRU. Any attempt to reduce unemployment below the NRU is therefore foolhardy and irresponsible. In the short run it accelerates inflation, while in the long run it perversely increases the NRU to an unnecessarily high level.

If the government realises it made a mistake when expanding the economy to point B, it can stabilise the rate of inflation at 5%. Workers and employers 'see through' their money illusion and realise that they have confused money quantities

with real quantities. As soon as this happens, they refuse respectively to supply and to demand the labour necessary to keep unemployment below the NRU. The economy now moves to point *C*. Once point *C* is reached, any further increase in aggregate demand moves the economy to point *D* and an inflation rate of $\dot{P}_2$ and to a repeat of the process just described, but starting from a higher initial rate of inflation.

Rational expectations

The theory I have just described is based on the theory of **adaptive expectations**, in which workers and firms form expectations of what will happen in the future only on the basis of what is happening currently and upon what has happened in the recent past. However, new-classical economists favour an alternative theory of how expectations are formed, called the theory of **rational expectations**. According to this theory, it is unrealistic to assume that workers and firms, acting rationally in their self-interest, form expectations of future inflation solely on the basis of current or recent inflation.

Key *term*

Adaptive expectations describe how economic agents adapt their expectations of what is likely to happen in the future on the basis of what has happened in the recent past.

Rational expectations explain how economic agents form expectations of what is likely to happen in the future on the basis of the most up-to-date and relevant information that is available.

Extension material

The difference between adaptive expectations and rational expectations
To understand the difference between the theories of adaptive and rational expectations, consider the situation of a gambler deciding whether to place a bet on a particular horse winning a race. Three races ago, the horse ended the race in fourth position, improving to third place two races ago and to second place recently. Forming his expectations adaptively, the gambler decides to bet on the horse, expecting it now to win. But gambling on the basis of recent form alone could be less successful than a strategy that makes use of all the information available, including past form. Information about the quality of the jockey, and about other matters such as the qualities of the other horses and their jockeys, the length of the race, the state of the track, and perhaps 'inside information' provided by a stable boy, might lead to a more rational gambling decision.

This story does not mean that a gambler, forming expectations rationally, always wins his bets. He may win or lose, just as bets made on decisions formed adaptively or by picking a name out of a hat, may be right or wrong. However, over a long sequence of races, it is likely that gambling decisions formed on the basis of rational expectations produce better outcomes than decisions formed adaptively or randomly. The more 'perfect' the information on which rational expectations are formed, the more likely it is that the expectations prove correct. It is less sensible to gamble on the basis of limited information when more up-to-date and relevant information is available.

Returning to the causes of inflation, new-classical economists argue that it is unrealistic to assume that a rational economic agent, acting on self-interest, forms expectations of future inflation solely on the basis of past or experienced inflation. Self-interest requires quick modification of economic behaviour in line with expectations formed on the basis of the most up-to-date information available. This means that it is *not* in people's interests to suffer money illusion.

As a result, new-classical economists reject the idea that economic agents suffer money illusion for quite long periods. If expectations are formed rationally rather than adaptively, people don't suffer from money illusion and any attempt by a government to reduce unemployment below its natural rate fails, leading solely to accelerating inflation. The correct way to reduce unemployment is to reduce the natural rate itself, rather than to increase demand to try to reduce unemployment below the NRU. To do this, the government should use appropriate free-market supply-side policies.

The incorporation of the theory of rational expectations into the explanation of the inflationary process represents the third stage in the development of monetarist and free-market theories of inflation. New-classical economists continue to accept the Friedmanite concept of the natural rate of unemployment. But whereas Milton Friedman believed that, in the short run at least, governments can trade off along a short-run Phillips curve and reduce unemployment below the natural rate, the theory of rational expectations rejects this possibility.

In new-classical thinking, it is in workers' and employers' interests to realise instantly any mistakes made when forming expectations, and to see through any attempt by an 'irresponsible' government to reflate the economy beyond the full employment level. New-classical economists believe that in this situation, attempts by government to increase aggregate demand to stimulate output and employment are anticipated fully by private economic agents. Workers and firms modify their behaviour to offset or neutralise the effects intended by the government, so the increase in aggregate demand has no effect upon real activity and employment. In extreme new-classical economics this is the case in both the short run and the long run because output and employment are always assumed to be at their natural or equilibrium levels.

An important difference separating the adaptive and rational expectations of free-market economics is the length of time unemployment must remain above its natural rate as the cost or penalty of an attempt to reduce unemployment below the natural rate. In Friedmanite theory, the economy experiences a lengthy period of unemployment above its natural rate, to 'bleed' the system of inflationary expectations built up during the period of fiscal or monetary expansion.

In contrast to this gradualist theory, new-classical theory assumes that economic agents immediately reduce expectations of future inflation, providing they believe in the credibility of a tough free-market government's commitment to reducing inflation. Believing that the government means business in pursuing tight fiscal and monetary policies to control inflation, workers and firms immediately build a lower expected rate of inflation into their wage-bargaining and price-setting behaviour. Inflation falls quickly and painlessly, without the need for a lengthy period of unemployment above its natural level.

In effect, a firmly free-market government reduces inflation by 'talking down' inflation. However, if credibility in government policy were to disappear, its ability to control inflation would also be lost. People would now expect higher prices, and would alter behaviour accordingly. Expectations of higher prices would become self-fulfilling.

Inflation psychology

It is now widely agreed by Keynesians as well as by free-market economists that what made inflation particularly difficult to control in the UK, until quite recently, was the existence, built up over decades, of an **inflation psychology**. Over the years, many groups in UK society, including house owners and wage earners in strong bargaining positions, did extremely well out of inflation. For example, house owners with large mortgages had a vested interest in allowing inflation to continue, in order to reduce the real value of their personal debt. Indeed, house owners did even better when house price inflation exceeded the general rate of inflation. In this situation, the real value of houses increased while the real value of mortgages fell.

Between the late 1990s and 2007, the UK government and the Bank of England succeeded in reducing peoples' expectations of inflation (except with regard to house price inflation). Therefore, because of the benign effect on people's behaviour, it became much easier to control inflation. The authorities had successfully 'talked down' the rate of inflation. However, as the burst of cost-push inflation in 2007 and early 2008 showed, circumstances can quickly change for the worse and that while inflation can be dormant, it is never dead.

The possible problem of price deflation

In the late 1990s and early 2000s, when the UK inflation rate fell toward 1%, some economists argued that inflation would soon be replaced with deflation (i.e. a continuously falling price level). The fear of deflation resurfaced in 2008 and 2009. If price deflation does occur, it may bring its own problems. When people believe prices are going to fall, they postpone **big ticket** consumption decisions, for example replacing their cars. This may erode business confidence and trigger recession or deepen and lengthen an already existing recession. However, this assumes that falling prices are the result of a *bad* deflation rather than a *good* deflation.

The difference between the two is illustrated in Figure 17.8. A good deflation, shown in panel (a) of Figure 17.8, results from improvements in the economy's supply side, which reduces business costs of production. Both the *SRAS* curve and the *LRAS* curve shift to the right and assuming the *AD* curve does not itself shift, the price level falls, but output and employment rise. However, in the recessionary conditions existent in the UK economy in 2009, if deflation occurs, it is much more

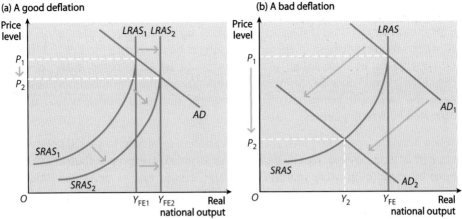

Figure 17.8 *Good and bad deflations*

likely to be the bad deflation shown in panel (b). A bad deflation is caused by a collapse of aggregate demand, negative multiplier effects, and possibly by a credit crunch.

Box 17.2 Does deflation lie ahead?

Within 6 months, during the course of 2008, the fear of an unacceptably high rate of inflation gave way to the opposite fear of deflation. The following extract published late in 2008 indicates what may happen in a period of deflation.

Yesterday's headache returns to haunt us

Periods of deflation were common in Britain right up until the Second World War. In the nineteenth century there were as many years of falling prices as of rising prices, with the result that the cost of living was lower when the First World War broke out in 1914 than it had been when Wellington triumphed at Waterloo in 1815. But since 1945, deflation has been considered yesterday's problem — in the UK at least. The last time the published inflation rate went negative in Britain was in 1947.

Jonathan Loynes of Capital Economics said that a short burst of deflation driven by tumbling oil and food prices might help the economy, since falling prices mean consumers can buy more with their income. Rising spending power would provide a boost to confidence and could help lift the economy out of recession. A longer period of deflation would not be such good news, as the experience of Japan in the 1990s illustrates. Expecting prices to be lower in the future than they are at present means consumers defer purchases and thereby cause or prolong recessions.

The Guardian, 13 November 2008

Follow-up questions

1 Who may benefit from deflation in an economy?
2 Why may deflation either cause or prolong a recession?
3 Research whether deflation has occurred in the UK since this article was written.

The costs and benefits of inflation

Everybody agrees that inflation can have serious adverse effects or costs. However, the seriousness of the adverse effects depends on whether inflation is anticipated or unanticipated. If inflation could be anticipated with complete certainty, it would pose few problems. Households and firms would simply build the expected rate of inflation into their economic decisions, which would not be distorted by wrong guesses.

When inflation is relatively low, with little variation from year to year, it is relatively easy to anticipate next year's inflation rate. Indeed, **creeping inflation**, which is associated with growing markets, healthy profits and a general climate of business optimism, greases the wheels of the economy. Viewed in this way, a low rate of inflation — but not absolute price stability — may be a necessary side-effect of expansionary policies to reduce unemployment.

A low, but stable inflation rate may also be necessary to make labour markets function efficiently. Even if average real wage rates are rising, there will be some labour markets in which real wages must fall in order to maintain a low rate of unemployment. To save jobs, workers may be willing to accept falling real wages caused by nominal wage rates rising at a slower rate than inflation. However, workers are much less willing to accept absolute cuts in nominal wage rates. Thus, with zero inflation, the changes required in real wage rates to make labour markets function efficiently fail to take place. Labour markets function best when inflation is low, but also stable. By contrast, absolute price stability produces real wage stickiness, which then results in unnecessarily high unemployment.

However, the adverse effects of inflation begin to exceed the benefits as soon as inflation becomes difficult to anticipate. An inflation rate that varies unpredictably from year to year is difficult for people to anticipate fully. Additionally, an inflation rate that is both high and difficult to anticipate creates distortions, which increasingly destabilise normal economic activity. Free-market economists generally argue that when inflation creeps upward, all too soon it acts as sand thrown in the wheels of the economy, making markets less efficient and competitive. When the *sand in the wheels* effect becomes stronger than the *greasing the wheels* effect, the costs of inflation exceed the benefits. The costs of inflation are described below.

Distributional effects

One cost of inflation is that weaker social groups in society, such as pensioners on fixed incomes, lose while others in strong bargaining positions gain. Moreover, in times of rapid inflation, real rates of interest are often negative. In this situation, lenders are really paying borrowers for the doubtful privilege of lending to them and inflation acts as a hidden tax, redistributing wealth from creditors to debtors.

> **examiner's voice**
> Exam essay questions may ask for explanation of the costs and benefits of inflation, followed by an assessment of whether the costs exceed the benefits.

Distortion of normal economic behaviour

Inflation actually distorts consumer behaviour by causing households to bring forward purchases and hoard the goods they buy if they expect the rate of inflation to accelerate. Similarly, firms may divert funds out of productive investment in fixed investment projects into unproductive commodity hoarding and speculation. People are affected by **inflationary noise**, which occurs when changes in relative prices are confused with a change in the general price level.

Breakdown in the functions of money

In a time of severe inflation, money becomes less useful and efficient as a medium of exchange and a store of value. Rapidly changing prices also erode money's functions as a unit of account and standard of deferred payment. In a hyperinflation, in which the inflation rate may accelerate to several hundred per cent a year or even higher, less efficient bartering replaces money and imposes extra costs on most transactions.

Stacks of worthless banknotes during the German hyperinflation of 1923

International uncompetitiveness

When the inflation rate is higher than in competitor countries, exports increase in price, making them uncompetitive. This puts pressure on a fixed exchange rate. With a floating exchange rate, the rate falls to restore competitiveness, but rising import prices may fuel a further bout of inflation.

Shoe leather and menu costs

With rapid inflation, consumers incur **shoe leather costs**, spending time and effort shopping around to check which prices have or have not risen. By contrast, **menu costs** are incurred by firms having to adjust price lists and vending machines more often.

Summary

➤ Control of inflation is a major macroeconomic objective.

➤ Inflation can be defined as a persistent or continuous rise in the price level or as a continuing fall in the value of money.

➤ Deflation can be described a persistent or continuous fall in the price level or as a continuing increase in the value of money.

➤ The price level is measured by a price index and the rate of inflation is measured by annual changes in the level of the index.

➤ The consumer prices index (CPI) and the retail prices index (RPI) measure consumer price inflation in the UK.

➤ The construction of a price index requires choice of a sample (the national shopping basket) and the weighting of all items in the sample.

➤ Theories of inflation can be divided into demand-pull and cost-push theories.

➤ The quantity theory of money, which is the oldest theory of inflation, is a demand theory of inflation.

➤ Cost-push theories came into fashion in the Keynesian era in the 1960s and 1970s.

➤ A short-run Phillips curve illustrates the conflict between controlling inflation and reducing unemployment, but is not itself a theory of inflation.

➤ The monetarist theory of inflation stems from the modern quantity theory of money, but also incorporates the role of expectations in the inflationary process.

➤ Monetarist and free-market economists argue that the long-run Phillips curve is vertical, located at the economy's natural level of unemployment.

➤ In recent years economists have feared that the problems of deflation may replace the problems of inflation.

➤ At low and stable inflation rates the benefits of inflation may exceed the costs, but at higher and more variable inflation rates the reverse is true.

Questions

1 Distinguish between inflation, deflation and reflation.

2 Why is the rate of inflation measured by changes in the CPI usually different from the rate of inflation measured by changes in the RPI?

3 What is the quantity theory of money?

4 What are the similarities of, and the differences between, the quantity theory of money and the Keynesian demand-pull theory of inflation?

5 Analyse the causes of cost-push inflation.

6 Explain the Phillips curve relationship.

7 Distinguish between short-run and long-run Phillips curves.

8 Distinguish between the theories of adaptive expectations and rational expectations.

Chapter 18

Money, banks and monetary policy

Besides being a mixed economy, the economy we live in is a monetary economy, in which most of the goods and services produced are traded or exchanged via the intermediary of money. This chapter describes the nature and functions of money in a modern economy, before explaining how bank deposits, which are created by the private enterprise and commercial banking system, form the largest part of modern money. The second half of the chapter surveys the changes that have taken place in monetary policy in the UK, showing how the main features of current monetary policy developed out of the monetary policies implemented by UK governments and the Bank of England over the last 20–30 years. The chapter concludes by explaining how a significant sea change may be taking place in the nature of monetary policy, at least with the recessionary conditions hitting the UK and global economies in recent times.

Learning outcomes

This chapter will:
- describe the nature and functions of money
- explain how the private enterprise banking system creates the lion's share of modern money
- develop your understanding of monetary policy, focusing on the use of interest rates to try to control inflation
- evaluate the success of monetary policy before 2008
- discuss whether the nature of monetary policy changed during the 2008 recession

What you should already know

At AS you learnt that in the UK monetary policy is implemented by the Monetary Policy Committee (MPC) of the Bank of England, which raises or lowers interest rates to try to achieve the government's target rate of inflation. You also learnt how monetary policy can involve the use of the

money supply and exchange rates. However, the Bank Rate set by the Bank of England has been the main instrument of monetary policy affecting other interest rates and thence the level of aggregate demand in the economy. Essentially, monetary policy is a demand-side policy, which shifts the aggregate demand curve in the *AD/AS* macroeconomic model.

The nature and functions of money

Money is best defined by focusing on the two principal functions money performs in the economy. Money functions as:

 Key *term*

> **A medium of exchange (means of payment).** The economy we live in is a monetary economy in which most of the goods and services produced are traded or exchanged via the intermediary of money, rather than through **barter** (i.e. swapping goods). Whenever money is used to pay for goods or services, or for the purpose of settling transactions and the payment of debts, it performs this function.

Money is both a medium of exchange and a store of value.

> **A store of value (wealth).** Instead of being spent, money may be stored as a **wealth asset**, in preference to holding other *financial* assets, such as stocks and shares. When stored rather than spent, money's purchasing power is transferred to the future, although inflation may erode money's future purchasing power.

Box 18.1 The development of modern money

Barter

Before the development of money, exchange and trade took place in simple and primitive village economies, based on barter: the swapping of goods and services. However, barter is inefficient and impractical in a more complex economic system. Successful barter requires a **double coincidence of wants**, which means that a person wishing to trade a television set for a refrigerator must not only establish contact with someone with equal but opposite wants (that is, an individual possessing a refrigerator who wishes to exchange it for a television set); they must also agree that the television set and refrigerator are of equal value.

Barter is inefficient because the time and energy spent searching the market to establish the double coincidence of wants results in unnecessary search costs, shoe-leather costs and transaction costs. These, in turn, promote a much greater inefficiency: namely, preventing the development of specialisation, division of labour and large-scale production.

Commodity money

Figure 18.1 shows the three main forms of money that have developed since money replaced barter. The earliest form of money was **commodity money**. Commodities

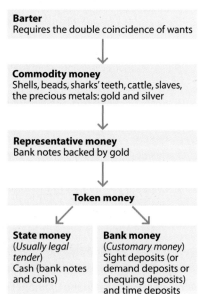

Figure 18.1 *Barter and the different forms of money*

that functioned as money had an intrinsic value of their own: they yielded utility and consumer services to their owners. Beads, shells, sharks' teeth and other commodities could be used for decorative purposes while being stored as wealth and some commodities used as money, such as cattle, could be slaughtered and eaten.

Representative money

As money evolved, gold and silver gradually replaced other forms of commodity money because they possessed, to a greater degree, the desirable characteristics necessary for a commodity to function as money: relative scarcity, uniformity, durability, portability and divisibility. All of these help to create confidence in money, which is necessary for its acceptability. Nevertheless, gold and silver are vulnerable to theft and are difficult to store safely. Eventually, wealthy individuals deposited the precious metals they owned with goldsmiths for safekeeping.

At the next stage, the goldsmiths developed into banks, and the receipts they issued in return for deposits of gold became the first banknotes or paper money. These notes were **representative money**, representing ownership of gold. Early banknotes were acceptable as a means of payment because they could be exchanged for gold on demand. They were issued by privately owned banks rather than by the state, although the state continued to issue gold and silver coinage. Although worthless in themselves, banknotes functioned as money because people were willing to accept them as long as there was confidence that notes could be changed into gold, which does have an intrinsic value.

Token money

Modern money is almost all token money with no intrinsic value of its own. It takes two main forms: **cash** and **bank deposits**. In the UK, the state, or rather its agent, the Bank of England, has a monopoly over the issue of cash (although, Scottish and Northern Ireland banks also have a limited ability to issue banknotes). However, cash is literally the *small change* of the monetary system; bank deposits form by far the largest part of modern money. Most modern money takes the form of bank deposits created by the private enterprise banking system.

Follow-up questions

1 Why does money provide a more *efficient* means of payment than barter?
2 What are the advantages and disadvantages of using cash as the main form of personal wealth?

Banks and bank deposits

A **bank** is an institution that:
➤ accepts deposits from the general public that can be transferred by cheque or debit card
➤ creates deposits owned by the general public when it makes advances or bank loans; these can either be **overdrafts** or **term loans**

Gold has long been considered a form of money

PHOTODISC

 Key *term*

A **bank** is an institution that accepts deposits and creates deposits when lending to customers who wish to borrow.

Almost all banks in the UK are commercial companies. Most banks aim to make a profit for their owners. The Bank of England is an exception, since its aims are primarily to oversee the financial system and to implement the country's monetary policy. Commercial banks divide into retail banks such as HSBC and Barclays, whose main business is with the general public and **wholesale banks**, which deal with each other and with other financial institutions largely located in the City of London. Wholesale banks are often called **investment banks**, although until recently they were generally known as merchant banks.

BARCLAYS

examiner's voice
You should understand that bank deposits are the main form of money and that cash is a relatively small part of total money.

Barclays is a retail bank

In contrast to cash, which is tangible and can be seen and touched, bank deposits are intangible. Customers only 'see' a bank deposit when reading the statement of a bank account, or when viewing the electronic display in a cash-dispensing machine. Bank deposits are the main form of money because banks possess the ability to create new deposits, almost out of thin air, where none previously existed. I explain the essential features of the deposit-creating process in the Extension material that follows.

Extension material

How banks create money

Bank deposits make up by far the largest part of modern money, between about two-thirds and 90% depending on how money is defined.

Many students are completely mystified as to how bank deposits are created. A good starting point for developing an understanding is provided by the following story:

Suppose I write my signature on a scrap of paper, together with the words 'I owe the bearer £100'. I then give you the scrap of paper and ask you to go to a shop and buy £100 worth of goods. Then, when the time comes to pay, you must give the scrap of paper to the shop assistant. Now we all know that, in real life, shops refuse to accept such an 'I owe you'. But just suppose the shop did accept my scrap of paper, believing it could then use the note to buy goods from its suppliers. My 'I owe you' note would have become money.

Now while ordinary individuals can't generally create money in the manner in which I have described, banks can. I shall now use a highly simplified model of the banking system to explain how.

Bank deposits are the main form of money because banks possess the ability to create **credit**. To explain how, I am going to make three simplified (and unrealistic) assumptions about the banking system. These are:

- There is only one bank in the economy (a monopoly bank).
- The bank possesses only one reserve asset, namely cash, which it uses to meet any cash withdrawals by customers.
- The bank decides that, to maintain confidence and to prevent customers wanting to withdraw all their funds, it must always possess cash equal to 10% of total customer deposits.

The first assumption means that, unlike in a system in which there are many banks, customers cannot withdraw and transfer cash from one bank to another. The second and third assumptions taken together mean that, for prudential reasons, the bank chooses to operate a 10% **cash ratio**.

Suppose that a member of the general public deposits £1,000 cash in the bank. From the bank's point of view, the £1,000 is simultaneously a **liability** and an **asset**, and will be recorded as such in the bank's balance sheet:

Liabilities	Assets
Deposits £1,000	Cash £1,000

As things stand, all the bank's deposit liabilities are backed with cash (i.e. the bank's cash ratio is 100%). If this remained the position, the bank would not be a bank at all, but a safe-deposit institution, guarding, for a fee, the cash deposited by customers. The difference between a bank and a safe-deposit institution is that a bank uses the cash deposited with it as a monetary base, from which to launch the profitable loans it grants to customers.

Unlike the customer depositing cash in the bank, i.e. lending the cash to the bank in return for a deposit credited to the customer's name, other customers may have little or no cash and need to borrow from the bank. Providing they are credit worthy, the bank is in a position to lend exactly £9,000 to these customers This takes the form of an interest-earning advance on the assets side of the bank's balance sheet, which is matched by a £9,000 created deposit on the liabilities side of the balance sheet:

Liabilities	Assets
Initial deposit £1,000	Cash £1,000
Created deposit £9,000	Advances £9,000
Total deposits £10,000	Total assets £10,000

Both the customer who made the initial deposit of £1,000 and the customers in receipt of the advances can draw cheques equal to £10,000 in total on their deposits. The £1,000 cash deposit has increased total deposits to £10,000.

As I have said, my assumption of a monopoly bank is completely unrealistic. However, it has allowed me to illustrate in a simplified way that the banking system as a whole can expand bank deposits, and hence the money supply, to a *multiple* of the reserve assets (in this case cash) that back the created deposits. The resulting *money multiplier* measures the maximum expansion of deposits (low-powered money) that is possible for a given increase in cash (high-powered money) deposited in the banking system. In my example, the money multiplier is 10, which means that total bank deposits can expand the money supply to ten times the cash held by the banking system.

Box 18.2 A brief history of banking

To understand how a bank such as Barclays operates, it is useful to divide the bank's customers into two different groups: those in credit and those in debit. Members of the former group deposit cash in the bank, while members of the latter group borrow from the bank. The bank makes a profit by charging borrowers a higher interest rate than it pays to attract deposits.

Before the middle of the nineteenth century, banks printed their own banknotes. Some of these were given to customers depositing gold in the banks, but the rest were lent to customers borrowing from the banks. By printing and lending notes in this way, the banks' note issue grew to exceed the gold deposits held by the banks. Prudent banking requires a bank to keep sufficient reserve assets (in this case, gold) to meet all likely calls by customers on the bank's liabilities.

However, greedy or imprudent banks were often tempted, in pursuit of profit, to over-extend their note issue by printing and lending banknotes greatly in excess of the gold they owned. In these circumstances, the banks' holdings of gold might prove insufficient to meet the demand by customers to convert banknotes (the banks' liabilities) into gold. Imprudent over-extension of the note issue thus led to bank crashes, which occurred periodically when banks ran out of gold. The large number of bank crashes that occurred in the early nineteenth century led to the 1844 Bank Charter Act, which largely removed the right of British banks to issue their own notes.

However, the 1844 Bank Charter Act encouraged a new monetary development, namely the creation of **deposit money**, which is now the main form of modern money. Apart from Scottish and Northern Irish banks (which have to deposit an equivalent amount of gold at the Bank of England), banks can no longer print and issue their own notes. However, banks get round this inconvenience by simply *crediting a deposit* to the account of a customer to whom a loan is given. Whenever loans are made, bank deposits are created.

Sight deposits or **demand deposits**, which in the UK are known as **current account deposits** upon which cheques can be drawn, are money because they are both a store of value and a medium of exchange.

Note that the *deposit* is money and not the *cheque*. The cheque is just an instruction to make a cash withdrawal or to shift ownership of a bank deposit from one person to another. However, the fact that cheques are customarily acceptable as a means of payment turns bank deposits into money. These days, **debit cards** are increasingly used instead of cheques to make payments and to transfer ownership of bank deposits.

Cash became mere token money, rather than representative money, when the state withdrew the promise to convert its notes and coins into gold on demand: that is, when the currency came off the **gold standard**. Cash is also usually **legal tender** — *fiat money* made legal by government decree — which must be accepted as a medium of exchange and in settlement of debts. Like cash, bank deposits created by the private enterprise banking system are token money, but they are also **customary money** rather than legal tender. This means that bank deposits are generally accepted because of people's confidence in the banks and in the monetary system. However, people can refuse to accept payment by cheque or debit card, demanding instead payment in legal tender. In the UK, the use of cheque guarantee cards adds to the acceptability of bank deposits as a medium of exchange, since banks guarantee in advance to honour a payment by cheque up to a certain value, usually between £100 and £500 per transaction.

Follow-up questions

1 Explain the difference between a bank's customer being in credit or in debit.
2 What is the difference between legal tender and customary money?

Money, money substitutes and near money

As I have explained, to function as money, an asset must be both a medium of exchange and a store of value or wealth. Bank **demand deposits** (**sight deposits** or **current account** deposits) are money because they possess both of these functions. Bank **time deposits** (**savings accounts** and **deposit accounts** in the UK) are not quite as liquid as demand deposits. In the past, customers had to wait several days to convert a time deposit into cash and a chequing facility was not usually available. Nevertheless, these days banks usually allow time deposits to be converted into immediate cash, but with the loss of a few days interest.

To understand fully the nature of money, it is useful to compare money with substitutes for money and near money. These are all shown in Table 18.1.

Table 18.1 *Money, money substitutes and near money*

Money substitutes	Money	Near money
Medium of exchange but not a store of value (e.g. credit cards and charge cards)	Medium of exchange and store of value (e.g. cash, bank and building society deposits)	Store of value, but insufficiently liquid to be a medium of exchange (e.g. national savings securities)

Over the last 30 years, credit cards, mostly operating in the Visa and MasterCard networks, have increasingly replaced cash and the use of cheques as a means of payment. However, although they serve as a medium of exchange, most credit cards cannot be used as a store of wealth. Indeed, the use of a credit card builds up a personal liability in the form of a debt with the credit card company, which must eventually be settled with a cash or cheque transaction. Because a credit card transfers rather than settles a debt, it is a substitute for money rather than money itself.

**e*xaminer's voice*

You must understand the money supply as well as interest rates. However, detailed knowledge is not required of the financial assets that function as money, the money supply, or the structure of interest rates.

Whereas a money substitute such as a credit card is a medium of exchange but *not* a store of value, the reverse is true for near money. A financial asset such as a National Savings security provides an example, being too illiquid to be a means of payment. In the past, building society deposits were also near moneys rather than money. However, most building society deposits can now be converted into cash and withdrawn on demand and without penalty and building societies now issue chequebooks and allow cheques to be drawn on deposits. Thus, building society deposits have developed into money, since they have become a medium of exchange as well as a store of value.

Extension material

The problem of defining the money supply

Before the advent of monetarism, few economists gave much attention to the precise definition of the money supply or stock of money in the economy. This reflected the

Keynesian view that money did not matter in the macroeconomic management of the economy. However, when monetarism replaced Keynesianism as the new prevailing orthodoxy in the 1970s, money did begin to matter — particularly in the years before monetarism itself drifted from favour around 1985. For a few years from the mid-1970s to the mid-1980s, during the 'monetarist era', control of the money supply became an important part of monetarist economic management in general and monetary policy in particular. During this period, monetarist economists devoted considerable attention to the problem of deciding which assets to include and exclude when defining the money supply.

A significant problem that faced the monetarists stemmed from what has become known as **Goodhart's Law**. This is named after Charles Goodhart, formerly a professor at the London School of Economics and a member of the Bank of England's Monetary Policy Committee (MPC). Goodhart argued that, as soon as a government tries to control the growth of a particular measure of the money supply, any previously stable relationship between the targeted measure of money and the economy breaks down. The more successful the Bank of England appears to be in controlling the rate of growth of the financial assets defined as the money supply, the more likely it is that other financial assets, regarded previously as near money outside the existing definition and system of control, will take on the function of a medium of exchange and become money.

In this way, attempting to control the money supply is rather like a man trying to catch his own shadow. As soon as he moves, his shadow also moves. Although what is defined as money may be controlled, when other financial assets become money, this becomes irrelevant. The difficulties of first defining the money supply, and second, exerting control over its rate of growth, contributed to the downfall of monetarism after 1985.

Over the years, the Bank of England has used more than one definition of the money supply. These divide into measures of narrow money and broad money. **Narrow money**, which restricts the measure of money to cash and bank and building society sight deposits, reflects the medium of exchange function of money, namely money functioning as a means of payment. **Broad money** also measures time deposits, which are a store of value rather than a medium of exchange.

The Bank of England and monetary policy

Most banks are commercial banks, whose main aim is to make a profit for their owners. Although it makes a considerable profit, the most significant exception is the Bank of England, which is the UK's **central bank**. For most of the

> **Key term**
>
> The **central bank** is the bank that implements monetary policy and also issues and controls fiat money or cash.

period since its formation in 1694, the Bank of England was a private enterprise company. The Bank is now a nationalised industry and its surplus profit goes to the state. The Bank of England's principal function (besides overseeing and trying to maintain confidence in the whole of the financial system) is to implement **monetary policy** on behalf of the UK government.

Monetary policy is the part of economic policy that attempts to achieve the government's macroeconomic objectives using monetary instruments, such as controls over bank lending and the rate of interest. Before 1997, monetary policy was implemented more or less jointly by central government and the Bank of England, which were known as the *monetary authorities*. But the Treasury abandoned its hands-on role in implementing monetary policy in 1997 when the incoming Labour government made the Bank of England operationally independent. Unless the Bank is put under pressure by the Treasury, there is now only one monetary authority: the Bank of England.

Objectives and instruments of monetary policy

To understand monetary policy, it is useful to distinguish between policy *objectives* and policy *instruments*. A policy objective is the target that the Bank of England aims to hit. By contrast, a policy instrument is the tool of control used to try to achieve the objective.

Monetary policy objectives and instruments can be classified in different ways. Policy objectives can be divided into *ultimate* and *intermediate* objectives. Policy instruments separate into those that affect the supply of new deposits that the commercial banks can create and those that affect the demand for loans or credit.

Monetary policy objectives

For over 30 years, *control of inflation* has been the main objective of UK monetary policy. The government needs to control inflation in order to create conditions in which the ultimate policy objective of *improved economic welfare* can be attained. However, before 1992, the Bank of England tried to control inflation by first meeting an *intermediate* monetary policy objective. There have been two intermediate monetary policy objectives. First, from the mid-1970s to 1985, under the influence of monetarist economic theory, the *money supply* was the intermediate target of monetary policy. Second, from 1985 to 1992, the *exchange rate* replaced the money supply as the intermediate policy objective. Intermediate policy objectives were finally abandoned in 1992 when the pound was forced out of the **exchange rate mechanism** (ERM) of the **European monetary system** (EMS).

examiner's voice
You must understand that control of inflation is the main objective of monetary policy, but that there can be other objectives.

Since 1992, monetary policy has targeted the control of inflation directly, without the use of any intermediate policy objectives.

Extension material

Monetarism and monetary policy

Monetarist economists believe that inflation is caused by a prior increase in the quantity of money in the economy. The quantity theory predicts that if the quantity of money increases and people end up holding money balances larger than those they wish to hold, the excess money holdings will be spent. This creates excess demand for real goods and services in the economy, which in turn pulls up the price level in a demand-pull inflation.

From the late 1970s until the mid-1980s, monetary policy was based on announcing, first, a target rate of growth of the money supply, and second, that policy would then be implemented to achieve the announced target. Suppose, for example, growth of real GDP is 2% and the government aims for a maximum inflation rate of 3%. Under these conditions, the target rate of growth of the money supply should be set at a maximum rate of 5%, to enable goods and services to be purchased at prices up to 3% higher than last year's prices.

The monetarist period in UK monetary policy ended in 1985 when Thatcher's Conservative government abandoned setting formal money supply targets. There were two main reasons for the collapse of monetarism, both suggested by Goodhart's Law. First, the growth of the money supply proved difficult if not impossible to control. Second, the relationship between the growth of the money supply and the rate of inflation, which had seemed stable *before* monetarist policies were implemented, broke down *after* the attempt was made to control the growth of the money supply.

Monetary policy instruments

As you learnt at AS, policy instruments are the tools used to achieve policy objectives. There are two categories of monetary policy instrument: those that affect the retail banks' ability to *supply* credit and to create bank deposits; and those that affect the general public's *demand* for bank loans. The success or lack of success of both types of monetary policy instrument depend on the extent to which they control or influence the commercial banks' ability to create the main form of money, namely bank deposits.

Controlling the supply of credit

In the Keynesian era, the Bank of England limited the ability of commercial banks to supply more credit and bank deposits in two main ways. The first method was to impose **required reserve ratios** on the banks, which then had to reduce total lending and bank deposits when the Bank of England reduced the supply of reserve assets available for the banks to hold.

With the second method, the Bank of England imposed **direct controls on bank lending**. Two types were used: **quantitative** and **qualitative controls**. Quantitative controls impose maximum limits on the amount that banks can lend or on the rate at which banks can expand total deposits. By contrast, qualitative controls are 'directional' controls that instruct or persuade banks to lend only to certain types of customer. For example, business customers requiring credit to finance investment or exports might be given a high priority, with consumer credit being relegated to a much lower position in the queue for advances.

In the 1980s, the Bank of England abandoned these policies. Two main factors explain why. First, Thatcher's Conservative government believed that free markets are far more effective than interventionist policies in achieving efficient and competitive resource allocation. Second, abolition of foreign exchange controls in 1979 meant that UK-based banks, which were subject to restrictive controls, could no longer compete profitably for banking business with overseas competitors. The controls meant that UK banks competed internationally on an un-level playing field. Because the controls encouraged banking business to move offshore, the government decided to abolish them to attract the business back to the UK.

How interest rates influence the demand for credit

Whereas the direct controls on bank lending described above ration the supply of credit available, at least until 2009, modern monetary policy has operated almost solely through interest rate policy. To influence the quantity of bank deposits being created (and also the level of aggregate demand in the economy), the Bank of England rations demand for credit by raising or lowering its official rate of interest. In recent years, the Bank of England has reverted to an older tradition of calling its key interest rate the **Bank Rate**.

> **examiner's voice**
> You should understand that different interest rates reflect different risks and that short-run interest rates differ from long-run interest rates.

> **Key term**
>
> The **rate of interest** is the cost of borrowing and the reward paid to savers for foregoing consumption.

Applying the *AD/AS* model to analyse monetary policy

When using *AD/AS* analysis to explain how monetary policy affects the economy, a good starting point is the aggregate demand equation I explained in Chapter 15:

$$AD = C + I + G + (X - M)$$

Whereas fiscal policy can affect aggregate demand by changing the level of government spending (*G*), monetary policy affects the other components of aggregate demand, *C*, *I*, and (*X – M*). A cut in interest rates causes the

> **examiner's voice**
> You don't really need to learn any more about *AD/AS* analysis and monetary policy than you learnt a year ago at AS. In fact, in all your economics, simple things done well are always preferable to complicated analysis gone wrong.
>
> Monetary policy shifts the *AD* curve in the economy rather than the *AS* curve. This reflects its role in the management of aggregate demand.

AD curve illustrated in Figure 18.2 to shift to the right from AD_1 to AD_2.

There are three main ways in which a cut in interest rates increases aggregate demand. Two of these are:

➤ Lower interest rates reduce household consumption (C). First, lower interest rates discourage saving, which means that more income is available for consumption. Second, the cost of house-hold borrowing falls, which cuts the cost of servicing a mortgage and credit card debt. Borrowers have more money to spend on consumption because less of their income is used for interest payments. Third, lower interest rates may cause asset prices to increase, e.g. the prices of houses and shares. Higher house and share prices increase personal wealth, which in turn increases consumption. Fourth, rising house and share prices lead to an increase in consumer confidence, which further boosts consumption.

➤ Lower interest rates increase business investment (I) — the purchase of capital goods such as machines by firms. Businesses bring forward investment projects they would have cancelled or postponed at a higher cost of borrowing, believing that new capital goods can now be profitably used. A rise in business confidence is also likely to boost investment.

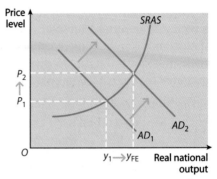

Figure 18.2 *How a decrease in the interest rate causes the AD curve to shift to the right*

How changes in interest rates affect exports and imports via the exchange rate

The third way in which a fall in interest rates increases aggregate demand works through the effect of lower interest rates on net export demand (X − M). Lower UK interest rates lead to the selling of pounds or sterling, as owners of international capital decide to hold other currencies instead. This causes the pound's exchange rate to fall, which increases the price competitiveness of UK exports in world markets. At the same time, the prices of imports rise and they become less competitive in the UK market. The UK's balance of payments on current account improves, with the increase in net export demand shifting the AD curve to the right.

> **examiner's voice**
>
> *Sterling* is a word often used when describing the role of the pound in the international economy. For example, economists write about the demand for sterling or for the pound sterling.

By contrast, a rise in interest rates triggers a capital inflow in the balance of payments, which increases the exchange rate. Exports lose their competitiveness, and the current account of the balance of payments deteriorates. Aggregate demand falls and the AD curve shifts to the left.

Box 18.3 The transmission mechanism of monetary policy

The Bank of England believes that monetary policy affects aggregate demand and inflation through a number of channels, which form the transmission mechanism of monetary policy. The flow chart in Figure 18.3 shows the routes through which changes in the Bank's official interest rate (the instrument of monetary policy), shown at point 1 in the diagram, eventually affect inflation (the objective of monetary policy), shown at point 11.

Official interest rate decisions (point 1 in Figure 18.3) affect **market interest rates** (point 2), such as mortgage rates and bank deposit rates set by commercial banks and financial institutions. At the same time, policy actions and announcements affect **expectations** about the future course of the economy and the **confidence** with which these expectations are held (point 4). They also affect **asset prices** (point 3) and the **exchange rate** (point 5).

These changes in turn affect **aggregate demand** in the economy (point 8). This comprises **domestically generated demand** (point 6) and **net external demand** (point 7), which is determined by export and import demand.

Domestic demand results from the spending, saving and investment behaviour of individuals and firms within the economy. Lower market interest rates increase domestic demand by encouraging consumption rather than saving by households and investment spending by firms. Conversely, higher market interest rates depress domestic spending. If the official interest rate falls, asset prices rise and people feel wealthier and generally more confident about the future. As a result, consumption increases. A lower official interest rate causes financial capital to flow out of the pound and into other currencies, which in turn causes the exchange rate to fall. A falling exchange rate reduces UK export prices, while raising the price of imports. Demand for UK-produced goods increases.

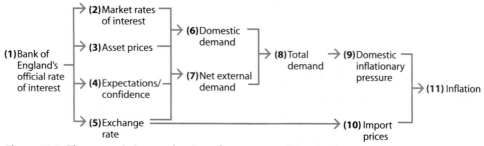

Figure 18.3 *The transmission mechanism of monetary policy*

Changes in aggregate demand (relative to the economy's ability to supply output) affect **domestic inflationary pressures** in the economy (point 9). Changes in aggregate demand affect demand-pull inflationary pressures. However, there are also cost-push pressures from the effects of changes in aggregate demand on domestic wage rates. Changes in **import prices** (point 10) brought about by changes in the exchange rate affect inflation in two ways. Changes in the prices of imported food and consumer goods affect inflation directly, while changes in the prices of imported raw materials affect cost-push inflationary pressures.

The Bank of England estimates a time lag of up to 2 years between an initial change in the Bank's official rate of interest (point 1) and the resulting change in the rate of inflation (point 11). Output is affected within 1 year, but the fullest effect on inflation occurs after a lag of 2 years. In terms of the size of the effect, the Bank believes a 1% change in its official interest rate affects output by about 0.2–0.35% after about a year and inflation by around 0.2–0.4% per year after 2 years.

Follow-up questions

1 What is meant by an 'asset price'? Explain how an increase in interest rates affects asset prices.
2 How does a fall in interest rates affect import prices in the UK?

Box 18.4 Libor and Bank Rate

Until quite recently, high-street banking was a boring form of business. For each borrower, a bank had to have around ten savers to provide the funds being lent. The need to attract savers was a significant constraint on the banks' ability to provide new loans or credit.

All this changed in the deregulated and liberalised financial world created in the 1980s and 1990s. The traditional business of 'boring' banking went out of the window as high-street banks moved onto a much more interesting business plan. Out went household savings as the banks' principal source of liquidity and in came the borrowing of funds on the London interbank wholesale money market.

The rate of interest at which banks lend to each other is called the **Libor**, which is the acronym for the London interbank offered rate of interest. Unlike **Bank Rate**, which is set monthly by the Bank of England, the Libor rate is determined on a daily basis by the demand and supply for funds as banks lend to each other to balance their books.

In normal times, the 3-month Libor rate trades at a small premium of around 0.15% above where the market thinks Bank Rate will be in 3 months' time. However, when the credit crunch spread from America in 2007, Libor shot up to around 1.5% above Bank Rate. As Figure 18.4 shows, for most of the time, Libor remained well above Bank Rate through 2008 and into 2009.

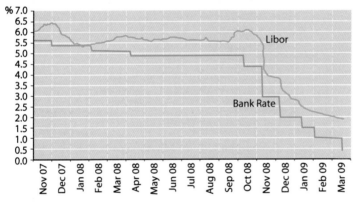

Figure 18.4 Libor and the Bank Rate, November 2007–March 2009

Source: Bank of England

The divergence between Bank Rate and Libor has made it difficult for the Bank of England to operate monetary policy effectively. For example, a cut in Bank Rate aimed at reducing the interest rates that the general public have to pay when borrowing from high-street banks is ineffective if the rates the banks charge is determined by Libor rather than by Bank Rate and monetary policy.

Follow-up questions

1 How are changes in Bank Rate expected to affect mortgage interest rates?
2 What has happened to the divergence between Bank Rate and Libor in the months or years since January 2009?

UK monetary policy from 1992 to 2009

Since 1992, UK monetary policy has been directed explicitly at a published inflation rate target. In this *pre-emptive* monetary policy the authorities announce that they are prepared to raise interest rates even when there is no immediate sign of accelerating inflation, in order to anticipate and head off a rise in the inflation rate that would otherwise occur many months in the future. The policy-makers at the Bank of England estimate what the inflation rate is likely to be 18 months to 2 years ahead (the medium term), if policy (that is, interest rates) remains unchanged. If the forecast rate of inflation is different from the target rate set by the government, the Bank changes interest rates to prevent the forecast inflation rate becoming a reality in the future. Interest rates are also raised or lowered to pre-empt any likely adverse effect upon the inflation rate of an adverse outside shock hitting the economy.

In 1997 the inflation rate target was made *symmetrical*. This means that the Bank of England must stimulate aggregate demand, which will generally raise the rate of inflation, whenever actual inflation is below the target rate, just as the Bank must try to reduce the rate of inflation whenever actual inflation is above the target rate. The Labour government stated that although the primary objective of monetary policy is price stability, the Bank of England must also support the government's economic policy objectives, including those for growth and employment. The fact that the Bank of England now has a duty to use monetary policy to protect economic growth and employment helps to explain why UK monetary policy changed so radically in 2009, when quantitative easing replaced interest rate changes as the main instrument of monetary policy.

The credit crunch, the 2008 recession and the crisis in monetary policy

In Chapter 17, I described how the UK and other economies suffered from a sudden burst of cost-push inflation in 2007 and the first half of 2008. The rising cost of oil, natural gas, raw materials and food took the CPI inflation rate up to 5.2%, well above the upper target limit of 3% set by government. By December 2008, the effect of rising input prices and the burst of cost-push inflation had passed through the system. Real national output was now falling, with the recession threatening to deepen and lengthen in a way not seen since the Great Depression of the 1930s. Not only were energy and raw material costs now falling, aggregate demand was also falling dramatically. In part, this was caused by the drying up of bank lending and liquidity resulting from the credit crunch. In these conditions, with demand collapsing and unemployment rapidly rising, many economists believed that the rate of inflation would fall to close to zero, with some even predicting a falling price level or deflation.

Box 18.5 What is quantitative easing?

In Box 18.4, I suggested that, when the gap between the Bank Rate and Libor widens, cutting the Bank Rate to reduce the cost of borrowing from banks can become ineffective. However, there is another possibly greater problem involved. Suppose that at the same time, the inflation rate becomes negative and the price level falls. Nominal interest rates, including Libor and mortgage rates, may also fall but they cannot become negative. The real interest rate is the nominal interest rate minus the rate of inflation. For example, if nominal interest rates fall very low to 1% but the inflation rate in a deflation is minus 3%, real interest rates are actually quite high at plus 4%. But if the behaviour of people living in the 'real economy' is influenced by real, rather than by nominal, interest rates, the policy in a recession of relying on Bank Rate cuts to stimulate aggregate demand may be completely ineffective.

In 2008, the fear of what I have just outlined led to the recommendation that interest rate cuts must be backed up by quantitative easing, which is the equivalent of printing more money.

The Bank of England began to implement a policy of quantitative easing on 5 March 2009. The following extract, taken from an article published in the *Daily Telegraph* on 8 January 2009, explains the main features of quantitative easing:

Quantitative easing is the modern way to print money. Ultimately the impact is not very different from dropping dollar bills from a helicopter. Its aim is to get money flowing around an economy when the normal process of cutting interest rates isn't working — most obviously when interest rates are so low that it's impossible to cut them further.

The way to do this is for the central bank to buy assets in exchange for money. In theory, any assets can be bought from anybody. In practice, the focus of quantitative easing is on buying securities (like government debt, mortgage-backed securities or even equities) from banks.

Where, one might ask, does the central bank get the money to buy all these securities? The answer is that it just waves a magic wand and creates it. It doesn't even need to turn on the printing presses. It simply increases the size of banks' accounts at the central bank. These accounts held by ordinary banks at the central bank go by the name of 'reserves'. All banks have to hold some reserves at the central bank. But when there is quantitative easing, they build up 'excess reserves'.

If banks swap their securities for reserves, the size of their own balance sheets shrinks just as the central bank's balance sheet expands. Assuming they want to keep their own balance sheets static, they will then start lending to borrowers and so start putting more liquidity into the economy.

Even if quantitative easing isn't necessarily effective, it would certainly be worth a try if it carried no danger. But its safety is far from certain. It could theoretically lead to the debauchment of a nation's currency and inflation.

Follow-up questions
1 To what extent has quantitative easing been successful since it was introduced in 2009?
2 Why might quantitative easing lead to inflation?

Summary

➤ Money is best defined by its two principal functions, as a medium of exchange and store of value or wealth.

➤ Virtually all modern money is token money with no intrinsic value.

➤ Cash (notes and coins) is fiat money, issued by the state.

➤ Cash is the 'small change' of the system and bank deposits are by far the largest part of modern money.

➤ Banks can create deposits, which in total form a multiple of the cash or monetary base the banks possess.

➤ Cash can be thought of as *high-powered* money, while bank deposits are *low-powered* money.

➤ The main function of the Bank of England is to implement the government's monetary policy.

➤ Under monetarism, monetary policy aimed to control the rate of growth of the money supply.

➤ In recent years, the rate of interest has been the main monetary policy instrument, aimed at targeting the rate of inflation.

➤ In an *AD/AS* diagram, monetary policy is illustrated by shifts of the *AD* curve to the right (expansionary monetary policy) and to the left (contractionary monetary policy).

➤ UK monetary policy was successful from 1992 until 2008.

➤ Monetary policy became much less successful with the onset of recession in 2008 and the threat of falling price level.

➤ In 2009, monetary policy switched away from relying solely on interest rate changes to a policy of quantitative easing, through which the Bank of England creates more money for people to spend.

Questions

1 List and briefly explain the two main functions of money.

2 What is token money?

3 Distinguish between money, near money and money substitutes.

4 What is Goodhart's Law?

5 What is the money multiplier?

6 Define monetary policy.

7 Why are direct controls no longer imposed by the Bank of England on commercial banks?

8 How do changes in the Bank of England's official interest rate affect bank lending and the economy?

9 What is meant by pre-emptive monetary policy?

10 What is quantitative easing?

Chapter 19

Fiscal policy and supply-side policy

Fiscal policy is the part of economic policy in which the government attempts to achieve policy objectives using the fiscal instruments of government spending, taxation and the government's budgetary position (balanced budget, budget deficit or budget surplus).

In this chapter I explain how the main thrust of UK fiscal policy has changed over the years from 'sound finance' and balanced budgets to the management of aggregate demand in the Keynesian era running from the 1950s to the 1970s.

In the 1980s and 1990s, fiscal policy became an important part of supply-side economic policy, which itself was part of the anti-Keynesian free market revival. Supply-side economics encompasses more than just fiscal policy, but tax cuts and reductions in public spending, which aim to increase personal incentives and to free resources for the private sector to use, lie at the heart of supply-side economic policies.

At the time of writing this book in the spring of 2009, fiscal policy has been changing once again. Although supply-side elements of fiscal policy continue to be important, fiscal policy has reverted back, for a few months or years at least, to Keynesian demand management. As I explain in the chapter, this is a response to the recession which hit the British economy in 2008 and to the collapse of aggregate demand which has both caused and deepened the severe downturn the UK economy is experiencing in 2009.

Learning outcomes

This chapter will:
> provide a brief history of UK fiscal policy
> describe the structure of public finance in the UK
> compare Keynesian and supply-side fiscal policy
> explain automatic stabilisers, crowding out and the structural and cyclical components of a budget deficit

> ➤ use *AD/AS* diagrams to analyse Keynesian and supply-side fiscal policy
> ➤ update your knowledge of the Code for Fiscal Stability and the demise of fiscal rules
> ➤ remind you of the wider meaning of supply-side economics
> ➤ introduce you to European Union fiscal policy

What you should already know

At AS, you learnt the meaning of fiscal policy and about how fiscal policy is both similar to, and different from, monetary policy. At the start of the A2 course, you should understand how fiscal policy has both macroeconomic and microeconomic functions, influencing both aggregate demand and aggregate supply and how, through the fiscal instruments of government spending and taxation, fiscal policy affects the pattern of economic activity.

A brief history of UK fiscal policy

From the 1850s onward, until the birth of Keynesian economics just before the Second World War, UK governments generally followed the principles of 'sound finance' (fiscal orthodoxy). This tradition is associated with the nineteenth-century prime minister, William Gladstone, who in his earlier role as chancellor of the exchequer aimed to balance the government's budget and to keep both government spending and taxation as low as possible.

For three decades from the 1950s to the end of the 1970s, Keynesian economics fundamentally changed the nature of UK fiscal policy. In his *General Theory*, published in 1936, Maynard Keynes legitimised the use of fiscal policy as a means of managing the level of aggregate demand in the economy. In the Keynesian era, deficit financing became respectable and part of the new Keynesian orthodoxy.

However, under Margaret Thatcher in the 1980s, demand management was rejected and there was a return to the principles of 'sound finance' and balanced budgets. During the free-market revival and the relatively short-lived monetarist years of the early 1980s, there was of course still a fiscal policy, but now used in a supply-side way to improve the economy's ability to produce. In these years, income tax rates were cut, not to stimulate aggregate demand, but to improve personal incentives to work harder, save, invest, and to be entrepreneurial.

In the 1990s, although demand management policies were reintroduced, monetary policy and *not* fiscal policy was used to influence demand, with control of inflation as the policy objective. Fiscal policy continued to be used in a supply-side way and also to promote macroeconomic stability. This policy became formalised in the fiscal rules set out in 1997 in the Labour government's Code for Fiscal Stability.

*e*xaminer's voice
Exam questions may ask you to describe the main UK taxes and/or forms of public spending, or to describe the pattern of public spending.

Chancellor Alistair Darling leaves No 11 on Budget Day, 2008

In 2008, there was again a significant U-turn in UK fiscal policy. To try to prevent the collapse of aggregate demand from turning the *recession* (which arguably began in the third quarter of 2008) into a deep *depression*, the Labour government began to use fiscal policy to manage aggregate demand. In the November 2008 Pre-Budget Report, the fiscal rules in the Code for Fiscal Stability were suspended, government spending was dramatically increased and value added tax was cut. At the time of writing in April 2009, it is impossible to say whether this marks a sea change in UK fiscal policy, or whether its use to manage demand will be dropped when and if the economy recovers from recession. Change of government in 2009 or 2010 may lead to a return to a non-Keynesian fiscal policy, providing that the state of the economy allows such a change.

The structure of public finance in the UK

Taxation and other sources of government revenue
A tax is a compulsory levy charged by government or by a public authority to pay for its expenditure. **Taxation** is the principal source of government revenue for most economies.

In the UK about 89% of total taxation is levied by central government, with local government taxation (currently the council tax and business rates) accounting for the remaining 11% of taxation levied by government.

Progressive, proportionate and regressive taxation
In a **progressive tax** system, the proportion of a person's income paid in tax *increases* as income rises, while in a **regressive tax** system, the propor-

Key **terms**

Taxation is compulsory levies charged by the government to raise revenue, primarily to finance government spending.

A **progressive tax** is a tax for which the proportion of a person's income paid in tax rises as income increases.

tion paid in tax *falls* as income increases. A tax is **proportionate** (a **flat tax**) if exactly the same proportion of income is paid in tax at all levels of income. Progressivity can be defined for a single tax or for the tax system as a whole.

The word *progressive* is value-neutral, implying nothing about how the revenue raised by the government is spent. Nevertheless, progressive taxation has been used by governments, particularly during the Keynesian era, to achieve the social aim of a 'fairer' distribution of income. But progressive taxation cannot by itself redistribute income — a policy of transfers in the government's public expenditure programme is required for this. Progressive taxation used on its own merely reduces post-tax income differentials compared to pre-tax differentials.

> **Key terms**
>
> A **regressive tax** is a tax for which the proportion of a person's income paid in tax falls as income increases.
>
> A **proportionate tax** or **flat tax** is a tax for which the proportion of a person's income paid in tax stays the same as income increases.

Average and marginal rates of income tax

For individual taxes such as income tax or inheritance tax, we can identify whether the tax is progressive, regressive or proportionate by examining the relationship between the average rate at which the tax is levied and the marginal rate. In a progressive income tax system, the **marginal tax rate** is higher than the **average tax rate**, although the average rate, which measures the proportion of income paid in tax, rises as income increases. Conversely, in a regressive income tax system, the marginal tax is less than the average rate, while the two are equal in the case of a proportionate tax.

For income tax, the average tax rate is calculated as total tax paid divided by total income. By contrast, the marginal tax rate is calculated as the *change* in total tax paid divided by the *change* in total income.

$$\text{average tax rate} = \frac{\text{total tax paid}}{\text{total income}} \quad \text{or:} \quad \frac{T}{Y}$$

$$\text{marginal tax rate} = \frac{\text{change in total tax paid}}{\text{change in total income}} \quad \text{or:} \quad \frac{\Delta T}{\Delta Y}$$

As a general rule, the *average* tax rate indicates the overall burden of the tax upon the taxpayer, but the *marginal* rate may significantly affect economic choice and decision making. In the case of an income tax, it influences the choice between work and leisure when deciding how much labour to supply. The marginal rate of income tax also influences decisions on whether to spend income on consumption or to save.

The principles of taxation

Taxpayers commonly view all taxes as 'bad', in the sense that they do not enjoy paying them, although most realise that taxation is necessary in order to provide for the useful goods and services provided by the government. A starting point for analysing and evaluating whether a tax is 'good' or 'bad' is Adam Smith's four

principles (or canons) of taxation. Adam Smith suggested that taxation should be equitable, economical, convenient and certain, and to these I may add the canons of efficiency and flexibility. A 'good' tax meets as many of these canons as possible, although because of conflicts and trade-offs, it is usually impossible for a tax to meet them all at the same time. A 'bad' tax meets few if any of the guiding principles of taxation.

Key *term*

A **principle (or canon) of taxation** is a criterion for judging whether a tax is a good tax or a bad tax.

➤ **Equity.** A tax system should be fair, although there may be different and possibly conflicting interpretations of what is fair or equitable. Specifically, a particular tax should be based on the taxpayer's *ability to pay*. This principle is one of the justifications of progressive taxation, since the rich have a greater ability to pay than the poor.

➤ **Flexibility.** If the tax system is used as a means of economic management then in order to meet new circumstances the tax structure and the rates at which individual taxes are levied must be capable of easy alteration.

Public expenditure

The measurement of **public expenditure** is usually restricted to spending by central government and local government. Taken together this is called **general government expenditure**.

The measurement of public spending can also include spending on net investment in new capital by nationalised industries. However, most spending by nationalised industries is excluded on the grounds that it is financed by revenue raised from the sale of the industries' output and is not dependent on finance from the taxpayer. In any case, privatisation of most of the former nationalised industries means that spending by the few enterprises that remain in the state sector is very small, though recent bank nationalisations have changed this.

Government spending includes defence

Perhaps more significant than the *absolute* totals of public expenditure is the **ratio of public expenditure to national income**, which indicates the share of the nation's resources taken by the government. Apart from the periods 1914–18 and 1939–45, which saw rapid, but temporary, increases in government spending to pay for the First and Second World Wars, the twentieth century witnessed a steady but relatively slow increase in government expenditure from around 10% to over 40% of GDP, reaching 46.75% in 1982/83. The ratio rose in the early 1980s, but fell in the late 1980s, before rising and falling again in the 1990s. By 2005/06, the ratio had increased again to over 42%, and at the time of writing in April 2009, it looks set to rise well above 50%.

A major explanation lies in changes taking place in employment and unemployment, which in turn relate to the economic cycle. Spending on social security, which includes unemployment-related benefits, is by far the largest single category of public spending. Before the 2008 recession, the main unemployment benefit, the **jobseeker's allowance**, only amounted to about 5% of total welfare benefits. The **income-support benefit** claimed by poor families and the **state pension** were much more important. When the economy booms, unemployment falls, so spending on social security also falls. The reverse is true in a recession. I revisit this issue later in the chapter when explaining the cyclical and structural components of the government's budget deficit and borrowing requirement, and the role of automatic stabilisers in the economy.

The ratio of public spending to GDP is an accurate measure of the share of the nation's total financial resources under the command of the government. However, because a large part of government expenditure is on **transfers**, such as the unemployment-related benefits just described, it is a misleading indicator of the share of national output produced by the government itself. Transfers do not involve a claim by the government on national output, or a diversion of resources by the government away from the private sector. Rather, spending on transfers merely redistributes income and spending power from one part of the private sector to another: from taxpayers to recipients of state benefits and pensions.

When transfers are excluded, government spending falls from around 40% or more of GDP to between only 20 and 30%. This figure is a more accurate measure of the share of national output directly commanded by the state (and thus unavailable for use in the private sector) to produce the hospitals, roads and other goods and services that the government collectively provides and finances, mostly out of taxation.

In 2008/09, interest payments on the **national debt** were expected to be £34 billion, or 5.5% of public spending. For an obvious reason, this item of public spending increases when interest rates rise. However, *total* interest payments are also affected by the government's budgetary position. A budget deficit generally increases interest payments because it increases the total *stock* of government debt. Conversely, a budget surplus allows the government to reduce the national debt by paying back past borrowing. As a result total interest payments fall. In the early

2000s, low interest rates and a budget surplus both reduced debt repayments as a proportion of public spending and of GDP. By 2005, however, a budget deficit was once again increasing debt repayments, although to some extent this was offset by interest rates remaining low. From 2008 onwards until at least 2010, the government's budget deficit will grow larger. Interest payments on the national debt are likely to increase because the government has to borrow more. However, the rise in the debt repayment burden may be partially offset because nominal interest rates have been falling toward zero as the Bank of England tries to combat recession.

The aims of taxation and public spending

An obvious aim of taxation is to raise the revenue required to finance government spending. In addition, you learnt when studying microeconomics at AS, taxes and subsidies can be used to alter the relative prices of goods and services in order to change consumption patterns.

Ultimately, the aims of both taxation and public spending depend on the underlying philosophy and ideology of the government in power. They differ significantly, for example, between Keynesian and free-market or supply-side inspired governments. I shall divide the aims or objectives of public spending and taxation into three main categories: allocation, distribution and economic management.

> **examiner's voice**
>
> The aims of taxation should not be confused with the principles of taxation, though an aim might be to organise the tax system in accordance with the principles of taxation as much as possible.

Allocation

As I have just noted, taxes are used to alter relative prices and patterns of consumption. Demerit goods, such as alcohol and tobacco, are taxed in order to discourage consumption, while merit goods, such as museums, are untaxed and subsidised and sometimes directly provided by the state. Taxes are also used to finance the provision of public goods, such as defence, police and roads. Also, under the 'polluter must pay' principle, taxes are used to discourage and reduce the production and consumption of negative externalities, such as pollution and congestion. Likewise, subsidies are used to encourage the production or provision of external benefits or positive externalities. Taxation can be used to deter monopoly by taxing monopoly profit through removing the windfall gain accruing to a monopolist as a result of barriers to entry and inelastic supply.

Distribution

The price mechanism is value-neutral with regard to the equity or social fairness of the distributions of income and wealth resulting from market forces in the economy. If the government decides that the distributions of income and wealth produced by free market forces are undesirable, taxation and transfers in its public spending programme can be used to modify these distributions and reduce the alleged market failure resulting from inequity.

Before 1979, UK governments of all political complexions used progressive taxation and a policy of transfers of income to the less well off in a deliberate attempt — albeit with limited success — to reduce inequalities in the distribution of income. Governments also extended the provision of merit goods such as free state education and healthcare, in order to improve the **social wage** of lower-income groups. The social wage is the part of a worker's standard of living received as goods and services provided at zero price or as income in kind by the state, being financed collectively out of taxation.

Between 1979 and 1997, Conservative governments changed the structure of both taxation and public spending to *widen* rather than *reduce* inequalities in the distributions of income and wealth. The reason for this change relates to the conflict between two of the principles or canons of taxation I mentioned earlier: equity and efficiency. The Conservatives believed that greater incentives for work and enterprise were necessary in order to increase the UK's growth rate. For free-market economists and politicians, progressive taxation and transfers to the poor meant that people had less incentive to work hard and to engage in entrepreneurial risk. Moreover, the ease with which the poor could claim welfare benefits and the level at which they were available created a situation in which the poor rationally chose unemployment and state benefits in preference to low wages and work. In this so-called **dependency culture**, the unwaged were effectively 'married to the state', but some of the poor, obviously not enjoying this marriage, drifted into antisocial behaviour, attacking bus shelters and other public property, as well as privately owned property.

The Conservatives argued that income tax rates and benefit rates should *both* be reduced. They believed that tax and benefit cuts would alter the labour/leisure choice in favour of supplying labour, particularly for benefit claimants who lack the skills necessary for high-paid jobs. They also believed that to make everyone eventually better off, the poor must first be made worse off. Increased inequality was necessary to facilitate economic growth from which all would eventually benefit. Through a *trickle down* effect, the poor would end up better off in absolute terms, but because inequalities had widened, they would still be relatively worse off compared to the rich.

After 1997, policy was again reversed, particularly in the late 1990s. Using initiatives such as the New Deal, New Labour governments tried to reduce income inequalities. But although the real incomes of most of the poor increased, income inequalities continue to grow, largely because high incomes have grown at a much faster rate than low incomes.

examiner's voice
Make sure you don't confuse fiscal and monetary policy, but understand the links between the two.

Economic management and fiscal policy

Everything I have written when discussing the allocative and distributional aims of taxation and government spending broadly relates to fiscal policy. However, the term fiscal policy is normally used in relation to the economic management of the economy, usually, though not always, at a macro level.

Before proceeding further I shall remind you of the definition of fiscal policy previously learnt at AS. **Fiscal policy** is used to achieve the government's economic objectives through the use of the fiscal instruments of taxation, public spending and the government's budgetary position. As an economic term, fiscal policy is often associated with Keynesian economic theory and policy. I noted earlier how, in the 1950s and 1960s, Keynesian governments abandoned the fiscal neutrality of sound finance and balanced budgets, preferring an active fiscal policy based on managing the level of aggregate demand.

However, it is misleading to associate fiscal policy exclusively with Keynesianism. Until recently, the Keynesian fiscal policy implemented in the UK in the three decades before 1979 was replaced by a very different supply-side fiscal policy. I shall now explain first **Keynesian fiscal policy** and then **supply-side fiscal policy**.

Key terms

Fiscal policy is the use of government spending, taxation and the government's budgetary position to achieve the government's policy objectives.

Keynesian fiscal policy is used to manage aggregate demand and is named after John Maynard Keynes.

Supply-side fiscal policy is used to increase personal incentives and is favoured by free-market economists.

Keynesian fiscal policy

During the Keynesian era, fiscal policy took on a meaning more narrow and specific than the rather general definition I gave earlier. In the Keynesian era, fiscal policy came to mean the use of the overall levels of public spending, taxation and the budget deficit to manage the level of aggregate demand in

examiner's voice
Students often define fiscal policy too narrowly simply in terms of Keynesian fiscal policy and demand management.

the economy. The aim was to achieve full employment and to stabilise the economic cycle, without at the same time creating excessive inflationary pressures. Keynesian fiscal policy was implemented with varying degrees of success in the decades before 1979. The key elements of the theory behind Keynesian fiscal policy were:

➤ Left to itself, an unregulated market economy results in unnecessarily low economic growth, high unemployment and volatile business cycles.
➤ A lack of aggregate demand, caused by a tendency for the private sector to save too much and invest too little, can mean that the economy settles into an under-full employment equilibrium characterised by demand-deficient unemployment.
➤ By deliberate **deficit financing**, the government can, using fiscal policy as a demand management instrument, inject demand and spending power into the economy to eliminate deficient demand and achieve full employment.
➤ Having achieved full employment, the government can then use fiscal policy in a discretionary way (that is, changing tax rates and levels of public spending to meet new circumstances) to fine-tune the level of aggregate demand. For much of the Keynesian era, governments believed that fiscal policy could achieve full

employment and stabilise the economic cycle, while avoiding an unacceptable increase in the rate of inflation.

➤ The overall stance of fiscal policy and, indeed, of economic policy in general, was orientated towards the demand side of the economy. The more microeconomic elements of fiscal policy, such as transfers to industry, were aimed at improving economic performance on the supply side. But on the whole, supply-side fiscal policy was treated as subordinate to the macroeconomic management of aggregate demand and to the assumption that output would respond to demand stimulation. In any case, the microeconomic elements of Keynesian fiscal policy were generally interventionist rather than non-interventionist, extending rather than reducing the state's role in the mixed economy.

➤ Central to Keynesian fiscal policy was the assumption that the government spending multiplier has a high value. At this stage you should refer back to Chapter 15 and refresh your knowledge of the national income multiplier in the context of shifts of the economy's aggregate demand curve. If the national income multiplier is large with respect to real output, for example eight, an increase in government spending of £10 billion increases aggregate demand and money national income by £80 billion. A large multiplier means that changing the levels of government spending, taxation and the budget deficit (or surplus) can be extremely effective in managing aggregate demand.

Supply-side fiscal policy

In the Keynesian era, fiscal policy played a central role in the creation of a mixed economy based on the political consensus that the UK economy should contain a mix of market and non-market economic activity, and of public and private ownership. The more supply-side and free-market fiscal policy pursued since 1979 has been very different. Along with policies such as privatisation and deregulation, fiscal policy has been used to change the mixed economy by increasing the role of markets and private sector economic activity, and by reducing the economic role of the state.

The main elements of the fiscal policy implemented first by Conservative governments and then by Labour governments in the UK since 1979 are as follows:

➤ The government ceased using taxation and public spending as discretionary instruments of demand management. Under supply-side influence, recent governments, at least up until 2008, argued that a policy of using fiscal policy to stimulate or reflate aggregate demand to achieve growth and full employment is, in the long run, at best ineffective and at worst damaging. They argued that any growth of output and employment resulting from an expansionary fiscal policy is short-lived and that in the long term the main effect of such a policy is inflation, which quickly destroys the conditions necessary for satisfactory market performance and wealth creation.

➤ One explanation of the supply-side view I have just described lies in the supply-side approach to the government spending multiplier. If the multiplier is small in size with respect to real output, for example one, then fiscal policy used in a

Keynesian expansionary way has little stimulatory effect on real national output, with its main effect falling on inflation.

➤ A medium-term policy 'rule' was recommended (in place of short-term discretionary fiscal changes) to reduce public spending, taxation and government borrowing as proportions of national output. Besides wishing to reduce what they see as the inflationary effects of 'big government spending', many supply-side economists believe that the high levels of government spending, taxation and borrowing of the Keynesian era led to the crowding out of the private sector. (Crowding out is explained later in this chapter.)

➤ Microeconomic fiscal policy became more important than macroeconomic fiscal policy. Governments subordinated the more macroeconomic elements of fiscal policy, which were dominant during the Keynesian era, to a much more microeconomic fiscal policy, intended to combine an overall reduction in the levels of taxation and public spending with the creation of incentives aimed at improving economic performance on the supply side of the economy.

➤ As well as being subordinated to a more microeconomic supply-side orientated fiscal policy, the macroeconomic elements of fiscal policy became subservient to the needs of *monetary* policy. Control over public spending and borrowing was seen as a precondition for successful control of monetary growth and inflation. Again, I explain this later in the chapter.

The government's budgetary position

Using the symbols G for government spending and T for taxation and other sources of revenue, the three possible budgetary positions of the government (and of the whole of the public sector) are:

$G = T$ (**balanced budget**)

$G > T$ (**budget deficit**)

$G < T$ (**budget surplus**)

A **government budget deficit** occurs when public spending exceeds revenue from taxation and other sources of revenue. A budget deficit can be eliminated by cutting public spending or raising taxation, both of which can balance the budget or move the budget into surplus. However, assuming that a deficit persists, the extent to which spending exceeds revenue must be financed by public sector borrowing. The Treasury uses various official terms for public sector borrowing, including the **public sector net cash requirement** (PSNCR) and **public sector net borrowing** (PSNR). However, because the Treasury frequently changes its official terminology, the most important thing to learn is that public sector borrowing repre-

Key terms

A **balanced budget** means total government spending equals total government revenue in a particular time period.

A **budget deficit** means total government spending exceeds total government revenue in a particular time period.

A **budget surplus** means total government spending is less than total government revenue in a particular time period.

The **government budget** is total government spending minus total government revenue in a particular time period, e.g. a year.

sents 'the other side of the coin' to the budget deficit. Whenever there is a budget deficit there is a positive **borrowing requirement**. Conversely, a budget surplus means that the government can use the tax revenues that it is not spending to repay previous borrowing. In this case, the borrowing requirement is negative.

Key *term*

The **borrowing requirement** is the amount the government or public sector must borrow to finance a budget deficit.

Box 19.1 Sound finance and balanced budgets

The passage below is an extract from a budget speech delivered by Conservative chancellor Nigel Lawson during a period known as the 'Lawson boom'. The budget followed nearly 6 years of economic growth. During these years the public finances moved from deficit into surplus. Margaret Thatcher, the prime minister, hoped that the budget would remain in balance or in surplus and that budget deficits were a thing of the past. This was not to be. The severe recession that followed the Lawson boom in the early 1990s led to the return of a budget deficit. Thatcher probably hadn't understood the cyclical nature of budget surpluses and deficits.

> At one time, it was regarded as the hallmark of good government to maintain a balanced budget; to ensure that government spending was fully financed by revenues from taxation, with no need for government borrowing.
>
> Over the years, this simple and beneficent rule was increasingly disregarded. Profligacy not only brought economic disaster and the national humiliation of a bail out by the IMF; it also added massively to the burden of debt interest, not merely now but for a generation to come.
>
> Thus, one of our main objectives, when we first took office in 1979, was to bring down government borrowing. In 1987–88, the year now ending, we are set to secure something previously achieved only on one isolated occasion since the beginning of the 1950s: a balanced budget.
>
> Indeed, we have gone even further. It looks as if the final outturn for 1987–88 will be a budget surplus of £3 billion. Instead of a PSBR, a PSDR: not a public sector borrowing requirement, but a public sector debt repayment.
>
> Some two thirds of this substantial undershoot of the PSBR I set at the time of last year's Budget is the result of the increased tax revenues that have flowed from a buoyant economy; while the remaining third is due to lower than expected public expenditure, again the outcome of a buoyant economy: less in benefits for the unemployed.
>
> A balanced budget is a valuable discipline for the medium term. It represents security for the present and an investment for the future. Having achieved it, I intend to stick to it. In other words, henceforth a zero PSBR will be the norm. This provides a clear and simple rule, with a good historical pedigree.
>
> Nigel Lawson's budget speech, 15 March 1988

Follow-up questions

1 Explain the meaning of a *balanced budget*.

2 Relate the two terms *PSBR* and *PSDR* to the state of the public finances.

3 Research the changes that have taken place in the state of the public finances from 1988 to the present day. In which years was there a budget surplus? How has the 2008 recession affected the public finances?

Automatic stabilisers

The previous sections might indicate that the fiscal policy choice facing a government lies between Keynesian-style discretionary demand management and balancing the budget as advocated by many supply-side economists. But in reality, there is an alternative approach that lies between these extremes, in which a government bases fiscal policy on the operation of **automatic stabilisers**. These dampen or reduce the multiplier effects resulting from any change in aggregate demand within the economy.

Key *term*

An **automatic stabiliser** is a factor that changes in such a way as to automatically stabilise aggregate demand and the economic cycle. Examples are progressive taxation and unemployment benefits.

Suppose, for example, that a collapse of confidence or export orders causes aggregate demand to fall. National income then also begins to fall, declining by the initial fall in demand. But as national income falls and unemployment rises, *demand-led* public spending on unemployment pay and welfare benefits also rises. If the income tax system is progressive, the government's tax revenues fall faster than national income. In this way, increased public spending on transfers and declining tax revenues inject demand back into the economy, thereby stabilising and dampening the deflationary impact of the initial fall in aggregate demand, and reducing the overall size of the contractionary multiplier effect.

Automatic stabilisers also operate in the opposite direction to dampen the expansionary effect of an increase in aggregate demand. As incomes and employment rise, the take-up of means-tested welfare benefits and unemployment-related benefits automatically falls, while at the same time tax revenues rise faster than income. By taking demand out of the economy and reducing the size of the expansionary multiplier, automatic stabilisers reduce **overheating** in the boom phase of the economic cycle.

It is now widely agreed that automatic stabilisers such as progressive taxation and income-related transfers contributed to milder economic cycles experienced by the UK, prior to 2008 at least. Before 1939, economic cycles – or trade cycles, as they were then known – were much more volatile, displaying greater fluctuations between boom and slump than in the years between the Second World War and 1979. Keynesians claimed that recent relatively mild economic cycles prior to 1979 are evidence of the success of Keynesian demand management policies in stabilising cyclical fluctuations.

However, the economic cycle was relatively mild both in the UK and in countries such as Germany, which did not use fiscal policy to manage aggregate demand in a discretionary way. This suggests that the automatic stabilisers of progressive taxation and the safety net provided by welfare benefits for the poor – both of which were introduced widely in western industrialised economies after 1945 – were more significant than discretionary fiscal policy in reducing fluctuations in the economic cycle. Either way, economists now generally agree that a deficit should grow in the downswing of the economic cycle, provided the deficit is matched by a surplus in the subsequent upswing.

The cyclical and the structural budget deficit and borrowing requirement

To understand fully the links between the government's budgetary position and the wider economy, it is useful to distinguish between the cyclical and the structural components of the budget deficit and borrowing requirement. As the previous paragraphs indicate, the **cyclical budget deficit** is the part of the overall budget deficit that rises and falls with the downswings and upswings of the economic cycle as automatic stabilisers kick in. In the downswing of the economic cycle, tax revenues fall but public spending on unemployment and poverty-related welfare benefits increases. As a result, the government's finances deteriorate. Conversely, in the recovery and boom periods, tax revenues rise and spending on benefits falls.

If all the growth of the budget deficit and the related borrowing requirement were cyclical, the problem of a growing budget deficit would disappear when economic growth occurred, providing growth was sufficiently buoyant and sustained. But this does not happen if the cyclical changes are overridden by more powerful structural changes operating in the reverse direction. As the name suggests, growth in the *structural* component of the budget deficit and borrowing requirement relates to the changing structure of the UK economy. In recent years, a number of factors and trends, ranging from **deindustrialisation** and **globalisation** eroding the tax base via the movement of industries to eastern Europe and Asia, through to an ageing population and the growth of single-parent families dependent on welfare benefits, have contributed to the growth of the **structural budget deficit**.

The growing structural deficit carries the rather dispiriting message that a government that seriously wishes to improve public sector finances will need to introduce significant tax increases or public spending cuts, or possibly both. At the time of writing, the rapid deterioration in the UK's public finances caused by the 2008 recession, and by the Labour government's attempt to spend its way out of the recession, has worsened this problem.

Using *AD/AS* diagrams to illustrate Keynesian and supply-side fiscal policy

I shall first remind you of the aggregate demand equation or identity you learnt when studying Unit 2 last year:

$$AD = C + I + G + (X - M)$$

Government spending (G) is one of the components of aggregate demand. An increase in government spending and/or a cut in taxation increases the size of the budget deficit (or reduces the size of the budget surplus). Either way, an injection into the circular flow of income occurs and the effect on aggregate demand is expansionary.

Figure 19.1 illustrates the effect of such an expansionary or reflationary fiscal policy. Initially, with the aggregate demand curve in position AD_1, macroeconomic equilibrium occurs at point X. Real income or output is y_1, and the price level is P_1.

To eliminate the demand-deficient unemployment, the government increases the budget deficit by raising the level of government spending and/or by cutting taxes. The **expansionary fiscal policy** shifts the AD curve to the right from AD_1 to AD_2, and the economy moves to a new macroeconomic equilibrium at point Z.

However, the extent to which expansionary fiscal policy *reflates* real output (in this case from y_1 to y_2), or creates excess demand that leads to demand-pull inflation (in this case an increase in the price level from P_1 to P_2), depends on the shape of the AS curve, which in turn depends on how close the economy was to full employment. The nearer the economy gets to full employment, the greater the inflationary effect of expansionary fiscal policy and the smaller the reflationary effect. Once the full-employment level of real income is reached on the long-run aggregate supply curve at y_{FE}, a further increase in government spending or a tax cut inflates the price level. In this situation, real output cannot grow (except possibly temporarily), because there is no spare capacity. The economy is producing on its production possibility frontier.

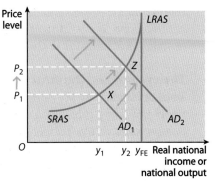

Figure 19.1 *Keynesian or demand-side fiscal policy*

Key terms

Expansionary fiscal policy uses fiscal policy to increase aggregate demand and to shift the AD curve to the right.

Contractionary fiscal policy uses fiscal policy to decrease aggregate demand and to shift the AD curve to the left.

Figure 19.1 can be adapted to illustrate the effect of a **contractionary** (deflationary) **fiscal policy**. In this case a cut in government spending and/or an increase in taxation shifts the AD curve to the left. The extent to which the demand deflation results in the price level or real income falling once again depends on the shape and slope of the *SRAS* curve.

Along with other supply-side policies, which I mention briefly later in this chapter, supply-side fiscal policy is used to try and shift the economy's long-run aggregate supply (*LRAS*) curve to the right, thereby increasing the economy's potential level of output. The effect of successful supply-side fiscal policy on the *LRAS* curve is shown in Figure 19.2. (Note that

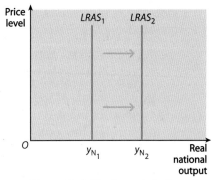

Figure 19.2 *The intended effect of supply-side fiscal policy*

an outward movement of the economy's production possibility frontier can also illustrate the intended effect of supply-side policies.)

Crowding out

As I previously mentioned, many supply-side economists believe that government spending and taxation *crowds out* private sector spending and output. There are two forms of **crowding out**: resource crowding out and financial crowding out.

Resource crowding out is associated with two basic economic concepts: scarcity and opportunity cost. Because it is impossible to employ real resources simultaneously in both the private and public sectors, the opportunity cost of employing more capital and labour in the public sector inevitably involves sacrificing the opportunity to use the same resources in private employment.

Financial crowding out results from the method of financing an increase in public spending. As I have explained, public spending can be financed by taxation or borrowing. Taxation obviously reduces the spending power of the private individuals and firms paying the taxes. Note, however, that if extra tax revenues paid by high income earners with a relatively low marginal propensity to consume are transferred as welfare benefits to poorer people with higher marginal propensities to consume, higher taxation may *increase* private sector spending, although at the probable cost of reduced personal incentives.

However, suppose, for example, that the government increases public spending by £40 billion, financing the resulting budget deficit with a sale of new gilt-edged securities (gilts) on the capital market. In order to persuade insurance companies, pension funds and the other financial institutions in the market for gilts to buy the extra debt, the guaranteed annual interest rate offered on new gilt issues must increase. But the resulting general rise in interest rates makes it more expensive for firms to borrow and to raise capital. Private sector investment thus falls.

Crowding out versus crowding in

The resource crowding out argument assumes full employment of all resources, including labour. But when spare capacity and unemployed labour exist in the economy, increased public spending does not necessarily reduce the private sector's use of resources. Instead, by using previously idle resources, increased government spending merely takes up the slack in the economy. Indeed, with unemployed resources, increased public spending financed by a budget deficit may, via the multiplier process I explain in Chapter 15, stimulate or *crowd in* the private sector. For example, increased spending on a public works road-building programme creates orders for private sector construction firms that, through their own spending in the subsequent stages of the multiplier process, generate further business for the private sector.

Resource crowding out and crowding in are illustrated in Figure 19.3. The production possibility frontier drawn in the diagram shows maximum levels of output that can be produced with various combinations of public sector and private sector spending and output. There is full employment at all points on the frontier. Assuming the economy is initially at point A, an increase in public sector spending from Pu_1 to Pu_2 crowds out or displaces private sector spending, which falls from Pr_1 to Pr_2, shown at point B. The size of the multiplier with respect to real output is therefore zero. Indeed, extreme free-market economists go further, arguing that the multiplier may be negative because an increase in public sector spending causes the production possibility frontier to shift inward.

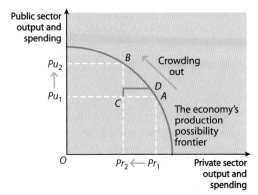

Figure 19.3 *Crowding out and crowding in illustrated on a production possibility diagram*

According to this extreme free-market view, real output falls because unproductive or wealth-consuming public sector spending displaces wealth-creating private sector spending. In the extreme, this argument is rather silly, since it implies that *all* private sector spending, such as gambling, is 'wealth-producing', while *all* public sector spending, for example on roads or hospitals, is 'wealth-consuming' or unproductive.

Keynesians agree that crowding out occurs if the economy is initially fully employed with no spare capacity. But suppose that to begin with the economy is producing inside the frontier, at a point such as *C* in Figure 19.3. In this situation, crowding in rather than crowding out may occur. An increase in public sector spending that is sufficient, via the multiplier process, to increase output to point *D* on the frontier, brings idle capacity into production. The stimulus is shown by the thick kinked line running from *C* to *D*. The line contains a vertical section and a horizontal section. The vertical section shows the initial increase in public spending, which triggers the multiplier process. By contrast, the horizontal section shows the resulting increase in private sector spending and output following on from the initial increase in public spending.

Whether an increase in public sector spending crowds out or crowds in the private sector should depend on whether the economy is initially on its production possibility frontier, at a position such as *A*, or inside the frontier, such as at *C*. Keynesians argue that the size of unemployment indicates whether or not the economy is *on* or inside the production possibility frontier, and that, in periods of recession, the economy is definitely inside its frontier. Free-market economists respond by arguing that unemployment figures provide a misleading indicator of whether the economy is on its production possibility frontier. The correct indicator is the existence of spare and competitive capacity capable of producing goods and services of a quality that people actually want. According to this view, increased public

spending can crowd out the private sector even when unemployment is high. If the required supply-side production capacity is not in place to respond to the stimulus of extra government spending, the economy behaves as if it is fully employed.

The subordination of fiscal policy to the needs of monetary policy

UK Governments (and the Bank of England) now realise that, because monetary and fiscal policy are *interdependent* rather than *independent* of each other, the success of monetary policy depends on the fiscal policy implemented by the Treasury. As I have explained, whenever it runs a budget deficit, the government has to borrow to finance the difference between spending and revenue. Conversely, a budget surplus enables repayment of past borrowing and a fall in the national debt. The government borrows in two main ways: by selling short-dated debt or Treasury bills and by borrowing long term by selling government bonds or gilt-edged securities, commonly known as gilts.

New issues of gilts are largely sold to non-bank financial institutions such as pension funds and insurance companies. To persuade these institutions to finance a growing budget deficit, the government may have to raise the rate of interest offered on new gilt issues. However, higher interest rates discourage investment in capital goods by private sector firms. This is the financial crowding out process I referred to earlier.

Before the 2008 recession kicked in, both methods of government borrowing were regarded as rather undesirable. As I have just indicated, a large new gilt issue raises interest rates, which may lead to crowding out and a fall in private sector investment. Conversely, a new issue of Treasury bills increases bank deposits and the money supply. This was thought to be inflationary.

The UK government's fiscal rules, 1998–2008

The realisation that fiscal policy has a significant effect on monetary conditions helps to explain how fiscal policy was used in the UK between 1998 and November 2008. Throughout these years, up until the Pre-Budget Report of November 2008, monetary policy rather than

> **examiner's voice**
> You must know about the UK government's fiscal rules and about what has happened to them in recent years.

fiscal policy was used to manage the level of aggregate demand. Fiscal policy's main macroeconomic role centred on achieving macroeconomic stability and thereby creating conditions in which competitive markets could function efficiently. The Labour government believed that households and firms should not be hit by unexpected tax increases that adversely affect consumer and business confidence and distort economic decision making. However, this did not stop the introduction of 'stealth' taxes.

Having set out the **Monetary Policy Framework** in 1997 to inform people of the way monetary policy is implemented, the newly elected Labour government then published the **Fiscal Policy Framework**. This included four fiscal policy objectives; two short term and two medium term.

The short-term objectives of fiscal policy, concerned with demand management, were:

➤ to allow automatic stabilisers to smooth the path of the economy
➤ to take other necessary action so that fiscal policy supports the role of monetary policy

By contrast, fiscal policy's medium-term objectives were:

➤ to fulfil the government's tax and spending commitments, while avoiding a damaging and unsustainable increase in the burden of public sector debt
➤ to make sure that the generations who benefit from public spending, as far as possible, pay the tax revenues needed to finance the spending

Seeking to ensure the credibility of fiscal policy (that is, to maintain the general public's belief in the government's ability to achieve these objectives), the Fiscal Policy Framework included a **Code for Fiscal Stability**. The code committed the UK government to the five principles of transparency, stability, responsibility, fairness and efficiency. To perform in accordance with these principles, the code required the government to publish each year a number of reports and information on fiscal policy and the state of the public finances. These include the **Pre-Budget Report**, published in the late autumn, and the **Financial Statement and Budget Report** (nicknamed the *Red Book*), which as the name indicates, is published on Budget day, usually in March.

 Key *term*

The **Code for Fiscal Stability** is the framework through which fiscal policy was implemented after 1997. The code contained two rules: the **golden rule** and the **sustainable investment rule**.

Central to the code were two fiscal rules:

➤ The **golden rule.** Over the economic cycle, net government borrowing should only be to fund new social capital such as roads and schools, and not to fund current spending, such as welfare benefits.
➤ The **sustainable investment rule.** Over the economic cycle, public sector debt (mostly central government debt: that is, the national debt) is held at a 'stable and prudent' level of less than 40% of GDP.

The difference between current and capital spending explains the golden rule. **Current spending** (for example, on public sector wages and salaries) does not create assets for future generations to use. If long-term debt is used to finance current spending, future generations have to pay taxes to pay back past borrowing without receiving any benefit in the form of useful goods and services. It is a case of 'live now, pay later'.

This is not the case with **capital spending** on assets such as roads, hospitals and schools. Providing social capital is properly maintained, future generations benefit from public sector investment undertaken now. Future generations should therefore pay part of the cost of capital spending undertaken now.

For these reasons, the government decided that, over a single economic cycle, the public sector's budget should balance with regard to current public spending, but

run a deficit with regard to capital spending on assets that future generations will use.

The general public tends to notice cuts in current spending more than it notices cuts in capital spending. This is because cuts in current spending affect the general public immediately, whereas the effect of cuts in capital spending will mainly be noticed in the future. In the past, therefore, governments have generally cut infrastructure projects when faced with the need to rein in public expenditure. The golden rule was meant to prevent politicians succumbing to this temptation. It aimed to protect necessary investment in social capital from public spending cuts.

The golden rule also allowed fiscal policy to be used in support of monetary policy to manage aggregate demand, although not in a discretionary way. Because the rule allowed deficits and surpluses to occur on current spending, within the constraint that the current spending budget must balance over the economic cycle, automatic stabilisers could operate and dampen fluctuations during the cycle. The fact that the government makes the decision on when a cycle begins and ends also added to flexibility, although at the cost of possibly destroying credibility in the golden rule.

Over the ten or so years of the Code's life, the government fudged the distinction between current and capital spending. This significantly reduced the credibility of the golden rule. Before 2008, the credibility loss was offset by greater credibility in the government's ability to meet the sustainable investment rule. Keeping public sector debt within 40% of GDP increased the confidence of financial markets in the government's handling of the public finances.

The publication of the Code for Fiscal Stability meant that the government officially recognised that, for the most part, fiscal policy should not be used in a discretionary way to manage aggregate demand. However, two qualifications must be made, even for the years when the Code appeared to work well. First, the growth of the structural budget deficit caused the government to introduce new 'stealth' taxes that it hoped people wouldn't notice. Having, for electoral reasons, announced its unwillingness to increase income tax to reduce the budget deficit, the government had to find other ways of raising revenue.

Second, when in 2003 *nominal* interest rates fell towards zero, monetary policy became less effective for stimulating aggregate demand. Some economists then argued that fiscal policy should once again be used primarily as a demand-side policy. This problem reappeared in 2008. Read carefully Box 19.2, which gives the reasons why the Labour government suspended its fiscal rules in November 2008.

Box 19.2 The suspension of the two fiscal rules

In the November 2008 Pre-Budget Report, the chancellor of the exchequer announced the suspension of the two fiscal policy rules (the golden rule and the sustainable investment rule) that had operated since the introduction of the Code for Fiscal Stability in 1998. The chancellor replaced the rules with a looser 'temporary operating rule', which will run until the two fiscal rules are reintroduced. However, there are a number of reasons why they may never be reintroduced. These

include the fact that the rules were too rigid and inflexible, a change of government with a new Conservative administration adopting a policy of its own choosing and the possibility that the state of the economy may remain so poor that circumstances will not allow a return to the old fiscal system.

The passage below is extracted from the 'Green Budget' published in January 2009 by the leading independent authority on fiscal policy, the Institute for Fiscal Studies (IFS) and is accessible on **www.ifs.org.uk/publications/4417.**

On coming to power in 1997, Chancellor Gordon Brown set himself two fiscal rules that were supposed to limit how much the government could borrow and to what purpose.

The government claims to have met both rules over the last economic cycle, but now concedes that it is on course to miss them by a large margin over the next cycle as a result of the credit crunch. For the time being, the government will be suspending its previous fiscal rules and instead be adhering to a temporary operating rule.

The perception that Mr Brown 'moved the goalposts' to ensure that the rules would be met — and his decision not to address the over-optimism of his forecasts through tax-raising measures and cuts in spending plans until just after the 2005 election — undermined the credibility of the rules. In its 2007 New Year survey of the views of independent economists, the *Financial Times* concluded that 'Almost none use the chancellor's fiscal rules any more as an indication of the health of the public finances'.

The November 2008 Pre-Budget Report (PBR) insisted that the government's 'fiscal policy objectives remain unchanged' and that it would merely 'depart temporarily from the fiscal rules until the global shocks have worked through the economy in full'.

In the meantime, Chancellor Alistair Darling replaced them with a much less restrictive 'temporary operating rule' under which the government only promises to strengthen the public finances over the medium term.

That task has not been made any easier by the fact that the government's famous fiscal rules had lost credibility as a meaningful constraint on its tax and spending decisions long before the impact of the credit crunch required them to be suspended.

Under these circumstances, we cannot expect people to have a great deal of faith in the 'temporary operating rule' that has replaced them for the time being. Given the huge uncertainties around the current fiscal outlook, it is not clear that any temporary limits on borrowing and debt could be tight enough to act as a constraint without offering a hostage to fortune if the recession is deeper or longer than expected. For now, credibility rests more on the government's ability to persuade people that it will indeed deliver the spending squeeze and tax increases that it has signalled from 2010–11 onwards — and more if that turns out to be necessary.

The 'Green Budget' published by the Institute for Fiscal Studies, January 2009

Follow-up questions

1 How did Gordon Brown, in his then role as chancellor of the exchequer, 'move the goal posts' with regard to the two fiscal rules?

2 Explain how the history of the two fiscal rules illustrates the importance of first establishing and then maintaining credibility in government economic policy.

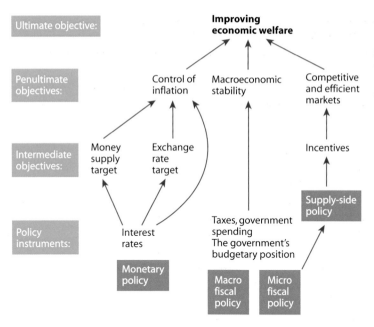

Figure 19.4
Comparing fiscal policy and monetary policy on a flow-line diagram, pre-November 2008

The flow chart I have set out in Figure 19.4 shows some of the possible links between monetary policy, fiscal policy and supply-side policy instruments and the objectives they are be intended to meet.

The left-hand side of the flow chart shows the instruments and objectives of monetary policy (before the introduction of quantitative easing in 2009), whereas the right-hand side allows us to relate monetary policy to fiscal policy and supply-side policy. The left-hand side shows control of inflation as the principal objective of monetary policy. However, control of inflation is best viewed as a penultimate policy objective, since improving economic welfare (shown at the top of the flow chart) should be regarded as the true ultimate policy objective.

The diagram predates the recent return of fiscal policy as a means of managing aggregate demand. Instead, the diagram reflects the role of fiscal policy between the introduction of the Code for Fiscal Stability in 1998 and the suspension of the Government's fiscal rules in November 2008. The macroeconomic element of fiscal policy thus focuses not on demand management but on creating conditions of macroeconomic stability. By contrast, the microeconomic element of fiscal policy is set out much in the way it is still used today, to create the personal incentives deemed necessary to create competitive and efficient markets. This is supply-side fiscal policy.

The Laffer curve

Supply-side economists believe that high rates of income tax and the overall burden on taxpayers create disincentives that, by reducing national income as taxation

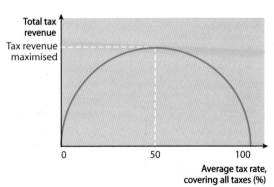

Figure 19.5 *The Laffer curve*

Key *term*

The **Laffer curve** shows tax revenue first rising and then falling as tax rates increase.

*e***xaminer's voice**

You should refer to the Laffer curve when discussing the incentive and disincentive effects of taxation.

increases, also reduce the government's total tax revenue. This effect is illustrated by the **Laffer curve** in Figure 19.5.

The Laffer curve is named after the leading supply-side economist, Arthur Laffer. Laffer's curve shows how the government's total tax revenue changes as the average tax rate increases from 0% to 100%. Tax revenue must be zero when the average tax rate is 0%, but the diagram also shows that total tax revenue is again zero when the tax rate is 100%. With the average tax rate set at 100%, all income must be paid as tax to the government. In this situation, there is no incentive to produce output other than for subsistence, so with no output produced, the government ends up collecting no tax revenue.

Between the limiting tax rates of 0% and 100%, the Laffer curve shows tax revenue first rising and then falling as the average rate of taxation increases. Tax revenue is maximised at the highest point on the Laffer curve, which in Figure 19.5 occurs at an average tax rate (for all taxes) of 50%. Beyond this point, any further increase in the average tax rate becomes counter-productive, causing total tax revenue to fall.

Supply-side economists argue that the increase in the tax burden in the Keynesian era, needed to finance the growing size of the government and public sectors, raised the average tax rate towards or beyond the critical point on the Laffer curve at which tax revenue is maximised. As noted, in this situation any further tax increase has the perverse effect of reducing the government's total tax revenue. This means that if the government wishes to increase total tax revenue, it must cut tax rates rather than increase them. A reduction in tax rates creates the incentives needed to stimulate economic growth. Faster growth means that *total tax revenue* increases despite the fact that *tax rates* are lower. Arguably, the effect is reinforced by a decline in tax evasion and avoidance, as the incentive to engage in these activities reduces at lower marginal tax rates.

The wider meaning of supply-side economic policy

Supply-side economic policy now encompasses more than just fiscal policy. In a rather broader interpretation, supply-side economic policy can be defined as the set of government initiatives that aim to change the underlying structure of the economy and improve the economic performance of markets and industries and of individual firms and workers within markets. For the most part, **supply-side policies** are also microeconomic rather than simply macroeconomic, since they act on the motivation and efficiency of individual economic agents within the economy to improve general economic performance.

Supply-siders, along with other members of the free-market revival, believe that the economy is usually close to its natural levels of output and employment. However, due to distortions and inefficiencies resulting from Keynesian neglect of the supply side, towards the end of the Keynesian era these natural levels became unnecessarily low. To increase the natural levels of output and employment and to reduce the natural rate of unemployment (NRU), supply-side economists recommend the use of appropriate microeconomic policies to remove distortions, improve incentives and generally make markets more competitive.

During the Keynesian era of the 1960s and 1970s, government microeconomic policy in the UK was generally interventionist, extending the roles of the state and of the planning mechanism. The policy became known as industrial policy. Aspects of industrial policy, such as regional policy, competition policy and industrial relations policy, generally increased the role of the state and limited the role of markets. By contrast, supply-side microeconomic policy is anti-interventionist, attempting to roll back government interference in the activities of markets and of private economic agents and to change the economic function of government from *provider* to *enabler*. The fiscal policy elements of supply-side economic policy include: tax cuts to create incentives to work, save and invest, and cuts in welfare benefits to reduce the incentive to choose unemployment rather than a low-paid work alternative. There are many other supply-side policies in addition to fiscal policies. These include policies of privatisation, marketisation (commercialisation) and deregulation, which I described in Chapter 9.

In essence, the supply-siders, together with the other free-market economists, wish to create an **enterprise economy**. In this broad interpretation, supply-side policies aim to promote entrepreneurship and popular capitalism and to replace the dependency culture and statism. Indeed, for free-market economists in general, the Keynesian *mixed economy* could perhaps best be described as a *mixed-up economy*.

The European Union fiscal policy

The European Union (EU) does not as yet have a common fiscal policy. However, if the EU ever achieves full economic union, member countries will have to dispense with large elements of national fiscal policies. They would have to have

similar tax structures and tax rates and would lose the freedom to use budget deficits and surpluses to manage demand within their countries. But, so far, this has not happened, and many argue it never will, at least in the foreseeable future.

The EU's **common monetary policy** and the **single currency** (the euro) within the eurozone means that countries such as Ireland and Greece can no longer use monetary policy to manage demand within their borders. As a result, member states try to use fiscal policy for this purpose. This freedom is limited because, in an increasingly globalised economy, financial markets exert discipline over any government that implements an irresponsible national fiscal policy. Financial markets simply refuse to supply the funds to finance the government's budget deficit, except at a much higher interest rate than before.

EU tax harmonisation

Currently, the EU imposes two main limits on a member state's fiscal freedom. These result from **tax harmonisation** and the **Stability and Growth Pact**. The logic behind tax harmonisation is as follows. Although trade barriers have been eliminated in the EU's single market, the common market is incomplete. A genuine common market also requires that indirect taxes among the member countries are brought closely into line or harmonised. For eventual economic union to occur, tax harmonisation is indispensable, though this does not necessarily imply the complete equalisation of tax rates.

The European Union requires all new member states to introduce **value added tax (VAT)**. However the rate at which VAT is levied varies between states. Although some progress has been made in harmonising VAT rates by agreeing maximum and minimum rates, it has been harder to persuade member states to end zero-rating of certain items (e.g. newspapers and books within the UK). Harmonisation of excise duties has been even less successful and the big difference in duties between member states leads to phenomena such as the 'booze-cruises' that transport alcoholic drink and cigarettes between France and Britain.

The Stability and Growth Pact

The Stability and Growth Pact (SGP) is an agreement to limit budget deficits in countries that are members of the eurozone. Establishing the eurozone meant that control of interest rates passed from member state governments to the European Central Bank, whose task is to keep inflation under control. At the time, Germany and France feared that so-called 'club-med' countries in southern Europe would try to escape the deflationary impact of the ECB's tough monetary policy by increasing public spending and by running large budget deficits. The

Key *term*

The **Stability and Growth Pact** is an agreement by EU countries to limit budget deficits in order to promote economic convergence among the member states of the European Union.

eurozone's northern member states therefore insisted that *all* member countries agreed to limit their budget deficits as a proportion of GDP.

The basic principle of the SGP is simple. In normal times all members of the European Union (and not only the eurozone members) are meant to aim for government budgets that are 'close to balance or in surplus'. Governments that run fiscal deficits bigger than 3% of GDP must take swift corrective action. If a eurozone country breaks the 3% limit for more than 3 years in a row, it is liable to fines of billions of euros.

> **examiner's voice**
> Don't confuse the EU's Stability and Growth Pact with the UK's Code for Fiscal Stabillity.

These provisions were meant to be so intimidating that no government would dare breach the 3% rule. It has not worked out like that. By 2003, Germany and France were themselves trying to fend off the threat of recession by breaking the SGP rules they had insisted on a few years earlier. Recession meant that the income Germany and France received from taxes declined, while high and growing unemployment meant greater spending on welfare benefits. To boost their economies, the German and French governments decided to defy the European Commission by cutting taxes. Not surprisingly, the governments of smaller eurozone countries, who had themselves already tasted the bitter medicine of sharp budget cuts to keep their own deficits in line, were furious.

In theory, as I have already stated, the Council of European Finance Ministers can heavily fine countries that breach the Pact. But in practice, it has been difficult if not impossible to get elected politicians to agree on large fines that would further damage a country's economy. Enforcement of the Pact therefore relies on the public shaming of countries that breach the rules. In the outcome, however, this is ineffective because governments rarely feel shamed.

Many observers have argued that the Pact is too rigid. Countries should be allowed to run larger deficits if there is a major recession, and money borrowed for productive investment in infrastructure projects like roads and schools should also be allowed. But on the other hand, some economists say that the eurozone does need a rule to control fiscal irresponsibility — otherwise countries could free ride and gain the benefits of eurozone membership without having to pay the costs. Given the difficulty of enforcing any rule without a central government in the EU, the Stability and Growth Pact is better than having no rules at all. With recession hitting almost all EU countries in 2008 and the suspension of the UK's own fiscal rules, the call for a relaxation of the Pact's rules have become more strident.

However, the current rules are written into European law. Getting agreement to change them would require the consent of most EU governments. But those countries that have been virtuous over deficits will be reluctant to help the countries that have broken the rules.

Summary

➤ Over more than a century, UK fiscal policy developed from balanced budgets and 'sound finance' to Keynesian demand management, to supply-side fiscal policy, and in 2008 back to Keynesian demand management.

➤ Taxes can be progressive, regressive or proportionate.

➤ The principles or canons of taxation are used to judge whether a tax is good or bad.

➤ Public spending is used to provide economic services, to transfer income from rich to poor and to pay interest on past government borrowing.

➤ Taxation and public spending have allocative, distributional and economic management aims.

➤ Keynesian fiscal policy centres on using the budget deficit to manage aggregate demand, through shifts of the aggregate demand (*AD*) curve.

➤ Supply-side fiscal policy focuses on shifting the long-run aggregate supply (*LRAS*) curve to the right via increases in personal incentives.

➤ Progressive taxation and means-tested welfare benefits function as automatic stabilisers.

➤ Supply-side economists believe that increased public spending crowds out the private sector, whereas Keynesians believe it crowds in or stimulates private spending.

➤ The Code for Fiscal Stability is aimed to promote macroeconomic stability.

➤ The Laffer curve is used to justify supply-side tax cuts.

➤ The European Union's Stability and Growth Pact should not be confused with the UK's Code for Fiscal Stability.

Questions

1 What are the main forms of taxation in the UK?

2 Distinguish between direct and indirect taxation.

3 What are the main forms of public spending?

4 Distinguish between the cyclical and the structural components of a budget deficit.

5 What is an automatic stabiliser?

6 How may public spending lead to crowding out?

7 Explain the link between fiscal policy and monetary policy.

8 What is (or was) the Code for Fiscal Stability?

9 Distinguish between the golden rule and the sustainable investment rule.

10 What does the Laffer curve show?

11 Explain the case for and against a flat-rate income tax.

12 What is the purpose of tax harmonisation?

13 What is the Stability and Growth Pact, and why has the Pact failed?

Chapter 20

International trade and globalisation

This chapter explains the case for international specialisation and trade, the benefits of the international division of labour and the principle of comparative advantage, and weighs up counter-arguments to justify import controls or protectionism. This section of the chapter is followed by an analysis of the welfare gains resulting from free trade and of the welfare losses caused by tariffs.

The chapter goes on to explain changes in the patterns of world trade and UK trade. The main changes have been a switch from a North–South pattern to a North–North pattern of trade and the growth of exports of manufactured goods produced in newly industrialising countries (NICs), particularly China. I develop the chapter by linking trade theory, in part via the role of the World Trade Organization (WTO), to globalisation. However, globalisation covers much more than just trade liberalisation, including the effects of increased capital and labour mobility and the growing ability of multinational corporations (MNCs) to exert power over the national economies in which they operate. I survey these and other features of globalisation in the concluding sections of the chapter.

Learning outcomes

This chapter will:
> explain the case for free trade
> describe different forms of protectionism
> survey patterns of trade, both for global trade and for the UK
> discuss the meaning of globalisation
> examine the main elements of globalisation
> describe the role of the World Trade Organization (WTO)

unit 4

At AS you came across the concepts of specialisation and the division of labour and exchange, but you learnt little about international trade. What you did learn was in the context of the current account of the balance of payments and exchange rates. For example, you learnt about the meaning of the balance of trade in goods and the balance of trade in services and how changes in exchange rates can affect these balances. International trade is best regarded as a completely new topic at A2, which you must learn from scratch.

The case for international trade

Widening choice

Imagine a small country such as Iceland in a world without international trade. As a **closed economy**, Iceland's production possibilities are limited to the goods and services that its narrow resource base can produce. This means that Iceland's average costs of production are likely to be high because the small population and the absence of export markets mean that economies of scale and long production runs cannot be achieved. At the same time, the consumption possibilities of Iceland's inhabitants are restricted to the goods that the country can produce.

 Key terms

A **closed economy** is an economy that undertakes no trade with the rest of the world.

An **open economy** is an economy completely open to trade with the rest of the world.

Compare this with Iceland's position in a world completely open to international trade. In an **open economy**, imports of raw materials and energy greatly boost Iceland's production possibilities. In theory at least, Iceland can now produce a much wider range of goods. In practice, however, Iceland produces the relatively

International trade improves consumer choice

few goods and services that it is good at producing, and imports all the rest. By gaining access to the much larger world market, Iceland's industries benefit from economies of scale and long production runs. Likewise, imports of food and other consumer goods present Iceland's inhabitants with a vast array of choice and the possibility of a much higher living standard and level of economic welfare than are possible in a world without trade.

Box 20.1 The collapse of Iceland's economy

Since first writing the above section about Iceland's economy several years ago, the country has become a case study, first of the benefits of opening up its economy to free trade, but more recently of the disadvantages of such openness.

Iceland has a population just larger than 300,000, which is roughly equal to the population of Cardiff. Following the deregulation of the country's financial system in 2000, Iceland's banks grew to become the nation's largest industry. Because of the small size of Iceland's economy, this growth could only happen if the banks expanded overseas, particularly in Britain. Iceland began to 'export' financial services and accumulated assets in the rest of the world equal to about ten times the country's GDP. In return, it imported luxury goods to maintain the lifestyles of Iceland's newly rich population. Before the crash of 2008, Iceland was ranked first in the United Nation's Human Development Index.

But it all ended in tears. Iceland's banks had grown to be far larger than the domestic economy could sustain. They owned 'toxic' assets and were allegedly riddled with fraud. The financial system collapsed in 2008, the economy shrunk, the exchange rate lost most of its value and unemployment grew very rapidly. Although other factors were involved, much of this debacle resulted from over-exposure to free trade and to the free movement of capital in little-regulated and increasingly globalised financial markets.

Follow-up questions
1 For Iceland, financial services have been an invisible export. What does this mean?
2 What is meant by financial deregulation?

Specialisation and the division of labour

Before explaining the benefits of international trade, I must first introduce you to two important economic principles: the **division of labour** and the **principle of comparative advantage**.

Over 200 years ago, the great classical economist, Adam Smith, first explained how, within a single production unit or firm (he took the example of a pin factory), output can increase if workers specialise in different tasks in a manufacturing process. Smith established one

> **examiner's voice**
> You must appreciate the different contexts in which the division of labour occurs: locally, regionally and internationally.

of the most fundamental of all economic principles: the benefits of **specialisation** and the division of labour. According to Adam Smith, there are three main reasons why specialisation increases total output:

➤ Workers don't need to switch between tasks, so time is saved.

> More and better machinery or capital is employed. Increasing capital at the same rate at which the labour force is increasing is called **capital widening**. Increasing the amount of capital per worker is called **capital deepening**.
> Practice makes workers more efficient and productive when performing specialised tasks (although because of 'deskilling', boredom and the creation of alienation towards employers, this can easily become a disadvantage).

The principle of the division of labour not only explains specialisation *between* workers *within* a factory: it can also be extended to explain the specialisation between plants or factories within a firm; specialisation between separate firms; and, lastly, geographical or spatial specialisation both internally within a country and externally between countries. Such *international* specialisation is the main subject of this chapter.

Absolute advantage

The benefits of the **international division of labour** suggest that if each of the world's countries, with its own endowment of natural resources such as soil, climate and minerals, and of man-made resources such as capital, know-how and labour skills, specialises in what it does best, total world output or production can increase compared to the outcome without specialisation. Being 'better at' producing a good or service means that a country can produce the good at the lowest cost in terms of resources used. Using microeconomic terminology, the country is technically and productively efficient in producing the good. We can also say that a country that is absolutely 'best at', or most technically efficient at, producing a good or service, possesses an **absolute advantage** in the good's production. Conversely, if it is not the best, the country suffers an absolute disadvantage compared to other more technically efficient producers.

Key terms

The international division of labour describes different countries specialising in producing different goods.

Absolute advantage occurs when a country is absolutely best (or more technically efficient) than other countries in a particular industry.

To explain absolute advantage, I shall assume just two countries in the world economy, Atlantis and Pacifica. Each country has only 2 units of resource. Only two goods can be produced: guns and butter. Each unit of resource, or indeed a fraction of each unit (because I shall assume that resources or inputs are divisible), can be switched from one industry to another, if so desired, in each country. In each country the production possibilities are such that 1 unit of resource can produce:

> in Atlantis: 4 guns or 2 tonnes of butter
> in Pacifica: 1 gun or 6 tonnes of butter

Quite clearly, in terms of technical efficiency, Atlantis is 'best at' — or has an absolute advantage in — producing guns. It is four times more technically efficient in gun production than Pacifica. However, this is not the case for butter production. Pacifica is three times more technically efficient in butter production and so possesses an absolute advantage in this good.

Suppose that both countries devote half their total resources to each activity (that is, 1 unit of resource out of the 2 units available for each country). Atlantis produces 4 guns, Pacifica produces 1 gun, which means that 5 guns are produced in total. Likewise, total butter production is 8 tonnes. Atlantis produces 2 tonnes and Pacifica produces 6 tonnes.

Now let's see what happens when each country produces only the good in which it has an absolute advantage. Atlantis devotes both its resource units to guns, producing 8 guns. Likewise, Pacifica completely specialises, producing 12 tonnes of butter with its 2 units of resource.

➤ Without specialisation, outputs are 5 guns and 8 tonnes of butter.
➤ With specialisation, outputs become 8 guns and 12 tonnes of butter.

In this example, specialisation produces a net output gain of 3 guns and 4 tonnes of butter.

But for output gains to translate into gains from trade, two further factors have to be taken into account. First, administration and transport costs occur whenever trade takes place. As a result, the output gains from trade are:

(3 guns + 4 tonnes of butter) – transport and administration costs

Clearly, specialisation and trade are not worthwhile if transport and administration costs exceed the output gains resulting from specialisation.

Second, assuming that only two countries trade with each other, for output gains to transfer into *welfare* gains for the inhabitants of both countries, the goods being traded must be in demand in the importing country. Given this assumption about demand, I shall further assume that each country exports its surplus to the other country once it has satisfied its own inhabitants' demand for the good in which it specialises. (This **double coincidence of wants** is not necessary when more than two countries trade together.)

But suppose Atlantis's inhabitants are vegans who refuse to eat animal products, while Pacifica's inhabitants are pacifists who hate guns. For Atlantis's inhabitants, butter is a *bad* rather than a *good*. Likewise, guns are a bad for Pacifica's residents. (A **good** yields **utility** or **economic welfare** to consumers, but a **bad** yields **disutility** or **negative welfare**.) Atlantis refuses to import butter, and Pacifica refuses to buy guns. Specialisation and trade do not take place. Without suitable demand conditions, the case for specialisation and trade disappears.

Comparative advantage

Absolute advantage must not be confused with the rather more subtle concept of **comparative advantage**. However, understanding *absolute* advantage is a stepping-

examiner's voice
It is important to understand the difference between absolute and comparative advantage.

Key term

Comparative advantage is measured in terms of opportunity cost. The country with the least opportunity cost when producing a good possesses a comparative advantage in that good.

stone to understanding *comparative* advantage. To introduce and illustrate this very important economic principle, I shall change the production possibilities of both countries so that Atlantis possesses the absolute advantage for *both* guns and butter (which means that Pacifica has an absolute disadvantage in both goods).

One unit of resource now produces:
➤ in Atlantis: 4 guns or 2 tonnes of butter
➤ in Pacifica: 1 gun or 1 tonne of butter

Although Atlantis is 'best at' — or has an absolute advantage in — producing *both* guns and butter, the country possesses a comparative advantage *only* in gun production. This is because comparative advantage is measured in terms of **opportunity cost**, or what a country gives up when it increases the output of an industry by 1 unit. The country that gives up *least* of the other commodity when increasing output of a particular commodity by 1 unit possesses the comparative advantage in that good. Ask yourself how many guns Atlantis has to give up in order to increase its butter output by 1 tonne. The answer is 2 guns. But Pacifica only has to give up 1 gun to produce an extra tonne of butter. Thus Pacifica possesses a *comparative* advantage in butter production even though it has an *absolute* disadvantage in both products.

When one country possesses an absolute advantage in both industries, as in the example above, its comparative advantage always lies in producing the good in which its absolute advantage is greatest. Similarly, the country that is absolutely worst at both activities possesses a comparative advantage in the industry in which its absolute disadvantage is least.

In this example, *complete* specialisation results in *more* guns but *less* butter being produced, compared to a situation in which each country devotes half its total resources to each activity. Without specialisation, the combined output of both countries is 5 guns and 3 tonnes of butter. With complete specialisation, this changes to 8 guns and 2 tonnes of butter. While production of guns has increased, production of butter has fallen.

When one country has an absolute advantage in both goods, *complete* specialisation in accordance with the principle of comparative advantage does not result in a net output gain. The output of one good rises, but the output of the other good falls.

Students often get puzzled by this, thinking (wrongly) that specialisation cannot lead to gains from trade. However, *partial* specialisation can produce a net output gain. For example, suppose Pacifica (which suffers an *absolute* disadvantage in *both* goods) completely specialises and produces 2 tonnes of butter. By contrast, Atlantis (which has the absolute advantage in both goods) devotes just enough resource (half a unit) to top up world production of butter to 3 tonnes. This means that Atlantis can still produce 6 guns using 1.5 units of resource. Total production in both countries is therefore 6 guns and 3 tonnes of butter. At least as much butter and more guns are now produced compared with the no-specialisation outcome.

This example shows that specialisation can produce a net output gain, even though one country is absolutely better at both activities.

The assumptions underlying the principle of comparative advantage

When arguing that definite benefits result when countries specialise and trade in accordance with the principle of comparative advantage, I made a number of rather strong but not necessarily realistic assumptions. Indeed, the case for trade — and hence the case *against* import controls and other forms of protectionism — is heavily dependent upon these assumptions. Likewise, some of the arguments in favour of import controls and against free trade, which I shall explain shortly, depend on showing that the assumptions necessary for the benefits of specialisation and trade to occur are simply not met in real life. These assumptions are as follows:

➤ Each country's endowment of factors of production, including capital and labour, is fixed and immobile between countries, although factors can be switched between industries within a country. In the course of international trade, *finished goods* rather than *factors of production* or inputs are assumed to be mobile between countries.

➤ The principle of comparative advantage assumes **constant returns to scale**. In my example, 1 unit of resource is assumed to produce 4 guns or 2 tonnes of butter in Atlantis, whether it is the first unit of resource employed or the millionth unit. But in the real world, increasing or decreasing returns to scale are both possible and indeed likely. In a world of **increasing returns to scale**, the more a country specialises in an activity in which it initially has an absolute advantage, the more its productive efficiency and advantage increases. Countries that are 'best' to start with become even 'better'. But if **decreasing returns to scale** occur, specialisation erodes efficiency and destroys a country's initial advantage. A good example occurs in agriculture, where over-specialisation can result in monoculture or the growing of a single cash crop for export. Monoculture often leads to soil erosion, vulnerability to pests and falling future agricultural yields.

➤ The principle of comparative advantage implicitly assumes relatively stable demand and cost conditions. Over-specialisation can cause a country to become particularly vulnerable to sudden changes in demand or to changes in the cost and availability of imported raw materials or energy. Changes in costs, and new inventions and technical progress, can quickly eliminate a country's

earlier comparative advantage. The greater the uncertainty about the future, the weaker the case for complete specialisation. Indeed, if a country is self-sufficient in all important respects, it is neutralised against the danger of importing recession and unemployment from the rest of the world when international demand collapses.

Extension material

Comparative advantage and competitive advantage

Comparative advantage must not be confused with *competitive* advantage. A country, or a firm within a country, enjoys a **competitive advantage** when it produces better-quality goods at lower costs and better prices than its rivals. Competitive advantage is more similar to *absolute* advantage than to comparative advantage.

Dynamic factors that promote the growth of firms can create competitive advantage. Successful investment undertaken over many years equips a country with modern, 'state-of-the-art' production capacity, capable of producing high-quality goods that people want to buy. Properly funded and organised research and development (R&D) contributes in a similar way, while the stock of human capital resulting from investment in education and training adds to competitive advantage.

Factors that create competitive advantage can trigger a **virtuous spiral** of larger profits, higher investment, better products and greater sales, which in turn leads to even higher profits, and so on. Conversely, countries and firms that are not competitive may enter a **vicious spiral** of decline. Inability to compete causes profits to fall, which in turn reduces investment. The quality of goods declines and sales are lost to more competitive countries or firms. Profits again fall (maybe disappearing altogether), and a further round in the vicious circle of decline is unleashed.

The case for import controls and protectionism

Import controls can be divided into quantity controls such as **import quotas**, which put a maximum limit on imports, and **tariffs** or **import duties** (and their opposite, **export subsidies**), which raise the price of imports (or reduce the price of exports).

 Key term

Import controls include tariffs or import duties, quotas, export subsidies and informal controls.

Supporters of free trade believe that import controls prevent countries from special-ising in activities in which they have a comparative advantage and trading their surpluses. As a result, production takes place inefficiently and economic welfare is reduced. But as I have already noted, the case for free trade depends to a large extent upon some of the assumptions underlying the principle of comparative advantage. Destroy these assumptions, and the case for free trade is weakened.

Below are some of the contexts in which import controls have been justified.

➤ **Infant industries.** As I have already explained, many economic activities benefit from increasing returns to scale, which mean that the more a country specialises in a particular industry, the more productively efficient it becomes. This increases its competitive advantage. Developing countries justify the use of import controls to protect infant industries from established rivals in advanced economies. Protectionism is needed while newly established industries develop full economies of scale.

➤ **Strategic trade theory.** The infant industry argument is closely related to strategic trade theory, a relatively new theory that has grown in influence in recent years. Strategic trade theory argues that comparative and competitive advantage are often not 'natural'. Rather, governments try to create competitive advantage by nurturing strategically selected industries or economic sectors. This justifies protecting the industries while competitive advantage is being built up. The skills that are gained will then spill over to help other sectors in the economy. Strategic trade theory also argues that protectionism can prevent exploitation by a foreign-based monopoly.

➤ **Agricultural efficiency.** As I noted earlier in the context of agriculture, monoculture erodes efficiency and destroys comparative advantage that existed before specialisation took place. Decreasing returns to scale weaken the case for complete specialisation.

➤ **Changes in demand or cost conditions.** Over-specialisation may cause a country to become particularly vulnerable to sudden changes in demand or to changes in the cost and availability of imported raw materials or energy.

➤ **Sunset industries.** A rather similar case to the infant industry argument is sometimes made in advanced industrial economies such as the UK to protect older industries from the competition of infant industries in developing countries. Keynesian economists have sometimes advocated the selective use of import controls as a potentially effective supply-side policy instrument to prevent unnecessary deindustrialisation and to allow orderly rather than disruptive structural change in the manufacturing base of the economy. According to this view, import controls are justified, at least on a temporary basis, to minimise the social and economic cost of the painful adjustment process, as the structure of an economy alters in response either to changing demand or to changing technology and comparative and competitive advantage.

➤ **Anti-dumping.** When a country produces too much of a good for its own domestic market, the surplus may then be 'dumped' and sold at a price below cost in overseas markets. Import controls are sometimes justified as a means to prevent this supposedly 'unfair' competition.

➤ **Demerit goods and 'bads'.** In the case of narcotic drugs and weapons, an *output* gain does not necessarily lead to a *welfare* gain. Governments argue they have a moral duty to ban imports of heroin, cocaine and handguns to protect the welfare of their citizens.

examiner's voice
When answering an exam question requiring evaluation of the case for free trade (or the case for import controls) it is best to avoid a 'shopping list' approach. Instead, select, develop, analyse and evaluate three or four arguments or counter-arguments.

➤ **Self-sufficiency.** Politically, it is often argued that protection is necessary for military and strategic reasons to ensure that a country is relatively self-sufficient in vital foodstuffs, energy and raw materials in a time of war.

➤ **Employment.** Trade unions argue that import controls are necessary to prevent multinational firms shifting capital to low-wage developing countries and exporting their output back to the countries from which the capital was moved. They further argue the case for employing labour, however inefficiently, in protected industries rather than allowing labour to suffer the greatest ineffi-ciency of all: mass unemployment. This is an example of **second-best theory**. The second-best argument stems from the fact that the 'first best' (free trade in a world of fully employed economies and perfect markets) is unattainable. Therefore, a country can settle legitimately for the second best. Employing resources inefficiently, protected by tariffs, is better than not employing resources at all. This justification for protecting domestic industries and main-taining employment came into prominence around the time that Barack Obama took over the US presidency in 2009.

Box 20.2 Paul Krugman and strategic trade theory

In 2008, Paul Krugman, professor of economics at Princeton University, USA, was awarded the Nobel Prize in Economics, in part for his pioneering work in developing strategic trade theory in the 1980s and 1990s. In contrast to the orthodox free-market approach to international trade, firmly grounded in the principle of comparative advantage, strategic trade theory argues that import controls can sometimes be justified. Krugman argued that rich developed countries benefited from protec-tionism while they established their national wealth. However, they now put pressure on poor countries to abandon import controls and to allow overseas-based multi-national corporations unlimited access to their economies. As I explain later in the chapter, opponents of globalisation argue that free trade theory is used to justify first-world economic imperialism.

Below is an extract from the beginning of a paper Krugman wrote in 1987. The full article can be found online at: **bss.sfsu.edu/jmoss/resources/Is%20Free%20Trade%20Passe.pdf**

If there were an Economist's Creed, it would surely contain the affirmations 'I understand the principle of comparative advantage' and 'I advocate free trade'. For 170 years, the appre-ciation that international trade benefits a country whether it is 'fair' or not has been one of the touchstones of professionalism in economics.

Yet the case for free trade is currently more in doubt than at any time since the 1817 publica-tion of Ricardo's *Principles of Political Economy*. This is not because of the political pressures for protection, which have triumphed in the past without shaking the intellectual foundation of comparative advantage theory. Rather, it is because of the changes that have recently taken place in the theory of international trade itself.

In the last 10 years the traditional <u>constant returns</u>, <u>perfect competition</u> models of interna-tional trade have been supplemented and to some extent supplanted by a new breed of models that emphasise <u>increasing returns</u> and <u>imperfect competition</u>. These new models call into doubt the extent to which actual trade can be explained by comparative advantage.

Showing that free trade is better than no trade is not the same thing as showing that free trade is better than sophisticated government intervention. The view that free trade is the best of all possible policies is part of the general case for laissez-faire in a market economy and rests on the proposition that markets are efficient. If increasing returns and imperfect competition are necessary parts of the explanation of inter-national trade, we are living in a <u>second-best</u> world where government intervention can in principle improve on market outcomes.

'Is free trade passé?' by Paul Krugman, published in *The Journal of Economic Perspectives*, 1987

Follow-up questions

1 Briefly define each of the underlined terms in the extract.

2 How do increasing returns to scale and imperfect competition weaken the case for unlimited free trade based on the principle of comparative advantage?

International trade

Welfare losses and welfare gains

In this and the next two sections of the chapter, I bypass the justifications for tariffs put forward by economists such as Paul Krugman and return to the free-market case for free trade. Analysis of the welfare gains from free trade and the welfare losses caused by import controls centres on the concepts of **consumer surplus** and **producer surplus** you learn when studying Unit 3.

If a country does not enter into international trade, which means its economy is *closed*, domestic demand for a good within a country can only be met by domestic supply (that is, by firms producing *within* the country). Such a situation is shown in Figure 20.1, in which market equilibrium for the good occurs at point X. Consumers pay price P_1 for the good, and the quantity bought and sold is Q_1. Consumer surplus, which measures **consumer welfare,** is shown by the triangular area bounded by points XZP_1. Likewise, **producer welfare** (producer surplus) is the triangular area bounded by points XP_1U.

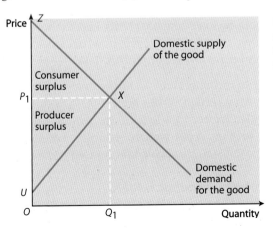

Figure 20.1 *Consumer and producer surplus in a market closed to international trade*

But consider what happens in a world of completely free trade, in which domesti-cally produced goods have to compete with cheaper imports. In the next diagram, Figure 20.2, imports are priced at the ruling world price of P_W, which is lower than

P_1. In this situation, equilibrium now occurs in the domestic market at point V. Although domestic demand has increased to Q_{D1}, domestic supply (located where the domestic supply curve cuts the horizontal price line at P_W) falls to Q_{S1}. Imports (equal to $Q_{D1} - Q_{S1}$) fill the gap between domestic demand and supply.

examiner's voice

You should practise drawing and explaining this diagram and the diagrams that follow to show the welfare gains and losses resulting from trade and import controls. Remember, however, the assumptions that underpin free-trade theory that I explained earlier. Question these assumptions and the case for free trade weakens.

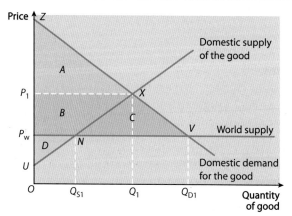

Figure 20.2 *The welfare gains and losses resulting from the introduction of a tariff*

To understand how imports affect economic welfare within the country, it is important to understand how consumer surplus and producer surplus change after the price of the good falls to the world price P_W. Consumer surplus increases by the wedge-shaped area bounded by the points $P_W V X P_1$. This divides into two parts, shown on the diagram by areas B and C. Look closely at the area B. This shows a welfare transfer away from domestic firms to domestic consumers. The fall in the price from P_1 to P_W, brought about by lower import prices, means that part of the producer surplus domestic firms previously enjoyed now becomes consumer surplus. The consumers 'win' and the domestic producers 'lose'.

But this is not the end of the story. Consumers enjoy a further increase in consumer surplus, which is brought about by receipt of the area C. As a result, the total increase in consumer surplus gain exceeds the size of the welfare transfer from producer surplus to consumer surplus. A **net welfare gain** thus results, equal to area C, that makes up part of the consumer surplus that households now enjoy.

How a tariff or import duty affects economic welfare

I shall now assume that domestic firms pressure the government to introduce a tariff to protect the home market. If the tariff equals the distance between P_1 and P_W, the domestic market for the good reverts to the original equilibrium position that existed before imports entered the country. But suppose the government imposes a smaller tariff, which is just sufficient to raise the price of imports (and also of domestically produced goods) to $P_W + t$ in Figure 20.3. At price $P_W + t$,

AQA A2 Economics

domestic demand falls to Q_{D2}, while domestic supply rises to Q_{S2}. Imports fall from $Q_{D1} - Q_{S1}$ to $Q_{D2} - Q_{S2}$.

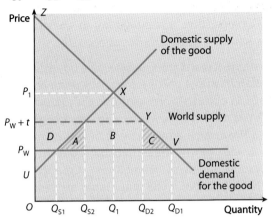

Figure 20.3 The effect of imposing a tariff

At the higher price, consumer surplus *falls* by the 'wedge' shaped area $P_W V Y P_W + t$, — which equals the areas $D + A + B + C$. The higher price increases producer surplus by the area D, and the government gains tariff revenue shown by the area B. The areas D and B are *transfers* of welfare away from consumers respectively to domestic producers and to the government. The *net* welfare *loss* resulting from the tariff, which is the sum of triangles A and C in the diagram, is:

$$(D + A + B + C) - (D + B), \text{ which equals } A + C.$$

Changing comparative advantage and the pattern of world trade

When, over two centuries ago, Adam Smith first explained the advantages of the division of labour, and a few years later in the early nineteenth century another distinguished classical economist, David Ricardo, developed Adam Smith's ideas into the principle of comparative advantage, they were not just interested in abstract theory. Instead, like most great economists, they wished to change society for the better by influencing the politicians of their day. Smith and Ricardo believed in the virtues of a competitive market economy and industrial capitalism. Ricardo, in particular, believed that a single country such as the UK, and indeed the whole world economy, can only reach their full productive potential, maximising output, welfare and living standards, if the market economy is truly international. He argued that each country should specialise in the activities in which it possesses a comparative advantage and trade the output that is surplus to its needs in a world free of tariffs and other forms of protectionism.

To many people living in industrial countries during the nineteenth century and the first half of the twentieth century, it must have seemed almost natural that the earliest countries to industrialise, such as the UK, had done so because they possessed a competitive and comparative advantage in manufacturing.

examiner's voice

Exam questions may ask you to describe and explain patterns of trade, either global or for the UK. Make sure you can distinguish between geographical and commodity patterns of trade.

It probably seemed equally natural that a pattern of world trade should have developed in which the industrialised countries in what is now called the *North* exported manufactured goods in exchange for foodstuffs and raw materials produced by countries whose comparative advantage lay in the production of primary products – in modern parlance, the countries of the *South*.

However, in recent years, the pattern of world trade has become quite different from the North–South exchange of manufactured goods for primary products that characterised the nineteenth century. In a North–North pattern of trade, which is illustrated in Figure 20.4, the developed industrial economies now exchange goods and services mostly with each other. However, a growing fraction of their trade, particularly in the case of imports, is with **newly industrialising countries** (NICs) or **emerging markets**, particularly India, China and South Korea. A group of countries known as the **BRIC** countries (Brazil, Russia, India and China) are responsible for exporting large quantities of goods and services to the North. India, China and South Korea now export manufactured goods to countries in the North such as the UK and the USA, and import raw materials or commodities such as copper from developing countries such as Zambia. They also import a growing fraction of the crude oil produced by oil-exporting developing countries such as Saudi Arabia and Venezuela.

The shift of manufacturing to China and other NICs reflects changing competitive and comparative advantage and the **deindustrialisation** of Britain and North America. Only a relatively small proportion of the trade of North countries is with poorer countries in the non-oil-producing developing world.

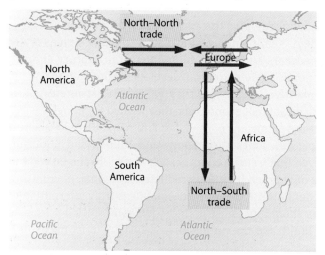

Figure 20.4
North–North and North–South patterns of trade

Extension material

The Heckscher–Ohlin theory of international trade
In the 1930s two Swedish economists, Heckscher and Ohlin, explained the then dominant North–South exchange of manufactured goods for primary products in terms of factor

endowments. The **Heckscher–Ohlin theory**, which is really an extension of the principle of comparative advantage, argues that a capital-rich country is likely to industrialise and export capital-intensive manufactured goods. However, if capital is scarce relative to labour, the country specialises in and exports labour-intensive primary products. The Heckscher–Ohlin theory was grasped by pro-free market economists because it appeared to give legitimacy to a pattern of trade in which rich counties exploited the poorer countries, over which they often exerted military and political control.

The UK's international trade

Table 20.1 shows that over the 52-year period from 1955 to 2007, the pattern of the UK's international trade changed from a 'North–South' to a 'North–North' pattern in terms of the global regions with whom the UK trades. The UK now trades mainly with other developed countries in the North, and especially with other EU countries. In 1955, only 15% of UK exports and 12.6% of UK imports were with countries that eventually formed the EU. By contrast, 32.9% of UK exports and 31.4% of UK imports were with developing countries. By 2007, this situation was reversed: respectively 58% and 54.5% of UK exports and imports were with EU countries, while exports to other developing countries had fallen to 13.2% for exports, though imports had recovered somewhat to 20.6%, from their lower percentage in 2000.

Table 20.1 *The changing pattern of the UK's international trade with other world regions*

	1955		1992		2000		2007	
UK trade with	**Exports (%)**	**Imports (%)**	**Exports (%)**	**Imports (%)**	**Exports (%)**	**Imports (%)**	**Exports (%)**	**Imports (%)**
EU	15.0	12.6	56.4	52.5	57.3	51.0	58.0	54.5
Other west European countries	13.9	13.1	7.9	11.6	4.0	6.0	4.1	7.9
North America	12.0	19.5	13.0	12.6	18.0	15.4	16.3	10.4
Other developed countries	21.1	14.2	3.6	7.1	5.8	8.3	3.8	4.5
Oil-exporting developed countries	5.1	9.2	5.6	2.5	3.3	2.0	4.6	2.1
Other developing countries	32.9	31.4	13.5	13.7	11.6	17.3	13.2	20.6

Source: *Annual Abstract of Statistics*, various, ONS

In contrast to Table 20.1, which shows changes in the global pattern of UK trade, Table 20.2 (on page 342) focuses on changes in the commodities traded over a rather shorter time period – 2000–07. The table shows that, despite the impact of deindustrialisation, which has reduced manufacturing output to less than 15% of GDP, the UK's trade in goods is still dominated by the export and import of manufactured goods, though with the country importing significantly more than it exports. I shall take up this story again in the next chapter, when investigating the UK's balances of trade in goods and in services.

Table 20.2 *Changes in selected items in UK trade in goods by type of commodity, 2000–07 (£m),* *(percentages of total trade in goods shown in brackets)*

	2000		2002		2005		2007	
	Exports	**Imports**	**Exports**	**Imports**	**Exports**	**Imports**	**Exports**	**Imports**
Food	5,827 (3.1%)	13,310 (6.0%)	5,693 (3.0%)	14,874 (6.3%)	6,552 (3.1%)	18,593 (6.6%)	7,390 (3.3%)	21,291 (6.9%)
Drink and tobacco	4,081 (2.2%)	4,350 (2.0%)	4,300 (2.3%)	4,501 (1.9%)	4,095 (1.9%)	5,102 (1.8%)	4,395 (2.0%)	5,434 (1.8%)
Raw materials	2,447 (13.0%)	5,816 (2.6%)	2,645 (1.4%)	5,420 (2.3%)	3,745 (1.8%)	6,129 (2.2%)	5,177 (2.3%)	8,068 (2.6%)
Fuels and energy	17,057 (9.1%)	10,016 (4.5%)	16,000 (8.6%)	10,279 (4.4%)	21,496 (10.2%)	26,921 (9.6%)	24,767 (11.2%)	31,262 (10.1%)
Chemicals	24,992 (13.3%)	20,663 (9.4%)	26,386 (11.1%)	23,967 (10.2%)	33,388 (15.8%)	29,208 (10.4%)	38,913 (17.6%)	34,831 (11.3%)
Machinery and transport equipment	87,812 (46.7%)	102,420 (46.3%)	84,395 (45.2%)	107,556 (45.9%)	87,379 (41.3%)	117,318 (41.8%)	82,669 (37.4%)	116,258 (37.7%)
Other manufactures	43,879 (23.3%)	62,030 (28.1%)	43,822 (23.5%)	65,624 (28.0%)	52,597 (24.9%)	75,644 (27.0%)	56,047 (25.4%)	87,578 (28.4%)
Total exports	**187,936**		**186,524**		**211,608**		**220,857**	
Total imports		**220,912**		**234,239**		**280,397**		**308,506**

Source: *Annual Abstract of Statistics*, ONS, 2008

Globalisation

Globalisation is the name given to the processes that integrate all or most of the world's economies, making countries increasingly dependent upon each other. Some economists argue that globalisation has occurred over centuries, going back at least as far as the creation of a system of relatively free worldwide trade in the nineteenth century. Perhaps it extends even further back to the Spanish and Portuguese occupation of much of South America.

Key *term*

Globalisation is the process of growing economic integration of the world's economies.

In the late nineteenth century and the period before 1914, communication and transport networks expanded throughout much of the world and international trade grew significantly. At the same time, older industrial countries, and particularly the UK, began to invest their surplus savings in capital projects located overseas rather than in their domestic economies.

However, these changes are better described as aspects of **internationalisation** rather than globalisation. Globalisation, which has come to mean rather more than mere internationalisation of economic relationships, began to feature in the economics literature of the mid-1980s. The use of the term has increased dramatically ever since.

Recent globalisation has been made possible by improvements in information and communication technology (ICT), as well as by developments in more traditional forms of technology. Examples of globalisation include service industries in the UK dealing with customers through call centres in India and fashion companies designing their products in Europe, making them in southeast Asia and finally selling most of them in North America.

The debate about globalisation

Free-market economists generally support globalisation and regard its growth as inevitable. They argue that the benefits of further global economic integration, which include the extension of political freedom and democracy as well as the economic benefits of more production and higher living standards, significantly exceed the disadvantages, such as the destruction of local cultures. However, opponents argue that globalisation is a respectable name for the growing exploitation of the poor, mostly in developing countries, by international capitalism and US economic and cultural imperialism.

For its critics, low-paid workers in sweat-shops, farmers in the developing world being forced to grow genetically modified crops, the privatisation of state-owned industry to qualify for IMF and World Bank loans, and the growing dominance of US corporate culture and multinational companies symbolise what is wrong with globalisation. According to this view, global-isation has led to a 'McDonaldisation' or 'Coca-Colonisation' of significant parts of the world's economy, which involves the

A Thai Coca-Cola advert

destruction of local and national products, identities and cultures by US world brands. What is needed is a counter-process of 'glocalisation', or local action that prevents or offsets the damage done by globalisation to vulnerable local cultures. However, this view is not taken seriously by supporters of globalisation, who believe that people in the rest of the world demand US products because they consider them superior to traditional local produce.

Features of globalisation

Some of the main features of globalisation are:

> the growth of international trade and the reduction of trade barriers — a process encouraged by the World Trade Organization (WTO)

> greater international mobility of capital and to some extent of labour

> a significant increase in the power of international capitalism and multinational corporations (MNCs) or transnational companies

> the deindustrialisation of older industrial regions and countries, and the movement of manufacturing industries to newly industrialising countries (NICs)

examiner's voice

Exam questions may focus on the nature of globalisa-tion and on the benefits and costs of the process. This is likely to feature in the global context data-response question in the Unit 4 exam.

> more recently, the movement of internationally mobile service industries, such as call centres and accounts offices, to NICs
> a decrease in governmental power to influence decisions made by MNCs to shift economic activity between countries

Employment practices resulting from globalisation

Closely related to the 'world brand' process has been the alleged treatment of local labour by multinational corporations. This works in two ways. First, companies such as Nike are accused of selling trainers and footballs in developed countries such as the UK at prices far above the cost of raw materials and the low wages paid to workers in developing countries making the goods. In response, the multinationals argue that the 'low wages' they pay far exceed the local wages paid by firms indigenous to the countries in which they manufacture. They believe this encourages local wages to rise. MNCs also claim to improve health and safety and other labour market conditions in the poor countries in which they operate.

Second, by threatening to close down factories and to move production to poor countries, it is argued that MNCs reduce wages and living standards in developed countries. Whether this is true depends on the type of jobs that emerge in developed countries to replace those lost through deindustrialisation and globalisation. Are the new jobs created in the highly skilled service sector, or are they menial, low-paid, unskilled 'McJobs'?

Globalisation in the service sector

Until quite recently, it was said that manufacturing was much more internationally mobile than service sector employment. This is no longer true. Call centres became one of the fastest-growing sources of employment in the UK in the 1980s and 1990s. At that time, UK-based companies favoured locating call centres in regions of high unemployment (and relatively low wages) *within* the UK. To some extent this has now changed. Call centres and back office activities of firms in industries such as financial services are being moved to the Indian subcontinent. This results from the *death of distance*, which is a part of the globalisation process. The rapid development of electronic methods of communication means that many service activities can now be located anywhere in the world, with little or no effect on a company's ability to provide the service efficiently to its customers.

Four factors encouraging the overseas location of call centres are:
> relatively low wages
> highly reliable and cheap telecommunications
> 24-hour shift employment to overcome the problem of time zones
> workers fluent in English, which is now the world's business language

However, for call centres, a fifth factor is often lacking: many overseas workers are insufficiently familiar with UK culture and habits, which for call centres leads to a communication problem. This disadvantage is much less significant for back office employment: for example, employing people in India to administer a UK company's accounts.

Global labour and capital mobility

As the previous paragraphs indicate, globalisation involves moving capital to lower-cost labour much more than it involves allowing low-paid workers born in poor countries to enter rich countries in North America and Europe. However, since the late nineteenth century there has been a much greater movement of poor people into rich countries than ever before. To some extent, immigration controls introduced by countries such as the USA and Australia, which replaced an earlier completely free movement of labour, have slowed this process. But this has been offset by illegal immigration and by the fact that rich countries informally encourage migration to fill the relatively low-paid jobs that their own citizens do not wish to do.

Enlargement of the EU is increasing both labour and capital mobility on a regional basis. Western European firms have been moving eastward, but this is balanced by workers from countries such as Poland and Hungary migrating westward. Nonetheless, it is still much easier in a globalised world for a brain surgeon or a highly paid business executive to move between countries than it is for a Chinese or Indian peasant.

Globalisation and the power of national governments

In recent decades, globalisation has considerably reduced the power of national governments, certainly in smaller countries, to control multinational firms operating within their boundaries. National governments have also lost much of the freedom to undertake the economic policies of their choice with respect to managing domestic economies. Governments enjoy less freedom to introduce tariffs and other import controls. At the same time, capital flows into and out of currencies severely constrain a government's ability to implement an independent monetary policy, even when the country's exchange rate is freely floating.

The World Trade Organization's role in promoting globalisation

Economists and politicians who believe that the benefits of globalisation far exceed any disadvantages involved claim there has been *too little* rather than *too much* international integration of countries' economies. In their view, if countries get rid of *all* protectionist measures, then Adam Smith's 'invisible hand' of the market promotes international trade,

> **examiner's voice**
>
> Along with the European Union, the WTO may figure in Unit 4 exam questions. By contrast, knowledge of the other main international economic institutions, the IMF and the World Bank, is useful but not essential.

which then benefits poor countries as well as rich ones. This view of the world lies behind the creation of the **World Trade Organization (WTO)**, the international organisation established to remove trade barriers and liberalise world trade.

To understand the WTO, it is necessary to go back to events occurring in the 1930s and 1940s. In the 1940s, during the Second World War, it was widely believed (especially in the UK and the USA) that the worldwide Depression and mass unemployment of the 1930s had been made worse, and was possibly caused, by a

collapse of international trade. 'Beggar my neighbour' protectionist policies intro-duced by countries desperately trying to save local jobs were blamed. By 1945 the USA and the UK had decided to try to create a postwar world of free trade. Because this required international agreement, the **General Agreement on Tariffs and Trade (GATT)** was established as a multilateral organisation of member countries whose aim was trade liberalisation. To begin with, GATT was supposed to be a temporary organisation, to be replaced with a WTO as soon as member countries could agree. However, because member countries were unable to agree, the 'temporary' organisation lasted much longer than intended, from the 1940s until the mid-1990s, when the WTO at last replaced GATT.

GATT and later the WTO organised rounds of talks among member countries to reduce import controls. The rounds, which took place at roughly 5-year intervals, were often named after the city or country in which the talks were initiated: for example, the Tokyo round, the Uruguay round and, more recently, the Doha round. Out of respect, the Kennedy round in the mid-1960s was named after the then recently assassinated American president. Each round of talks ends with an agreement to reduce import controls. GATT, and latterly the WTO, have then tried to get member countries to implement the tariff cuts they have agreed.

GATT and WTO agreements have been successful in reducing import controls on manufactured goods. There has been much less success in securing agreement to reduce tariffs and quotas on trade in services and agricultural goods. Recently, the WTO has tried to get the developed countries of the EU and the USA to open their markets to cheap food imports from the developing world. However, the most recent rounds of talks organised by the WTO at Cancún (in Mexico) and Doha (in Qatar) were not successful. Economists and politicians in many developing countries claim that this lack of success provides further evidence of globalisation and international organisations serving the interests of rich countries at the expense of the poor.

The belief that globalisation benefits most countries, poor as well as rich, has been attacked by supporters of the **dependency theory** of trade and development. Dependency theorists argue that developing countries possess little capital because the system of world trade and payments has been organised by developed industrial economies to their own advantage. The **terms of trade** — the ratio of a country's export prices to its import prices — have as a general rule moved in favour of industrialised countries and against primary producers. This means that, by exporting the same amount of manufactured goods to the developing world, a developed economy can import a greater quantity of raw materials or foodstuffs in exchange. By the same token, the developing country must export more in order to buy the same quantity of capital goods or energy vital for development. Globally, the movement of the terms of trade in favour of developed nations has raised levels of income and standards of living in the richer countries at the expense of poorer developing countries. However, there have been some exceptions, namely NICs and the oil-producing non-industrial countries, which have benefited from substantial increases in the price of oil.

Economists of the dependency school argue that the transfer of wealth and resources to the richer countries is further promoted by profit flows and interest payments. On an international scale, dividends and profits flow to multinational corporations with headquarters in North America, western Europe and Japan from their subsidiaries in the developing world. Similarly, there is a flow of interest payments to western banks from loans originally made to finance development in developing countries. In most years, flows of dividends and interest payments from South to North exceed aid flows in the opposite direction.

> **examiner's voice**
>
> The more or less continuous economic growth enjoyed by advanced industrialised countries in the 1990s and the first few years of the 2000s contributed to the globalisation process — and was also partially the result of globalisation. By contrast, the negative economic growth and recession that hit these (and other) countries in 2008 and 2009 has been blamed (in part) on globalisation, leading to renewed calls for an end to globalisation processes.

Box 20.3 Recession, globalisation and de-globalisation

In January each year, the world's leading economists, businessmen and women, and politicians meet at the Swiss mountain resort of Davos to discuss the economic problems facing the world. In January 2009 one of the problems was **de-globalisation**, or a reversal of the globalisation process. I have extracted the following passage from an article published immediately after the 2009 Davos meeting.

Globalisation under strain

At the annual pilgrimage to Davos last month, politicians were united in agreement: the biggest danger facing the world economy is protectionism. Many of the mountaintop sermons picked out the risk of financial mercantilism, a reflux of capital from foreign markets to home ones. Britain's prime minister preached against a 'retreat into domestic lending and domestic financial markets'. But back in the real world the barriers to the free flow of capital are rising fast.

In Britain, data from the Bank of England show that in the fourth quarter of 2008 local banks sharply cut lending to foreign customers. British borrowers are themselves suffering from the withdrawal of Icelandic, Irish and other foreign lenders, which provided a big chunk of their credit at the peak of the bubble. Things are worse in emerging markets. Central and eastern Europe is under the greatest strain, having binged on international borrowing in recent years. In places such as Russia and Ukraine, local banks that had relied on borrowing abroad to finance their expansion were the first to suffer when credit dried up. Banks with foreign parents are also feeling the pinch.

The imponderable is just how much this retraction in banks' foreign lending owes to political pressure to focus credit on domestic customers. Politicians may not be able to stop the drying-up of cross-border credit. Then again, there is little sign that they want to. Many are employing what one banker terms the 'moral suasion' of repeated calls to lend more at home. Last month George Provopoulos, the governor of Greece's central bank, warned Greek banks not to send rescue funds abroad. Banks that have not taken taxpayers' money can resist this more easily than others. State support is increasingly accompanied by explicit obligations to lend at home. The Obama administration has signalled that it will require

American banks that benefit from its forth-coming rescue package to lend more.

This is economic nationalism, but of an insidious type. The purpose is to steer banks towards supporting businesses and jobs at home, not abroad. That has the whiff of protectionism about it.

The Economist, 5 February 2009

Follow-up questions

1 Explain why the global financial crisis that began in 2007 should slow down or even reverse the globalisation process.

2 Assess the effect of the global recession that hit the world economy in 2008 and 2009 on different aspects of globalisation.

Summary

➤ International trade widens a country's production possibilities and also its consumption possibilities.

➤ International trade enables countries to benefit from specialisation and the division of labour.

➤ Absolute advantage means that a country is technically more efficient in producing a good than other countries, being absolutely best at the activity.

➤ Comparative advantage is measured in terms of opportunity cost.

➤ Specialisation and trade in accordance with the principle of comparative advantage can lead to a net output gain.

➤ The net output resulting from trade gain can translate into a net welfare gain. In contrast, protectionism may lead to a net welfare loss.

➤ Import controls have been justified by strategic trade theory, the protection of infant industries and by other arguments.

➤ The North–South pattern of world trade has largely given way to a North–North pattern.

➤ The older industrialised economies of western Europe and North America also import many of the manufactured goods they use from Asian NICs.

➤ Much of the UK's trade is with other European Union (EU) member states.

➤ Globalisation is the name given for the increasing integration of the world's economies.

➤ Trade liberalisation, international capital and labour mobility and the increased power of multinational corporations (MNCs) are important elements of globalisation.

➤ The World Trade Organization (WTO) promotes trade liberalisation, and some would say the interests of rich countries against the poor.

Questions

1 Explain how international trade widens choice.

2 What are the benefits of the division of labour?

3 Why is a 'double coincidence of wants' unnecessary when more than two countries trade together?

4 Distinguish between absolute advantage and comparative advantage.

5 Distinguish between comparative advantage and competitive advantage.

6 Outline two arguments used to support import controls.

7 How has the pattern of world trade changed?

8 Explain one reason for the changing pattern of world trade.

9 How important is the EU for UK trade?

10 What is meant by globalisation?

11 Outline the main features of globalisation.

12 How have multinational corporations promoted globalisation?

13 Why is capital generally more internationally mobile than labour?

14 Explain the role of the WTO in the world economy.

Chapter 21

The balance of payments

Many years ago, UK newspapers regularly featured headlines such as: 'Britain in the red — sterling crisis looms'. Then all went quiet for 30 or more years, not because the UK balance of payments current account deficit was necessarily small, but because fixed exchange rates had been replaced with floating exchange rates. Newspaper headlines were now more likely to be: 'Balance of payments problem? What problem?' By 2009, history had come full circle. Even though the pound's exchange rate still floated, the huge size of the UK's current account deficit was again viewed as an economic problem.

Learning outcomes

This chapter will:

> remind you of the difference between the current account and capital flows in the balance of payments

> examine the structure of and recent changes in the UK balance of payments

> discuss the meaning of balance of payments equilibrium and disequilibrium

> question whether a current account deficit poses a problem

> compare expenditure-reducing and expenditure-switching policies aimed at reducing a current account deficit

> explain the J-curve effect

> discuss whether a current account surplus poses problems

> recap on how *AD/AS* diagrams can be used to illustrate the effect of changes in the current account

What you should already know

At AS, the Unit 2 specification on the National Economy required candidates to understand the main items in the current account of the balance of payments, namely trade in goods, trade in services, investment income and transfers. An understanding of the meaning of current account deficits and surpluses was also required, together with the fact that achieving a satisfactory current account can be an important macroeconomic policy objective.

The meaning of the balance of payments

The **balance of payments** is the part of the national accounts that attempts to measure all the currency flows into and out of the country in a particular time period, for example a month, quarter or year. The balance of payments is only an estimate of currency flows. Activities such as smuggling, money laundering and late recording of data or sending inaccurate data to the government mean that there are always errors in the balance of payments.

Key term

The **balance of payments** measures all the currency flows into and out of an economy in a given time period.

The structure of the UK balance of payments

Since the balance of payments is an official record collected by a government, the presentation of the currency flows depends on how the government decides to group and classify all the different items of payment. Until quite recently, the UK government divided the balance of payments into two main categories:

➤ the current account
➤ the capital account

But to fit in with the method of classification used by the **International Monetary Fund** (IMF), the format of the UK's balance of payments has been changed. Unfortunately, the new method of presentation, which is shown in slightly simplified form in Table 21.1, is confusing. Capital flows, which used to form the *capital account*, are now listed in the *financial account* of the balance of payments. Misleadingly, the capital account now comprises various transfers of income that

Table 21.1 *Selected items from the UK balance of payments, 2008 (£m)*

The current account (mostly trade flows)	
Balance of trade in goods	−92,876
Balance of trade in services	+48,878
Net income flows	+33,129
Net current transfers	−13,624
Balance of payments on the current account	**−24,493**
The capital account	
(Transfers, which used to be in the current account)	**+3,505**
The financial account	
(Capital flows, which used to be in the capital account)	
Net direct investment	+361,995
Net portfolio investment	−230,058
Other capital flows *(mostly short-term 'hot money' flows)*	−234,622
Drawings on reserves	+36,283
Financial account balance	**−66,402**
The balance (errors and omissions)	**+87,390**

Source: National Statistics website (**statistics.gov.uk**), 27 March 2009

were previously part of the current account before the new method of classification was adopted.

For this reason, this chapter presents a general survey of the current account and capital flows and tries to avoid unnecessary detail. The examination boards, including AQA, no longer require knowledge of official methods of presentation of balance of payments accounts.

Recent changes in the UK current account

Figure 21.1 shows the changes that took place in the UK current account and in the main items in the current account between 1997 and 2007. 1997 was the last time that the UK current account more or less balanced, without a deficit or surplus. The graph clearly shows the massive deterioration that occurred in the UK's balance of trade in goods in the late 1990s and the early 2000s. Although the balance of trade in services showed a growing surplus, the services surplus was not sufficient to offset the trade in goods deficit. As a result, the overall current account deteriorated from its initial position of more or less balanced to the deficit at the end of 2007 of nearly £40 billion. However, as Table 21.1 shows, the current account improved in 2008.

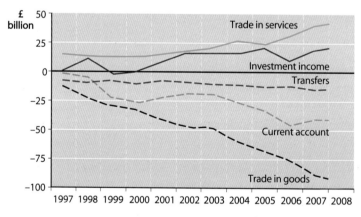

Figure 21.1
Changes in the UK current account and its main items, 1997–2007

Source: National Statistics website (**statistics.gov.uk**), 21 February 2009

More up-to-date statistics extending into 2009 will reflect the effect of the credit crunch and the decline in the overseas earnings of UK financial services industries. By the time you read this chapter, the UK's balance of trade in services (of which financial services were by far the main item) may have dramatically changed.

The current account of the balance of payments

For the most part, the balance of payments on the current account measures the *flow* of expenditure on goods and services, broadly indicating the country's income gained and lost from trade. The **current account** is usually regarded as the most important part of the balance of payments because it reflects the economy's international competitiveness and the extent to which the country may or may not be living within its means.

To measure the balance of payments or current account, we first add together the **balance of trade in goods** and the **balance of trade in services**. (The balance of trade in goods can also be called the **balance of visible trade**, while the balance of trade in services comprises **invisible trade** items.) If receipts from exports of goods and services are less than payments for imports of goods and services, there is generally a **current account deficit**. Conversely, a **current account surplus** occurs when receipts from trade exceed payments for trade. However, because there are other items in the current account besides trade flows, this is not always true. The other items are **net income flows** and net current **transfers**.

Net income flows

Net income flows are made up mostly of **investment income** flows generated from profit and interest payments flowing between countries. In the chapter's next section, I explain how UK-based multinational companies (MNCs) invest in capital assets located in other countries. The profit income generated when an investment is complete flows back to the parent company and its UK shareholders. The investment itself is an *outward* capital flow, but the income it generates is *current* income, figuring in the current account of the balance of payments.

Profits also flow out of the UK to the overseas owners of assets located in the UK — for example, to Japanese or US multinational companies owning subsidiary companies in the UK. In Table 21.1, the item **net income flows** shows the difference between these inward and outward profit flows resulting from capital investment undertaken in the past. The fact that the UK's net income flows were +£33,129 million in 2008 seems to indicate that UK companies own more profitable assets in the rest of the world than overseas-based MNCs own in the UK. However, not all income flows are profit payments by multinational companies. Interest payments on loans within the international banking system, which form part of the overseas earnings of the City of London, contribute significantly to net income flows.

Key terms

The **current account** is the part of the balance of payments measuring income currency flows, especially payments for exports and imports.

Transfers are payments flowing between countries in forms such as foreign aid, grants, and gifts.

Investment income is profit and interest income flowing into a country that is generated from assets the residents of the country own abroad.

examiner's voice
This book does not include tables or details of the balances of trade in goods and services for the UK. These are AS topics, which I explain in some detail in the *AQA AS Economics* textbook.

Capital flows

As the previous paragraph indicates, it is important to avoid confusing *capital* flows with *investment income*. As explained, *outward* capital flows generate *inward* investment income flows in subsequent years. The capital outflow enlarges the *stock* of capital assets located in other countries, owned by MNCs based in the country exporting the capital. **Net capital flows** are the difference between inward and outward capital movements. Positive net outward capital flows, over a period of years, mean that the country acquires capital assets located in other countries that are greater in value than the country's own assets bought by overseas companies.

As Table 21.1 shows, net investment income flows into the UK were over £33 billion in 2008. A positive net investment income *flow* (in the current account) suggests that, in previous years, UK residents and MNCs invested in a larger and more profitable *stock* of capital assets in the rest of the world than that acquired by overseas residents and MNCs in the UK. Following the UK's abolition of virtually all foreign exchange controls in 1979, the UK became a large net exporter of capital, presumably because UK MNCs believed that investment abroad would be more profitable than investment within the UK. During the 1980s, the positive net capital outflow meant that the UK became a large owner of overseas capital assets. By contrast, the USA became a 'debtor' nation in the 1980s: that is, assets owned in the USA by other countries grew to exceed those owned by the USA in the rest of the world. This position remains largely true today.

Long-term capital flows

In order to understand properly the importance of capital flows in the balance of payments, it is useful to distinguish between long-term and short-term capital flows. Long-term capital flows are dividable into direct investment and portfolio investment flows:

> **Direct overseas investment** involves acquisition of real productive assets, such as factories, oil refineries, offices and shopping malls, located in other countries. On the one hand, a UK-based MNC may decide to establish a new subsidiary company — for example, in the USA. On the other hand, direct investment can also involve acquisition, through merger or takeover, of an overseas-based company. In 2007 the UK bank RBS invested £10bn in acquiring the Dutch bank ABN Amro — a move that is now seen as catastrophic, both for RBS and for the UK banking industry. This was an example of outward direct investment. Conversely, the decisions in the 1980s and 1990s by the Japanese vehicle manufacturers Nissan, Toyota and Honda to invest in automobile factories in the UK led to inward direct investment, or **foreign direct investment** (FDI).

> **Portfolio overseas investment** involves the purchase of financial assets (that is, pieces of paper laying claim to the ownership of real assets) rather than physical or directly productive assets. Typically,

Key terms

Direct overseas investment occurs when firms invest in or buy real productive assets located in foreign countries.

Portfolio overseas investment occurs when financial services firms buy financial assets such as shares and government bonds issued in foreign countries.

portfolio investment occurs when fund managers employed by financial institutions such as insurance companies and pension funds purchase shares issued by overseas companies, or securities issued by foreign governments. The globalisation of world security markets or capital markets and the abolition of exchange controls between virtually all developed countries have made it easy for UK residents to purchase shares or bonds that are listed on overseas capital

Honda is one of many Japanese car companies with factories in the UK

markets. This has led to a massive increase in portfolio investment. UK residents can now buy shares and corporate bonds that were previously only available on the capital market of the company's country of origin. Securities issued by foreign governments, such as US Treasury bonds, can also be bought.

The credit crunch, which began in America in 2007, and the so-called 'financial meltdown' that followed, had a significant adverse effect on portfolio investment both within and between countries. Many financial assets, particularly those bought and sold by banks, became known as 'toxic assets'. This term arose from the fact that a potential purchaser of a package of financial assets offered for sale by a bank could not know in advance whether assets in the package were of high risk and potentially little value or a sound investment (even the bank trying to make the sale might not know). In such conditions of imperfect information, trading in many types of financial asset collapsed.

Short-term capital flows

Long-term capital flows can partly be explained by comparative and competitive advantage. The flows are a response to people's decisions to invest in economic activities and industries located in countries that have a competitive advantage. Comparative advantage (which, as Chapter 20 explains, must not be confused with competitive advantage) may also rest in the same country. But since changes in competitive and/or comparative advantage usually take place quite slowly, long-term capital flows tend to be relatively stable and predictable.

This is not true of short-term capital flows. Short-term capital movements, which are also called 'hot money' flows, are largely speculative. The flows occur because the owners of funds, which include companies and banks as well as wealthy private individuals, believe that a quick speculative profit can be made by moving funds between currencies. Speculating that a currency's exchange rate is about to rise, owners of funds move money into that currency and out of other currencies whose exchange rates are expected to fall. 'Hot money' movements are also triggered by differences in interest rates. Funds flow into currencies with high interest rates and out of currencies with lower interest rates. International crises,

such as the outbreak of a war in the Middle East, also cause funds to move into the currency of a safe-haven country, regarded as politically stable.

If the pool of hot money shifting between currencies was small, few problems would result. However, short-term capital flows have grown significantly over the last 50 or so years. A large-scale movement of funds from one currency to another creates an excess supply in the former currency and an excess demand for the second currency. To eliminate excess supply and demand, the exchange rates of the two currencies respectively fall and rise. As a result, the movement of funds between currencies produces the changes in exchange rates that speculators were expecting. More importantly, a large-scale hot money flow of funds between currencies destabilises exchange rates, the current accounts of balance of payments and, indeed, domestic economies. Such destabilisation occurred late in 2008 and early in 2009 when owners of hot money shifted their funds out of the pound on a massive scale.

Speculative capital flows between currencies such as the dollar, the pound and the euro, which occupy a central place in the finance of international trade, can destabilise the international monetary system. The most recent examples of destabilisation followed the credit crunch and the financial meltdown I referred to earlier. Banks and other financial institutions, and also governments, within a range of countries (which included the UK) lost their international credit ratings. To fight the recession hitting their economies, governments built up massive budget deficits, which governments tried to finance by borrowing overseas.

However, once a government loses a triple A credit rating, international investors lend only on highly unfavourable terms. The government and its central bank may then resort to quantitative easing, which is virtually the same as printing more money.

Key terms

Speculative capital flows occur when companies, banks and rich individuals buy a currency in order to earn higher interest rates on bank deposits held in that currency, or when they speculate that a rise in the currency's exchange rate will enable them to make a capital gain in the future.

Balance of payments equilibrium occurs when the current account more or less balances over a period of years.

This precipitates fear of a future uncontrollable inflation, which in turn leads to mass selling of the country's currency by owners of hot money. In turn, this leads to a collapse of the country's exchange rate, which creates a further reason for international speculators to decide against financial assets denominated in the country's currency.

Balance of payments equilibrium

It is important to avoid confusing balance of payments *equilibrium* with the last item in Table 21.1, which ensures that the balance of payments *balances*. **Balance of payments equilibrium** (or external equilibrium) occurs when trade and capital flows into and out of the country are more or less equal over a number of years. Sometimes, balance of payments equilibrium is more narrowly defined, referring only to the current account. In this narrow sense, the balance of payments is in equilibrium when the current account more or less balances over a period of years. Defined in this way, balance of payments equilibrium is perfectly compatible with the occurrence of a short-term current account deficit or surplus. However, fundamental disequilibrium exists when there is a persistent tendency for payments for imports to be greater or less than payments for exports over a period of years.

Extension material

'Balance' in the balance of payments

The balance of payments is a balance sheet and, like all balance sheets, must balance in the sense that all items must sum to zero. In the UK balance of payments, this means that all items in the current account, the capital account and the financial account must sum to zero. In practice, this never happens because items are inaccurately measured and recorded — hence, the need for a **balancing item** to make the balance of payments sum to zero. The balancing item is a *mistakes* item equalling the number required to make the balance of payments sum to zero.

Government statisticians who construct the UK balance of payments use a *continuous revision* method of measurement. When the balance of payments statistics for a particular year are first published, soon after the end of the year in question, the balancing item may be quite large. In this situation, too much trust should not be placed in the figures. In subsequent months and years, the balancing item gradually decreases. In the light of new and previously unavailable information, the statisticians whittle away the balancing item, allocating elements of the item to one or more of the flows in real trade, investment income or capital.

Does a current account deficit pose a problem?

While a *short-run* deficit or surplus on the current account does not pose a problem, a persistent or *long-run* imbalance indicates a fundamental disequilibrium. However, the nature of any resulting problem depends upon the size and cause of the deficit or surplus, and also upon the nature of the exchange rate regime. The larger the deficit, the greater the problem is likely to be. The problem is also likely to be serious if the deficit is caused by the uncompetitiveness of the country's industries. In the short run, a deficit allows a country's residents to enjoy living standards boosted by imports, higher than would be possible from consumption of the country's output alone. But in the long run, the decline of the country's industries in the face of international competition may lower living standards.

A balance of payments deficit poses more problems when the exchange rate is fixed than when it floats freely. In both cases, the immediate cause of a deficit usually lies in the fact that exports are too expensive in overseas markets, while imports are too cheap at

examiner's voice
Exam candidates often assert that balance of payments deficits are bad and that surpluses are good. This does not necessarily follow.

home. Obviously, there can be more deep-seated causes of over-priced exports and under-priced imports, relating, for example, to domestic wage costs being higher than in other countries. However, in a floating exchange rate regime, the exchange rate simply responds to market forces and falls, thereby restoring export competitiveness and curing or reducing balance of payments disequilibrium. I explain this in the next and final chapter of this book.

By contrast, in a fixed exchange rate system, currencies may remain more or less permanently overvalued or undervalued. An overvalued fixed exchange rate leads to a large current account deficit, which then puts downward pressure on the exchange rate. However, in a fixed exchange rate system, the country's central bank takes action to prevent the exchange rate falling. In a process known as **exchange equalisation**, the central bank uses reserves of gold and hard currencies to purchase its own currency on the foreign exchange market.

Official reserves are limited, so a country cannot go on propping up a fixed exchange rate and financing a deficit for ever. In a fixed exchange rate system, eventually a country must take action to try to reduce or eliminate a persistent payments deficit.

Box 21.1 Does a balance of payments deficit matter?

There are a number of well-respected economists who argue that large balance of payments deficits are not something for policy-makers to be concerned about. If there is a net inflow of capital, there must of necessity be a current account deficit. Because that is what a current account deficit actually means — a net inflow of capital. If the current account were in balance, there would be no net capital inflow. If the current account was in surplus, it would mean that there would be a net capital outflow. Those who say, and many do, that New Zealand needs an inflow of capital to finance its future development are in effect saying that New Zealand must continue to have a current account deficit. So in that sense, part of the reason for our current account deficit is simply a reflection of the enthusiasm which foreign institutions, companies, and indeed individuals have had for investing in New Zealand in recent years.

As foreign capital flows into New Zealand, it is matched by a current account deficit. A current account deficit is simply an indication that investment being undertaken in New Zealand exceeds the savings of New Zealanders

and that this excess of investment over savings simply reflects the decisions of countless individual New Zealanders in the private sector to borrow to finance investment. In the longer-term, this process will be self-correcting as either New Zealanders decide not to take on additional debt or foreigners decide not to extend additional credit. The balance of payments is expected to adjust relatively smoothly, without the involvement of governments or central banks.

Even economists who do not take quite such a sanguine view of current account deficits concede that deficits are of much less concern today, with a floating exchange rate and the virtually complete abolition of the distortions which previously affected the allocation of investment, than was the case, say, prior to 1984. At that time, deficits were often the result of substantial fiscal deficits and had to be covered by government borrowing overseas in foreign currency.

Donald Brash, Governor of New Zealand's central bank, accessed on 30 January 1998 at **rbnz.govt.nz/speeches/0056822.html**

Follow-up question
At the time of the Governor's speech, the New Zealand government was running a budget surplus. The UK government now has a large budget deficit. Why may a large current account deficit be regarded as bad when the government's finances are in a bad state?

Policies to cure or reduce a balance of payments deficit

A government (or its central bank) can use three different policies to try to cure a persistent deficit caused by an overvalued exchange rate. These are the '3 Ds' of **deflation**, **direct controls**, and **devaluation** or currency **depreciation**, which are shown in Figure 21.2.

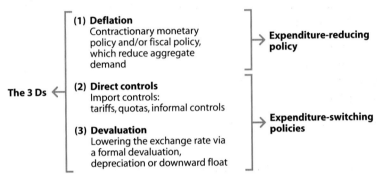

Figure 21.2 *The '3 Ds' of deflation, direct controls and devaluation*

Deflation, or a reduction in the level of aggregate demand in the economy, reduces a current account deficit because it is mainly **expenditure reducing**. By contrast, import controls and devaluation are primarily **expenditure switching**.

Deflationary policies
Deflationary policy involves using contractionary monetary and/or fiscal policy to reduce the demand for imports. For example, if the marginal propensity to import in the economy is 0.4, reducing aggregate demand by £10 billion should cause spending on imports to fall by £4 billion. This is an expenditure-reducing policy.

Key term

Deflationary policy involves contractionary monetary or fiscal policy that shifts the *AD* curve to the left.

Although deflation is primarily an expenditure-reducing policy, it also has an expenditure-switching element. By reducing the rate of domestic price inflation relative to inflation rates in other countries, deflation increases the price competitiveness of exports and reduces that of imports.

However, in modern economies this is usually quite a small effect and the main effect of deflationary policies is to reduce aggregate demand and to depress economic activity in the domestic economy. Output and employment tend to fall rather than the price level. Unfortunately, as well as reducing the demand for imports, deflation affects the domestic economy. Falling demand for domestic output may force firms to seek export orders, so as to use spare production capacity. However, because exports are generally less profitable than domestic sales, a sound and expanding home market may be necessary for a successful export drive.

In summary, when deflating aggregate demand to achieve the external objectives of supporting the exchange rate and reducing a current account deficit, a government sacrifices the domestic economic objectives of full employment and economic growth. For this reason, governments may choose to use expenditure-switching policies of import controls and devaluation, in preference to expenditure-reducing deflation.

Direct controls

The direct controls used to reduce a payments deficit are import controls. **Embargoes** and **quotas** directly prevent or reduce expenditure on imports, while **import duties** or **tariffs** discourage expenditure by raising the price of imports. Import controls do not, however, cure the underlying cause of disequilibrium, namely the uncompetitiveness of a country's goods and services. Moreover, because a country essentially gains a 'beggar my neighbour' advantage at the expense of other countries, import controls tend to provoke retaliation.

Arguably, protectionism reduces specialisation and causes world trade, world output and economic welfare all to fall. Because of this, international organisations such as the EU and the World Trade Organization (WTO) have reduced the freedom of individual countries to impose import controls unilaterally to improve their current accounts. However, the EU uses its common external tariff to provide protection for all its members.

Devaluation

The word **devaluation** is used in a number of different ways. In a strictly narrow sense, a country devalues by reducing the value of a fixed exchange rate or an adjustable peg exchange rate. (Fixed exchange rates and adjustable peg exchange rates are explained in Chapter 22.) However, the term is also used in a looser way to describe a downward float or **depreciation** of a floating exchange rate. The word 'depreciation' can also confuse. Devaluation or a downward float causes an *external* depreciation of the currency; more units of the currency are needed to buy a unit of *another* currency. Don't confuse this with an

Key term

Devaluation is a fall in a currency's exchange rate brought about either formally by a government and its central bank or informally through a downward float or depreciation of the exchange rate.

internal depreciation of the currency, occurring when there is inflation *within* the economy.

Unavailability of import controls means that a country must generally choose between *deflation* and *devaluation* if it wishes to reduce a current account deficit. As with import controls, devaluation has a mainly expenditure-switching effect. By increasing the price of imports relative to the price of exports, a successful devaluation switches domestic demand away from imports and towards home-produced goods. Similarly, overseas demand for the country's exports increases in response to the fall in export prices.

examiner's voice

The Unit 4 exam is synoptic so the examination may require application of AS microeconomic concepts such as elasticity.

Price elasticity of demand and devaluation

The effectiveness of a devaluation in reducing a payment deficit depends to a significant extent upon the price elasticities of demand for exports and imports.

As Figure 21.3 shows, when the demands for exports and imports are both highly price elastic, a devaluation can reduce a current account deficit. Following a devaluation, the domestic price of imports rises from P_1 to P_2, while the overseas price of exports falls from P_3 to P_4. As a result, domestic residents spend less on imported goods following an increase in their relative prices. At the same time, residents of overseas countries spend more on the country's exports, whose relative prices have fallen.

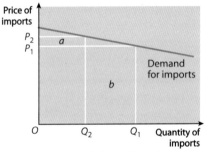 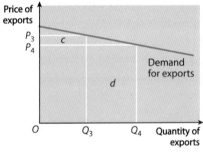

Figure 21.3 *The effect of a devaluation (or downward float) of an exchange rate on the current account of the balance of payments*

On the import side, area *b* in Figure 21.3 shows reduced expenditure on goods produced in other countries. Higher import prices mean that consumers switch to the now cheaper domestically produced substitutes. However, expenditure on the goods still being imported rises by area *a*. When demand for imports is price elastic — as in Figure 21.3 — total domestic expenditure on imports falls by area $(b - a)$.

examiner's voice

Deflationary policies and devaluation should best be regarded as complementary policies rather than as substitutes.

In a similar way, expenditure on the country's exports increases by area $(d - c)$, providing overseas demand for the country's exports is price elastic. Area *d* shows increased expenditure on exports because prices of exports fall relative to prices of

overseas produced substitutes. However, the foreign exchange earned by the goods exported before the devaluation falls by area *c*.

Overall, the current account improves by $(b - a) + (d - c)$, assuming the demand for imports and the demand for exports are both price elastic.

Extension material

The Marshall–Lerner condition

It is more difficult to see what may happen to the current account when, for example, the demand for exports is price inelastic but the demand for imports is price elastic. Fortunately, the **Marshall–Lerner condition** provides a simple rule to assess whether a change in the exchange rate can improve the current account. The condition states that when the *sum* of the export and import price elasticities is greater than unity (ignoring the minus sign), a fall in the exchange rate can reduce a deficit and a rise in the exchange rate can reduce a surplus. When, however, the export and import price elasticities of demand are both highly inelastic, summing to less than unity, a fall in the exchange rate can have the perverse effect of worsening a deficit (while a revaluation might increase a surplus).

The Marshall–Lerner condition is a *necessary* condition, but not a *sufficient* condition, for a fall in the exchange rate to reduce a payments deficit. For a devaluation or downward float to be successful, firms in the domestic economy must have spare capacity with which they can meet the surge in demand brought about by the fall in the exchange rate. This means that expenditure-reducing deflation and expenditure-switching devaluation should best be regarded as complementary policies rather than as substitute policies for reducing a current account deficit. Deflation *alone* may be unnecessarily costly in terms of lost domestic employment and output, yet may be necessary to provide the spare capacity and conditions in which a falling exchange rate can successfully cure a payments deficit.

The J-curve

Even if domestic demand for imports and overseas demand for exports are both price elastic and spare capacity exists in the economy, firms within the country may still be unable immediately to increase supply following a fall in the exchange rate. In the short run, the Marshall–Lerner condition (explained in the *Extension material*) may not hold because elasticities of demand are lower in the short run than in the long run. In these circumstances, the balance of payments may worsen before it improves. This is known as the **J-curve** effect, which is illustrated in Figure 21.4.

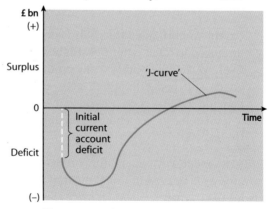

Figure 21.4 *The J-curve effect*

The initial worsening of the balance of payments that follows the fall in the exchange rate may reduce confidence in the idea that changing the exchange rate is the most appropriate method for reducing a payments imbalance. Falling confidence may, in turn, cause capital outflows that destabilise both the balance of payments and the exchange rate. The J-curve effect thus reduces the attractiveness of exchange rate adjustment as an instrument to correct payments disequilibrium. Even when the benefits of a falling exchange rate are realised, they may be short-lived. The increased price competitiveness produced by the devaluation is likely to be eroded as increased import prices raise the country's inflation rate.

 Key terms

The **J-curve** is a curve, shaped like the letter 'J', that maps the possible time path of the state of the current account following a devaluation.

Nevertheless, if conditions are right, a devaluation can reduce a current account deficit. Despite occurring on so-called 'Black Wednesday', the pound's devaluation in September 1992 was extremely successful, at least for a number of years. There were two main reasons for this. First, expenditure reduction in the severe recession of the early 1990s created the spare capacity that enabled successful expenditure switching following the pound's devaluation. Second, the factories built in the UK by Japanese companies such as Honda and Toyota had just come on stream, producing goods of a quality that people wanted, in the UK and overseas.

Box 21.2 UK trade deficit drops to £7.4bn in December 2008

In the autumn of 2008 and the early months of 2009, the UK government seemed to adopt a policy of 'benign neglect' with regard to the pound's exchange rate, i.e. allowing and almost encouraging the exchange rate to fall. The aim was to improve the price competitiveness of UK exports. The extract below gives some indication as to whether the policy was successful.

A sharp fall in imports as the economy slowed dragged Britain's trade deficit to its lowest in 18 months at the end of 2008, official figures showed today. The Office for National Statistics said the UK's visible trade gap — the difference between goods sold overseas and those coming into the country — came down from a record £8.1bn in November to £7.4bn in December. With the fall in the value of the pound making goods from the rest of the world dearer, the ONS said Britain's import bill was cut by 2.5% in December. Exports, despite the boost from the lower exchange rate, were only slightly higher.

Despite the improvement in December, the total deficit in goods for 2008 as a whole increased to a record £93.2bn from £89.3bn in 2007. City analysts said there were some signs that the lower pound was boosting growth. David Page, economist at Investec, said: 'It's certainly encouraging. It's suggesting that there is an underlying improvement coming through in the structural trade position for the UK and we're very hopeful that as global activity picks up we'll see a significant stimulus to the UK.'

The *Guardian*, 10 February 2009

Follow-up questions

1 To what extent, if any, does the information in the extract illustrate the J-curve effect?

2 Why might the global recession being experienced in December 2008 have adversely affected the recovery in UK exports that might be expected following the fall in the pound's exchange rate?

Does a current account surplus pose a problem?

While people readily agree that a persistent current account deficit can pose serious problems, fewer people realise that a balance of payments surplus on the current account can also lead to problems. Indeed, because a surplus is often seen as a sign of national economic virility and success, it is frequently argued that the bigger the surplus, the better the country's economic performance.

This is true to the extent to which the surplus measures the competitiveness of the country's exporting industries. There are, nevertheless, two reasons why a *large* payments surplus is undesirable, although a small surplus may be a justifiable policy objective.

One country's surplus is another country's deficit

Because the balance of payments must balance for the world as a whole, it is not possible for all countries to run surpluses simultaneously. Unless countries with persistently large surpluses agree to take action to reduce their surpluses, deficit countries cannot reduce their deficits. This means that deficit countries may be forced to impose import controls from which all countries, including surplus countries, eventually suffer. In an extreme scenario, a world recession may be triggered by a resulting collapse of world trade.

> *e*xaminer's voice
> Possibly because the UK current account has been in deficit for many years, exam questions on current account surpluses have been rare. Nevertheless, the topic can always appear in future exams.

At various times since the 1970s, the current account surpluses of the oil-producing countries have led to this problem, as have the Japanese and latterly the Chinese payments surpluses, which have largely matched the US trade deficit. On several occasions, the US government has faced pressure from US manufacturing and labour interests to introduce import controls and other forms of protectionism. When introduced, US protectionism undoubtedly harms world trade.

Almost without exception, non-oil-exporting developing countries also suffer chronic deficits, although these are different from the US trade deficit. The imbalance of trade between more developed and less developed countries cannot be reduced without the industrialised countries of the North taking action to reduce surpluses that have been gained at the expense of the developing economies of the South.

The current account surpluses of oil-producing countries can lead to problems

A balance of payments surplus is inflationary

It is often forgotten that particularly when the exchange rate is fixed a balance of payments surplus can be an important cause of domestic inflation. This is because a balance of payments surplus is an injection of aggregate demand into the circular flow of income, which, via a multiplier effect, increases the equilibrium level of nominal or money national income. If there are substantial unemployed resources in the economy, this has the beneficial effect of reflating real output and jobs. However, if the economy is initially close to full capacity, demand-pull inflation results. Note also that a balance of payments deficit has the opposite effect. The deficit is a leakage or withdrawal of demand from the economy, which deflates the equilibrium level of income.

Policies to cure or reduce a balance of payments surplus

The policies available to a government for reducing a balance of payments surplus are the opposite of the '3 Ds' of deflation, direct controls and devaluation appropriate for correcting a payments deficit. The policies are the '3 Rs' of **reflation**, **removal of import controls** and **revaluation**.

➤ Reflating demand, via expansionary monetary policy or fiscal policy, increases a country's demand for imports.

➤ Trade can also be liberalised by removing import controls.

➤ There have been calls on countries with large payments surpluses, such as Japan and China, to revalue in order to reduce global payments imbalances. But because there is much less pressure on a surplus country to revalue than on a deficit country to devalue, such calls have not usually been successful. It is also worth noting that, for a revaluation to reduce a current account surplus, the Marshall–Lerner condition must be met. In addition, a reverse J-curve, illustrated in Figure 21.5, may operate, causing the payments surplus to get bigger immediately after the revaluation, before it eventually starts to get smaller.

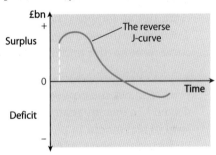

Figure 21.5 The reverse J-curve

Applying *AD/AS* analysis to the current account of the balance of payments

I shall now round off the chapter by reminding you about how to use *AD/AS* analysis to explain how a change in the current account of the balance of payments affects the level of real output and the price level in the economy.

As I explained earlier in the chapter, the current account includes non-trade items (income and transfers) as well as exports and imports. However, for the sake of simplicity, I shall pretend that exports and imports are the only items in the current account. Given this assumption, there is a current account surplus when net

exports are positive, i.e. $X > M$, and a deficit in the current account when net exports are negative, i.e. $X < M$.

As I also mentioned earlier, exports are an injection of spending into the circular flow of income, whereas imports are a leakage or with-drawal of spending from the flow.

Suppose that initially $X = M$, which means there is neither a surplus nor a deficit in the current account. Note also that in this situation, given my assumption that there are no non-trade flows in the current account, foreign trade injections into the circular flow of income exactly equal foreign trade withdrawals from the flow. To put it another way, when $X = M$, the current account has a *neutral* effect on the state of aggregate demand and on the circular flow of income.

@xaminer's voice

This final section of the chapter is almost identical to the similar section in the chapter in my AS book on the balance of payments. This results from the fact that in almost all instances, you don't need to learn any more about AD/AS at A2 over and above what you first learnt at AS.

However, suppose that at the next stage, overseas demand for British exports increases, but UK demand for imports remains unchanged. This means there is a net injection of spending into the circular flow of income. The current account moves into surplus, with $X > M$.

In the AD/AS diagram drawn in Figure 21.6, the increase in exports shifts the AD curve to the right. What happens next in the economy depends on the shape and slope of the $SRAS$ curve around the initial point of macroeco-nomic equilibrium (point X in Figure 21.6).

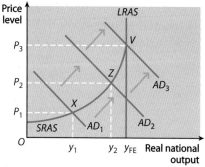

Figure 21.6 *How an increase in exports can affect the national economy*

Point X shows the economy in deep recession, suffering from deficient aggregate demand. In this situation, *any* event that increases aggregate demand increases the level of real output in the economy and causes demand-deficient unemployment to fall. An increase in exports is just such an event. In the diagram, increased exports shift the AD curve rightward from AD_1 to AD_2. This causes real output to rise from y_1 to y_2, though at the cost of inflation, since the price level rises from P_1 to P_2.

Following the shift to the right of the aggregate demand curve to AD_2, macroeconomic equilibrium is now shown at point Z. But as the $SRAS$ curve becomes steeper, moving up the curve, the diagram tells us that the main effect of a further shift of the AD curve from AD_2 to AD_3 falls on the price level rather than on output and jobs. Output increases, from y_2 to y_{FE}, but the price level also increases to P_3. As full employment approaches, export demand becomes *inflationary* rather than *reflationary*.

@xaminer's voice

You must be able to use the AD/AS model and the circular flow of income to analyse how changes in exports and/or imports affect macroeconomic performance, i.e. growth, employment, inflation and international competitiveness.

Nevertheless, in this situation the growth in export demand eliminates the demand deficiency previously existent in the economy. The economy ends up on its long-run aggregate supply (*LRAS*) curve, with macroeconomic equilibrium at point *V*.

Once point *V* has been reached, what may happen next in the economy depends on assumptions made about the nature of short-run and long-run aggregate supply. According to Figure 21.6, when the economy produces on the vertical *LRAS* curve any further increase in the demand for exports leads only to the price level rising above P_3, without any increase in real output. However, there is another possibility. Foreign demand for a country's exports often creates favourable supply-side conditions in which the *LRAS* curve shifts to the right. This means the economy can produce and supply the goods needed to meet the increase in export demand without generating inflation. This is an example of **export-led growth**. The German and Japanese economies certainly enjoyed export-led growth from the 1960s to the 1980s and China has recently enjoyed similar benefits. However, before the onset of global recession in 2009, the growth of demand for Chinese exports also caused inflation in the Chinese economy.

A fall in export demand and/or an increase in domestic demand for imports triggers an opposite effect to the one just described. There is a net leakage of demand from the circular flow of income, the *AD* curve shifts to the left, and both real output and the price level fall (or, more realistically in the latter case, the rate of inflation slows down). Overall, the effect is *deflationary*.

examiner's voice

You would illustrate the desired effect of supply-side policies aimed at increasing export competitiveness by shifting the vertical *LRAS* curve to the right. This could lead to a fall in the relative prices of exports. Quality and productivity improvements brought about by the supply-side policies could be depicted by the fall in the average price level.

Summary

➤ The balance of payments is the part of the national accounts that measures all the currency flows into and out of the country in a particular time period.

➤ The two main parts of the balance of payments are the current account and capital flows.

➤ The two main parts of the current account are the flows of spending on exports and imports.

➤ Net income from abroad, which is mostly net investment income, and current transfers are also items in the current account.

➤ Net investment income results from capital flows. For example, an outward capital flow generates an inward flow of investment income in future years.

➤ Capital flows divide into direct investment, portfolio investment, and speculative or 'hot money' flows.

➤ 'Hot money' flows can destabilise the exchange rate, the balance of payments, and indeed the whole economy.

➤ Balance of payments equilibrium occurs when the current account more or less balances over a number of years. As a simplification, when $X = M$. Disequilibrium is when there is a large and persistent current account deficit or surplus.

➤ A large deficit is not necessarily a problem, particularly if the exchange rate is floating, with capital flows financing the deficit.

➤ The expenditure-reducing policy of deflation and/or the expenditure-switching policies of import controls and devaluation can be used to reduce a current account deficit. Sometimes deflation and devaluation should be used in tandem.

➤ Likewise reflation, removal of import controls and revaluation can be used to reduce a surplus.

➤ Contrary to popular opinion, a large and persistent surplus may be undesirable.

➤ Current account deficits are themselves deflationary and surpluses may be inflationary.

➤ An increase in a current account deficit leads to a shift to the left of the *AD* curve in an *AD/AS* diagram. A decrease in a deficit or an increase in a surplus causes the *AD* curve to shift to the right.

Questions

1 How has the UK balance of payments changed in recent years?

2 What is a long-term capital flow?

3 Why do short-term capital flows take place?

4 Explain the meaning of balance of payments equilibrium.

5 Must a large current account deficit necessarily pose problems?

6 Outline the policies that may be used to reduce a payments deficit.

7 Distinguish between an expenditure-reducing and an expenditure-switching policy.

8 Explain the J-curve.

9 How may a balance of payments surplus be reduced?

10 With the help of an *AD/AS* diagram, explain why successful supply-side policies may be needed to bring about a long-term and sustainable improvement in the balance of payments.

Chapter 22

Exchange rates, the pound, the dollar and the euro

Although domestic currencies are used to pay for internal trade within countries, imports are usually paid for in the currency of the country exporting the goods or services. An exchange rate measures how much of another currency a particular currency can buy; it is the external price of the currency quoted in terms of the other currency. Exchange rates can also be measured against gold, or against a weighted average of a sample or 'basket' of currencies. Currencies are bought and sold in the foreign exchange market, which is now an international 24/7 electronic market. On a global scale, the market never closes, and ICT-based buying and selling takes place throughout the day and night.

The chapter begins by describing different ways to measure a country's exchange rate, outlines the main types of exchange rate system, and explains and analyses how balance of payments disequilibrium is dealt with in floating and fixed exchange rate systems. Towards the end of the chapter, I shall explain the special features of and the relationships between a number of key world currencies. These are the UK pound, the US dollar and the euro.

Learning outcomes

This chapter will:
- ⮞ explain the meaning of an exchange rate and how an exchange rate is measured
- ⮞ describe the different types of exchange rate system or regime
- ⮞ analyse exchange rate and balance of payments equilibrium and disequilibrium in a freely-floating exchange rate system
- ⮞ assess the advantages and disadvantages of freely-floating exchange rates
- ⮞ examine how fixed and managed exchange rates operate
- ⮞ survey the roles of the pound, the US dollar and the euro in world payments systems, historically and at the present day

At AS, you learnt about the link between monetary policy and the exchange rate, however, you did not learn fully how exchange rates are determined. You did learn how changes in exchange rates affect export and import prices, the balance of payments on current account and indeed the level of domestic economic activity in the national economy.

The meaning and measurement of an exchange rate

These days the **exchange rate** of a currency is simply the external price of the currency in terms of another currency, such as the US dollar. The convention of quoting exchange rates in terms of the US dollar is of fairly recent origin. Before 1914 most exchange rates were expressed in terms of gold and only after 1945 did the dollar become the near universally accepted standard by which the external values of other currencies were measured.

Key *term*

The **exchange rate** is the external price of a currency, usually measured against another currency.

In recent years, in response to the changing pattern of UK trade, the pound's exchange rate is as often quoted against the euro as it is against the dollar. The **sterling index** is also used to measure the pound's exchange rate. The sterling index, which is sometimes called the **effective exchange rate index**, does not measure the pound's external value against a particular currency. Rather it is a trade-weighted average of the pound's exchange rate against a number of leading trading currencies, calculated to reflect the importance of each currency in international trade.

At the close of market trading on 14 April 2009, the sterling index was 78.03 compared to its 1990 index of 100. This means that over the years since 1990, the sterling exchange rate had depreciated or fallen in value by 21.97% when measured against the exchange rates of the UK's most important trading partners. Much of the collapse of the pound's exchange rate occurred in 2007 and after.

Figure 22.1 shows what happened to the pound's exchange rate against the US dollar during the course of 2007 and 2008, together with the forecast exchange

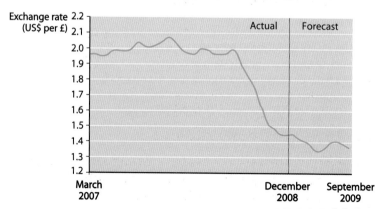

Figure 22.1
The UK pound's exchange rate measured against the US dollar, actual and forecast, March 2007– September 2009

rate (which may be inaccurate) between January and September 2009. The graph clearly shows the 30% or so fall in the value of the pound, measured against the dollar in the late summer and autumn of 2008.

The real exchange rate

The different exchange rates mentioned so far are all *nominal* exchange rates. These must not be confused with the *real* exchange rate, which measures the rate at which home-produced goods exchange for imports, rather than the rates at which currencies themselves are traded. The real exchange rate, which is a measure of competitiveness, is calculated by the following formula:

examiner's voice

It is useful but not vital to understand the difference between the nominal and the real exchange rate.

$$\text{pound's real exchange rate} = \text{sterling index} \times \frac{\text{domestic price level}}{\text{weighted foreign price level}}$$

The different types of exchange rate system

Figure 22.2 shows the main types of exchange rate system. The two extreme types are **freely-floating exchange rates** (also known as **cleanly floating exchange rates**) and rigidly **fixed exchange rates**. A fixed exchange rate is the most extreme form of a **managed exchange rate**.

examiner's voice

Exam questions are set more often on floating exchange rates than on other types of exchange rate. However, questions *may* be set on fixed or managed exchange rates..

Key term

A **freely-floating exchange rate** is determined solely by demand and supply, i.e. by market forces.

The managed exchange rates that lie between the extremes of freely-floating and rigidly fixed exchange rates take two main forms: **adjustable peg** and **managed floating** (or **dirty floating**) exchange rates. Adjustable peg exchange rates resemble fixed exchange rates in many respects, but the rate at which the exchange rate is fixed may be changed from time to time. A formal devaluation reduces the fixed exchange rate, while revaluation increases the fixed rate.

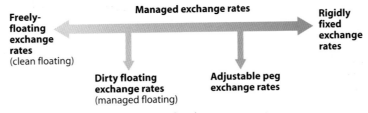

Figure 22.2 *The different types of exchange rate system*

By contrast, as its name indicates, a **managed floating exchange rate** is closer to a freely-floating exchange rate than to a fixed exchange rate. Market forces or supply and demand 'officially' determine the exchange rate, but the country's

central bank intervenes 'unofficially' behind the scenes, buying or selling reserves and raising or lowering interest rates to move the exchange rate upward or downward.

Freely-floating exchange rates

In a regime of freely-floating ('cleanly' floating) exchange rates, the external value of a country's currency is determined on foreign exchange markets by the forces of demand and supply alone. Later in this chapter, I shall explain that in recent years capital flows and speculation have been extremely significant in influencing the supply of and demand for a currency, and hence its exchange rate. However, I shall first simplify by assuming that a currency is demanded on foreign exchanges solely for the payment of trade and that trade flows alone determine exchange rates. I shall assume, too, that any holdings of foreign currencies surplus to the immediate requirement of paying for trade are immediately sold on the foreign exchange market.

Explaining the slope of the demand and supply curves for pounds

When the exchange rate of the pound falls, UK exports become more competitive in overseas markets. The volume of UK exports increases, leading to greater overseas demand for pounds to finance the purchase of these exports. This explains the downward-sloping demand curve for pounds, which is illustrated in Figure 22.3.

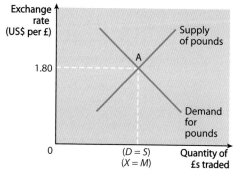

Figure 22.3 *Exchange rate equilibrium in a freely-floating exchange rate system*

But just as UK exports generate a demand for pounds on foreign exchange markets, so imports into the UK generate a supply of pounds. The explanation lies in the fact that UK trading companies generally pay for imports in foreign currencies. Importers must sell sterling on the foreign exchange market in order to purchase the foreign currencies needed to pay for the goods they are buying. As the pound's exchange rate rises, fewer pounds are needed to buy a given quantity of foreign currency. This means that the sterling price of imports falls. UK consumers are likely to respond to

*e*xaminer's voice

It is useful but not essential to understand why the demand curve for a currency slopes downward and why the supply curve slopes upward. By contrast, it is essential to understand exchange rate equilibrium and disequilibrium and to be able to link both concepts to the balance of payments.

the falling price of imports by increasing total spending on imports (which happens as long as the demand for imports is price elastic). A greater total quantity of sterling must be supplied on foreign exchange markets to pay for the imports — even though the sterling price of each unit of imports has fallen. The result is the upward-sloping supply curve of sterling depicted in Figure 22.3. This shows that at higher exchange rates, more sterling is supplied on the foreign exchange market.

Exchange rate equilibrium in a freely-floating exchange rate regime

Exchange rate equilibrium occurs at the market-clearing exchange rate at which the demand for pounds on foreign exchange markets equals the supply of pounds. In Figure 22.3, this is determined at Point *A*. The equilibrium exchange rate is $1.80 to the pound.

At this exchange rate, the money value of exports (paid in sterling) equals the money value of imports (paid in foreign currencies). If I assume that exports and imports are the only items in the country's balance of payments, the balance of payments is also in equilibrium.

Because I am assuming away any complications introduced by capital flows, exchange rate equilibrium implies balance of payments equilibrium on current account and vice versa. The two equilibria are just different sides of the same coin: exchange rate equilibrium is price equilibrium, whereas balance of payments equilibrium (where $X = M$ in Figure 22.3) means that the quantity of the currency flowing into the country equals the quantity flowing out. Given the simplifying assumptions I have made, once the balance of payments is in equilibrium, there is no pressure for the exchange rate to rise or fall.

The adjustment process to a new equilibrium exchange rate

I shall now assume that some event or 'shock' disturbs the initial equilibrium, for example an improvement in the quality of foreign-produced goods causes UK residents to increase demand for imports whatever the exchange rate. In Figure 22.4, the increase in demand for foreign exchange to pay for imports causes the supply curve of sterling to shift to the right from S_1 to S_2. (Remember, when more foreign currencies are demanded, more sterling must be supplied.) In the new situation, the current account of the balance of payments is in deficit by the amount ($X < M$) in the diagram — as long as the exchange rate

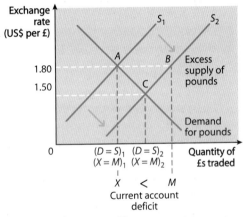

Figure 22.4 *How a current account deficit is eliminated in a freely-floating exchange rate system*

stays at $1.80. At the $1.80 exchange rate, UK residents supply or sell more sterling than before to pay for imports, but because overseas residents still demand the same quantity of UK goods (assuming that their views on the quality of UK goods relative to foreign goods has not changed), the overseas demand for sterling to pay for UK exports remains at its previous level.

At the exchange rate of $1.80 to the pound, there is an excess supply of sterling on the foreign exchange market, equal to the distance *B* minus *A*. The market mechanism now swings into action to restore equilibrium — both for the exchange rate and for the balance of payments. When the excess holdings of sterling accumulated at the

exchange rate of $1.80 are sold on the foreign exchange market, the pound's exchange rate falls. This increases the price competitiveness of UK exports while making imports less price competitive. The exchange rate falls until a new equilibrium exchange rate is reached at Point C, where the exchange rate is $1.50 to the pound.

Note that the current account of the balance of payments is once again in equilibrium, but at $(X = M)_2$ rather than at $(X = M)_1$. This means that at the new equilibrium exchange rate, although they are again equal in size, the money values of exports and imports have both increased.

Conversely, if the initial equilibrium is disturbed by an improvement in the quality of UK goods or services, the demand curve for sterling shifts to the right. This moves the current account into surplus, causing the pound's exchange rate to rise or appreciate in order to relieve the excess demand for sterling. Providing UK residents don't change their views on the relative quality of imports, the exchange rate rises until the balance of payments and exchange equilibrium are once again restored.

examiner's voice

You should practise drawing demand and supply graphs to show a floating exchange rate.

Key *term*

A **disequilibrium exchange rate** is the rate at which there is excess demand for, or excess supply of, the currency.

Extension material

The theory I have just outlined can be called the **traditional approach** to floating exchange rates. The traditional approach, which largely ignores capital flows, contrasts with the **monetary approach**, developed in the 1950s and 1970s by the monetarist economists Milton Friedman and Harry Johnson. The monetary approach argues that capital flows, brought about by conditions in global money and financial markets, are much more important than trade flows in determining changes in exchange rates.

The monetary approach to floating exchange rates provides better explanations of recent volatility in foreign exchange markets and wild swings of exchange rates than does the traditional approach, which side-steps the problems created by capital flows.

The advantages of floating exchange rates

Economists generally agree that providing there are no distorting capital flows, freely-floating exchange rates have the following advantages.

Balance of payments equilibrium

The exchange rate (which is the external price of the currency) should move up or down to correct a payments imbalance. Providing the adjustment mechanism operates smoothly, a currency should never be overvalued or undervalued for long. In the event of an overvalued exchange rate causing export uncompetitiveness and a payments deficit, market forces should quickly adjust towards an equilibrium exchange rate, which also achieves equilibrium in the balance of payments. Similarly, undervaluation should be quickly corrected by an upward movement of the exchange rate.

Resource allocation

If the world's resources are to be efficiently allocated between competing uses, exchange rates must be correctly valued. For efficient resource allocation in a constantly changing world, market prices must accurately reflect shifts in demand and changes in competitive and comparative advantage that result from technical progress and events such as discoveries of new mineral resources. In principle, a freely-floating exchange rate should respond and adjust to these changes. By contrast, a fixed exchange rate may gradually become overvalued or undervalued, as demand or competitive and comparative advantage move against or in favour of a country's industries.

Domestic policy objectives

It is sometimes argued that when the exchange rate is freely floating, balance of payments surpluses and deficits cease to be a policy problem for the government, as it is then free to pursue the domestic economic objectives of full employment and growth. Market forces look after the balance of payments while governments concentrate on domestic economic policy. If, in the pursuit of domestic objectives, the inflation rate rises out of line with other countries, in a freely-floating world the exchange rate simply falls to restore competitiveness.

Inflation

In much the same way, a responsible country with a lower than average inflation rate should benefit from a floating exchange rate because the exchange rate insulates the country from 'importing inflation' from the rest of the world. If inflation rates are higher in the rest of the world, a fixed exchange rate causes a country to import inflation through the rising prices of goods imported from high-inflation countries. By contrast, a floating exchange rate floats upward, which lowers the prices of imports, insulating the economy against importing inflation.

Independent monetary policy

With a floating exchange rate, monetary policy can be used solely to achieve domestic policy objectives, such as the control of inflation. This is called an *independent* monetary policy. By contrast, with a fixed exchange rate, interest rates may be determined by events in the outside world (and in particular by capital flows out of and into currencies), rather than by the needs of the domestic economy. To maintain a fixed exchange rate, interest rates may have to be raised to prevent the exchange rate from falling. In this situation, monetary policy is no longer independent, in the sense that it can no longer be assigned to pursuing purely domestic policy objectives.

The disadvantages of floating exchange rates

Freely-floating exchange rates nevertheless have some disadvantages, particularly relating to the fact that in the modern globalised world in which financial capital is internationally mobile, capital flows rather than exports and imports are the main determinants of floating exchange rates.

Speculation and capital flows

The argument that a freely-floating exchange rate is never overvalued or undervalued for very long depends crucially upon the main assumption of the traditional theory of exchange rates, that currencies are bought and sold on foreign exchange markets only to finance

> **e*xaminer's voice*
> Refer back to Chapter 21 and reread the section on hot money flows.

trade. This assumption means that speculation and capital flows have no influence on exchange rates. But as the monetary theory of exchange rates argues, this is at odds with how the modern globalised economy works. These days, well over 90% of currency transactions taking place on foreign exchange markets stem from capital flows and from the decisions of individuals, business corporations, financial institutions and even governments to switch wealth portfolios between different currencies. In the short run, exchange rates are extremely vulnerable to **speculative capital** or **hot money** movements into or out of currencies. Just like a fixed exchange rate, a floating exchange rate can be overvalued or undervalued, which means it does not reflect the trading competitiveness of the country's goods and services.

International trading uncertainty

It is sometimes argued that, whereas fixed exchange rates create conditions of certainty and stability in which international trade can prosper and grow, the volatility and instability caused by floating exchange rates slow the growth of, and even destroys, international trade. In fact, *hedging*, which involves the purchase or sale of a currency in the 'forward' market 3 months in advance of the actual delivery of the currency and payment for trade, considerably reduces the trading uncertainties associated with floating exchange rates. Indeed, fixed and managed exchange rates may also cause uncertainty, especially when a currency is overvalued and a devaluation is expected.

Cost-push inflation

Floating exchange rates sometimes contribute to cost-push inflation. Suppose a country has a higher rate of inflation than its trading partners. Trading competitiveness and the current account of the balance of payments both worsen, causing the exchange rate to fall in order to restore competitiveness. This may trigger a vicious cumulative downward spiral of faster inflation and exchange rate depreciation. The falling exchange rate increases import prices, which raise the rate of domestic cost-push inflation. Workers react by demanding pay rises to restore the real value of the eroded real wage. At the next stage, increased inflation erodes the export competitiveness initially won by the fall of the exchange rate, which in turn triggers a further fall in the exchange rate to recover the lost advantage, and so the process continues. The resulting downward spiral can eventually destabilise large parts of the domestic economy, causing unemployment and reducing economic growth.

Demand-pull inflation

Floating exchange rates can trigger demand-pull inflation as well as cost-push inflation. With a floating exchange rate, there is no need to deflate the domestic economy to deal with a balance of payments deficit on the current account. But suppose a large number of countries with floating exchange rates simultane-

examiner's voice

It is important to understand the links between exchange rates and inflation.

ously increase aggregate demand. This can lead to excess demand on a worldwide scale, which fuels global inflation. This happened in the 1970s, when a worldwide expansion of demand created conditions in which oil and primary goods producers could raise prices and still sell in world markets. In countries such as the UK, the resulting inflation appeared to be import cost-push inflation, caused by the rising cost of imported energy and raw materials. However, the true cause lay in excess demand created by the simultaneous effects of demand expansion and floating exchange rates, when world supply could not increase, at least in the short run, to meet the surge in global demand. A similar situation occurred in 2007 and early 2008.

Box 22.1 Is Britain going bust?

In September 1992, two currency speculators, George Soros and Jim Rogers, effectively 'broke' the Bank of England. They speculated against the pound on a massive scale and forced the UK chancellor and the governor of the Bank of England to withdraw the pound from the semi-fixed exchange rate regime known as the Exchange Rate Mechanism of the European Monetary System. The day on which this happened is known as 'Black Wednesday'.

Seventeen years later in January 2009, Jim Rogers famously again said that Britain is bust. Rogers advised young British people to 'Move to China; learn Chinese'. Below is an extract from an interview Jim Rogers gave to Sky News in January 2009 in which he described sterling as 'finished' and London's financial services as a disaster. He went on to say that the government had made a 'horrible mistake' in spending billions of pounds to stop Britain's banks collapsing and added that Britain would soon have little to offer the world.

After years of enjoying a strong currency and thriving financial sector, the winds of change blowing across the UK are fast turning into a storm.

The fact is that the UK has had two things to sell to the world over the last 25 years, the North Sea oil and that's drying up — within a decade the UK is going to be importing oil — and

the City of London. The UK's financial asset (the City) is a disaster and it's not going to revive.

Sterling has got to go lower over the next decade or two because when the North Sea dries up I do not know what the UK is going to sell to the world.

Jim Rogers, 21 January 2009

Follow-up questions

1 Research what happened to the pound's exchange rate in September 1992 and assess whether this was good or bad for the UK economy.

2 In recent years the UK economy has often been said to be 'unbalanced'. What is meant by this and, if true, what have been the consequences?

Extension material

The purchasing power theory and long-term determinants of the exchange rate

Over three decades from the 1970s to the early 2000s, the pound's exchange rate generally fell against those of other currencies. Indeed, the downward trend occurred through most of the twentieth century and has continued right up to the present day. The **purchasing power parity** (PPP) theory provides the best explanation for such long-term changes in exchange rates.

Consider a situation in which a country's inflation rate is 10% higher than the inflation rates of its main competitors. The PPP theory predicts that, in this situation, the country's exchange rate falls by approximately 10% to offset the loss of trading competitiveness caused by the higher domestic inflation rate. As a result, the purchasing power of exports over imports returns to its earlier level: that is, the level existing before the domestic inflation rate moved out of line with inflation rates in the rest of the world.

Although the PPP theory provides a good explanation of long-term changes in exchange rates (taking place over many decades), it is less useful for explaining short-term changes. As I have indicated, short-term changes in exchange rates result mainly from speculative capital flows. Hot money flows cause exchange rates to overshoot, in which case the currency becomes overvalued, or to be undervalued. However, because speculative flows tend to even out over periods longer than a few years, hot money movements are less significant for explaining long-term changes in exchange rates.

Fixed exchange rates

With a freely-floating exchange rate system, a currency's external value rises or falls to eliminate a balance of payments surplus or deficit on the current account. By contrast, with **fixed exchange rates**, a currency's external value remains unchanged, while the internal price level, or more usually the level of domestic economic activity and output, adjusts to eliminate balance of payments disequilibrium.

 Key term

A **fixed exchange rate** is an exchange rate fixed at a certain level by the country's central bank and maintained by the central bank's intervention in the foreign exchange market.

Although most exchange rates now float freely, fixed exchange rates have been important for long periods in the last 100 or more years. In a rigidly fixed system, devaluation is ruled out as a means of reducing a current account deficit. This means that deflationary policies that decrease aggregate demand have to be used to improve the current account. As a result, deflation harms the domestic economy, which explains why modern governments generally reject a return to rigidly fixed exchange rates. Governments prefer to be able to devalue, or at least to be able to engineer a downward float of the currency.

The longest period of rigidly fixed exchange rates occurred in the nineteenth century and in the early years of the twentieth century. During this period, most major world currencies were fixed against gold in a system known as the **gold standard**. In addition, from 1999 until 2002, 12 currencies of the countries committed to adopting the euro were rigidly fixed against each other in preparation for their eventual disappearance when replaced by euro notes and coins in 2002. These countries, together with other counties such as Malta and Slovenia, which adopted the euro more recently, now form the eurozone. The eurozone will grow in size when the local currencies of other new EU member countries are eventually replaced by the euro.

> *examiner's voice*
>
> A rigidly fixed exchange rate is the most extreme form of managed exchange rate.

> *examiner's voice*
>
> Historical knowledge of the gold standard is useful, but by no means essential.

The advantages of fixed exchange rates

Because the advantages and disadvantages of fixed exchange rates are closely but oppositely related to those of floating rates, which I have already explained in some depth, I shall provide only a brief summary here.

The main advantages of fixed exchange rates are:

> ➤ certainty and stability
> ➤ the anti-inflationary discipline imposed on a country's domestic economic management and upon the behaviour of its workers and firms. I explain this in greater depth in the Extension material later in the chapter, which covers the relationship between fixed exchange rates and monetary policy.

> *examiner's voice*
>
> Make sure you can adapt my earlier coverage of the advantages and disadvantages of floating exchange rates so as to be able to explain the advantages and disadvantages of fixed exchange rates.

The disadvantages of fixed exchange rates

By contrast, the principal disadvantages of fixed exchange rates include:

> ➤ a possible increase in uncertainty if devaluation or revaluation is expected
> ➤ continued overvaluation or undervaluation of the currency
> ➤ severe deflationary costs of lost output and unemployment for a deficit country and the importing of inflation by a surplus country
> ➤ a possible balance of payments or currency crisis in a country whose currency is overvalued
> ➤ tying up of resources in official reserves, which could be used more productively elsewhere

Managed exchange rates

An exchange rate is managed when the country's central bank actively intervenes in foreign exchange markets, buying and selling reserves and its own currency to influence the movement of the exchange rate in a particular direction. By managing the exchange rate, a country's monetary authorities hope to achieve the stability and certainty associated with fixed exchange rates combined with a

floating exchange rate's ability to avoid overvaluation and undervaluation by responding to market forces.

However, critics of **managed exchange rates** argue that, instead of combining the advantages of both fixed and floating exchange rates with the disadvantages of neither, in practice the opposite happens. Exchange rate management too often achieves the disadvantages of uncertainty and instability combined with the ineffective and wasteful use of official reserves in frequent fruitless attempts by governments to stem speculative hot money flows out of currencies.

As well as by maintaining a rigidly fixed exchange rate, which is the extreme example of a managed exchange rate, exchange rates can be managed in two ways. These are through an adjustable peg (or fixed peg) system and by managed floating (or dirty floating).

Key terms

A **managed exchange rate** is similar to a fixed exchange rate (which itself is the extreme form of a managed exchange rate) in that the central bank intervenes in the foreign exchange market to determine its currency's exchange rate.

An **adjustable peg exchange rate** is a managed exchange rate similar to a rigidly-fixed exchange rate except that the central bank may alter the exchange rate's central peg by devaluing or revaluing.

Adjustable peg exchange rate systems

An **adjustable peg exchange rate** has a closer resemblance to a rigidly fixed exchange rate than to a freely-floating exchange rate. Nevertheless, adjustable pegs are more flexible than rigidly fixed exchange rates. This is because the exchange rate is adjusted upwards or downward from time to time by the country's central bank. An upward *revaluation* corrects an undervalued exchange rate, whereas a downward adjustment or *devaluation* is used to correct overvaluation.

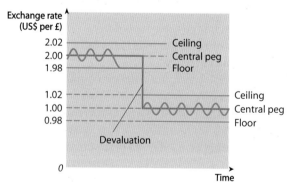

Figure 22.5 *A devaluation of an adjustable peg exchange rate*

Figure 22.5 illustrates devaluation of the pound in an adjustable peg exchange rate system. The exchange rate is initially fixed at a *central peg* of $2.00. Supply and demand then determine the day-to-day exchange rate. Providing the exchange stays between a ceiling and a floor set at the time that the central peg was fixed, the exchange rate is correctly valued for trade. There is no need for central bank intervention. However, the graph shows the exchange rate falling to the floor of $1.98, possibly because of a speculative capital flow against the currency. At this point the central bank intervenes, raising domestic interest rates to attract capital flows into the currency and using reserves to support the fixed exchange rate. By selling reserves and buying its own currency, the central bank creates an artificial demand for its own currency. A policy of buying and selling currencies to support an exchange rate is known as **exchange equalisation**.

Key term

Exchange equalisation takes place when a central bank buys or sells its own currency to maintain its exchange rate at a particular level.

As Figure 22.6 shows, maintaining the exchange somewhere between the ceiling and the floor is almost identical to the way a buffer stock agency buys or sells stocks of an agricultural good or a metal to stabilise the price of the primary product.

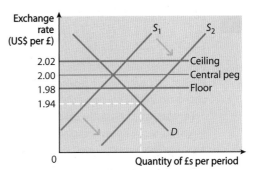

Figure 22.6 *How managing the exchange rate resembles buffer stock intervention*

If you refer back to Figure 22.1, you will see that the pound's exchange rate against the dollar was around the $2.00 dollar mark in the first half of 2008. However, from August onwards, a hot money flow out of the pound and into the dollar led to a collapse of the exchange rate, with the pound's value falling in the latter months of 2008 by about 30% against the dollar. At the time, the pound's exchange rate was floating, as it still is, but consider what would probably have happened had the pound's value been fixed against the dollar, say at $2.00 to the pound. In its early days, the outflow of speculative funds would have shifted the supply curve of pounds to the right, say to S_2 in Figure 22.6. In a floating system, the capital outflow would have taken the exchange rate down to $1.94 (at least to start with). However, with a managed exchange rate, support-buying by the Bank of England would be triggered at $1.98 to prevent the pound diving below the floor. If buying up its own currency was successful, the Bank of England would have succeeded in maintaining the fixed exchange rate. However, given the massive size of the speculative flow out of the pound, it is much more likely that the $2.00 peg would be abandoned, either by devaluing to a lower central peg, or by waving goodbye to the managed exchange rate.

Persistent support for a currency means that its exchange rate is overvalued, condemning the country to over-priced exports, under-priced imports and a current account deficit. In a rigidly fixed exchange rate system (which can be illustrated by the left-hand part of Figure 22.5), this is the end of the story. The country's government has to deflate the domestic economy and/or impose import controls, since devaluation and revaluation are not permitted in a rigidly-fixed system.

However, Figure 22.5 goes on to show the authorities devaluing the exchange rate to a new central peg of $1.00 so as to correct the imbalance. This illustrates the difference between adjustable peg and rigidly fixed exchange rate systems.

Box 22.2 Caution! Falling pound

Except for the lucky few that still have money to burn, the years of Christmas shopping in New York have come to an end. From your Upper East Side hotel to your hoard of electronic goodies, each dollar sign is worth about 30% more in pounds than it was worth this time last year. And if you thought that a trip to the Parisian Centre Pompidou might be a substitute, *pensez encore une fois*. Sterling has lost almost as much value against the euro and shows no sign of reaching the bottom.

For this we can partly thank Mervyn King, governor of the Bank of England, whose monetary policy committee's decision to cut the base rate sent sterling plunging once again. Where one pound was worth $2.11 last November, it was trading at $1.46 last week. This might still be within levels seen as recently as 2002, but everything from the state of British finances to the woeful housing market is prompting many to wonder how far it could yet drop.

The worry is that investors will sell pounds en masse on the back of cheap interest rates and fears about the long-term health of the economy and public finances. A mass sell-off would see the pound crash in value and push up the price of imported goods — particularly worrying for a post-manufacturing, import-dependent economy. This would force the Bank of England to spend billions to defend the currency and push up interest rates to quell inflation just when rates should be low to stimulate demand and stave off a slump.

Professor Catherine Schenk at the University of Glasgow, says: 'There is now the danger of sterling becoming a one-way bet. If you get speculators in the market and this becomes the consensus, it can be a self-fulfilling prophecy. If enough people are selling a currency, it will put pressure on it to fall.' Schenk believes that sterling is still less at risk than many other European countries because it is traded more heavily.

Nick Stamenkovic, a macro-strategist at Edinburgh's RIA Capital Markets, believes that a run on the pound is still unlikely: 'We are only back to where we were when we left the ERM, Europe's Exchange Rate Mechanism, in 1992. The pound for many years has been massively over-valued. The Bank of England's cutting of interest rates is a strategy of benign neglect.'

The *Scottish Sunday Herald*, 7 December 2008

Follow-up questions

1 In the context of the passage, explain the meaning of the terms 'one-way bet' and 'benign neglect'.

2 Research what has happened to the pound's exchange rate since December 2008.

Managed or dirty floating

Fixed and adjustable peg exchange rate systems have now been abandoned throughout most of the world. Virtually all exchange rates now float, though there is a difference between 'clean' and **dirty floating**. Clean floating is the same as free floating and pure floating, i.e. there is absolutely no central bank intervention to prop up the exchange rate or to manipulate its value. In earlier sections of this chapter I have explained clean or pure floating. By contrast, 'dirty' or 'managed'

Key **term**

Dirty floating is a managed exchange rate system in which the central bank intervenes in the foreign exchange market when the exchange rate is still floating.

floating occurs when the exchange rate is *officially* floating, in the sense that a country's monetary authorities announce that market forces are determining the exchange rate, but in fact they intervene *unofficially* behind the scenes to buy or sell their own currency to influence the exchange rate.

At one extreme, dirty or managed floating is simply a *smoothing operation* for a clean or freely-floating exchange rate. However, at the other extreme, currency intervention may try to secure and then maintain an unofficial exchange rate target. China regularly intervenes in foreign exchange markets to keep its currency, the renminbi (rnb), low against the dollar. The currencies of some of the smaller EU countries that have not as yet adopted the euro have also tried to maintain the exchange rates of their currencies against the euro.

The pound, the dollar, and reserve currency roles

The US dollar is the world's **reserve currency**. A reserve currency is a currency that governments and central banks outside the country that issues the currency wish to hold.

 Key term

A **reserve currency** is a currency widely held in the foreign currency reserves of other countries and used by them to pay for trade.

The US dollar is the world's reserve currency

To take on a world reserve role, a currency must be transmitted into overseas ownership. In the second half of the nineteenth century, the pound became the world's reserve currency, alongside gold. At the time, the pound was on the gold standard, which meant that the Bank of England fixed the pound's exchange rate against gold and guaranteed to exchange pounds for gold on demand at this fixed rate.

This brings me to the two rather paradoxical circumstances that enable a currency to become a reserve currency. On the one hand the currency must be

> **examiner's voice**
> It is useful but not essential to know about reserve currencies.

'hard', i.e. one which people and banks in other countries wish to hold. However, on the other hand, there must be a mechanism that transmits ownership of the currency on a large scale to people and banks in other countries. The transmission mechanism is the country's balance of payments deficit.

Normally when a country runs up a huge balance of payments deficit, its currency's exchange rate falls or 'softens' because of its excess supply on foreign exchange markets. In the case of a reserve currency, this is generally not so. People and banks in the rest of the world are only too happy to get their hands on and then to keep the currency without feeling the need to sell it. In this way, large holdings of the currency are transmitted into ownership outside the currency's country of origin.

In the late nineteenth century and up to 1914, Britain benefited from its *hegemonic* position in the world economy. Because of the UK's military, political and economic power in the nineteenth century, the residents of other countries wanted to hold the pound. The accumulation of pounds owned outside the UK led to the currency taking on a world reserve role.

After 1918, the UK's economy had weakened and this led to a quick decline in the pound's reserve role. The role was finally finished by the Second World War. After the war, the pound was not freely convertible into other currencies and therefore undesirable to hold. By this time, the US dollar had become the world reserve currency, reflecting the hegemonic power that the USA now enjoyed. The dollar continues to be the world's main reserve currency, though to some extent it is rivaled by the euro. As was the case with the pound over 100 years ago, the USA's huge balance of payments deficit on the current account has provided the main transmission mechanism, along with the willingness of governments and people worldwide to hold the dollar.

Vast overseas ownership of the dollar renders the currency vulnerable to a mass-selling panic. To some extent this happened late in 2004, encouraged in part by the US government's policy of benign neglect with respect to the dollar's exchange rate. The US administration seemed to encourage the dollar's fall, hoping that, by making US goods more competitive in world markets, the problem of a growing US payments deficit would diminish.

However, two factors temper mass selling of dollars. First, a large-scale sale of dollars inevitably involves mass purchase of other currencies, such as the euro. For this to occur, dollar holders' confidence in the euro and in the economies of eurozone countries must exceed their doubts about the dollar and the US economy. The sheer size and hegemonic role of the US economy means that the dollar is still generally regarded as a better bet than other currencies. Second, the USA's huge current account deficit means that other countries, including the eurozone countries, have surpluses, which means that their currencies are in short supply on foreign exchange markets. This in turn means a lack of a transmission mechanism to convey the currencies into widespread overseas ownership and into a world reserve role equalling the past role of the dollar

Indeed, the reserve currency status of the dollar also means that individuals and companies worldwide, for example in South America and Africa, hold the dollar as a wealth asset in preference to their national currencies.

Extension material

Fixed exchange rates and monetary policy

At various times in recent decades, UK governments used a high exchange rate as a policy instrument with which to control inflation. A high exchange rate reduces inflation in three different ways. In the first place it causes the prices of imported food and consumer goods to fall. The second effect operates through falling prices of imported raw materials and energy. These reduce costs of production, which in turn reduce cost-push inflationary pressure within the domestic economy. The third effect is more subtle, since it operates through changes in human behaviour. If the exchange rate remains high, firms that raise prices by more than their international competitors suffer falling profits and even bankruptcy. At the same time, workers who push for higher wage increases than those on offer in competitor countries face the risk of unemployment. Realising it is against self-interest to behave in an inflationary way, firms and workers choose to moderate price rises and wage claims. The economist, Sir Alan Budd, argues that the pound's membership of the ERM at a high exchange rate had precisely this effect, 'bleeding' the economy of inflationary expectations between 1990 and 1992.

A high exchange rate thus disciplines or constrains domestic inflationary pressures. However, if devaluation is expected, the counter-inflationary discipline provided by the high exchange rate quickly disappears. If the government's commitment to a high exchange rate is questioned, the credibility of counter-inflation policy may vanish. In this situation, inflationary pressures are unleashed, which reduces international competitiveness and causes the current account to deteriorate. An overvalued exchange rate leads to a hot money outflow, which puts downward pressure on the exchange rate. To prevent the exchange rate from falling, the country's central bank may have to increase domestic interest rates. Higher interest rates contract or deflate aggregate demand in an economy already suffering a loss of export competitiveness brought about by the high exchange rate.

Using a high exchange rate in this way to reduce domestic inflation means that monetary policy in general, and interest rates in particular, are not available to stimulate or reflate aggregate demand within the economy. Indeed, the deflationary effects of a high exchange rate and high interest rates mean that the domestic policy objectives of full employment and economic growth have to be sacrificed to the external objective of supporting the exchange rate.

The euro

For most people, the European Union's single currency, the **euro**, came into existence on 1 January 2002 when euro notes and coins entered circulation. However, economists usually date 1 January 1999 as marking the euro's introduction, as this was the date on which the exchange rates of the 12 countries that became the first members of the **eurozone** or euro area were irrevocably fixed against each other. (The eurozone and the euro area are the names used for the group of EU countries that have replaced their national currencies with the euro.)

 Key terms

The **euro** is the single currency used in some, but not all, European Union member states.

The **eurozone** contains the EU countries in which the euro has replaced national currencies, also known as the euro area.

Currently, the UK is *inside* the EU but *outside* the eurozone, retaining the pound as the national currency and implementing a strictly national UK monetary policy. By contrast, eurozone member countries are subject to the monetary policy implemented in Frankfurt by the **European Central Bank** (ECB). The pound's exchange rate floats against the euro, but as I have indicated, some of the other non-eurozone EU currencies are more or less fixed against the euro.

At the time of writing in April 2009, in addition to the 12 original members of the eurozone, a further eight EU countries have adopted the euro, taking eurozone membership to 20 countries. The most recent is Slovakia, which joined on 1 January 2009.

A euro

Key term

The **European Central Bank** (ECB) is the central bank for eurozone countries.

European monetary union (EMU) and the euro

The euro was created to facilitate greater economic integration among EU member states. Indeed, the euro is a stepping stone to full **monetary union** (EMU) between EU states and, possibly in the future, to a much fuller **economic union**.

At this point it is worth noting that EMU means two different things. The official EU meaning is *economic* and monetary

Key term

Economic and monetary union (EMU) involves common monetary arrangements among EU countries to create a common currency and then to achieve fuller economic union among EU member states.

union. Defined in this way, EMU suggests that common monetary arrangements adopted by EU member countries are part of a grander scheme to integrate the national economies of member states. More narrowly defined, the acronym means *European* monetary union, which involves a common monetary policy applied to all EU member states adopting the euro. In the latter meaning, EMU can be interpreted simply as a step towards making the EU's single market work better and more efficiently.

The process of creating the euro and EMU began in the early 1990s, around the time the exchange rate mechanism disintegrated. The first step in the process centred on the publication of a timetable for introducing the single currency. The timetable required a European Central Bank to be established prior to the euro's introduction.

The impact of the euro upon eurozone economies

The introduction of the euro has had the following effects on the member countries of the eurozone.

➤ **Economic integration.** The euro has replaced national currencies such as the French franc and the German Deutschmark in the countries adopting the single currency. For supporters of greater economic integration in the EU, the single currency is a necessary step towards a much fuller economic union. In this view, monetary union and the euro will enable EU firms and consumers to benefit in future years from increased specialisation, a larger market, faster growth and higher living standards. Opponents of the euro argue that these supposed advantages are more than countered by the single currency's adverse effects.

➤ **Price competitiveness.** Whichever view is preferred, each member country is now locked in to the single currency at the exchange rate agreed prior to entry. This means that eurozone countries have lost the freedom to lower or raise national exchange rates to correct overvaluation or undervaluation against each other. Countries such as Greece that entered at too high an exchange rate face having to deflate domestic demand to restore competitiveness within the eurozone. Conversely, the countries that arguably entered the eurozone at too low an exchange rate, such as Germany, can reap the benefit of artificially high price competitiveness.

➤ **Speculation.** One of the reasons for creating the euro was to prevent the national currencies of member countries being 'picked off' by international speculators, as had occurred in the early 1990s. When the euro was launched, many economists believed that the strength of eurozone economies (and the euro's potential role as a world reserve currency) would deter speculative selling or buying of the currency. Nevertheless, the euro itself is could be vulnerable to a speculative attack. Although eurozone countries can no longer devalue or revalue against each other, the euro itself floats against the rest of the world's currencies.

➤ **Monetary policy.** Eurozone member countries can no longer implement independent monetary policies. In an important sense, national central banks such as Germany's Bundesbank and the Bank of France are now just branch banks of the European Central Bank, which sets an interest rate for the whole of the eurozone.

➤ **One size fits all.** The fact that the ECB sets an interest rate for the whole of the eurozone has led to the 'one size fits all' problem. In the 1990s, before launching the euro, the EU tried to get eurozone countries to converge their national economic cycles. Without convergence, each country might be in a different phase of its economic cycle. Some countries might be in recession or on the verge of recession, while others were in the recovery or boom phases of the economic cycle. Complete convergence, by contrast, means that every country is in the same phase of the economic cycle. In times of rapid economic growth, a lack of convergence means that a high interest rate is needed to dampen demand-pull inflationary pressures in the fastest-growing countries, while low

interest rates may be required to stimulate economic recovery or to ward off recession in other countries. The one size fits all problem stems from the fact that these requirements are mutually exclusive. However, *realpolitik* within the EU usually means that the needs of core economies, particularly Germany and France, override the requirements of peripheral countries such as Ireland and Portugal.

➤ **Interest rates.** However, somewhat in conflict with my last sentence, the ECB has been criticised for being too cautious and deflationary when setting interest rates for eurozone countries. If true, this may reflect the influence in the eurozone of the German fear of high inflation, which stems from memories of the disastrous effect of German hyperinflation in the early 1920s. In the German view, interest rates must at all times be set sufficiently high to pre-empt inflationary pressures, especially those arising in supposedly less responsible 'club-med' members of the eurozone, namely Greece, Spain, Portugal and Italy.

➤ **Fiscal policy.** The German view just outlined helps to explain the fiscal policy imposed on eurozone countries by the Stability and Growth Pact. The Pact limits the freedom of the eurozone member states to choose their own national fiscal policies. To prevent expansionary fiscal policies fuelling excess demand and inflation, the Pact tries to prevent eurozone countries from increasing budget deficits to more than 3% of GDP and national debts to more than 40% of GDP. When first implemented, the Stability and Growth Pact was meant to rein in profligate fiscal policies of some of the smaller EU countries. In the outcome, the Pact more or less disintegrated in 2003 and 2004 when the budget deficits and national debts of supposedly responsible Germany and France began to break the Pact's rules. Opponents of the Stability and Growth Pact believe that the Pact has really been fighting yesterday's problem of inflation instead of the current problem of stagnation, possible deflation and unemployment. As long as it exists in its original form, the pact reduces the chance of a eurozone government successfully using expansionary fiscal policy to get out of recession or a slow-growth economic environment.

Summary

➤ An exchange rate is the external price of the currency in terms of another currency.

➤ There are three types of exchange rate: freely floating, fixed and managed.

➤ A freely-floating (clean floating) exchange rate is determined by supply and demand.

➤ Provided there are no capital flows, a freely-floating exchange rate should automatically eliminate a current account deficit or surplus.

➤ Free floating enables a country to pursue an independent monetary policy.

➤ There are, however, disadvantages with a freely-floating exchange rate system, for example, exchange rate instability or volatility.

➤ Speculative or hot money capital flows also destabilise floating exchange rates, sometimes leading to severe overvaluation or undervaluation.

➤ In a rigidly fixed exchange rate system, the exchange rate cannot rise or fall to eliminate or reduce a payments surplus or deficit.

➤ The advantages of a fixed exchange rate relate closely to the disadvantages of a floating rate, while the disadvantages relate to a floating system's advantages.

➤ Adjustable peg and 'dirty' floating are types of managed exchange rates.

➤ In an adjustable peg system, the exchange rate can be revalued or devalued to try to correct a payments imbalance.

➤ The pound and the US dollar have both been reserve currencies. The dollar continues to have this status and the euro is developing a world reserve role.

➤ The euro has replaced national currencies for the EU member states in the eurozone.

➤ The UK is not in the eurozone and continues to use the pound.

Questions

1 State three ways in which a country's exchange rate can be measured.

2 Distinguish between a currency's nominal exchange rate and its real exchange rate.

3 Using a demand and supply diagram, show how a freely-floating exchange rate is determined.

4 Outline the advantages and disadvantages of a floating exchange rate.

5 How may a fixed exchange rate discipline inflationary behaviour?

6 Describe two types of managed exchange rate.

7 Distinguish between 'dirty' and 'clean' floating.

8 Why has the exchange rate sometimes been targeted as a macroeconomic policy objective?

9 Does the euro have a fixed or a floating exchange rate? Explain your answer.

10 Why did most members of the EU decide in the 1990s to replace their national currencies with the euro?

11 Why was convergence deemed a necessary condition for a successful eurozone?

12 Explain two possible effects on the British economy if the UK were to adopt the euro.

Index

Page numbers in **bold** indicate definitions of key terms.

E

X